GOOD FORM

GOOD FORM

The Ethical Experience of the Victorian Novel

JESSE ROSENTHAL

PRINCETON UNIVERSITY PRESS
PRINCETON AND OXFORD

Published by Princeton University Press,
41 William Street, Princeton, New Jersey 08540
In the United Kingdom: Princeton University Press,
6 Oxford Street, Woodstock, Oxfordshire OX20 1TR
press.princeton.edu

ISBN 978-0-691-17170-8

Library of Congress Control Number: 2016931465

British Library Cataloging-in-Publication Data is available

This book has been composed in Sabon Next LT Pro

Printed on acid-free paper. ∞

Printed in the United States of America

10 9 8 7 6 5 4 3 2 1

For Masha

The *Universality* of this *moral Sense*, and that it is antecedent to *Instruction*, may appear from observing the Sentiments of *Children*, upon hearing the Storys with which they are commonly entertain'd as soon as they understand Language.

—FRANCIS HUTCHESON, *INQUIRY INTO THE ORIGINS OF OUR IDEAS OF BEAUTY AND VIRTUE*

The moralist, as well as the poet, must give us back the image of our mind. He must show to us the connection of moral truths which had governed our thoughts, though we had not unfolded them into reasonings.

—WILLIAM WHEWELL, *LECTURES ON SYSTEMATIC MORALITY*

CONTENTS

ACKNOWLEDGMENTS

This book has been a part of my life, in one form or another, for a decade now. It started as a graduate dissertation at Columbia University, where I had the great good fortune to work with Sharon Marcus, Nicholas Dames, and Bruce Robbins. This book simply would not exist without their influence, patience, and generosity. Amanda Claybaugh, Erik Gray, and Edward Mendelson might not have overseen my dissertation, but all three contributed greatly through their encouragement and wisdom. Friends from Columbia argued with me, and taught me, and helped me learn to think; though I'm sure I'm leaving some names out, I am especially grateful to Eugene Vydrin, Casey Shoop, Allison Deutermann, Andy Lynn, and Garrett Ziegler. Saharah Moon Chapotin provided sanctuary and understanding, an escape from New York, and far more patience than I deserved. Dehn Gilmore deserves special thanks: her intelligence and friendship are everywhere in the pages that follow.

I am also grateful to my colleagues at Johns Hopkins, who have helped me grow up as a thinker, and have helped my book grow up as well: Frances Ferguson, Richard Halpern, Eric Sundquist, Sharon Cameron, Chris Nealon, Mark Thompson, Sharon Achinstein, Drew Daniel, Jared Hickman, Jeanne-Marie Jackson, and Yi-Ping Ong. I am particularly grateful to Amanda Anderson, Jonathan Kramnick, and Douglas Mao, all of whom provided insightful comments on the manuscript. I am indebted to my editors at Princeton University Press, and two anonymous outside readers, who provided valuable suggestions as the book took its final form.

I started writing this book as an attempt to describe the points of connection between two experiences: the fraught pleasures of reading, and the often too-quiet call to right action. What I know of both of these I owe entirely to my parents, Pam and Michael Rosenthal. I was lucky enough to be raised among meaningful words: books, debates, humor, convictions. I have tried to enact, in my life and my writing, the lessons of two people who follow so faithfully a joint commitment to literature and the just society. Thanks for everything.

Since I started writing this book, I've become a parent too, and I can only hope that I will be able to offer something similar to my daughters. Sasha and Rory: you've made my life rich. If, in later years, you happen to read this book, know that I was happy while I wrote it, because of you. And Masha—for a million reasons, but mainly because you're my brilliant best friend, this book is for you.

An abbreviated version of chapter 5 appeared in "The Large Novel and the Law of Large Numbers, or Why George Eliot Hates Gambling," *ELH* 77, no. 3 (Fall 2010). A few paragraphs of chapter 3 appeared in "Being in the Plot: Action, Intuition, and Trolleys," *boundary 2* 40, no. 2 (Summer 2013). There is some overlap between chapter 2 and the entry "The Newgate Novel," and between chapter 3 and the entry "Wit and Humor" in the *Blackwell Encyclopedia of Victorian Literature* (London: Wiley-Blackwell, 2015).

GOOD FORM

INTRODUCTION

"MORALISED FABLES"

riedrich Nietzsche, writing at the close of the nineteenth century, offered an account of the "origin of English morality." Victorians had
replaced their religion with morality, Nietzsche argued, and in place
of God, now believed that the source of right action lay within.[1] No one,
for Nietzsche, exemplified this better than the zealous-Calvinist-turned-
secular-novelist, George Eliot:

> They are rid of the Christian God and now believe all the more firmly
> that they must cling to Christian morality. That is an English con-
> sistency; we do not wish to hold it against little moralistic females
> *à la* Eliot. In England one must rehabilitate oneself after every little
> emancipation from theology by showing in a veritably awe-inspiring
> manner what a moral fanatic one is. . . . When the English actually
> believe that they know "intuitively" what is good and evil, when they
> therefore suppose that they no longer require Christianity as the guar-
> antee of morality, we merely witness . . . that the origin of English
> morality has been forgotten.[2]

Nietzsche is wrong here, in the ways that he is often wrong: a lack of dis-
crimination in the spectrum of the religious and the secular, a characteristic
contempt for the figure of the "the literary female."[3] But in the essentials, he
is correct. Over the course of the nineteenth century, an "intuitive" faith in
an internalized sense of right and wrong did come to take an increasingly
prominent, if fraught, place in English moral life. And it was to be "moralistic" figures like George Eliot—that is, novelists—who would provide the
most lasting expression of this prominence.[4] One more thing Nietzsche was
correct about, albeit not quite in the way he intended: the origin of this
connection—between novel-writing, intuition, and morality—would come
to be largely forgotten.

What do we mean now when we say that the progress of a narrative
"feels right"? How did feeling, form, and the sense of right and wrong get

1

mixed up, in the nineteenth century, in the experience of reading a novel? This book is an attempt to answer these questions. The compulsion of narrative, a reader's feeling of being drawn through a text, was a key term in the developing novel art of the nineteenth century. Thackeray, for example, would describe Dickens's novelistic skill in these terms: "The power of the writer is so amazing, that the reader at once becomes his captive, and must follow him whithersoever he leads."[5] The metaphor of physical motion, which Victorians applied to the reading experience, came to offer a means of describing the movement from what *is* to what *ought to be*—or at least the yearning for that movement. At the same time, the moral valence that readers placed on the stories they read came to shape, in terms of both market forces and creative tradition, the principles that now define the well-plotted realist novel.

This book, then, will make two joined arguments. First: when Victorians discussed—as they so often did—the moral dimensions of novel reading, a closer look will demonstrate that they were being a good deal more attentive to the formal properties of the novel than we have tended to give them credit for. And, second: that the moral principles that attached to the Victorian understanding of the novel form have persisted, and become an implicit part of our own ongoing critical practice. We have begun, with the recent work of critics such as Nicholas Dames and Caroline Levine, to give the Victorians credit for their formal understanding of literature.[6] Yet even in these discussions, the moral dimensions of Victorian thought still remain a bit of an embarrassment for critics: a sort of stuffy, stiff-necked rectitude that can obscure more meaningful scientific or aesthetic insights. By offering a fuller context for the ethical discourse of the British nineteenth century, *Good Form* argues that Victorian formalism was inextricably tied to moral thought. This not only impacts our reading of Victorian literary and philosophical history but also offers a new perspective on our own approaches to literature. We cannot understand the formal principles of the novel that we have inherited from the nineteenth century without also understanding the moral principles that have come with them. Key Victorian insights into the theory and practice of narrative came in the guise of morals arguments, much as more recent insights have taken the form of linguistics or cultural history. And the force of these moral readings has so shaped the structure of novels, and our understanding of them, that we continue to reenact these readings today. Victorian moral thought, in other words, has become part of the fabric of both novel theory and canonical formation: what we read and how we read it.

At the center of my argument lies the term, "intuition," which Nietzsche singled out to describe what he saw as a typically Victorian approach to moral concerns. His use of the word was not arbitrary, and corresponds to its frequent usage in the philosophical debates of the day.[7] As Bernard

Williams puts it, "Intuition used to be taken as an intellectual power of arriving at abstract truths, and its application to ethics lay in the idea that ethical truths could be grasped *a priori* by such a faculty."[8] The school that this term came to apply to, philosophers like William Whewell and H. L. Mansel, situated itself in opposition to the consequentialist and deliberative utilitarianism of Bentham and the Mills. Intuitionists argued in the tradition of Lord Shaftesbury and Frances Hutcheson for an internal basis for moral ideas. As Mansel put it in an 1854 lecture, "conceptions of right and wrong without an intuitive moral faculty are as impossible as conceptions of colours without a sense of sight."[9] Now, we normally remember the period for its utilitarianism, but at the time, the intuitionist side had enough currency that John Stuart Mill opens *Utilitarianism* by setting himself in opposition to it: his work, he says, will refuse to have "recourse to the popular theory of a natural faculty, a sense or instinct, informing us of what is right and wrong."[10] Discussions of the nineteenth century, therefore, which stress the dominance of utilitarianism to such an extent that there seems to be little else on the ethical landscape, have little to say about the role of the moral sense and intuitionist thought. As J. B. Schneewind has noted, "the intuitionist standpoint is, quite surprisingly considering its importance for the thought of the period, almost completely neglected in histories of philosophy no less than in surveys of literature."[11] If we want to understand how Victorians understood themselves as moral beings, then, we need to broaden the scope of our conversation to try to explain the experience of intuitive judgment.

This means looking beyond the narrow confines of utilitarianism—but it also means reconsidering the stereotype of the moralizing Victorian.[12] Such a stereotype is a legacy of the *fin-de-siècle* and modernism, and contends that Victorian novels suffered from having their morality bolted on: opinionated narrative intrusions that did not serve an aesthetic or formal purpose. In an 1885 review of a biography of George Eliot, Henry James took the occasion to sum up the author's "general attitude with regard to the novel": "not primarily a picture of life, capable of deriving a high value from its form, but a moralised fable, the last word of a philosophy endeavouring to teach by example."[13] This reading of Eliot, and of the Victorian novel in general—moralism over formalism, good intentions over good writing—took hold in the early part of the twentieth century and has yet to let go. F. R. Leavis, for example, uses this quote in *The Great Tradition* as evidence that James "show[s] finer intelligence than anyone else in writing about George Eliot."[14] We see a similar approach taken by Virginia Woolf, when she introduces George Meredith as an example of the disparity between the nineteenth century and "the age we now live in—the year 1928." The Victorians, Woolf suggests, let their moralizing get in the way:

His teaching seems now too strident and too optimistic and too shallow. It obtrudes; and when philosophy is not consumed in a novel, when we can underline this phrase with a pencil, and cut out that exhortation with a pair of scissors and paste the whole into a system, it is safe to say that there is something wrong with the philosophy or with the novel or with both. Above all, his teaching is too insistent. He cannot, even to hear the profoundest secret, suppress his own opinion.[15]

Meredith's typically Victorian failing, then, as far as Woolf is concerned, is not so much that his work has a moral quality. Rather, it is that, like James's version of Eliot, he *moralizes*—that is to say, he presents a moral argument that seems to be separate, or separable, from his artistic product.

What I will argue in this book is that it would take a good deal more than even the formidable combined powers of Henry James and Virginia Woolf to separate out the moral content from Victorian novels. I am not talking here about Eliot's occasional harangues or Meredith's overt erudition; these are a certain sort of stylistic trait typical of, though by no means confined to, the nineteenth century. What is more deeply ingrained in the form of the Victorian novel is the sense of narrative necessity that underwrites naive novel reading and the most sophisticated narratologies alike. By focusing discussions of morals in Victorian novels on authorial intrusions and philosophic themes—on those non-narrative elements of the novel that seem to disrupt the novel's forward progress—we tend to miss the ways in which moral ideas can become a part of narrative structure itself. The central issue in the *Madame Bovary* obscenity trial, for example, was whether the novel was *about* Emma's sexual activities, or instead just featured them as a way of focusing on a moral lesson.[16] In other words, the moral questions surrounding Flaubert's novel became questions of whether the meaning of the novel was to be found in synchronic description or diachronic narrative development. The same question, it turns out, was operative in debates about the propriety of crime novels—"Newgate novels," as they were called—and their representation of vice. If vice and criminals were presented in the service of a Bunyanesque progress toward salvation, as many argued was the case with Dickens's *Oliver Twist*, then such details would be morally acceptable. If they were presented as an end in themselves—charges often leveled against other Newgate novels by Edward Bulwer-Lytton and William Harrison Ainsworth—then the novel could be considered immoral. In crime novels, then, morality or vice was a function of whether the details of the novel took on a diachronic or synchronic form. The feeling that Thackeray described in Dickens, of being "led," became the experience that allowed the novel its ethical dimension. I will discuss these points in greater depth in chapter 2, but the key point here is that when Victorian critics discussed the morality of novels, they were discussing a good deal more than its static elements: the explicit arguments and the choice of details. Instead, what we find when we look closely is that arguments about moral topics frequently turned on nuanced formal points.

And it is here—where Victorian theory and practice move back and forth between the formal and the moral—that we can locate the moral content that modernist critics would be unable, in Woolf's words, to "cut out . . . with a pair of scissors." What we have come to see as formal novelistic principles—narrative disclosure, character development, the relation of the one and the many—continue to echo the intuitionist moral ideas of the nineteenth century. Nietzsche saw moral intuition as the cross scratched in the sand, marking where the Victorians had buried, and forgotten, their dead God. But now, as Schneewind suggests, even that burial site—the tradition of intuitionist thought—has been forgotten, with the result that discussions of narrative form have come to seem ethically neutral. Still, we encounter the "intuitionist standpoint" every time we make reference to the propulsive force of the narrative, in terms like Georg Lukács's "poetic necessity," Roland Barthes's "constraint of the discourse," or Peter Brooks's "narrative desire."[17] Each of these terms relies on its own metalanguage—historical materialism, structural linguistics, psychoanalysis—and yet each is still dependent on the sniff-test, on a criterion of "I'll know it when I see it."

Moral intuition and these intuitions of theory: the similarity between the two goes beyond analogy. One intuition is not simply *like* another. Rather, in the moral conceptualizations of narrative form, through the give-and-take of literary evolution, Victorian reading practices codified a certain sort of text, and a certain way of understanding it. But—and this is important—I do not mean here that our reading is actually governed by moral intuitions: that some turns of events (a successful courtship, perhaps, or responsible maturation toward a vocation) actually appeal to our moral faculties. What I mean is that "moral intuition" is the name that Victorians gave to the experience of anticipated, developing, formal satisfaction. Over the nineteenth century, through the dialectic of production and reception, that moral description came to seem a part of the formal. It is easy now to miss the moral inflection when novel theories imply that we can all recognize a successfully completed narrative arc. But the central idea here—of an agreed-upon sense of what constitutes the right outcome of events—is where Victorian ideas of morality ended up. The understanding of moral intuitions shifted over the nineteenth century—from an innate faculty to tacit communal consensus—until we were left with a form and interpretive methods, shaped by moral concerns and yet somehow understood to be morally neutral. The moral concerns of the Victorians have taught us how to read their books.

Is it any wonder, then, that generations of critics have been troubled by the power of narrative form to naturalize, to *argue for*, certain moral positions? We don't read completely ingenuously; any generic understanding requires a sort of primitive novel theory. And part of that primitive novel theory—the part that finds that a certain sort of story feels right—has moral considerations built into it, which can act as the ground for any number of normative positions. This is all to say that the focus on ethical thought in this book should not be taken as a denial of the political or ideological work that novels can do. I agree, for the most part, that novel narrative can be subtly coercive. But what are the conditions of possibility for a novel narrative being political or ideological in the first place? We generally take it for granted that there can be something normative—or galvanizing, or politically inspiring—in a five-hundred-page account of the made-up experiences of made-up people. But how does a compelling story become a compelling argument? That is the question that this book seeks to address.

Fifteen years ago, a book like this would have needed to offer a justification for its focus on ethics. Now, on the other side of criticism's "turn to ethics,"[18] connecting moral thought and literary form hardly requires explanation. But this project does require, perhaps, some explanation of what it is not. While I am certainly anxious to vindicate Victorian literature from modernist caricatures of its overt moralism, I do not want my argument to be taken as a championing of the period's covert, formal, moral ideas. In particular, I would like to emphasize that this book does not take as axiomatic the transformative hypothesis: the idea that that reading novels actually alters people's moral or political character. This notion seems to be implicit in most discussions of novels, and particularly discussions of novel realism— even those that would not explicitly subscribe to it. When Fredric Jameson, in the *Political Unconscious*, characterizes "the bulk of garden-variety literary criticism" as "ethical," he is referring to a sort of criticism that looks to literature for "permanent features of human 'experience,' and thus . . . a kind of 'wisdom' about personal life and interpersonal relationships."[19] Even criticism that does not see itself as concerned with ethics will still tend to look for instructive examples: what Eliot, say, shows us about egoism, or what Dickens reminds us about the effects of dehumanizing bureaucracy. As we will see in chapter 1, the tradition of novel criticism, through its varied twentieth- and twenty-first-century forms, has tended to justify its institutional existence by calling on this broadly ethical model. Given this tacit disciplinary consensus, the sort of link between ethics and novel form that I am drawing in this book will, inevitably, sound like it is arguing for the mildly life-altering properties of reading. Suffice it to say here that this is not my intention. There is moral thought in these novels—even moral arguments implicit in their form—but I am not convinced that it is morally improving to read them.[20] This should not be taken as a jab at those who do draw lessons from their readings. This book is greatly indebted to the work of critics such as Amanda Anderson, Caroline Levine, and Andrew Miller, who have returned with care and precision to the moral concerns of

Victorians and shown how those concerns are still of relevance to us today.[21] In each of these cases, an ethical thrust of Victorian fiction—Habermasian communicative rationality for Anderson, imaginative reconsideration of social possibilities for Levine, radical self-improvement for Miller—becomes in some way an ethical challenge for readers.[22] While I remain skeptical about the suggestion that novels themselves can transform us, I am largely convinced that faithful, ethically charged criticism, acting in concert with these novels, can provide a useful model of attentive reading and can be a spur to moral thought. But, when it comes to moral intuition, setting such an example is not, for better or for worse, what I wish to do in this book.

And, after all, we certainly don't need the Victorians to tell us to be more intuitive in our moral lives. When it comes to morality, we are plenty intuitive enough already—*too* intuitive, I tend to think, when it comes to things like hiring, housing, and voting for public office. What a careful reexamination of Victorian moral thought does offer, though, is a greater understanding of the moral undercurrents of our critical and theoretical heritage. I am less concerned with pointing out what we might learn about right action from a careful reading of Victorian texts; I am more concerned with learning how we developed that practice of careful reading in the first place. The ethical intuitions that our literary practice has learned from the Victorians and internalized—the feeling of rightness, and the pull toward a better conclusion—are those feelings that we use to explain the rightness of a conclusion, or the familiarity of a text over space and time. *Good Form* does not propose to offer lessons, handed down from the Victorians, that we *ought to* learn. Rather, I want to show how their moral beliefs have inflected what we have already learned—and what we, as literary critics and cultural historians, already do. It seems clear to me that Victorians were indeed concerned, through and through, with moral questions. But it also seems clear to me that this did not produce only the rigid moralism so often associated with Victorianism. It also produced subtle thought on the nature of reading. Any encounter with their novels, and with many realist novels that we read in the same fashion, must take into account the moral stamp that their intuitions left on their work, and on us.

In my first chapter, "What Feels Right," I will pick up on the questions that I have raised in this introduction, in order to show how literary theory bears the mark of the ethical debates of the nineteenth century. Through a reading of two industrial novels, Elizabeth Gaskell's *Mary Barton* and Charles Dickens's *Hard Times*, as well as a discussion of a number of classic narrative theorists, I will show how narrative theory, underwritten by a principle of forward compulsion through the text, reiterates the position of the intuitionist thinkers of the Victorian period. By then turning to a discussion of the philosophical arguments of Bernard Williams—famous for his use of small narratives as philosophical argument—I will suggest how narrative form, having subsumed the tenets of intuitionism, itself became an effective argumentative practice.

In the chapter that follows, "The Subject of the Newgate Novel," I will focus what I take to be a central moment in the development of these moral narrative practices—one that is, at the same time, a moment in the coming into being of "the Victorian novel." Looking at *Oliver Twist* and the "Newgate novel" controversy of the 1830s, I offer an example of one way in which the experience of diachronic reading could be interpreted in an explicitly moral fashion. The specific formal technique that I will be discussing is "suspense," understood broadly as a novel's overt withholding of certain key elements from its readers. This is a pretty familiar part of a good deal of Victorian narrative—*Jane Eyre* and *Little Dorrit* come immediately to mind. Looking at Newgate novels, crime novels whose moment of popularity immediately precedes the appearance of such canonical figures as Dickens and Thackeray, I show that the basis for the contemporary condemnations and defenses of these works—specifically of Ainsworth's *Jack Sheppard* and Dickens's *Oliver Twist*—was not simply subject matter but also narrative method that produced the novels' moral, or immoral, effects. In particular, I show that Dickens's novel parts ways with the larger subgenre at the moments that it calls attention to the fact that there is a backstory that is both responsible for the events we read and inaccessible to us. In other words, it becomes both more morally acceptable to its contemporary readers and more of a familiar "Victorian novel"—the very first, according to some—to its modern readers. Ainsworth's novel, on the other hand, betrays a certain strangeness that was part and parcel of its moral unacceptability: a sense that it was not directed by any law outside of the events that it was describing. This chapter thus serves to introduce the moral themes of the Victorian novel and also to show an example of what storytelling that does not make use of moral sensibility might look like.

Suspense, though, was not the only narrative mechanism that an author could use to imply that there was a "law" governing the text. My third chapter, "Getting David Copperfield," finds another method in a rather unlikely place: humor. This is not, as I show through a discussion of Romantic and Victorian writings on the subject, a humor that was defined by its ability to make a reader laugh. Rather, I show that humor was a strategy used to produce, in the reader, the experience of unspoken agreement and shared community with others. What was withheld in *Oliver Twist* is here present, but forgotten as a part of everyday life. The narrative of David's progression is always measured against this backdrop of an anonymously judging public of which he is part, and the novel's narrative method seeks to move him into agreement with that public. The novel thus uses humor to underscore the idea that our individual intuitions are shared, though in ways that are difficult to conceptualize. Dickens's narrative technique thus makes use of an externalization, into the social sphere, of a reader's individual feeling.

Themes of the two previous chapters—canonicity and *sensus communis*—come together in the next chapter, on the *Bildungsroman*. "Back in Time" is a study of the philosophical and literary significance of the novel of development. Of particular interest will be the question of how this one particular narrative trajectory came to stand in, at least in the study of the Victorian novel, for the much larger body of nineteenth-century literature. Why does *Oliver Twist*, for example, follow its developmental narrative into the textual archive of Victorian studies, while *Jack Sheppard*, profoundly nondevelopmental, remain outside as historical context? Through readings of Margaret Oliphant's *Miss Marjoribanks*, Goethe's *Wilhelm Meister's Apprenticeship*, *Great Expectations* and Mill's *Autobiography*, I will suggest that the ethical foundations of the concept of *Bildung*—and in particular the idea of *sensus communis*—made form in the *Bildungsroman*, lay the groundwork for our own understanding of what makes a novel count as an object of study.

"The Large Novel and the Law of Large Numbers," on George Eliot's *Daniel Deronda*, exposes a suspicion with the very possibility of development—particularly as it relates to the connection between an individual and her larger community. In the process, I suggest that Eliot's final work calls into question the ethical implication of individual intuitions in general. I have been arguing that the nineteenth-century novel form linked developmental narrative, intuition, and a sense of social embeddedness; in Eliot's novel we can see a deep distrust of this connection. Looking at the novel in the context of changing understandings of statistics and probability, I show how Eliot's sweeping narrative structure highlights the divide she, and many of her contemporaries, had come to see between intuition and the outcomes that emerge from long durations and large numbers. By thematizing the counterintuitive nature of the statistical split between the one and the many, Eliot expressed her discomfort with the Victorian connection of individual intuition and the novelistic representation of larger groups.

Finally, as a conclusion, I turn briefly to a consideration of how the arguments in this book relate to the question of literary periodization. This is, without question, a book on Victorian literature, written in the context of Victorian moral thought. From that point of view, it is very much rooted to a specific time and place. On the other hand, many of the arguments and theoretical ideas in this book rely on a certain concept of realism that would seem to extend beyond Britain and beyond the nineteenth century. In these closing thoughts, I will consider just how much of my argument is portable to a larger discussion of literary realism. In so doing, I hope to elaborate the ways in which the Victorian novel, and the moral thought that attached to it, has continued to influence our larger sense of how works from the past can seem to be, in some odd way, about us.

CHAPTER 1

WHAT FEELS RIGHT: ETHICS, INTUITION, AND THE EXPERIENCE OF NARRATIVE

Georg Lukács, in a 1935 essay on Balzac's *Lost Illusions*, offers a defense of the "old-fashioned . . . methods of plot-building" against natural- ist accusations of clumsy contrivance.[1] Realist novelists like Balzac and Dickens, Lukács claims, produce such "subtle and multiple intercon- nections" in their novels that the events in their narratives take on a *"poetic necessity,"* which is more important than the plausibility of any individual event:

> Introduce an accident, however well-founded causally, into any tragic conflict and it is merely grotesque; no chain of cause and effect could ever turn such accident into a necessity. The most thorough and accurate description of the state of the ground which would cause Achilles to sprain his ankle while pursuing Hector or the most bril- liant medico-pathological explanation of why Antony lost his voice through a throat infection just before he was due to make his great speech over Caesar's body in the forum could never make such things appear as anything but grotesque accidents; on the other hand, in the catastrophe of Romeo and Juliet the rough-hewn, scarcely motivated accidents do not appear as mere chance. (56)

Here Lukács makes archly explicit something that lies implicit in most dis- cussions of narrative. Not all events are created equal; some seem right and some seem wrong, even if it is difficult to say precisely why or how. Still, Lukács claims, with what might seem like an almost naive insistence, there is really no alternative: "Romeo and Juliet's love *must* end in tragedy" and "Lucien must perish in Paris." These outcomes represent the "true neces- sity" that inheres in Shakespeare's tragedy or Balzac's novel.

But, of course, this "true necessity" is not *truly* necessary. There is no logical reason to assume that *Lost Illusions* could not have ended with Lucien staying in the country. What Lukács means is that, if such a novel were to exist, its conclusion would "appear grotesque." Is this just hindsight bias—the belief that because something happened, it *had* to happen—or an overreliance on teleology? While Lukács might be willing to subscribe to the latter, I would argue that it points to something far more basic in the way that critics discuss, write about, and read novel narrative. Novel theory in the twentieth and twenty-first centuries, for all its sophistication of critical metalanguage, has long rested on an important but largely unexamined premise: that certain directions in novel narrative will seem—or "appear," or "feel"—right, and others will seem wrong. The language that critics use to make these claims will usually involve some metaphor of vision, or physical sensation, or nonrational intuition. After all, there is no logical or rational reason Achilles could not have sprained his ankle. At the base of narrative theory has been a largely tacit agreement not only that narrative is a system of representation that we respond to in some nonrational way but also that we ratify narrative as either successful or unsuccessful at this nonrational level. If narrative "works," it does so because of how it makes us feel—and, so the story seems to go, there is no way to tell just how it will make us feel without actually engaging in the experience.

In this chapter, I will attempt to sketch out the history and consequences of this connection between novel narrative and a felt, intuitive experience over time. What I hope to show is that this hard-to-define quality of narrative—its ability to engage a reader and mobilize expectation toward a certain state of affairs—is intimately connected with the moral concerns of the nineteenth century. This is not only an issue for understanding individual narratives; since literary studies depends on distinguishing a few model texts for close study, the question of how we recognize a successful or well-formed narrative has a great impact on the discipline as a whole. This will be a theme in later chapters in this book: how these concerns helped to form the novelistic tradition into its recognizable shape by conflating certain morally inflected experiences with what we have come to see as satisfying narrative structure. First, though, it will be useful to reflect on how our own understanding of narrative form has been shaped, through and through, by a reliance on intuition—and just how much implicit morality that intuition has brought along with it.

NOVEL INTUITIONS

If we wish to look for the root of this reliance on intuition, a good place to start would be the principal metalanguage of narrative theory over the last half-century or so: linguistics.[2] Linguistics depends, in large part, on the un-reflective judgment of the competent speaker as its court of highest appeal. As Chomsky puts it, "linguistics as a discipline is characterized by attention to certain kinds of evidence that are . . . readily accessible and informative: largely, the judgments of native speakers."[3] These judgments are not based on a consciously held set of rules. Instead, as one popular linguistics textbook claims, "all the linguist has to go by . . . is the native speaker's intuitions."[4] While it is true that literary studies have been a good deal more influenced by a Saussurean social model than a Chomskyan model of deep grammar, the field still makes use of the idea of the native speaker. In fact, at the heart of a good deal of twentieth-century literary study is Chomsky's reformulation of the Saussurean distinction between *langue* and *parole* as *competence* and *performance*.[5] "Performance," as Jonathan Culler explains it, would allow a speaker to utter an ungrammatical statement through distraction or to make an effect of some sort; "competence" is based more on a "judgment": "Competence is reflected in the judgment passed on an utterance or in the fact that the rule violated is partly responsible for the effect achieved."[6] Culler's choice of emphasis here makes clear that a central inheritance that literary study takes from linguistics is the idea that we can understand the "rules" by imagining a judge—native or competent—who can tell when those rules are broken. More to the point, we can understand rules by imagining the "effects" they will have on the reader when they are broken.

This method is, by Culler's account, an essential element of literary study. As he puts it, "One cannot . . . emphasize too strongly that every critic, whatever his persuasion, encounters the problems of literary competence as soon as he begins to speak or write about literary works, and that he takes for granted notions of acceptability and common ways of reading" (124). We speak of a *langue* underwriting the narrative *parole*, in other words, but we prove it through the intuitive judgment that a competent reader passes on a literary performance. Obviously, Lukács is not claiming that all readers, everywhere, will react with disgust to the examples he offers. It may well be possible for someone to view Antony's sore throat with pleasure, but it would be someone lacking in competence and therefore not worth analyzing.

The problem that arises when this procedure of intuitive judgment is applied to literature, though, is that while most of us can easily imagine how to construct a sentence that we could intuit to be faulty—a glaring subject-verb disagreement would probably suffice—it is quite a bit harder to say what an "incorrect" narrative might be. Take, for example, Seymour Chatman's suggestion that all of the elements of a narrative must eventually be shown to be "relevant": "otherwise we object that the narrative is 'ill-formed.'"[7] The way Chatman proceeds here is through a standard method of argument in narrative theory: argument by contradiction, or *reductio ad absurdum*. Assume something to be the case, and then claim that this would lead to an unsuccessful narrative. And yet we note that, in order to classify the narrative as unsuccessful, Chatman has to imagine readers—"we" competent readers—"objecting" to it. The problem with this approach is one that I imagine many of Chatman's actual readers faced, if they paused over this: allowing he had a point, working through a few possible counterexamples, and ultimately concluding, "I'd have to read it and see." It is quite difficult to judge a narrative ill-formed, in other words, absent the intuition that only comes with the experience of reading it.

Novel theory generally tries to explain away its reliance on intuition and experience by reference to an underlying constraint based in a theoretical metalanguage. Thus, for example, Barthes will claim, in *S/Z*, that the narrative is propelled onward "by the discourse's instinct for preservation."[8] Barthes is here referring to a point in the Balzac story "Sarrasine," when the protagonist receives a mysterious warning, instructing him not to visit the castrato Zambinella. He chooses to disregard this warning, and the story continues. But, as Barthes tells us, there really never was a choice. For if Sarrasine does not make the right decision, "there would be no story." Again, "I'd have to read it and see," but it seems that there could very well be a story; this moment could produce something no more significant than a suspenseful delay. Counterfactual, to be sure, but what I have been suggesting is that discussions of narrative consistently turn to the counterfactual and then suggest that this course could not have been taken. Yet whatever their choice of metalanguage may be—Marxism, linguistics, psychoanalysis, history—narrative theorists do not actually mean that an underlying structure made a certain outcome *necessary*. What they mean is that, had another outcome come about, it would have somehow felt wrong.

My intention here is not to say whether these critics are right or wrong about the specific plot points that they analyze. Rather, what I wish to point out is that, for all their differences in theoretical approach, each implicitly assumes that given a traditional (realist, old-fashioned, readerly) narrative and a competent reader, that reader will feel that the narrative exerts some sort of compulsion, which necessitates that something "must" happen, or which "constrains" the direction of the story to one goal. But at the same time, they all are forced to allow that this compulsion, this felt necessity, only exists as a feeling that readers will intuit. What "should" happen in novel narrative, in other words, becomes a question of what feels right.

The idea persists in the language used—Lukács's sight metaphor, Barthes's reference to constraint—that there is something essentially physical in this feeling. Perhaps the most familiar physicalization of the experience of reading, in the twentieth century, is Peter Brooks's drive-based description of the experience as "narrative desire": the "desire that carries us forward, onward, through the text."[9] The idea of being somehow carried, though, stretches back to the nineteenth century. Thackeray, as we have seen, describes Dickens's "power" in similar terms of compulsion: the "reader at once becomes his captive, and must follow him."[10] Desire offers one way of describing an experience that seems almost physical; Thackeray takes the more direct approach of suggesting that the writer has simply taken the reader in hand.

Indeed, nineteenth-century England probably offered the most serious attempts to describe the seemingly physical nature of narrative experience. Nicholas Dames argues that "physiology was the metalanguage of nineteenth-century novel theory, as perhaps linguistics is of twentieth-century novel theory."[11] The philosopher and physiologist Alexander Bain, to take one example, offers the classification of the "mental attitude under a gradually approaching end, a condition of suspense" as either "Pursuit" or "Plot-interest."[12] As the first term suggests, Bain understands this to encompass all sorts of movements toward a desired goal, in animals as well as humans. As the second term suggests, though, the engagement with narrative is the example par excellence of this sensation. After a discussion of the various physical and mental effects of this phenomenon, Bain offers the following: "the composer of fiction and romance studies how to work up the interest to the highest pitch. The entire narration in an epic poem, or romance, is conceived to an agreeable end, which is suspended by intermediate actions, and thrown into pleasing uncertainty" (273). The fact that Bain feels comfortable using the engagement with narrative to encapsulate a wide array of physical phenomena with only a minimum of explanation suggests that there was some contemporary agreement on the idea that narrative mechanics such as suspense and delay could have a physical effect on a novel's readers.

The idea of the nonrational draw of narrative thus has a long—and, I think, familiar—connection with the reading experience. Yet this experience, call it what you will, has rarely received much consideration in the twentieth century as more than a guilty or, at best, empty pleasure. While novels' formal techniques could produce the sensation of being led or compelled, and make their readers intuit some sort of necessity, this was just the spoonful of sugar that made the more important work of the novel—intersubjective character studies, and examinations of relations with other intelligences—go down.

For, come the twentieth century, it was this relation to the lives of others that would be the central ethical lens through which the novel would be viewed. As Dorothy Hale has convincingly shown, post-Jamesian theories of the novel, despite their varied differences, largely agree that "the novel's primary ideological work [is] the promotion of sympathy."[13] Such theories are "committed to a moral belief in the intrinsic good of alterity—that humans are most fulfilled when they come to know sympathetically persons who are substantially different from themselves" (8). Novel reading, then, becomes an ethical act insofar as it becomes about the reader's relation with another person. Or, to be more precise, it becomes an ethical act when it induces the reader to respond to trope and convention in a way that resembles—and hopefully educates the reader in preparation for—encountering flesh-and-blood humans. In fact, some have gone so far as to suggest that this "ideological work" is not only the ethical dimension of novels but the novelistic domain of ethics. Martha Nussbaum, for example, argues that "the narrative styles of writers such as James and Proust" are at least as well suited as, if not better suited than, "abstract philosophical style" for exposing the reader to "the truths about human life."[14] Richard Rorty, meanwhile, goes even further, stating that narrative expression, especially that offered by novels, is the superior vehicle for expressing these truths:

> This process of coming to see other human beings as "one of us" rather than as "them" . . . is a task not for theory but for genres such as ethnography, the journalist's report, the comic book, the docudrama, and, especially, the novel. Fiction like that of Dickens, Olive Schreiner, and Richard Wright gives us details about kinds of suffering being endured by people to whom we had not previously attended.[15]

For Rorty, the central ethical categories of novel narrative are "us" and "them": our relation to others beside ourselves. Though not quite as explicit, Nussbaum suggests as much as well, by her reference to "human life"—presumably, exposure to lives other than our own offer us the potential for improvement. The ethical dimension of narrative methods, and particularly novel narrative methods, is at its base a social one.

Though Rorty lists a number of different genres, he accords pride of place ("especially") to the novel. This fits in well with the tradition that Hale describes. This "ideological work" is specific to the novel, according to the theorists that Hale discusses, because its effect derives from certain generic formal elements. Hale refers to this theoretical tradition, at once formal and concerned with our relation to others, as "social formalism." So for James and Lubbock, the key formal category becomes "point of view": a formal strategy that allows readers insight into human relations that they might not otherwise be able to obtain. For Bakhtin, it becomes the carnival and the dialogical: a formal strategy that allows characters and social classes to speak in their own voices, freed from the monological control of the author's own voice and identity.[16] As this latter example shows, the novel's moral work need not be strictly confined to sympathy after the fashion of Adam Smith. That is, it need not be only "our fellow-feeling with any passion" felt by another.[17] We can go even further and suggest that theoretical work that specifically *refutes* the value of intersubjective sympathy, as in the application of Emmanuel Levinas to novel criticism, still continues in this "social formalist" tradition.[18] Gayatri Chakravorty Spivak, in an essay dealing with J. M. Coetzee's *Disgrace*, focuses on the "inability" of David Lurie, the novel's main character, to "'read' [his daughter] Lucy as patient and agent" after she has been brutally raped.[19] She sees this as part of the novel's Levinasian approach to Lucy (21–22n). Yet even so, this refusal to allow for sympathetic identification ends up being a central technique of "[l]iterary reading [that] teaches us to learn from the singular and unverifiable"—in fact, she even goes so far as to say that if the neo-conservative Paul Wolfowitz, the architect of the wars in the Middle East that have spanned most of the last fifteen years, "had had serious training in literary reading and/or the imagining of the enemy as human, his position on Iraq would not be so inflexible" (23). The very formal techniques that work against sympathy in the novel, Spivak claims, would encourage a practice of reading, "literary reading," with the possibility of a deeply significant social impact. From the promotion of sympathy to its refutation, then, we can say that novel theory has been linked by a belief that the novel form's methods of encountering other intelligences—their thoughts, language, experience—are what makes the reading experience ethical.

What we should notice here is that these formal techniques are essentially different from the sort used to produce "narrative desire" or "plot interest." In social-formalist approaches to the novel, the key moments usually involve the sight of other people, represented in an essentially synchronic fashion. This has its roots, I believe, in the visual metaphors that surround the idea of sympathy. Smith founds his theory of moral sentiments on the figure of the "impartial spectator," who is able to imagine the experience of someone else—say, someone in pain. The encounter here is not one of empathy; the spectator does not actually experience the sufferer's pain as well. Instead, upon viewing it, "the spectator represents to himself the sentiments and sensations of the sufferer through a deliberate act of the imagination."[20] I am passing over a number of the fine points of Smith's theory here, because I want to stress the following: the interaction between the spectator and the sufferer in this case takes the form of a static representation. Traditionally, this form of representation has been taken to be visual. Audrey Jaffe, for example, stresses the importance of the visual sense for a Victorian novel-reading public: "sympathy in Victorian fiction takes shape in, and as, a series of visualized narratives."[21] Now, certainly, this "series" occurs over time, but the series that Jaffe describes is less the experience of moving through time, and more a comparable series of visual encounters. In other words, it is more a multiplicity of synchronic moments than any sense of the diachronic. Rae Greiner objects to this "questionable practice of characterizing Smithian sympathy as a predominantly visual affair," pointing to the importance of "imaginative reflection" in Smith's philosophy.[22] Greiner does so, though, in the service of a relation to other intelligences—chief among them what she calls "fellow-feeling"—that firmly places literary realism in the social-formalist tradition.

In the experience of narrative, though, the social engagement that gives social formalism its moral charge is largely absent. This is clearly true in the psycho-physiological cases of Brooks and Bain. And I would argue that it is present as well in Thackeray's metaphor of "following" the author's lead; there is no sign that he is particularly interested in what we might call the narrator's "point of view." Instead, his point is that the narrator makes us want to see what happens next. Our relation, therefore, is not with the narrator himself but rather with the compulsion to move through a sequence of events. The figure who leads is not so much a personified narrator as it is the compelling force, the personification of Brooks's psychic drives or Bain's animal instincts. The point is that this sort of experience of narrative necessity, instead of having something to say about our relations with other intelligences, is largely understood as an internal experience.

THE INTERNAL PRINCIPLE

In 1832—five years after *Pelham*, five years before *Pickwick*, during the period that with the benefit of hindsight we can designate as the dawning of the Victorian novel—the Reverend Adam Sedgwick delivered a sermon attacking the moral education at Cambridge.[23] *A Discourse on the Studies of the University*, as it was titled when published, was largely a critique of utilitarianism. This is not surprising; it fits nicely with the novelistic tradition which was then coming into being, a tradition that would, in its major works, return repeatedly to a pointed and explicit denunciation of the principle of utility. In the early 1830s, though, utilitarianism was less associated with Bentham or the Mills and more with the religious system of William Paley, whose *Moral and Political Philosophy* was the textbook of moral philosophy at Cambridge. And what concerned Sedgwick in Paley's work was not those points we now associate with an opposition to utilitarianism: dangers of egoism, irreducible dignity of the individual, artistic creativity. Rather, Sedgwick criticized Paley for his denial of "the sanction and authority of the moral sense."[24] As Sedgwick put it: "to reject the moral sense is to destroy the foundation of all moral philosophy." The public reaction to the *Discourse*, both positive and negative, was strong. The *Times of London* praised its "great and varied excellence";[25] John Stuart Mill, on the other hand, quickly penned a scathing review: "We shall show that Mr. Sedgwick has no right to represent Paley as a type of the theory of utility; that he has failed in refuting even Paley; and that the tone of high moral reprobation

which he has assumed toward all who adopt that theory is altogether un-
merited on their part, and on his, from his extreme ignorance of the subject, peculiarly unbecoming."[26] He still had harsh words for Sedgwick in
his autobiography, decades later.[27] Whether positive or negative, Sedgwick's
message, it seems, had found resonance.

But what is this "moral sense" that Sedgwick is so anxious to defend?
The term seems a naive one in the context of the rational utilitarianism
identified with the period. In fact, when discussed today, the moral sense
is most often associated with eighteenth-century philosophy, and the work
of Francis Hutcheson in particular. A theory of the moral sense claims, in
rough outline, that there are certain impressions that correspond to moral
ideas. Such impressions are not compounded out of simpler impressions; to
feel that something is "good" is not just another way of saying that we feel
approbation, pleasure, or sympathy at the sight of it. Instead, we possess a
faculty that allows us to perceive, or *sense*, the ethical quality of an action
or a state of affairs, just as we can perceive the color of an object. Such
moral sense theory was often also called "intuitionism," with the slightly
different connotation we have already seen the term to possess. The idea
that humans possess such an a priori faculty stood in direct opposition to
the causation-based principles of utility put forward, most importantly, by
Bentham and Mill.

If such an instinctive approach to ethics now seems rather naive, this is
due in no small part to the eventual triumph of utilitarianism in academic
circles. What opposition there may have been to the philosophy of Bentham and Mill now seems to be located in writers viewed as less strictly
philosophical, such as Carlyle and Ruskin. In what follows, however, I will
attempt to sketch out the development of the antagonistic relationship between ideas of the moral sense and utilitarianism. My claim will be that the
academic debate between these two schools of thought is actually indicative
of a deep-seated cultural uneasiness about the possibility of a connection between an individual's internal intuition and the external social world. The
philosophical debate can thus offer us a clearer picture of what the specific
stakes were in placing oneself in opposition to utilitarianism. Positions that
have been viewed as simply a negative response to utilitarianism, in other
words, can be viewed as more subtle positive arguments in favor of a specific sort of internality.

Victorian moral philosophers inherited a tradition of internally oriented
moral thought from the British philosophers of the seventeenth and eighteenth centuries. As Stephen Darwall puts it, "British moral philosophy of
[that] period saw the development of some of the first internalist theories of
moral obligation and practical normativity in the history of ethics."[28] Some
of the most influential intellectual descendants of these internalist thinkers,
in the period from the 1830s to the 1880s—from the time of William

Whewell to that of Henry Sidgwick—claimed, with some variation, that the rightness or wrongness of a given action or state of affairs could be located in a sensible or psychological faculty, with little or no reference to questions of advantage or consequence. And while intuitionists and utilitarians agreed on little, they did agree on the deeply drawn lines in ethical thought between moral sense theory and utilitarianism—or, as they were alternatively known, "intuitionism" and "inductivism."[29] William Whewell, in an 1854 lecture on the history of English moral philosophy, claims,

> Schemes of morality . . . are of two kinds:—those which assert it to be the law of human action to aim at some external object . . . , as for example, those which in ancient or modern times have asserted Pleasure, or Utility, or the Greatest Happiness of the Greatest Number, to be the true end of human action; and those which would relate human action by an internal principle or relation, as Conscience, or a Moral Faculty.[30]

Whewell's focus is on the aim, or object, of different moral systems. In their modern forms, these different systems are classified by their dependence on "Utility, or the Greatest Happiness . . ." on one side and a "Moral Faculty" on the other. This division of moral theories into those based on utility and those based on an internal faculty becomes a commonplace among Victorian moral thinkers. H. L. Mansel reiterates it in an 1854 lecture: "The various principles which have been at different times advocated as forming the foundation of Moral Philosophy, may ultimately be reduced to two."[31] One "starts from the assumption that right and wrong are positive qualities, discernible in individual acts by a peculiar faculty of the intuitive consciousness"; the other only believes in such qualities "as they finally lead to a greater amount of happiness or misery . . . to the individual committing them." W.E.H. Lecky opens his *History of European Morals* with a reference to "the great controversy, springing from the rival claims of intuition and utility to be regarded as the supreme regulator of moral distinctions."[32] This "great controversy" was no less clear to foreign explicators; in his *Morale anglaise contemporaine*, Jean-Marie Guyau refers to "l'opposition de la «morale inductive» et de la «moral intuitive», sur laquelle insiste si souvent l'école anglaise contemporaine."[33] There was, it seems, no single dominant Victorian moral outlook so much as a single dominant division in moral thought.

Given the seeming starkness of this opposition, though, it can be startling to turn back to the eighteenth-century roots of moral sense philosophy, where utility seems to reside rather comfortably. Though the term "moral sense" had been used earlier by Shaftesbury, it is in the works of

Francis Hutcheson that we find the first attempt at a systematization of the concept. In his *Inquiry into the Original of Our Ideas of Beauty and Virtue*, he defines the term as "that Determination to be pleas'd with the Contemplation of those Affections, Actions, or Characters of rational Agents, which we call virtuous."[34] Such a "determination," though, meets with some difficulty when an agent is forced to choose between a number of possibly virtuous actions. To address this, Hutcheson offers a formulation that now seems quite familiar: "that Action is best, which procures the greatest Happiness for the greatest Numbers; and that, worst, which, in like manner, occasions Misery" (125). This is one of the earliest, if not *the* earliest, instances of the principle of utility in its Benthamite form.[35]

How, then, in the space of little more than a century, does the moral sense go from accommodating utilitarianism to opposing it? The difference, it turns out, lies in the priority that utility assumes in the ethical formula. Hutcheson's use of the principle of utility comes only when questioning which of two possible actions one should take. The greatest happiness, therefore, is not the source for every moral decision but rather the means for deciding between two already morally valid decisions. Even more important, perhaps, is Hutcheson's reason for invoking the principle of utility in the first place: "we are led by our moral Sense of Virtue to judge thus" (125). Utility is not the ultimate sanction of moral actions; rather, it is our moral sense that sanctions the application of utility. Furthermore, the happiness that this utility produces is, for Hutcheson, of a very specific sort. For the moral sense is founded in "a benevolent universal Instinct," and "a little Reflection will discover . . . that this Benevolence is our greatest Happiness" (133–34). The sort of principle of utility that Hutcheson puts forward, then, extends our internal moral sense, almost by analogy, to the external world. That which *feels* right to us—in the sense of moral feeling—will *feel* right to others, in the sense of happiness. Unlike later utilitarianism, this connection is not something that the individual agent has to learn. Nor, conversely, does the outer world have to somehow accommodate itself to the individual's correct intuitions. Rather, the feelings of the inner and outer world seem to share a basic relation with one another. This connection of moral sense and utility can in fact be read as a gloss on Locke's highly ambiguous statement that "Good and Evil . . . are nothing but Pleasure or Pain, or that which Occasions or procures Pleasure and Pain to us."[36] Here moral quantities seem at once to be discoverable, in good empiricist fashion, only in our own sensations, while at the same time they are seen as those things which bring about those sensations. In other words, that which is indistinguishable from a sensation—we should note that Locke uses the existential verb "are"—will also be that which "occasions" that sensation. This seems to be at the base of Hutcheson's use of the principle of utility. That which we can find in our own sensations will bring about the same sensations in others.

It was in severing this analogy that the two schools of thought become separated in the nineteenth century. Whewell, as we have seen, bases morality on an "internal principle or relation." Though an "internal principle" had certainly been present in the previous century, there is now also a "relation" that is, in Whewell's terms, "independent" of any external end. There is no longer a reason to believe, in other words, that moral intuition will bear any relation to the world of others. Mansel goes so far as to classify even sympathy as ultimately based in an external calculation: "There is the theory of Sympathy, as maintained by Adam Smith, who tells us that we are so constituted as to feel pleasure or pain at an act which gives pleasure or pain to others . . . a theory which . . . is yet, in principle, identical with the ultimate form of the Utilitarian theory" (366). Thus even a theory of moral sentiments which relies on the relation of one's own feelings with the feelings of others is placed in opposition to the independent faculty of the moral sense. The issue here is using an external measuring stick as the mark of the good. As Whewell puts it, "Since we are . . . led directly to moral Rules, by the consideration of the internal conditions of man's being, we cannot think it wise to turn away from this method, and to try to determine such Rules by reference to an obscure and unmanageable external condition."[37] Mansel offers a similar opinion, claiming that the focus of the moral philosopher should be "the facts and laws of the soul within him." Such an approach is only possible through "psychological inquiry," which offers us a wholly internal subject for analysis: "Moral Science is possible, if an internal sense, call it by what name you please, presents us with the facts of moral approbation and disapprobation of this and that action in itself and for its own sake: and it is possible in no other way."[38]

And yet, in spite of all that, it would be overly simplistic to classify utilitarianism as strictly outward-facing, and intuitionism as strictly internal. Certainly they find the deciding voice of moral action in different places—utilitarianism in external effects, intuitionism in internal sense—but when we look at the sort of community they presuppose, the places are oddly reversed. Schneewind makes the point that "Utilitarianism presents a morality which is primarily impersonal, appropriate to the life of the large society or city and to the relation between strangers, while Intuitionism speaks more clearly for a personal morality, drawn from the life of the small group or the family, from the relations between old acquaintances or close friends."[39] Utilitarianism, then, offers an ethical solution in plural situations, in which people might be bringing different values or beliefs—or where their beliefs remain unknown. Intuitionism, on the other hand, functions best in situations in which people have a set of shared values or conventions. So while intuition is asserted, insistently, in the nineteenth century to be an internal faculty, it is one that, at the same time, seems dependent on a tacit sense of community.

CASE STUDIES: *MARY BARTON* AND *HARD TIMES*

My account thus far of this debate, while focusing on philosophy, is reflective of larger issues particular to a developing nineteenth-century *episteme*.[40] That is, it offers terms, in the language of philosophy, to describe the opposition we can see in other discursive forms. In what follows, I will offer a couple of short readings that illustrate how the intuitionist position—what I have suggested is also an "internalist" position—provided the grounds for an alternative to utilitarianism. In particular, what I want to suggest here is that the experience of diachronic narrative becomes the method the novels use for realizing this particular ethical opposition.

Victorian novelists concerned with the condition of England, from Disraeli to Eliot, frequently included more or less overt critiques of utilitarianism within their works.[41] I would like to start by looking at two works that put this issue front and center: Elizabeth Gaskell's 1848 *Mary Barton* and Charles Dickens's 1854 *Hard Times*. Both novels are examples of what we have come to call the "industrial novel," or the "social problem novel": a set of novels that focus on the condition of the working class. There is a strongly felt, if sometimes vague, ethical message in these novels' focus on the human misery inherent in capitalism: a general sense that it is necessary to treat other humans by some other standard than the bottom line. While the political message of industrial novels can range, as Ruth Bernard Yeazell puts it, "over a broad spectrum of Victorian belief," there tends to be greater consensus on the importance of protecting the ethical realm from the economic realm.[42] These novels are invested in distinguishing ethical relations from the ends-oriented teleological thought of laissez-faire political economy. In *Mary Barton*, Gaskell frequently measures her criticism, but she still has the saintlike Job Legh gently set human duty in opposition to the "higher good" of progress: "I have lived long enough, too, to see that it is part of His plan to send suffering to bring out a higher good; but surely it's also part of His plan that as much of the burden of the suffering as can be, should be lightened by those whom it is His pleasure to make happy."[43] Dickens, in *Hard Times*, is a good deal blunter and more explicit. Sissy Jupe is asked in school to remark on the proposition that "this schoolroom is an immense town, and in it there are a million of inhabitants, and only five-and-twenty are starved to death in the streets, in the course of the year." Her answer, that "it would be just as hard upon those who were starved, whether the others were a million, or a million million" is "of course" wrong, in terms of the greatest-happiness principle taught in the Benthamite Coketown schools.[44] Readers with competence in sarcasm, though, will know that Sissy is, of course, right. When Dickens sums up utilitarian political economy with "the Good Samaritan was a Bad Economist" (207), it is clear enough that it is better to be on the good side of the equation than the bad.

Now, it might seem like choosing these two novels at the outset is stacking the deck a bit. After all, who needs to turn to novel form when the content states the case so clearly? Yet the opinion that has long attached to both novels is that this content, clear though it might be, leaves something to be desired; Gaskell and Dickens, by this account, do not go far enough in imagining an alternative to the social ills they represent. Here the classic reading comes from Raymond Williams. Williams starts his discussion of *Mary Barton* by pointing out that, according to Gaskell, the title character was originally not going to be Mary but rather her father, John Barton: "Round the character of John Barton all the others formed themselves; he was my hero; *the* person with whom all my sympathies went."[45] This observation has become an essential part of the novel's twentieth-century reception history, due to Williams's short but influential reading. For Williams, John Barton is the site of the novel's most compelling social imagination; looking at the novel in terms of Mary leaves us only with a "Victorian novel of sentiment, . . . of little lasting interest."[46] Williams's reading thus presents the novel as a missed opportunity: a failure of nerve that ends up shying away from political difficulties in favor of a conventional romance plot. *Hard Times*, meanwhile, seems to Williams little more than a blunt, but effective, parody of utilitarianism. In this reading, Dickens's critique "is really negative": "There are no social alternatives to Bounderby and Gradgrind."[47] The attitudes in *Hard Times*, Williams concludes, "cancel each other out": Dickens "will use almost any reaction in order to undermine any normal representative position." In both cases, then, there is a sense that an original opposition to exploitative material conditions stops short of actually imagining—much less *representing*—a solution to those problems.

My larger argument, though, is that a good part of the ethical interpretation of novels in the nineteenth century did not derive strictly from explicit representation or exhortation but also from the experience of their narrative form. The polemical thrust of these novels lies not only in what they say, in other words, but also in how they feel. To a certain extent, this sounds like the work that sentiment has long done in literary representations of abjection: tugging on the heartstrings to produce feeling, instead of putting forward arguments. Here, though, it's worth stressing a point I made earlier: the experience of narrative is not the same as the experience of literary sympathy. Rather than responding to an imagined projection of "If I were in their place . . . ," narrative experience is a process over time, a relation between what is present in the text and what is suggested or withheld. We don't have to see characters, or even particularly identify with them, in order to experience the pull of narrative: its compulsion toward change. We should recall here Mansel's insistence that a theory of moral sentiment—an ethics of sympathy—is ultimately utilitarian in nature, since it assumes a connection between one's own ends and the ends of people in the outside world. In the intellectual landscape that I described in the previous section, the opposition to utilitarianism retreated from externality and representation and toward an ethics based on internal sense. Williams is right, perhaps, to characterize these novels as retreats from a representation of social conditions or their solutions. But it would be incomplete to read them simply as negations. *Mary Barton* and *Hard Times* struggle with the question of how to represent a solution precisely because they come to characterize external representation itself as a problem. Now, this might seem like a fairly serious problem for a realist novel. As we have seen, though, synchronic description is only one axis of the novelistic representation; there is also the internally felt experience of diachronic narrative. So, as we will see, these novels move away from moral sentiment. Indeed, they are both rather suspicious of sentiment altogether, insofar as it takes the form of static representation. But this doesn't mean that the novels turn away from an ethical project altogether. Instead, it means that the debate is shifted toward the internal.

Mary Barton offers a striking illustration of this shift away from sympathy to a more internally founded ethics. When John Barton is called to the side of a dying woman, the novel confronts us with a scene of abjection, clearly structured around provoking a sentimental response: "She sat up and looked round; and recollecting all, fell down again weak and passive despair. Her little child crawled to her, and wiped with its fingers the thick-coming tears which she now had strength to weep."[48] Yet for all the evocative power of this tableau—and it is considerable—the novel interrupts it with a scene that seems to complicate John's experience. Sent to the druggist for medicine, John is struck by the contrast between the death he has been witnessing in the cellar, and the well-fed middle-class obliviousness at street level:

> He thought they all looked joyous, and he was angry with them. But he could not, you cannot, read the lot of those who daily pass you by in the street. How do you know the wild romances of their lives; the trials, the temptations they are even now enduring, resisting, sinking under? You may be elbowed one instant by the girl desperate in her abandonment, laughing in mad merriment with her outward gesture, while her soul is longing for the rest of the dead, and bringing itself to think of the cold-flowing river as the only mercy of God remaining to her here. You may pass the criminal, meditating crimes at which you will to-morrow shudder with horror as you read them. You may push against one, humble and unnoticed, the last upon earth, who in Heaven will for ever be in the immediate light of God's countenance. Barton's was an errand of mercy; but the thoughts of his heart were touched by sin, by bitter hatred of the happy, whom he, for the time, confounded with the selfish. (63)

The passage highlights the failure of representation: we cannot know the internal experience of others from their outward appearance. The way that the passage wraps up, foreshadowing the murder of Harry Carson, can leave the final impression that the entire passage is an indictment of John: with his heart "touched by sin," he is unable to do anything but project his "bitter hatred of the happy." But though the passage starts and ends with a description of John, the majority of the passage is taken up with a description of "you." This is a familiar move in *Mary Barton*: Gaskell's narrator frequently brings the reader into the narrative, either with the second-person singular ("you") or the first-person plural ("we"). These are not just terms to refer to the general case ("you" meaning "one") since, as Robyn Warhol points out, Gaskell "frequently refers very openly to information she has previously related that the reader might have forgotten."[49] The novel's "you," in other words, often refers to its implied middle-class reader. And since Gaskell is not implying—I should hope—that her reader is "bitter" and "touched by sin," the limitation of sympathy is one that extends beyond either the personal failings of John or the collective failings of his class. Rather it is a limitation that affects the reader just as much in the present-tense act of reading: "he could not, you cannot, read . . ." John is misled, just as we readers are frequently misled, by a sentimental belief in the knowledge of others that can be gained from representations.

If we react to the people around us then—or to figures depicted in a novel—we are apt to be misled. But what else can we react to? In *Mary Barton*, the answer seems to be that we react more properly, and more meaningfully, to things and people that are not present. This is certainly something implicit in the novel's reception history, which, since Williams, has seemed to stress what the novel is *not* about. One of the first things any student studying the novel will learn is that it is a novel that *should* have been about John Barton but is not. By this reading, the social problem novel comes about by removing the "social"—public, political, male—figure, and leaving a conventional romance-novel romance that sketches his outlines. What is striking about this reading, and a large part of the reason why it seems to stick around despite so many critics pushing back on it, is that it points not just to the novel's history of composition but also to the mechanics of its plot. Most of the action happens offstage: the narrator does not describe Harry Carson's murder, and John Barton and Jem Wilson, the two characters Mary has the greatest emotional investment in, are absent for a large part of the novel. The character of Esther, Mary's fallen aunt, remains what Carolyn Lesjak has called an "absent presence" in the novel, who is at the same time largely responsible for the progress of the plot: "So insinuating is her influence that, in the end, Esther is directly or indirectly linked to every major event in the novel."[50] We don't need Gaskell's revelation of the novel's early form in order to sense that the novel is sketching the space around its absent figures. The plot of the novel is consistently structured around reactions to figures that are not present.

And here we can start to see the alternative to the sorts of sympathy that the novel presents as impossible. Mary spends a good deal of the novel isolated from the characters she feels the most strongly about, and yet this does not seem to inhibit the development of her feelings: in fact, she seems to be able to feel more truly and dependably when others are absent. To the extent that the novel displaces the political onto the romantic, it does so through the transfer of Mary's affections from the rich Harry Carson to the working-class Jem. Yet such a shift can hardly be said to be brought about through any sort of gradual narrative development. Mary is attracted to Carson; Jem proposes to her; Mary rejects him, spurred on in no small part by a desire to contradict her father: "one thing she was sure of; nothing he could say should make her have him. She would show them all *who* would be glad to have her" (129). And yet, as soon as Jem is out of her sight, she realizes that she loves him: "Her plan had been, as we well know, to marry Mr. Carson, and [rejecting Jem's proposal] was only a preliminary step. True; but it had unveiled her heart to her; it had convinced her she loved Jem above all persons or things" (131). It is hard to say whether or not this is *unrealistic*, exactly—the world is wide, after all, and love is strange—but it is certainly abrupt, and finds little preparation in what comes before it in the novel. It is not Jem's absence that is surprising here. We are prepared, in the nineteenth-century novel, for love to ripen in absence: think of Elizabeth Bennet alone in the portrait gallery at Pemberley. But we know *why* Elizabeth falls for Darcy (embarrassment over her misjudgment of Wickham, gratitude for the discreet assistance rendered to her family, admiration of his skill as landlord and employer); the reasons had been accumulating, and she has only now become aware of them. In Jem's case, no such reasons are represented. Mary seems to love him mainly by virtue of his absence.

This does not make for much of a romance, but then I imagine most readers understand that Mary's internal feelings are supposed to map onto a set of social concerns. Jem is the right person to love, in both moral and social terms. The novel encourages us to elide the emotional probability of Mary's change of heart altogether and implicitly switch tracks over to the social plot. Such a reading is supported by the fact that the relationship between Mary and Jem shares its signifiers with the more political story surrounding John Barton. Jem is accused of Harry Carson's murder—the murder that John committed—and it is only at the trial, testifying on his behalf, that Mary publicly states her love for him.[51] Far from being merely a private affair, then, Mary's preference for Jem—a love that seems a lot more like a moral choice—becomes a matter of public record. This is all to say that the novel does eventually put its vague moral argument into a politically meaningful form, but it only does so by refracting it through Mary's internal feelings. And it is when they are in this internal form that they produce the novel's most strongly felt compulsion: Mary's drive to appear at the trial. This compulsion—which is tied to the guilty knowledge that her father is a murderer—increasingly isolates her from the social world around her: "she's gone out of her wits!" says one observer (286). Social conscience takes the form of a sort of non-amorous love: a sort of desire for resolution. And this, in turn, produces a deeply internal drive.

It is important that Mary is responding here to a *false accusation*. Tzvetan Todorov, among other formalists, has pointed to this situation as one of the elements of an uncompleted narrative; a satisfying conclusion will generally require this accusation to be dismissed.[52] Todorov, following Viktor Shklovsky, offers this convention in a discussion of narrative techniques that draws from linguistics. The false accusation is, for Todorov, productive of the draw toward a complete narrative sentence. The reader, in other words, desires a correct syntactic resolution. But, of course, the implications of a false accusation are not just formal but ethical—to an extent that makes it quite difficult to disentangle the two. The feeling that something *ought* to happen is intuitive enough that Todorov would see it as the native speaker's tendency toward the well-formed (narrative) sentence. The compulsion has its root in the formal, in other words, but because of the ethical overtones, the interpretation of the affect that this technique produces is ethical. The reference to narrative syntax offers Todorov a way of describing the sense that the *parole* of Gaskell's narrative is controlled by some sort of underlying *langue* that determines what ought to happen next in the narrative sentence. But, since this *langue* is not present, what Todorov is saying is that narratives with a false accusation make it feel like some unconscious rule set is dictating what ought to come next. Just as Mary is compelled to go to Liverpool by an internal drive, the reader too feels the formal compulsion of the novel.

My point here is not to say that Mary's internally motivated love for Jem produces a useful alternative to politics. But Gaskell does seem to be committed to contrasting Mary's private and deeply felt drive—one that does not even need much in the way of an object—with the sort of false understandings of others that doom her father. John's corrupted sentimentalism gets it wrong, in other words, and Mary's romantic love-without-object gets it right. In the novel's conclusion, the reliably right-minded Job Legh discusses with Harry Carson's grieving father what is to be done. He repeatedly stresses that incommunicable feelings are a better guide to ethical action than a frank assessment of external social conditions:

"Still, facts have proved, and are daily proving, how much better it is for every man to be independent of help, and self-reliant," said Mr. Carson thoughtfully.

[Job replies,] "You can never work facts as you would fixed quantities, and say, given two facts, that the product is so and so. God has given men feelings and passions which cannot be worked into the problem. . . .

. . .

"What you say is very true, no doubt," replied Mr. Carson; "but how would you bring it to bear upon the masters' conduct,—on my particular case?" added he, gravely.

"I'm not learned enough to argue. Thoughts come into my head that I'm sure are as true as Gospel, though may be they don't follow each other like the Q.E.D. of a Proposition. . . . It's no business of mine, thank God. John Barton took the question in hand. . . . Then he grew bitter, and angry, and mad; and in his madness he did a great sin, and wrought a great woe." (385–86)

Job, then, provides the language for the opposition that we've seen between John and Mary: facts in opposition to feelings, propositional reason in opposition to incommunicable truth. But since the nature of incommunicable truth is that you cannot communicate it, Job has to preface his conclusion with a refusal to answer Mr. Carson's question directly. We are therefore left with an ethical solution that evades representation—not just because it is difficult to represent but because external representation would work against its more internal basis. We can take Job's rectitude on faith, perhaps, but we are not going to get any sort of definite proposition that we can share in. What we can share in, though, is the formal desire to see a false accusation removed: a formal desire that the novel uses to represent an internal state that is at once an emotion and a moral position. The experience of diachronic narrative, then, becomes the means by which the novel represents Mary's moral experience.

Turning to *Hard Times*, we see this opposition between fact and feeling taken to an extreme. Sissy Jupe is a character of "fancy" as opposed to "fact," and her "idle imagination" is presented as equivalent to an "idle story-book" (25). Similar to Mary, though, Sissy finds in her capacity for imagination and stories the ground for a moral faculty. Such a faculty becomes evident when Stephen Blackpool is falsely accused of theft. Sissy then joins Rachael in believing Stephen's innocence, against all inductive evidence to the contrary. This is certainly not due to any traditional sympathy for Stephen. Just like Jem—and John Barton and Esther, for that matter—Stephen is kept out of sight at the very moment when he is most motivating the narrative. (In the next chapter, we will see a similar fundamental moment of motivating intuition in *Oliver Twist*: Brownlow's vague recognition of Oliver, which only occurs after Oliver has been taken out of his sight.) Sissy's strength, in other words, is not just that she represents literature and the imagination but that these qualities lead her, later in life, to intuit correctly about moral matters. This link between stories and moral judgment echoes the point from Hutcheson's *Inquiry* (offered as an epigram to the current volume): "The Universality of this moral Sense, and that it is antecedent to Instruction, may appear from observing the Sentiments of Children, upon hearing the Storys with which they are commonly entertain'd as soon as they understand Language."[53] Children, Hutcheson claims, will naturally support the virtuous characters in stories. Sissy does so in Stephen's case as well. This offers an example of the sort of wisdom that Thomas Gradgrind refers to as a "wisdom of the Heart," in contrast to a "wisdom of the Head." Such wisdom of the heart, according to Gradgrind, is the "instinct" that he has lacked, or ignored, due to his utilitarian doctrine (217–18).

A character's position on Stephen's guilt or innocence becomes a moral measuring-stick of sorts in *Hard Times*. James Harthouse quickly comes to the conclusion that Stephen is guilty based on the evidence at hand; as he says to Louisa, "you saw and heard the case. . . . I only say what is reasonable, nothing worse" (198). This same character plainly admits later in the novel, "I am not a moral sort of fellow . . . and I never make any pretensions to the character of a moral sort of fellow. I am as immoral as need be" (226). This does not mean that he is immoral as a direct result of his belief in Stephen's guilt. Instead, the suggestion is that an immoral character specifically lacks the "instinct" to which Gradgrind refers, which would allow him to ignore external evidence. Louisa's redemption, on the other hand, is indicated by her statement, "I have once believed [in Stephen's guilt]. . . . I do not believe it now" (246).

This instinctive reaction, once again, comes as a product of neither sympathy nor sentiment. *Hard Times* is certainly sentimental enough, and its presentation of Stephen's hardships seems designed to make its readers sympathize with the hardships of the working class. But none of the characters who instinctively believe in his innocence do so because they identify with him or feel sorry for him. Some, such as Louisa, do in fact feel sorry for him, but this is not the source of their belief. Notably, the only character who bases his judgment on an imagined projection of "If I were in his place . . ." is Harthouse, who draws the wrong conclusion. It is precisely the character most willing to assume a consistency between his own feelings and those of others—"Fellows who go in for Banks must take the consequences. If there were no consequences, we should all go in for Banks" (180)—who is farthest from feeling correctly. The fact that Stephen is entirely absent during the part of the novel that I am discussing emphasizes the point; the instinctive belief in Stephen's innocence is based internally and has little to do with Stephen himself.

This emphasis on internality that I have been discussing, though, now leads us to a representational question. Just how internal can this instinct be if it is only presented externally? Dickens shows his prized characters making internal judgments with little regard for inductive evidence, but the only way that their intuitions can actually be shown to be correct is to have a conclusion that proves them to be so. In other words, the ultimate validity of the internal sense can still only be proved through the demonstration of external events. Dickens further hedges his bets here by making the reader privy to a conversation in which Tom Gradgrind tricks Stephen in order to make it seem that he robbed the bank. As a result, the characters' intuitions will not only be eventually shown to be correct; the reader knows they are correct from the moment suspicion falls on Stephen. I have already discussed the theme of the false accusation in relation to *Mary Barton*. We see something similar in *Hard Times*, where the reader intuits a felt necessity that Stephen should be vindicated.

Hard Times, for all its focus and social engagement, is not one of Dickens's finest productions of plot. Change occurs either abruptly or not at all. Outside of the related question of whether the young Tom Gradgrind will be found guilty of his crime, the plotline detailing Stephen's suspicion and ultimate, albeit posthumous, acquittal is one of the few sustained examples of narrative engagement in the novel. After Louisa returns to her father's house and Harthouse exits the scene, there is little movement of the other characters. The narrative of Stephen's accusation, then, carries the final third of the novel—carries the novel, that is, to its conclusion. This conclusion is repeatedly delayed, as Stephen, for various reasons, is unable to return to Coketown and face the charges against him. The reader's sense that the accusation ought to be dismissed, and desire for that dismissal to come about, grows with each delay. The reader's sensible reaction to the novel, then, produced through Dickens's narrative mechanics, mirrors the feelings of Rachael and Sissy. Dickens produces in the reader the intuitive moral desire—or, at least, a feeling that mimics it—that he depicts in his most valorized characters. Narrative method becomes the means by which the novel represents internal intuition. The specific objection that was raised numerous times to utilitarianism was that by basing its system on a calculable system, it denied the very existence of morals. The alternative to this that we see in the example of narrative was not only to make the case for a pre-existing morality. Rather, the alternative was to make the reader *feel* the internal, and sensible, existence of morality.

THE THEORETICAL ARGUMENT

My discussion of *Mary Barton* and *Hard Times* suggests the general two-part form that my readings in this book will take: first, locating the site of some sort of "poetic necessity," the formal technique that motivates the narrative progress of the work in question; and, second, demonstrating the moral implications of that site in the novel. I should say here that my goal will not be to show that reading actually produces a moral intuition, any more than reading *Clarissa* or *Uncle Tom's Cabin* would actually produce sympathy for another human being. In both cases, formal procedures are used to produce a readerly affect which, even though it is literally a response to tropes, is understood in ethical terms.

This claim about the relation of the formal and the ethical, though, can actually be taken a step further. It is not only the case that formal techniques of narrative compulsion *may* be understood in ethical terms; they can be understood more clearly, more precisely in ethical terms. In other words, ethics—and I will say a good deal more about what I mean by this term in a moment—is not just one metalanguage among others, at least not when it comes to Victorian narrative art. To be more precise, ethics is of particular use as an analytic tool whenever we are dealing with literary objects in which there is some sense of a controlling compulsion, a necessity, an "ought." I am not claiming that all work need be interpreted in an ethical light, or even that it necessarily could be. What I am claiming, though, is that readings that produce a "naive" sense of necessity already take the step of seeing in narrative a link between what exists and what should be— between, to use Hume's famous distinction, "is" and "ought." This binary distinction is present in most discussions of narrative, through one set of terms or another: synchronic and diachronic, paradigmatic and syntagmatic, the descriptive and the narrative, the discursive and the teleological. To the extent that the sort of narrative that we are used to in the Victorian novel brings these terms together, narrative form seems to offer in practice, if not in theory, an answer to Hume's question of how existence and obligation can be linked.[54] Geoffrey Galt Harpham, who has written well on the subject, offers a nice formulation: narrative, according to Harpham, is "a principle of formal necessity that governs the movement towards the union of *is* and *ought*."[55] We can say, in other words, that in *Mary Barton* and *Hard Times*, a false accusation is a state of affairs that *ought* to be rectified; the accusation ought to be dismissed.

I have thus far been using the term "ethics" in a highly general way, to describe the relation of "that which is" to "that which ought to be," or "that which one ought to do." This formulation—which is essentially the "O" operator in a deontic modal logic[56]—is too abstract for our purposes, since it could include something like the table of laws in a dogmatic society. Now, we could probably consider that table of laws ethical as a determining background to some sorts of narrative forms: highly traditional, conventional tales that always follow through a set series of events. But that does not work very well to describe the experience of the Victorian novel. Whether it is or is not the "most *lawless*" of all forms, as Gide called it,[57] or a Bakhtinian carnival, there is certainly a sense that the form allows at least some degree of freedom.

So, to describe the Victorian novel, a rather more refined sense of ethics is necessary. In particular, it has to be one that accounts for the seeming freedom of the novel, joined together with a sense of necessity that seems to shape the free play of events. The ethical tradition that I would like to turn to now, then, is the one that has concentrated most deeply on this joint sense of freedom and necessity: a tradition which can be described, broadly, as Kantian, and which is summed up well by John Rawls: "acting in accordance with a law that we give to ourselves."[58] Rawls here means to link Kant with the contractarian tradition of Rousseau, but the idea, taken broadly, can extend in some form to describe not only Kant and Rawls, but also such seemingly contradictory figures as Nietzsche, Hegel, and even the late Foucault.

These may seem an odd assembly of names, so I will say a few words on each. First, Nietzsche: I am taking his notion of the eternal return here, perhaps *contra* Nietzsche, more as a thought experiment than a statement of scientific fact. In particular, I take it as an attempt to solve the root problem of *ressentiment*: that "the will cannot will backwards."[59] To say "yes" to his demon's challenge—"This life, as you now live it and have lived it, you will have to live once more and innumerable times more"—is, in effect, to will the present moment into existence: to will backwards.[60] There is therefore a loopback effect: I am a product of, and subject to, only my own will. Hegel is perhaps an easier case, since in the *Philosophy of Right*, he specifically deals with the idea of institutional laws as a further step in our moral development. That is, the Hegelian state of *Sittlichkeit* is quite literally following laws that we have given ourselves. However, even at the level of the notion of the will—"the free will which wills the free will"—we see the a conception of freedom that overlaps with both Kant and the "loopback" I described above in Nietzsche.[61] The final example is what has come to be called "late" Foucault: the Foucault of the last two volumes of *The History of Sexuality*. Though he is not exactly consistent over this period, his Kantian education does show through in his understanding of ethics as a means of relating to oneself. He defines ethics, in one particularly nice phrase, as "the conscious [*réfléchie*] practice of freedom." This he opposes to a simpler "liberation," which he disowns.[62] The key point here is that his definition of ethics ends up being a freedom that is free precisely because one is always keeping a watch over oneself.

It is this tradition that allows us to address what I take to be the antinomy— the structuring paradox—of narrative theory: a sequence of events (or story, or *fabula*) comes logically prior to its telling (or discourse, or *sjuzhet*). The story is what gives the telling its coherence. But of course, rigorously speaking, the story, the *fabula*, is *not there*: all we have is the telling. All useful narrative analysis tries to address this problem in some way—stressing the interrelation between reader and text, but almost always ultimately favoring one side or the other as prior. But, as Harpham explains, when viewed in ethical terms, the reader does not just construct the meaning of the text; the reader constructs the "law of the text" that the reader then follows:

> An "ethical" approach to the dilemma of narrative theory would begin by conceding the strength of both formalist and reader-centered positions, and making of these apparently incompatible claims the cornerstone of its understanding. Plot is a construction of a particular narrative that uses only materials in that text. In one sense external to the narrative, arising from within and yet not precisely as its own, since the narrative is regulated by the plot. Interestingly, this account also describes the reader. The reader is free and autonomous, and responsible for his or her construction of the text; but in order to make a plot at all, readers must believe that they "perceive" it; they must submit to the text and try to understand it "on its own terms." Readers thus construct the text freely but construct it as the law of the text. Where, then, is the law? In both, that is, in the relation between the two: the relation of reader to narrative text provides a compelling instance of the free submission of the subject to the law.[63]

As we freely read, we produce the structure that dictates how we read. Of course, we do not do this completely arbitrarily; there are a number of formal indicators that point us in certain directions. But they point us to be compelled by a structure that we impose.

This relation between law and freedom helps to explain what is perhaps the most marvelous of realist effects: the fact that an assemblage of literary tropes, used to advance a pre-arranged plot, can take on the shape of a freely deciding human agent. Literary criticism has a long tradition of subordinating the character—which, after all, is not a real person—to the workings of underlying structure. We can find this idea, as Seymour Chatman has pointed out, in works ranging from Aristotle's to twentieth-century formalism.[64] Characters in classical tragedy, according to Aristotle, exist "for the sake of their actions" (9); the hierarchy he assigns here is strict: "plot is the origin and as it were the soul the tragedy, and the characters are secondary." Boris Tomashevsky echoes these sentiments nearly two and a half millennia later in "Thematics," though "motifs" now occupy the place of Aristotle's "action" and "plot": "The usual device for grouping and stringing together motifs is the creation of a character who is the living embodiment of a given collection of motifs. The assignment of this or that motif to a given character holds the attention of the reader. The character is a guiding thread which makes it possible to untangle a conglomeration of motifs and permits them to be classified and arranged" (87–88). Here too, characters exist only due to vulgar necessity: the reader's inability to pay attention to the actual thematic work of the narrative. Still, as Tomashevsky is at some pains to point out, they are nothing more than a means to an end. Lest there be any misunderstanding of his intention, Tomashevsky reiterates his point, with some evident distaste, asserting that this, alone, constitutes the purpose of character: "The reader must know how to recognize a character, and the character must attract at least some attention" (88). The language here is that of necessity: the reader *must*, the character *must*. Whatever readers might think about their relationship with the character, they are ultimately determined by the structure.

The ethical theorization of narrative laid out here can mediate between a naive sense of reader and character freedom, and the theoretical sense of the form's determinant nature. In this sense, it echoes the problem of free agency that Kant offers in *Groundwork of the Metaphysics of Morals*: "reason *for speculative purposes* finds the road of natural necessity much more traveled and more usable than that of freedom; yet *for practical purposes* the footpath of freedom is the only one on which it is possible to make use of our reason in our conduct."[65] I will return to Kant at greater length in my discussion of the *Bildungsroman* in chapter 4. For now, though, suffice it to say that Kant attempts to solve this problem by finessing the distinction he makes in the first *Critique* between the appearance of consciousness (which we have access to) and consciousness as thing-in-itself (which we do not). In a sort of idealistic precursor to the psychoanalytic unconscious, Kant suggests that our noumenal self—inaccessible to our reason or our senses—manages to be free of the laws of causal determinism as well.[66] Christine Korsgaard, in her introduction to the Cambridge edition of the *Groundwork*, offers a helpful gloss: "we must suppose that in our capacity as members of the world of understanding, we give laws to ourselves as members of the world of sense" (xxix). In other words, then, the law that we give to ourselves is the mediation between theoretical determinism and felt freedom.

We see this mediation in a number of forms throughout Victorian narrative; it is an essential part of realism's simultaneous demands for robust characters and compelling, forward-moving plots. The demands of a seemingly autonomous character would require that choices not be determined by a chain of causation; the demands of plot—"a narrative of events, the emphasis falling on causality," in E. M. Forster's formulation—require that we be able to causally interpret events and actions.[67] As one way of approaching this problem, it will be useful to turn to Victorian intellectual autobiography: "a genre," as Jonathan Loesberg puts it, "that transforms philosophy into narrative."[68] My interest in these sorts of texts—Cardinal

Newman's *Apologia pro Vita Sua*, along with John Stuart Mill's *Autobiography*, which I will discuss in chapter 4—is that they attempt to narrate fundamental reorientations of self, and thus face the same essential antinomy as novelistic realism. Change must seem necessary and not merely capricious; but, at the same time, the autobiographical form must narrate a development that exceeds the confines of determinism.

This point is especially pressing when it comes to the *Apologia*, which, as Newman describes it in his preface, was written to refute accusations that, while still in the Church of England, he had already secretly converted to Catholicism and had been using the Anglican pulpit to preach Catholic doctrine. In other words, his book is an attempt to show that he had not always been a Catholic but had, by slow and imperceptible processes, come to change his mind:

> I will draw out, as far as it may be, the history of my mind; I will state the point at which I began, in what external suggestion or accident each opinion had its rise, how far and how developed from within, how they grew, were modified, were combined, were in collision with each other, and were changed; again how I conducted myself towards them, and how, and how far, and for how long a time, I thought I could hold them consistently with ecclesiastical engagements which I had made and with the position which I held. . . . I shall account for that phenomenon which to so many seems so wonderful, that I should have left "my kindred and my father's house" for a Church from which once I turned away from dread . . . as if forsooth a Religion which has flourished through so many ages, among so many nations, amid such varieties of social life, in such contrary classes and conditions of men, and after so many revolutions, political and civil, could not subdue the reason and overcome the heart.[69]

This passage spells out the two joint aims that Newman has in his memoir. He has to show that on the one hand, he came to Catholicism by a series of accidents and insights, not through any predetermined plan, since a plan would be the sort of Romish dishonesty he is trying to defend himself against. But at the same time, he needs to show that Catholicism exerted a sort of draw—subdued his reason and overcame his heart—that moved him to it out of necessity. His progression, in other words, was not arbitrary; he could not have just as easily become, say, a dissenter. So the prose project he has assigned for himself in the *Apologia* is this: to depict a series of free and unconditioned choices that seem to lead by necessity to a certain conclusion.

And indeed, if we try to hunt down the actual moment of conversion—which certainly seems like it should be a significant moment in the

Apologia—we find ourselves lost in a mess of tenses and subordinate clauses. In the midst of a discussion of warnings from other Anglican clergymen and related theological debates, Newman mentions a tract he had been working on:

> I had begun my Essay on the Development of Doctrine in the begin-ning of 1845, and I was hard at it all through the year till October. As I advanced, my difficulties so cleared away that I ceased to speak of "The Roman Catholics," and boldly called them Catholics. Before I got to the end, I resolved to be received, and the book remains in the state in which it was then, unfinished. (181)

At the beginning of the second sentence, Newman is an Anglican, if a rather controversial one. He is still engaged in debates about doctrine and writing essays as a member of the Church of England. By the end of the third sen-tence, he is a Catholic. Of course, he is a Catholic before he begins writing the *Apologia*, but his textual presentation of himself, of his "mind," was of someone not yet Catholic. The conversion happens here, but it occurs in the middle of a sentence that is largely about an essay that Newman never finishes. To be more precise, it happens *before* the first clause in the sentence: "Before I got to the end . . ." In other words, by the time Newman references his "resolution," the resolution has already been made and has had an effect in his narrative—that is, his inability to get to the end of his essay. The com-bined dictates of freedom and necessity that underwrite Newman's *Apologia* lead him to imply that his surface narrative is determined by an underlying decision-making process that occurs prior to its manifestation in the text. Remember, as I said, that this served a rhetorical purpose: Newman's conver-sion was to seem understandable, even necessary, by the time it occurred—it had to be in keeping with a reader's expectations. By forcing the reader, for the sake of comprehension, to project back a change that would only mani-fest itself later in the text—to in effect will backwards—Newman made the reader provide the law that Newman would, himself, then follow.

MORAL FEELING AND ETHICAL EXAMPLES

What is at work in this passage from the *Apologia*, and what is implied by the discussion in the section preceding it, is something we might call an ethical unconscious. Newman acts in accordance with a decision he already made, though he does not yet know that he made it. For Kant, this is specif-ically a noumenal self that we do not have access to. But how can something that we do not have access to act as a moral incentive? Here, Kant intro-duces a rather fuzzy term: a "moral feeling," that is the "incentive" to moral action.[70] And this moral feeling takes the form of guilt. A human being, he writes, may see an act as necessary and yet, all the same, "he nevertheless finds that the advocate who speaks in his favor can by no means reduce to silence the prosecutor within him." In other words, when Kant wants to force the awareness in his agent of something going on behind the scenes, he does it in the form of the *failed* ethical experience, one that goes wrong. He implies that it is precisely our "moral feeling" about what went wrong that makes us aware of our ethical consciousness.

Kant also refers to this moral feeling as the "incentive" to moral action (5:79). This incentive, he takes great care to point out, must be separated at all costs from material incentives, which always have an object. The particular incentive to which Kant refers here, on the other hand, must have no object other than duty. Hence, for the sake of clarification, he also refers to it as "respect" (5:73). Still the usage of the term "incentive" should have some significance for us due to its close relation with the Freudian notion of the "drive"—in German, *Triebfeder* and *Trieb*, respectively. This terminological similarity points to the close relation between Kant's moral feeling and Freud's death drive; both produce in the subject desire without object. This is what Lacan means when he writes that Kant's "theory of consciousness, when he writes of practical reason, is sustained only by giving a specification of the moral law which, looked at more closely, is simply desire in its pure state."[71] It pushes forward, without object, only to push forward.

The drives are similar as well in that they both produce narrative. Brooks bases his theory in *Reading for the Plot* on the death drive and its interaction with the pleasure principle, both of which move in opposite directions toward satisfaction: "Between these two moments of quiescence, plot itself stands as a sort of divergence of deviance, a postponement which leads back to the inanimate" (103). Kant's moral feeling produces narrative in a different manner. This can perhaps be best understood through the fact that Kant, who begins his *Groundwork* with the demand that morality be "carefully cleansed of everything empirical" (4:388), still finds it necessary to demonstrate his principles through four examples (4:421–25). This may seem to be a dispensable clarification for some of his less abstractly oriented readers, but the fact remains that Kant, and ethical discourse in general, are drawn repeatedly to the illustrative example. J. Hillis Miller puts it well: "Narrative as a fundamental activity of the human mind, the power to make fictions, to tell stories to oneself or to others, serves for Kant as the absolute necessary bridge without which there would be no connection between the law as such and any particular ethical rule of behavior."[72] The law itself, since it has no content, must always be instantiated in concrete actions. The respect for the law, the moral feeling, is what pushes the agent toward this instantiation. Ethical discourse, then, is always pushed forward by this moral feeling, this *Triebfeder*, to produce narrative.

This formulation gathers its full meaning when we consider the other thrust of Kant's moral feeling, as seen by its manifestation as guilt in the second *Critique*. There it functions to point out the immorality—the "pathological" nature—of this instantiation. Instantiations of an abstract ethical law in concrete situations, in other words, never quite work. As Miller argues in his *Ethics of Reading*, the examples that Kant seems compelled to provide at the same time go "against the grain of [his] argument" (32). Such moments provide ample fodder for deconstruction, certainly. But rather than settling on the "unreadability of the example" as Miller does (38), we could also see this as an iterative procedure, which Harpham thus describes: "a process of reciprocal probing and stressing that tests the capacity of theory to comprehend and regulate practice, and the power of 'actual life' . . . to elude or deform theory."[73] Ethical argument takes place in the sphere of examples and counterexamples, speculative narratives of concrete situations that put ethical rules to the test.

It is this understanding of the relation of ethics and narrative, underwritten by a "moral feeling," that allows us, finally, to turn back to the debate between intuitionism and utilitarianism. As I mentioned earlier, the specific tradition of intuition that I have been discussing has not been in high academic repute since the publication of Sidgwick's *Method of Ethics* in 1874. But narrative methods—as described above—have actually made the notion of "moral feeling" axiomatic enough that they can continue this debate. The theoretical, in other words, has become formal.

By way of example, let us look at a more recent moment in the debate over utilitarianism, well past the high point of British moral intuitionism. In his entry in *Utilitarianism, For and Against*—he takes the "against" position—Bernard Williams points out that following utilitarian rules often "alienates one from one's moral feelings."[74] And to demonstrate this point, he offers two object lessons: about George, who is offered a job in chemical and biological warfare, which would help him support his family and would prevent someone with less compunction from taking the job; and Jim, who finds ten sympathetic prisoners about to be executed, and is offered the opportunity to kill one himself, with the effect that the other nine would go free (97–99). Though the examples are not very long, Williams spends a striking amount of time on details: George "is not very robust in health" and is "very attached" to his wife, who has fewer concerns about the job than he does; while Jim, "with some desperate recollection of schoolboy fiction, wonders whether if he got hold of a gun, he could hold the captain." The point is that Williams goes out of his way to make these proper names into some sort of literary creations, characters with implied backstories and pasts. The effect, for Williams, is to remove the discussion from the schematism of a blunt utilitarian rule—which would state, say, that one dead peasant, though regrettable, is a morally superior outcome to ten dead peasants[75]—and place it in the realm of people, possessed of some sort of "moral feeling," and protective of their "moral integrity" (104). George and Jim are not people, of course, any more than Sissy Jupe is a person, and so they do not actually possess these qualities. But Williams makes use of the techniques of literary mimesis to make them at least into somewhat "round" characters—enough so, at least, to make it clear that we are dealing with a familiar literary object.[76]

These literary objects, though, are also philosophical arguments. Miller suggested that this was the case with Kant: though he might have claimed he was just illustrating a theoretical point, he still needed recourse to instantiation. In Williams's case, it seems to me, the point is rather more clear. The stories not only have pride of place in his response to his utilitarian interlocutor, but the experience of reading them—he might say, "thinking through them," but it comes to the same thing—functions to introduce an important part of his disagreement with utilitarianism: the idea that certain choices can "feel wrong." In each case, Williams ends with a question to his reader, familiar from any introductory ethics course: "What should he do?" This is not a neutral question. Williams is asking with the knowledge that his reader will know the correct utilitarian response. He is also making the assumption that this response will feel wrong to the reader, that there will be some sort of resistance to it:

> To these dilemmas, it seems to me, that utilitarianism replies, in the first case, that George should accept the job, and in the second, that Jim should kill the Indian. Not only does utilitarianism give these answers but, if the situations are essentially as described and there are no further special factors, it regards them, it seems to me, as *obviously* the right answers. But many of us would certainly wonder whether, in (1), that could possibly be the right answer at all; and in the case of (2), even one who came to think that perhaps was the answer, might well wonder whether it was obviously the answer. (99)

In other words, he does not mean this to be a completely open-ended narrative. We play out the wrong ending in our head and are unsatisfied with it. This lack of satisfaction with the narrative—this sense that the story should not end this way—offers a response to a utilitarian calculus. Williams uses narrative methods here to produce a reminder of a necessity that does not seem to be present in the assumed theoretical structure.[77] At the same time, since it is a "dilemma," this feeling of necessity only comes about through being offered a choice, through the sense that the story *could* go in more than one way. The experience of narrative serves to bring together freedom and necessity in a way that would be absent from a static formulation.

To characterize Williams's work in terms of its relations to literature is to stay in keeping with the general thrusts of many of his arguments. Among Anglo-American philosophers, Williams shows a particular awareness of the literary nature of his approach, and of an example-based philosophical approach in general. Certainly, we get a sense of this in his famous essay "Moral Luck," when instead of choosing a George or a Jim, he focuses on Anna Karenina.[78] Implicit here seems to be the question of why a philosopher should bother making up an example from life, when someone else has already done such a good, and robust, job of it. Elsewhere, he makes this point explicit:

> In seeking a reflective understanding of ethical life . . . [philosophy] often takes examples from literature. Why not take examples from life? It is a perfectly good question, and it has a short answer: what philosophers will lay before themselves and their readers as an alternative to literature will not be life, but bad literature.[79]

Williams's point certainly seems to open up the discussion to the sort of post-structuralist analysis that would see the rhetorical base of writing across disciplinary lines. What I would like to concentrate on here, though, is simply the way in which a philosopher so adept at writing the micro-narratives of "ethical life"—ethical examples—understands these as connected with literature. Further, he suggests that even when philosophers deny this connection, it does not lead to something beyond or separate from literature; it just leads to literature that is not particularly effective.

The effective "literature" of the philosophical example, then, bears a relation to the sort of narrative literature that this book will be considering. Furthermore, this narrative-literary form of philosophical discussion becomes mobilized, as in the examples of Jim and George, against utilitarianism in particular. The alternative to the systematic argument, in other words, is to use the principles of narrative literature to produce an experience in the reader, a reaction which will stand in opposition to the stated rules of a utilitarian system. Williams's approach thus recalls the intuitionist stance of the nineteenth century, as we saw it in *Mary Barton* and *Hard Times*. This is the heritage of those philosophical debates: the idea that the argumentative response to a rational deliberative style is an *internal* argument, and that it works through a felt response to the experience of diachronic narrative.

I opened by pointing to the ways in which the critical tradition of the novel has implicitly made use of this same idea: that "poetic necessity" works because it "feels right" or, perhaps even more precisely, because something else would "feel wrong." Whether this is accurate, or whether it expresses a sort of naive confirmation bias, is ultimately beside the point—what matters is that it significantly represents the way that the phenomenology of novel reading has been understood over the last two hundred years. And in the nineteenth century, this experience of reading over time, motivated and sustained by the promise of an unknown conclusion, was understood to be a moral experience. We may have forgotten this, just as philosophical history has largely forgotten the intuitionist philosophers, but it is part of the novels, it is part of the way we talk about novels, and it is part of the way that we—intuitive, naive readers all—read even still.

CHAPTER 2

THE SUBJECT OF THE NEWGATE NOVEL: CRIME, INTEREST, WHAT NOVELS ARE ABOUT

The Victorian novel—whether we define the term by author, style, or monarch—has its beginning in a moment of moral controversy. *Oliver Twist*, Dickens's first work conceived as a novel from the outset, began publication in 1837 and continued through Victoria's ascension to the throne. While it never quite reached the heights of popularity achieved by *The Pickwick Papers*, this "first major Victorian novel"[1] was an undoubted success, spurring numerous imitations and theatrical adaptations. Yet, for a number of months toward the end of its run, the novel that a young queen, just six months into her reign, deemed "excessively interesting" was not the most popular novel dealing with underworld themes.[2] It was not even the most popular novel serialized in *Bentley's Miscellany*. That unofficial title belonged to William Harrison Ainsworth's *Jack Sheppard*, published alongside *Oliver Twist* in *Bentley's* beginning in 1839. Influenced in no small part by the popularity of *Oliver Twist*, and by the popularity of the highwayman Dick Turpin in his earlier *Rookwood*, Ainsworth focused his "romance" on the life of the famed eighteenth-century housebreaker who had three times escaped from Newgate Prison. The novel's popularity reached the levels of a full-scale cultural phenomenon. As John Forster wrote, in the *Examiner*, of the novel's numerous theatrical adaptations:

> Jack Sheppard is the attraction at the *Adelphi*; Jack Sheppard is the bill of fare at the *Surrey*; Jack Sheppard is the choice example of morals and conduct held forth to the young citizens at the *City of London*; Jack Sheppard reigns over the *Victoria*; Jack Sheppard rejoices crowds in the *Pavillion*; Jack Sheppard is the favourite at the *Queen's*; and at *Sadler's Wells* there is no profit but of Jack Sheppard.[3]

"Nix my dolly, pals, fake away," the "flash"—that is, slang—song from J. B. Buckstone's dramatization at the Adelphi became ubiquitous throughout London: "it deafened us in the streets. . . . It clanged at mid-day from the steeples of St. Giles . . . [I]t was whistled by every dirty guttersnipe, and chanted in drawing rooms by fair lips."[4] Thackeray reports that at the Coubourg, another theater, "people are waiting around the lobbies, selling *Shepherd-bags* [*sic*]—a bag containing a few locks that is, a screw driver, and iron lever."[5] As Keith Hollingsworth puts it, Ainsworth's novel, and the cultural phenomenon it inspired, became "the high point of the Newgate novel as entertainment."[6]

Jack Sheppard, then, was popular. But, as many critics hastened to point out, it was also bad: bad in quality, bad in morals. Worse, it was not an isolated incident. As a review in the *Athenaeum* put it in 1839, "Jack Sheppard . . . is a bad book, and what is worse, it is of a class of bad books, got up for a bad public."[7] More worrying than *Jack Sheppard* itself was the fact that the demands of the "bad public" would produce more of this "bad class of books." That genre—the "bad class of books"—were the Newgate novels: novels dealing with crime and criminals. Listing further characteristics, as is usually the case with literary moments, seems to be of limited utility. The stories usually, but not always, took place in the eighteenth century. They usually, but not always, were based on characters from the biographies found in the *Newgate Calendar*. They sometimes, but not always, took place in London. Yet, if we cannot say precisely what the Newgate novel was, as such, we can at least offer a reasonably complete list of what these novels were: Edward Bulwer-Lytton's *Paul Clifford* (1830) and *Eugene Aram* (1832),[8] Ainsworth's *Rookwood* (1834) and *Jack Sheppard* (1839), and Dickens's *Oliver Twist* (1838).[9]

Bulwer, Ainsworth, and Dickens—when it comes to literary history, clearly, one of these things is not like the others. But how do we explain the fact that, from this "bad class of books," *Oliver Twist* is the only one that is still read? When, in the context of larger discussions of the period, critics make reference to the Newgate novel—and there seems to be an increasing agreement on its importance—it is Dickens's novel that stands in for the rest. D. A. Miller, for example, refers to the "Newgate novel" as one of four traditions, along with sensation fiction, detective fiction, and realist fiction, that define, in practical terms, the "nineteenth-century novel."[10] Far from discussing a tradition as a whole, though, he confines his discussion to *Oliver Twist*. For Franco Moretti, Newgate novels play the role of describing the eastern part of London: "West of Regent Street, silver-fork novels; and east of it, in the City . . . not really City novels, but *Newgate* ones."[11] To describe this group of novels, Moretti takes the same approach as Miller: "Stories of crime, of criminals, like *Oliver Twist*." Differences in canonicity and

familiarity may indicate a quirk of literary history or a qualitative evaluation—we remember the good Newgate novel, and we forget the bad ones—
but it is not taken to say much about genre.

What I will argue in this chapter, though, is that a good part of the reason that *Oliver Twist* is read as our Newgate novel of choice, instead of the
more popular *Jack Sheppard*, is precisely because it is not a story "of crime,
of criminals"—it may have criminals in it, but it is not understood to be
about crime. During its publication, John Forster wrote approvingly of the
"delicacy of natural sentiment" evident in Dickens's novel, in contrast to
other novels on similar themes.[12] Though Forster was not the most impartial voice when it came to Dickens, we can see the same position taken in a
review published in the *Monthly Chronicle*:

> We have somewhere seen the names of Mr. Dickens and Mr. Ainsworth
> associated, as if they belonged to the same order; but this confusion
> must have arisen from the ignorance of the writings of one or the
> other. No two writers can be more unlike. Boz, it is true, has de-
> scended into the haunts of guilt and depravity; but he has brought
> back no foul airs with him, and, by a marvelous delicacy of percep-
> tions and treatment, has described vice faithfully, without shocking
> the moral sense of his readers by the coarseness of the portraiture. . . .
> [T]here is not a gleam [of Dickens's observations] to be detected in
> the tea-tray pictures of "Jack Sheppard": besides, there is a cordial hu-
> mour, a cheerful humanity, and a healthy purpose that we look for in
> vain throughout the pages of Mr. Ainsworth.[13]

Oliver Twist was to be distinguished from other similar novels, and particularly from *Jack Sheppard*, because of the ways in which it appealed to the moral
sensibilities of its reader: "natural sentiment," "moral sense." How it did this
is unclear from these descriptions—"cheerful humanity" and "healthy purpose" are terms that offer little analytical precision—but the general implications seem clear enough: *Oliver Twist* is more appealing to its readers' moral
feelings because it has other, "healthier," focuses than crime alone.

So, according to the novel's reviewers, our "moral sense" tells us that
Oliver Twist might feature crime, but unlike *Jack Sheppard*, crime is not
the novel's subject. Only the most "confused" or "ignorant" reader could
mistake it for a novel *about* crime. In fact, what a survey of the discourse
surrounding Newgate novels makes clear is how debated this question of
subject matter actually was. There are a number of rather easy generaliza-
tions that could be made about Victorian moral reactions to novels about
crime; yet these are overgeneralizations in no small part because they skim
over how difficult—then, as now—it is to say what it means for a novel to
be "about" anything.

In this chapter, I will look at the way in which morals and intuition come together around that tricky formal question of subject matter. This topic is a difficult one to discuss in any way but the most naive. The best definition for the term would probably be the one that Boris Tomashevsky offers for "theme": "The idea expressed by the theme is the idea that *summarizes* and unifies the verbal material in the work. . . . The development of a work is a process of diversification unified by a single theme."[14] Unfortunately, Tomashevsky does not offer much analytic method for determining what the theme of a particular novel might be. In the years since Russian formalism, there has been little development in the area, and our critical language remains somewhat impoverished. This critical aporia makes it particularly difficult to talk usefully about questions of moral praise and censure in novel history. To take just one famous example, the central issue in the *Madame Bovary* obscenity trial was whether the novel was *about* Emma's sexual activities or instead just featured them as a way of focusing on a moral lesson.[15] The moral critique of a novel, in other words, often comes down to the question of whether the novel is about the characters and actions it depicts, or whether its subject is more properly expressed by narrative structure: that is, the logic relating actions to their results, and characters to their punishments and rewards. And what we will see is that the "moral sense" that separates *Oliver Twist* from *Jack Sheppard* and the rest—that makes it a crime novel not about crime—is indeed based in the experience of the novel's narrative.

These formal elements that helped *Oliver Twist* win the moral debate are, as we shall see, many of those very elements that make the novel seem so familiar to us today. It is not coincidental, in other words, that narrative and moral intuition come together in the one novel that somehow remains recognizably "Victorian"—while the other Newgate novels have become museum pieces. The "high point" of the Newgate genre, as Hollingsworth called it, would also be an endpoint. The *Monthly Chronicle* wrote in February 1840, while London was still in the grips of "the Jack Sheppard mania," that Ainsworth's novel "has had no imitators—that it stands utterly alone— and that, whatever evils of another kind it may have produced, it has not inoculated our current literature."[16] In one year, *Jack Sheppard* had gone from being the most visible "bad book" of an entire "bad group of books" to being "utterly alone." Wishful thinking at the time it was written, this claim was nonetheless prescient. After 1840, British novels featuring prominent criminal characters became increasingly fewer and farther between. And today, with that one very pointed exception, the Newgate novels, and their authors, have all but disappeared from the nineteenth-century canon.

That Dickens's novel can be offered, almost two centuries later, as a synecdoche for an unread group, suggests that it is somehow distinct from the larger subgenre it is claimed to encompass. Hollingsworth writes, "What firmly draws the Newgate novels together is that most of them met firm opposition on the ground of morality or taste. . . . We are dealing with a school defined by its contemporary critics" (14). The continued acceptability of *Oliver Twist* throughout the nineteenth and twentieth centuries, and into our own, indicates that Dickens's novel managed to escape the critical censure that drove Bulwer to other genres and cast a long shadow over Ainsworth's career. *Oliver Twist* survives not as a Newgate novel but rather as a recognizable Victorian novel that represents some elements of the Newgate subgenre. Oliver manages to escape the Newgate genre, while Jack Sheppard, who escaped three times from Newgate Prison itself, fails.

The controversy at the moment of birth of the Victorian novel, then, is a moment where the formal and the moral cross, and it will allow us to understand better the moral principles that came to inform Victorian novelistic practice. The topic of subject matter—of whether a novel was really about crime or just depicted crime—lay at the heart of the Newgate novel controversy. But this concern went beyond just counting up how many crimes or criminals were in a novel. Rather, in a more complicated way, the loudest voices in the controversy turned again and again to the idea that what a novel was *really* about was not so much what was in the text, as what it was that kept a reader reading. But how can you define such a nebulous motivation? In what follows, I will suggest that there were specific narrative techniques that became central thematics. First, I will look at *Oliver Twist*, in order to show how the novel's subject matter is tied up not only in the narrative question of what *will* happen to Oliver but also in the moral question of what *should* happen to Oliver. In order to be generically legible, the novel relies, at a very basic level, on the reader's intuitive sense of the novel's correct outcome. The next section will look at Victorian criticism more generally, and in particular the topic of "interest": a term that Victorian critics used to describe the interplay of text and reader that I am describing. Finally, I will turn to Ainsworth's *Jack Sheppard*, in order to try to offer a sketch—based on the terms developed in the previous sections—of the Newgate novel genre as a whole. *Oliver Twist* and *Jack Sheppard* embark on their different historical paths at the dawn of Victoria's reign, at the moment of the coming into being of those literary careers and traditions by which we define the "Victorian novel." And in the moral outcry against the Newgate novel, we can see the beginnings of the connections of the formal and the moral, which continue to define the Victorian novel for us today.

THE FORM OF INTUITION: *OLIVER TWIST*

One way to address the question of what *Oliver Twist* might be about—crime, or the progress past crime—would be to ask which characters it is about. Those Victorian critics who saw the novel as being a novel about crime viewed the criminal characters as, intentionally or not, the focus of the novel. Thus, it is not surprising to see Thackeray, when he insists on the novel's moral danger, imagining a reader who is "[b]reathless to watch all the crimes of Fagin, tenderly to deplore the errors of Nancy, to have for Bill Sykes a kind of pity and admiration, and an absolute love for the society of the Dodger."[17] Notable here is the fact that Thackeray does not even find it necessary to suggest that Oliver is an unimportant character; he simply omits him from his discussion of the novel altogether. As for the criminal characters that he lists, he does not seem to find it interesting that three of them end up dead, and the other deported. Such endings, it would seem, have little impact on the reader's understanding of the novel. In this sense, Thackeray's view of the novel shows a striking lack of interest in any sort of narrative meaning. The description he offers of Fagin in a different context is telling. Fagin is "a clever actor," and the audience always receives "a knowing wink from the old man's eye"; he is "a clever portrait . . . a mask."[18] Such insistence on Dickens's "cleverness" is intended as a jab at the realism of the author's depiction, no doubt, but it also serves to highlight the lack of diachronic interest that the character might possess. Fagin is frozen: a still portrait, or an actor caught breaking character to mug for the audience.

Attempts to rescue the novel from such criticism, on the other hand, tended to focus on Oliver. This is not surprising; whatever critics might say about Oliver—usually in the context of sweeping statements about Dickens's "good" characters—it seems clear that if the novel moves away from crime, it does so by moving *him* away from crime. John Forster, in an 1837 review of the novel published in the *Examiner*, suggests that "No one can read [the novel's opening] without feeling a strong and sudden interest in Oliver, and that interest never ceases" (581). When he expands on this unceasing interest, though, he shifts his terms slightly: "We feel as deep an interest in little Oliver's own fate as in that of a friend we have long known and loved" (582). We are no longer interested in Oliver himself; instead our interest has become an interest in his "fate." Furthermore, at the same time that he extends this interest forward in time, he also extends it backward: "long known and loved." Unlike the tableau scenes of criminals that Thackeray seems to see in the novel, Forster sees, in the character of Oliver, a temporal continuity. More importantly, he sees this continuity as the reason for the reader's investment in the novel.

This method of redeeming the novel is not particular to Forster. In the twentieth century, Steven Marcus's insistence on the moral seriousness of the novel led him to claim that any relationship between *Oliver Twist* and the Newgate subgenre is "superficial and misleading."[19] His argument focuses on the Bunyanesque nature of the novel indicated by its subtitle: "The Parish Boy's Progress." Implicit in this claim is the fact that the novel is in fact about the *progress*—that is, the motion forward—of Oliver, the parish boy in question. The other characters then become backdrop, narrative elements in the forms of temptation, occurring as Oliver's story progresses. This close connection between the other elements in the story and Oliver's progression, Marcus argues, is why Dickens's "intricate and elaborate plots," and in particular the plot of *Oliver Twist*, should be excused from the oft-leveled charge of excess coincidence:

> [W]e cannot take it as an accident that the first time that Oliver is sent out with the Dodger and Charlie, the person whom they choose to rob turns out to be the man who was the closest friend of Oliver's father; it is no coincidence that the first time he walks out of Mr. Brownlow's house he is recaptured by the thieves; and the fact that the house the thieves break into, again when Oliver is first sent out, happens to be his aunt's beggars the very notion of accident. For the population of *Oliver Twist* consists only of persons—the wicked and the beneficent—involved with the fate of the hero. (78)

For Marcus, the novel does not rely on coincidence so much as it relies on the figure of Oliver. The presence and actions of other characters in the novels are only justified to the extent that they are connected with Oliver's fate. Marcus's claim, then, would be that *Oliver Twist* should not be grouped together with other Newgate novels because the criminal characters, as part of the novel's larger "population," are not the novel's focus of interest. Instead, they only play a supporting role in a novel really about Oliver—which is to say, Oliver's narrative.

Here, though, we come to a rather tricky—and counterintuitive—point: even if we grant that the novel is centrally concerned with Oliver's progression, why do we assume that it is a progression away from crime? Burton M. Wheeler offers textual evidence that it was only with his decision to extend his serial piece into a novel that Dickens "decided to rescue Oliver from a representative 'Parish Boy's Progress,' that is, from workhouse to criminal associates to deportation or the gallows."[20] Wheeler points to slight textual alterations that seem, in their original, to bear out this claim.[21] Even in the revised version, though, some moments in the early chapters remain ambiguous. After the chestnut scene in which Oliver asks for more, a Mr. Limbkins declares, "That boy will be hung. . . . I know that boy will be hung."[22] When the sentiment is repeated at the chapter's end, the narrator offers the following: "As I purpose to show in the sequel whether [Mr. Limbkins] was right or not, I should perhaps mar the interest of the narrative . . . if I ventured to hint, just yet, whether the life of Oliver Twist had this violent termination or no" (15). It is difficult not to read this as coyness on Dickens's part—in large part because it is difficult to imagine reading the novel unaware of its outcome—but the evidence indicates that when this chapter was written, the trajectory of the "life of Oliver Twist" was, at the very least, an open question.

A good point of comparison here—both in terms of generic convention and direct influence—would be Bulwer's 1830 *Paul Clifford*, understood at the time as the first Newgate novel, and still, while Dickens was writing, the representative work of the genre.[23] *Paul Clifford* attacked the criminal justice system by arguing that it was punishment that in fact produced criminals. As Bulwer put it in an 1840 preface, the novel sought to draw attention to both "vicious prison discipline and a sanguinary criminal code": "the habit of corrupting the boy by the very punishment that ought to redeem him, and then hanging the man, at the first occasion, as the easiest way of getting rid of our own blunders."[24] It was most likely this ostensible moral purpose that Dickens admired in the novel, though he at the same time maintained some distance. In the 1841 preface to *Oliver Twist* in which he defends himself against Thackeray's criticisms, Dickens invokes "Sir Edward Bulwer's admirable and most powerful novel of Paul Clifford" along with the *Beggar's Opera* as works that depict the underworld but have "other, wider, and higher aims" (liv).[25] In a scene from Bulwer's novel that seems to have provided a model for Oliver's mistaken arrest, a still relatively innocent Paul is sent to prison when his companion steals an esteemed lawyer's watch on the street (75).[26] Sent to prison to pick oakum, Paul falls in with criminal acquaintances and thus begins his life of crime. Picking oakum is also the task Mr. Limbkins assigns to Oliver when he arrives at the workhouse. Such generic similarities did not go unnoticed. *Punch*, in 1841, offered a "recipe" for a "startling romance," after the fashion of *Jack Sheppard*:

> Take a small boy, charity, factory, carpenter's apprentice, or otherwise as occasion may serve—stew him down in vice—garnish largely with oaths and flash songs—boil him in a cauldron of crime and improbabilities. Season equally with good and bad qualities—infuse petty larceny, affection, benevolence, and burglary, honour and housebreaking, amiability and arson—boil all gently. Stew down a mad mother—a gang of robbers—several pistols—a bloody knife. Serve up with a couple of murders—and season with a hanging-match.
>
> N.B. Alter the ingredients to a beadle and a workhouse—the scenes may be the same, but the whole flavour of vice will be lost, and the boy will turn out a perfect pattern.—Strongly recommended for weak stomachs.[27]

There is a sneer in the reference to *Oliver* at the end, to be sure, but there is also some insight into the effect of the novel. Whatever the reason that Oliver's path changes course, the end result is that the novel loses its "flavour of vice."

But when does it lose this "flavour"? Or, what comes to the same thing, when does it become apparent that Oliver will not become a criminal? Biography can be of some assistance here. In June 1837, Dickens's sister-in-law Mary Hogarth died, an event that plunged Dickens into grief, and left him—for the first and last time—unable to write. The June number of *Oliver Twist* did not appear in *Bentley's*. When the number, containing chapters nine, ten, and eleven, did appear a month later in July, the novel had started to move in a different direction. For it is in the tenth chapter that Mr. Brownlow, who will be Oliver's benefactor, and ultimately solve the mystery of his birth, first appears, and it is at the end of the eleventh chapter that Brownlow takes Oliver home with him. This marks a significant moment, for Brownlow is the first character to enter the novel from outside what D. A. Miller calls the "world of delinquency": made up of the workhouse, Fagin's lair, and the criminal justice system.[28] Generally speaking, he is the first character who is not involved in the corrupting process that Bulwer describes—a pattern Dickens, seemingly, had been following.[29]

It is as a direct result of Brownlow's entry into the novel that Oliver is able to cross over from the world of crime and the workhouse to the middle-class, domestic world. Such crossing between the two worlds is quite rare, because the novel keeps these separate worlds tightly segregated from one another. For Oliver to go from Fagin's clutches to Brownlow's protection, for example, he cannot simply walk (109). He seemingly cannot even have agency in crossing. He must be taken by force, first carried by Brownlow while unconscious, and then, upon returning, carried kicking and screaming by Nancy and Sikes. Similarly, when Brownlow later brings Monks to his house to answer for his plots against Oliver, it is only with the help of two unnamed enforcers. By contrast, both Oliver and, later, Noah Claypole, are able to walk directly from the world of the workhouse—what Miller classifies as part of the world of delinquency—to Fagin's lair. Nancy's attempt to come in contact with the other world, finally, will lead to her death. If the novel has one significant shift in its narrative sense, then, it most likely comes at this moment. Forster's comment on the interest we feel in "Oliver's fate," for example, appears in response to the following number.

The tendency here, I think, is to see this moment as a confirmation that Oliver has always been good, and therefore as the fulfillment of a Lukácsian "poetic necessity." But this interpretation seems to rest on an unjustified teleology, which explains away a significant shift in narrative trajectory by claiming that the shift is, itself, the natural outcome of a narrative trajectory. We should be careful not to assume, in other words, that the reason the novel shifts into a redemption narrative is that it had always been tending toward redemption. Such retrospective reading is subtly present, I think, in even the most sophisticated analyses of the novel. Miller, discussing Brownlow's disciplining desire to know everything about Oliver's past, writes that it is "clear what Oliver's story . . . is going to do: it will entitle him to . . . a full integration into middle-class respectability."[30] What Miller is referring to here, in "Oliver's story," is of course, the detailing of events of Oliver's life, up to and including the present moment. The story of *Oliver Twist*—the novel, in italics—is also the story of Oliver Twist, the boy. We see this later, when Oliver is asked, again, to tell his story to Dr. Losborne and the Maylies. What must be the longest uninterrupted speech that Oliver delivers in the novel—if not in his life—is described by the narrator without direct quotation: "The conference was a long one; for Oliver told them all his simple history. . . . It was a solemn thing, to hear, in a darkened room, the feeble voice of the sick child recounting a weary catalogue of evils and calamities which hard men had brought upon him" (233). By withholding Oliver's direct discourse, the narrator leaves the reader no choice but to assume that Oliver has given the same account to his protectors as the narrator has given to us. Miller's point about what Oliver's story will make "clear" to his domestic, middle-class listeners also seems to be a point about what this novel has already made clear to us: domestic, middle-class readers. This connection between us, as readers, and Brownlow makes sense, since Brownlow is a reader too: he first encounters Oliver while he is at a bookseller's stall, "reading away, as hard as if he were in his elbow-chair, in his own study" (73). And if Brownlow had read the novel that we have been reading, or so Miller suggests, then he would clearly see where it is heading. As I have been arguing, though, before Brownlow takes Oliver to his house, there has been no clear direction, or, if there is one, it tends toward the gallows. Brownlow does not take Oliver home in accordance with a redemption narrative—he *produces* that narrative. To rely on our sense of structural necessity to explain his actions, then, would be to reverse the order of operations.

Rather than occurring as a result of what has come before, Brownlow's action brings something new into the novel; and it is here, in what is new, that the novel has to rely in a fundamental way on intuition. Brownlow, after all, has never seen Oliver before. Yet his decision to take him home with him is not simply benevolence; the novel suggests that he would not have taken just any orphan boy. As he tells Oliver, "I feel strongly disposed to trust you . . . , and I am more interested in your behalf than I can well account for, even to myself" (104). And indeed, this seems to fit with the novel's general emphasis on the trustworthiness of Oliver's physiognomy. We have already heard, from Brownlow's point of view, that "it was impossible to doubt [Oliver]; there was truth in every one of its thin and sharpened lineaments" (90). Later on, a similar moment will occur when Rose Maylie not only understands his virtue but manages to intuit almost his entire story on sight: "think that he may never have known a mother's love, or the comfort of a home; and that ill-usage and blows, or the want of bread, may have driven him to herd with men who have forced him to guilt" (231).

Yet this later moment is of a different sort, because it occurs well after Oliver's first introduction into the domestic sphere, with the implications of the genealogical story—on which I will have more to say shortly—already underlying the narrative. When his goodness appears obvious to Rose, it is, for the most part, already obvious to the reader as well. Thus her intuition is a confirmation of sorts. Brownlow's intuition, on the other hand, actually plays a motivating role in the narrative; for it is due to this intuition that he moves not only Oliver, but also the novel, into the domestic sphere.

This intuition, though, should not be understood simply as a clumsy contrivance or deus ex machina. There is a motivation, even though Brownlow has never seen Oliver before. It is just not a motivation that is based in Oliver's story, as we have known it up until this point. Here is the moment when Brownlow first gets a good look at Oliver:

> "There is something in that boy's face," said the old gentleman to himself as he walked slowly away, tapping his chin with the cover of the book, in a thoughtful manner; "something that touches and interests me. *Can* he be innocent? He looked like—Bye the bye," exclaimed the old gentleman, halting very abruptly, and staring up into the sky, "Bless my soul!—where have I seen something like that look before?" (77)

Here the genealogical story, which will be developed in the novel's next chapter, and finally revealed in full in chapter forty-nine, enters the novel.[31] Oliver is an orphan, of course, and we are told that he looks like someone, even if we do not know whom. This seems to be a clear sign of some sort of familial connection, though not necessarily of parentage. It can be startling, given what we know of the novel, to look back and realize that this is the first time that Oliver's genealogy has even been treated as an enigma, much less an enigma that demanded a solution. Indeed, as the opening chapter indicates, Oliver's predicament is common enough to be a well-defined social situation: Oliver "fell into his place at once—a parish child—the orphan of the workhouse—the humble half-starved drudge—to be cuffed and buffeted through the world—despised by all, and pitied by none" (3). Dickens's quick succession through these phases, from "parish child" to "despised by all," depends on the familiarity of the figure of the orphaned pauper. And since it is so familiar, there is no expectation that more need be said on this front. Here, though, Brownlow not only articulates the enigma and starts to offer an answer ("He looked like—") but also cuts it off, and withholds the resolution ("Bye the bye"). Brownlow's felt motivation to bring Oliver over to the novel's other world is introduced with a new formal device in the novel: what Barthes would call the hermeneutic code, or what we might call, more simply, "suspense"—using Caroline Levine's broad definition of the term as "conspicuously withholding crucial pieces of knowledge" from the reader.[32] Here Brownlow's characteristic "absentmindedness" serves the purpose of the narrative, by holding this information back.

But that same absentmindedness—or, really, any sort of mindedness— also serves a second important purpose: it locates the source for this information elsewhere than in the events described in the novel. This is the first time in the novel that we are given access to private speech or recorded thought that indicates the existence of a knowledge of people and events that we, and Oliver, do not know. It is not surprising—in light of the lessons of Marxist and new historical criticism—that the introduction of the middle-class domestic world should bring with it the internal space of private subjectivity.[33] What I want to stress here, though, is that this glance inward is also a glance away from the world of the novel. Brownlow is drawing his intuitions from places and scenes to which the novel's reader has no access. As he tries to place Oliver's face, he retreats to his memory and imagination: comparing Oliver to a "vast amphitheatre of faces.": "There were the faces of friends, and foes, and of many that had been almost strangers peering intrusively from the crowd; there were the faces of young and blooming girls that were now old women" (77). Part of the function of these lines, of course, is personification: hammering home the point that Brownlow is old, is kindhearted, has suffered loss. At the same time, though, the lines makes it clear that whatever the nature of the genealogical plot will be, its possible cast of characters is much larger than that which is presented to us through the narration. Oliver's story, as Miller describes it, is inseparable from the accounts depicted in the novel. The genealogical story is a separate story, with its own timeline and characters. And it is based on *this* story—the existence of which he senses, even as the specifics elude him—that Brownlow first intuits Oliver's goodness.

To sum up, then: the chain of events that have taken place in the novel's Newgate plot—that is, in the world of the workhouse and criminals—do not in themselves make it clear that Oliver belongs in the domestic plot. Dickens instead introduces another story, which he vaguely hints at but does not elucidate, and uses this story as the basis of Brownlow's intuition. The one thing that we are given is that this story is, in some way, connected with Oliver's genealogy. As the novel continues, this underlying story comes to provide a logic of explanation for nearly everything that happens. Previously, Fagin's desire to corrupt Oliver had been explained by the fact that an innocent-looking child would make a good pickpocket, and Fagin had sought to retrieve Oliver from the police so that he could not "peach" about Fagin's organization. Starting in chapter twenty-six, though, the novel shows that Fagin's interest in Oliver to be due to payment from a mysterious figure. Along with this character, the novel also introduces groups of unknown characters, discussing a locket that we have never seen. The novel makes it clear, in other words, that the events that it is showing are determined by a story that its readers cannot fully access, except through its textual manifestations. The chapter titles self-consciously remind the reader of this: the title of the locket chapter explains that its contents "may be found of importance in this history"; the chapter describing Monks's first visit to Fagin advertises, "In which, a mysterious character appears upon the scene; and many things, inseparable from this history, are done and performed." From the moment of the introduction of the genealogical story, then, the novel draws attention to the fact that its events are determined by an underlying rationale, even as the specifics of this rationale are kept hidden.

Here, though, we are faced with what I referred to in the previous chapter as the "antinomy of narrative theory": the fact that the underlying story determines the narrative without pre-existing it. In the case of *Oliver Twist*, it is this genealogical story that is not actually there—at least not until chapter forty-nine, when Brownlow interrogates Monk and records the story into the textual narrative. Up until that point, the novel repeatedly asserts the existence of a determining logic but does not say what it is. In a rigorous sense, then, the genealogical story does not exist. This is true in a rather more practical sense as well: in March 1838, while the chapters mentioned earlier—the introduction of the locket as a MacGuffin,[34] Monks's machinations—were being published, Dickens famously wrote in a letter that no one would be able to produce a premature stage version, because "nobody can have heard what I mean to do with the different characters in the end, inasmuch as at present I don't quite know myself."[35] Though the novel insists on the existence of this underlying story, it only exists for the reader the same way it exists for Brownlow—as an internally felt certainty that there is a way that events *should* be occurring, that still only takes the form of nebulous intuition.

As soon as Brownlow begins to figure out the specifics of the story, we are no longer allowed access to his thoughts. The moment when Brownlow's intuition is proven correct comes when he has taken Oliver to his house. There, he sees Oliver sitting under a painting: "he pointed hastily to the picture over Oliver's head, and then to the boy's face. There was its living copy" (90). At this point, though, in a rather clumsy contrivance Oliver faints away from the surprise of it all, and Dickens offers a self-conscious "meanwhile" to deflect the reader away from Brownlow's discovery:

> Oliver knew not the cause of this sudden exclamation; for, not being strong enough to bear the start it gave him, he fainted away. A weakness on his part, which affords the narrative an opportunity of relieving the reader from suspense, in behalf of the two young pupils [the Dodger and Charley Bates] of the Merry Old Gentleman. (91)

Because Oliver has fainted, then, Dickens does not even follow Brownlow's finger to the wall, leaving us in a similar position to the one that Brownlow was in earlier: Oliver looks like—*someone*. What Dickens has done here, effectively, is to shift the onus of intuition from Brownlow to the reader. We know now that there is a genealogical story, which is producing the effects we see in the novel. But we don't know the specifics of that story. The narrator's claim, then, that he is "relieving the reader from suspense," is more than a little disingenuous, since it comes in the context of explicitly holding knowledge back from the reader. What it does indicate, however, is that the reader's engagement with the novel is now based on suspense: the belief that there is something to be known, which we do not yet know. The fact that the novel *seems* to know this, and to dole it out and withhold it, is what gives Oliver's narrative its sense of definite direction.

I started by suggesting that *Oliver Twist* was considered exempt from the Newgate genre insofar as the novel was considered to be about Oliver. What that means, though, is not so much that the novel is about Oliver at any one point in time but rather about his progress through, and away from, crime. In contrast, for Thackeray to see the novel as being not about Oliver, he has to see it not as a progression but rather as a static portrait. Fagin, Nancy, and Sikes are, for Thackeray, not characters whose deaths are ultimately important to how we perceive them. The moral reading of the novel, then, requires that a specific narrative trajectory be part of Oliver's characterization. As I have been trying to suggest, that narrative trajectory first enters the novel with Brownlow and takes the form of a moral intuition based on, and drawing from, the genealogy plot: from the belief that the sequence of events that we are reading has a specific direction, tending toward Oliver's final acceptance into middle-class society. In generic terms, we can also see the introduction of this underlying story as the move away from Newgate fiction, from novels *about* crime and criminals.

My argument, with its emphasis on the intuition of the direction of the novel's narrative, may seem to locate its object halfway between the reader and the text. For, what ultimately allows the novel its exemption in the Newgate novel controversy is also what gives it its familiar narrative form, the structured plot based on the intertwining of suspense and actions: suspense only being created insofar as the actions occur in the novel, the actions having meaning and coherence based on the determining knowledge that the reader must assume underwrites the text. It is this relation that produces the "ought" in *Oliver Twist*. Recall Harpham's formulation of the "ethical" dimension of reading: "Readers . . . construct the text freely but construct it as the law of the text."[36] The reader follows what seems like the underlying structure of the text while at the same time supplying that structure—building it from a mixture of textual clues and intertextual generic knowledge. Harpham is careful to keep his general formulation separate from any specific ethical content; this allows the "law of the text" to be specific to whichever text happens to be under consideration. In the case of *Oliver Twist*, though, we do not need to abstract so far, since its representations of vice were part of a debate situated not only in abstract normativity but in specific Victorian norms: What may be represented? What should we read? What I have been trying to suggest is that the answer to these questions, in *Oliver Twist*, was not simply about what appeared in the text. Rather, it was about how the text made the reader feel, at an intuitive level, in relation to what was depicted. Not only the underlying narrative structure but also the reader's role in the creation of that narrative structure determined the moral quality of the novel.

INTERESTING CRIMINALS: THACKERAY

The moral quality of *Oliver Twist*, then, can be traced back to the reader's role in the production of the novel's narrative trajectory. In this section, I would like to turn to the critical discourse that surrounded Newgate novels—the sum total of which we usually now refer to as the "Newgate novel controversy"—to show that Victorian critics took a consistent, if somewhat unconsidered, approach to the issue of novelistic morality, emphasizing the interaction between the novel and the reader. In the same way that critics located *Oliver Twist*'s moral quality in the way it oriented its reader toward an ending, so the Newgate novel controversy, in general, was not about what represented elements were *in* the novels so much as what methods the novels used to keep their readers reading—what, to use the term that critics of the time used, made the novels "interesting." I will be focusing particularly on Thackeray, who was one of the most vocal and consistent critics throughout the period.

First, though, we should address the reason most often given for Victorians' strong reaction to novels about crime: the fear of emulation. Literary history usually offers one case in particular as an example of this fear: the confession and execution of Benjamin François Courvoisier. Some background is in order: on May 5, 1840, the elderly Lord William Russell was murdered by Courvoisier, his valet. When the *Times* published his confession on June 25, it mentioned as well that, under questioning from the sheriff, Courvoisier had asked him "to let it be known to the world, that the idea was first suggested to him by reading and seeing the performance of *Jack Sheppard*."[37] The book, he said, had been lent to him by another servant, and "he lamented that he had ever seen it." Ainsworth then wrote a letter to the newspaper claiming that he had investigated the matter and found that "The wretched man declared he had neither read the work in question nor made any such statement."[38] Most available evidence indicates that

Ainsworth was closer to the truth, but that did not prevent parliamentary handwringing about the novel, or the eventual refusal on the mayor's part to grant any new licenses for plays bearing the name *Jack Sheppard*.[39]

In the journals and reviews of the time, though, we actually find considerable reticence to assign such immediate influence on Courvoisier to Ainsworth's novel. No less than many modern critics of cultural productions that glamorize violence or crime, the critics of the time had an ambivalent, if not equivocal, relation to the question of moral influence. In "Going to See a Man Hanged," his magisterial denunciation of the death penalty, Thackeray describes moment by moment the scene of Courvoisier's public execution. Yet he never once mentions Ainsworth or *Jack Sheppard*. This omission is particularly odd, since contemporary novels do play a part in his discussion. Noticing a prostitute "that Cruikshank and Boz might have taken as a study for Nancy," he concludes that she is quite unlike the portrayal of such women "in late fashionable novels."[40] Rather than point to the novel that had been tied in public discussions directly to the crime, Thackeray instead makes vague jabs at Dickens's novelistic verisimilitude. After insisting, famously, that since Dickens would not be able to "paint the whole portrait" of a prostitute, he "had better leave the picture alone altogether," Thackeray moves even further into generalization to make his final claim: "The new French literature is essentially false and worthless from this very error—the writers are giving us favourable pictures of monsters . . . (to say nothing of decency or morality)" (155). Eliding the very novel attached to the case he was seeing, Thackeray turns instead to Dickens. And then, when he turns to the possibility of indecency or immorality, he turns to an unnamed body of "French literature"—the ultimate point, furthermore, in parentheses. At what should have been—and was, by many historical accounts, perceived as—the proving grounds of Newgate novels' pernicious effects on public morality, Thackeray's interest seems to be drawn more to a discussion of selection of details. In other words, the discussion is not one of whether it is permissible to portray crime, but *how* one can portray crime without falling into error. If novelists cannot "paint the whole picture," that is a result of public morals, but it implies that painting the whole picture— even of criminals—would have at least artistic validity.

The depiction of vice, then, was not simply seen as morally pernicious. Thackeray may, at the time, have believed that public morals made it impossible to present crime in any other fashion, but this conclusion was largely his own. Other critical voices tried to distinguish between a novel that simply depicted vice and one that was *about* vice. In the *Athenaeum* review of *Jack Sheppard* mentioned earlier, for example, we find that the novel was not criticized simply for depicting vice. While casting *Jack Sheppard* as a "bad book," the review is at pains to point out that tales of criminals *could* be morally valuable. In what becomes a critical commonplace in reviewing the novel,[41] the *Athenaeum* draws a comparison between Ainsworth's novel and two famous eighteenth-century presentations of its principal characters: Fielding's *Jonathan Wild* and Gay's *Beggar's Opera*. These eighteenth-century works, we are told, had a moral plan behind their depictions: satirizing the economically and politically "great," to use Fielding's term, by showing their similarity to petty criminals.[42] What makes *Jack Sheppard* a "bad book" is the absence of any such purpose. It lacks a moral message and depends solely on its depiction of crime to engage its readers. In Ainsworth's novel, according to the *Athenaeum*, crime "is the one source of every interesting situation." This whole "bad class of books" is bad, then, not because of the depiction of crime but because of the way it relies on crime alone to produce the novel's interest.

This term, "interest," is nowhere explicitly defined, though, as we shall see, it recurs with startling regularity throughout discussions of Newgate novels. The discussion from the *Athenaeum* offers a useful context for understanding the term's usage. Novels that depict vice can have, in the terminology of modern American obscenity legislation, "redeeming social importance." This, for Victorian critics, was the value of a Gay or a Fielding. A novel like *Jack Sheppard*, on the other hand, simply presented crime for its own sake. This distinction is familiar enough, though notoriously difficult to pin down in a specific case. "Interest" becomes important in Victorian criticism specifically as a way to make clear what the central element of a novel is. Tomashevsky, as I have mentioned, offers an account of theme that correlates loosely with the idea of subject matter. But as Tomashevsky points out, a theme in a novel—crime, for example—is not by itself enough to structure a literary work. In addition, "interest must also be maintained, attention stimulated."[43] Something goes from being a theme of a book to an indispensable element of the book through focusing and maintaining the reader's interest.

If we turn back to *Oliver Twist*, we can see that what I have been describing as readerly engagement, or the production of intuition, can also be understood as "interest." When Brownlow first appears, he sees something in Oliver's face "that touches and interests" him; he later tells Oliver that he is "interested in [his] behalf." Or, as Forster similarly wrote: "No one can read [the novel's opening] without feeling a strong and sudden interest in Oliver, and that interest never ceases." Building on the discussion of narrative intuition in the previous chapter, we can extend Tomashevsky's claim that "the function of sympathy is primarily to direct interest and maintain attention."[44] Sympathy, in its various forms, can do this sort of work, and often did in Victorian and post-Victorian fiction. Yet sympathy is, in its novelistic form, a largely synchronic operation, operating through metaphors of the visual, as Audrey Jaffe argues when she points out "the powerful interplay between the specular quality of Victorian sympathy and the spectatorial character of Victorian culture."[45] There seems to be something different operating in the sort of diachronic narrative interest that we see with Oliver. Sympathetic representations can produce interest, but just as we should not assume that all criticism of Newgate novels was based on a fear of emulation, so we should not assume that interest in a character—criminal or otherwise—was necessarily based on sympathetic identification.[46]

As with the production of the genealogical plot in *Oliver Twist*, there is a certain ambiguity, in both Victorian and twentieth-century criticism, around who is actually responsible for the generation of interest. If reader's interest defines the subject of the novel, then what produces the interest? Tomashevsky strikes a middle ground, claiming that, though the reader's emotional reaction is essential to his theory, "this emotional coloration is inherent in the work; it is not imposed by the reader" (65). This qualification may contain a certain predictable formalism—locating meaning ultimately in the work itself—but it is not particularly different from the ideas put forward by Victorian critics. A novel's interest was not presented as an inherent quality, it is true; the reader's reaction was what was ultimately important. But the way in which a novel engaged the interest of the reader, as we shall see, would be presented as the novelist's responsibility.

The reader's interest thus plays a complicated role: at once the measuring stick of a novel's moral worth, and almost thoroughly under the control of the novelist. Thackeray's *Catherine* offers a usefully explicit rendering of these themes. This rather uneven novel was intended as a parody of Newgate conventions, one that would, in Thackeray's words, make it impossible for the reader to "mistake virtue for vice" or "allow a single sentiment of pity or admiration to enter his bosom for any character in the piece."[47] Perhaps suspicious of his own sneaking affection for his characters, Thackeray breaks from his parodic authorial voice to offer several explicit critiques. At the end of the first chapter of the parody, the author criticizes novels that depict crimes committed by virtuous characters: "if we *are* to be interested by rascally actions . . . let them be performed, not by virtuous philosophers, but by rascals" (19).[48] No better are those novels that *do* feature rascals but "create interest by making their rascals perform virtuous actions." "Interest" here seems to stand in for a certain sort of engagement that a reader has with a novel. Notable, though, is the fact that Thackeray's imagined reader has little control over how his or her interest is directed. Since we cannot help but be interested by rascally actions, it is up to the author, who "creates" the interest, to make sure that such actions are performed by rascals. The creation and maintenance of a reader's interest, we are left to infer, is at the novelist's discretion. Discussing Dickens's *Oliver Twist* in his afterword, Thackeray writes, "The power of the writer is so amazing, that the reader at once becomes his captive, and must follow him whithersoever he leads." The result: "No man has read that remarkable tale of *Oliver Twist* without being interested in poor Nancy and her murderer" (132). The novelist holds such sway over the reader's interest that "no man," Thackeray presumably included, can help but be interested. Such interest can even be quite against the reader's better judgment. Turning from Dickens to Ainsworth, from bad to worse, Thackeray has this to say of *Jack Sheppard*: "bad, ludicrous, monstrous as the idea of this book is, we read, and read, and are interested, too" (132). In a slightly later discussion of the works of Eugène Sue—we should recall that in his article on Courvoisier's hanging, Thackeray slipped easily from a critique of *Oliver Twist* to one of "fashionable" French novels— almost identical language is employed: "Read we must, and in spite of our- selves; and the critic . . . though compelled for conscience-sake to abuse this book, is obliged honestly to confess that he has read every single word of it, and with the greatest interest, too . . . though we know all this is sheer folly, bad taste, and monstrous improbability, yet we continue to read to the last page."[49] Apostrophizing the reader, finally, Thackeray asks, "Do you not blush to have been interested by brutal tales of vice and blood?" (234). The danger inherent in novelistic depiction of crime and criminals is not that the reader will believe the "bad," the "ludicrous," or the "monstrous" to be true. Instead, even knowing the novel to be false, we—Ainsworth's readers, Sue's readers, *all* readers—cannot help but read, and we cannot help but be interested.

This is not to say, however, that "interest" is a thoroughly negative term. Instead, it is a fact of novel reading; a reader's interest determines what a novel, in blunt terms, is *about*. When the *Athenaeum* writes that Ainsworth makes crime "the one source of every interesting situation," the contrast is with eighteenth-century authors who, according to the logic of the review at least, derived interest from other sources. In the case of Newgate novels, there was no shortage of alternative sources of interest. Bulwer's *Paul Clif-ford* was a political satire—early reviews and advertisements made much of its representations of royals and parliamentarians in the guise of thieves; *Eugene Aram* was a psychological novel; *Rookwood* was to be an English gothic, an attempt, as Ainsworth puts it, to write "a story in the bygone style of Mrs. Radcliffe";[50] *Jack Sheppard* was a historical romance. In fact, when Thackeray criticizes the novels, he takes care to point out that he is not crit- icizing them as a whole but only their "Newgate elements." In any of these novelistic subgenres, a certain thematics of crime might have been accept- able, as a means to an end other than entertainment through crime alone. In each of these cases, then, the claim that the novel was actually a Newgate novel meant that its portrayal of crime went beyond mere theme and ended up overtaking the subgenre it was supposed to support. The reader's interest came to rest, in other words, on the crime, and only on the crime.

John Forster's review of *Jack Sheppard* in the *Examiner*—perhaps the most damning review of the novel to see print—criticizes the novel on specifically these grounds. Ainsworth starts off promisingly enough, Forster writes, with "a few spirited scenes" of historical romance, and there is hope that "the nominal hero may be . . . a mere background" to a better sort of novel:

> Soon, however, is this illusion dissipated, and crime—bare, rascally, unmitigated, ferocious crime—becomes the idea constantly thrust before us. From that instant all of what we will call the interest of the book may be said to hang upon the gallows, and the reader finds himself suddenly launched on one undeviating and very dirty road to that pleasing and elevated object.[51]

Though the novel may be called *Jack Sheppard*, though it may feature Jack Sheppard, Forster begins the review by offering the hope that the novel might not be *about* Jack Sheppard. The interest of the book could have rested somewhere else: in "that sort of a picture of romance, for a correct rendering whereof Mr Ainsworth has indisputable requisites"—in other words, in historically meticulous descriptions of Jacobite intrigue. Certainly crime, and the world of Jack Sheppard and Jonathan Wild, would have played a part in such a picture, but it would not have been the source of interest. The historical verisimilitude of the romance, after the fashion of Scott, would have used crime to produce a different source of interest. Ainsworth, though, neglects this calling and uses "bare, rascally, unmitigated, ferocious crime" as an alternative to this other, better approach. Though he has a generic choice, Ainsworth's fault lies in allowing the Newgate themes to be the source of all "the interest of the book." A Newgate novel, in other words, is not only a novel with "Newgate themes" but rather a novel that uses those themes to keep a reader's interest.

These alternative sources of novelistic interest, though, go beyond generic themes; they derive as well from the novel's formal relation to narrative structure. We can glimpse this in Forster's offhand comment that *Jack Sheppard*'s interest "may be said to hang upon the gallows." The Tyburn gallows are not where the novel ends, precisely—there is a small amount afterward dealing with the noncriminal characters—but they are the end of Jack Sheppard's story. Insofar as the novel makes clear that crime is the source of its interest, that interest ends on, or hangs upon, the gallows. Not only that, but this ending is clear "from the instant" that it is clear that the novel's interest lies in crime. From this point forward, the rest of the novel is only an "undeviating and very dirty road" to Tyburn. This criticism of the novel suggests that, in its move to crime as its main source of interest, the novel also settles into a recognizable generic storyline, made familiar by the *Newgate Calendar*—or, more properly, one of the numerous collections of criminal biographies that bore that name.[52] If there is a positive generic feature in these novels it is this: as Hollingsworth puts it, "a Newgate novel was one in which an important character came (or, if imaginary, might have come) out of the Newgate calendar" (14). As the parenthetical qualification suggests, this classification is not absolute, nor is it absolutely reliable. Still, to the extent that a subgenre relies on certain readerly expectations, there could be little mystery of the final outcome of a Newgate story. *Newgate Calendar* biographies almost always ended on the Tyburn gallows. A large part of what separates the novel that simply *depicts* crime—the novel that *Jack Sheppard* might have been—from the novel that is *about* crime—the novel it turned out to be—seems to lie in the way it enacts certain generic conventions of the criminal story. Thus, for Forster, it is enough to say, by way of shorthand for all of the moral problems that Ainsworth's concentration on crime presents, that we know how the story will play out; we know its ending.

The alternative to such knowledge—the form of interest that kept a reader reading specifically through a lack of knowledge—took a form we have already seen: suspense. In an 1836 letter to his then-publisher John Macrone about his story, "The Black Veil," Dickens writes, "I am glad you like The Black Veil. I think the title is a good one, because it is uncommon, and does not impair the interest of the story by partially explaining its main feature."[53] The "interest of the story," by this usage, would be something ruined by an early revelation. This is hardly a peculiarity of Dickens's phrasing; we see a nearly identical usage in a review of Charlotte Brontë's *Shirley*: "while the interest of the story is generally well sustained, the *dénouement* is veiled with a greater tact than is usually employed in modern fictions."[54] The term, then, seems a shorthand for suspense, mystery, deferred knowledge. Of course, suspense is only sustained for so long, and deferred knowledge is ultimately conferred. So interest here displays its economic connotations as well: the promise of a narrative payoff for the time and attention invested. Victorian interest, then, appears to do what Peter Brooks has famously attributed to "narrative desire": the desire that "carries us forward, onward, through the text."[55] Brooks's reference to psychic drives is, as we shall see, somewhat stronger than the Victorian concept of interest. Still his terminology fits nicely with Thackeray's description of the reader who "must follow" the novelist "whithersoever he leads."

In the late 1860s, Alexander Bain's *Mental and Moral Science* would attempt to systematize, and make physical, the notion of the "interest of the story."[56] Drawing an explicit connection between novel reading and physical excitement, Bain refers to "the mental attitude under a gradually approaching end, a condition of suspense, termed Pursuit and Plot-interest."[57] "Plot-interest" here describes more than literature alone. Any activity that requires the pursuit of some end—"combining a small amount of uncertainty with a moderate stake" (270)—will, according to Bain, produce roughly the same reaction. As his name for the phenomenon indicates, however, narrative literature enjoys certain pride of place in his system. After moving through a series of increasingly refined experiences—"the excitement of pursuit as seen in the lower animals," "field sports," "the occupations of industry," "the sympathetic relationships," and "the search after knowledge"—Bain turns to "the literature of plot, or story." Such literature, he claims, is "the express cultivation of the attitude of suspense." The audience of a narrative will not actually be experiencing the events described, but the mechanics of plot will make it seem as if they were:

> An interesting stake, at first remote and uncertain, is brought nearer by degrees; and whenever it is visibly approaching to the decision, the hearer assumes the rapt attitude that takes him out of the subject sphere. . . . The entire narration in an epic poem, or romance, is conceived to an agreeable end, which is suspended by intermediate actions, and thrown into pleasing uncertainty; while minor points engage the attention and divert the pressure of the main plot. (272–73)

"Plot-interest," then, has two elements: the promise of an "agreeable end" combined with the "pleasing uncertainty" that the end will come about. The steadily increasing proximity of the conclusion not only engages the reader but actually makes the reader momentarily forget his or her own subjective circumstances and become engaged with the narrative's own actions and diversions.

This does not mean, though, that readers thoroughly forget themselves; and it is in this that we see why concerns about sympathy with criminal characters were different than concerns about actual emulation. We should recall Thackeray's reticence to attribute a complete loss of control in the Courvoisier case to a reading of *Jack Sheppard*. In fact, he turned away from that issue entirely to make a digression—one that, absent the larger context of Courvoisier's case, would appear to make little sense—through novelists' one-sided presentations of criminals. The critical position, in other words, would seem to be that a reader's engagement in a novel, even in its worst forms, does not lead to an absolute loss of subjectivity.

We see this in Bain's language, which consistently returns to the relative moderation of the sort of interest he is describing. The reader might be "rapt" and "thrown into pleasing uncertainty," but that uncertainty is still of a "small amount," and the stakes are "moderate." Plot-interest, according to Bain, must remain "within limits": "if the stake be high, the fear of losing it will deprive the situation of the favourable stimulus of plot-interest" (269–70). Interest, then, lies in a site between critical detachment and thorough identification. This mediate position, I would argue, is crucial for our understanding of nineteenth-century descriptions of novelistic interest.

As Albert Hirschman demonstrates in *The Passions and the Interests*, the idea of interest developed in the seventeenth and eighteenth centuries as a "countervailing" force, which could balance the passions that were coming to be seen as the principal motivations of human action.[58] Unlike concepts such as religion and rationality, which increasingly seemed ineffectual to control our baser desires, interest came to play the role of an inclination that, even while it was itself a natural inclination, exercised a moderating control over the other passions. Tracing the evolution of this concept from Machiavelli to Adam Smith and Hume, Hirschman suggests that this notion of a force at once primitive and moderating laid the philosophical groundwork for the eventual emergence and hegemony of market capitalism. Capitalism, founded on the notion of interest, became *naturally virtuous*: natural because it was inherent in all humans, virtuous because it resisted the animal passions that would lead a person, or a society, to ruin. Francis Hutcheson offers an evocative formulation: the impulses capable of moderating the passions take the form of the "calm desires."[59] Not desire in the sense of Brooks's psychic drives but moderate, *calm* desire—this perhaps best describes the way in which Thackeray imagines the experience of novel reading.[60] Readers are never imagined to thoroughly forget themselves; neither will they believe in the "ludicrous," nor will they become criminals—even though the novel exerts some force that keeps them reading, in "captivity" to the novelist. If we are to understand Victorian moral concerns about novel reading, then, it is necessary to see that the problem with misdirected sympathy was not simply that it would lead to an enacting of crimes.

In fact, the problem with such sympathy that emerges in Thackeray's criticism seems more related to questions of artistic honesty. Thackeray's main dispute with Newgate novels, recurring throughout his criticism, is that they engendered in their readers "a false sympathy for the vicious and criminal."[61] The "false" part of the accusation is every bit as important as the "sympathy," if not more so. Thackeray's main critique of *Oliver Twist*, after all, stems not only from the fact that Dickens "leads" the reader to "deplore the errors of Nancy, to have for Bill Sikes a kind of pity and admiration, and an absolute love for the society of the Dodger" (132). This is only an effect of Dickens's one-sided description of these characters. As Thackeray famously puts it, thieves and prostitutes may have their virtues, but they are "not good company for any man": "We had better pass them by in decent silence; for, as no writer can or dare tell the *whole* truth concerning them, and faithfully explain their vices, there is no need to give *ex-parte* statements of their virtues" (132). In "Going to See a Man Hanged," he makes a similar point. Since an author cannot present a full picture of a criminal, "he has no right to present one or two favourable points as characterising the whole; and therefore, in fact, had better leave the picture alone altogether."[62] Thackeray's central complaint seems to be not that these authors depict criminals, or even that they cast them in a favorable light. These come as side effects of the fact that the author does not, and cannot, present the *whole* criminal character to the reader.

Underlying this criticism is a belief that readers are all too comfortable with their romantic preconceptions about criminals. The novelists, when they conform to such presuppositions, are only giving the readers what they want. The *Athenaeum*, in fact, offered this as an apology of sorts for Ainsworth, suggesting that he is a "mere caterer to public appetite": "It is not his fault that he has fallen upon evil days, and that, like other trades-man, he must subordinate his own tastes to those of his customers" (803). Or, as Thackeray puts it, the "present popular descriptions of low life," while "shams," are "endlessly tickling to the reader."[63] So long as it remains in favor with readers, "the writer will not, of course, give up such a favourite mode of composition." When it comes to crime, then, the Newgate novel-ists under attack give the readers what they demand; but they also give the readers what the readers already know. There is no new information about the underworld. In fact, Thackeray goes so far as to suggest that the novel-ists themselves know little about their subject, albeit in roundabout form: "and when we say that neither Mr. Dickens, nor Mr. Ainsworth, nor Sir Lytton Bulwer, can write about what they know not, we presume that not one of these three gentlemen will be insulted at an imputation of ignorance on a subject where knowledge is not, after all, very desirable." So, between the novelist and the reader, there is only a repetition of familiar stereotypes and well-known caricatures.

Such depiction is a far cry from the sort of didactic depictions that Thac-keray believed should be offered, if any were to be offered at all. Thus, he writes to those who enjoy Eugene Aram, Dick Turpin, or "Biss Dadsy": "No, my dear Madam, you and your daughters have no right to admire and sympathize with any such persons, fictitious or real: you ought to be made cordially to detest, scorn, loathe, abhor, and abominate all persons of this kidney."[64] Note that the mother and daughters are not required to arrive at this outlook on their own; it is the novelist's imperative—the novelist "ought"—to make them hate criminals, and the only way to do so is "to paint such thieves as they are." This was what, in Thackeray's view, figures such as Fielding, Gay, and Hogarth did, and why they therefore stood as the point of comparison to which nineteenth-century novelists would never attain. In his more thoughtful moments, Thackeray would suggest that it was that they would not be *allowed* to attain it, for "[s]ince the author of *Tom Jones* was buried, no writer of fiction among us has been permitted to depict to his utmost power a MAN . . . . Society will not tolerate the Nat-ural in our art."[65] Thus, it is unclear whether Thackeray thought a moral novel concerning a criminal was even possible—a seeming equivocation that underlies both his affections for the character of Catherine and also his later insistence that *Vanity Fair* was a "novel without a hero."

Equivocations aside, this description of the "right" way to depict unsavory characters and situations has a good deal in common with the focus on narrative we saw in Forster. Thackeray believed that the only moral way to portray crime and criminals was to go beyond the reader's expectations and preconceptions. The novelist, therefore, must not only tell readers the truth but also tell them something new, something they did not already know. The only correct way to present crime would be by imparting knowledge that the author has and that the reader *should* have. For Thackeray in other words, if an author is to hold a character's interest in a criminal novel, that author can only do so by capitalizing not on what the reader already knows but on what the reader does not know. Recall that the central formal move in orienting *Oliver Twist* away from crime was the introduction of an explicitly withheld backstory. Just as Forster criticized *Jack Sheppard* for defaulting to a generic structure that the readers already know—and, implicitly, moving away from one whose source of interest would be less obvious—Thackeray holds out the possibility that even criminal novels could be read morally, if only readers were interested by the promise of something unknown. He might not have counted *Oliver Twist* among this list, but his critical ideas help to suggest why others did, and why we still do today.

WHEN YOU KNOW WHAT'S GOING TO HAPPEN: *JACK SHEPPARD*

Reading novelized accounts of real people and events can be an oddly powerless experience. History has already happened; Moscow was evacuated and burning when Napoleon arrived. I *know* that in a different way than I know that Jane Eyre married Rochester. Both are immutable, but somehow, as a reader, I feel involved in the re-creation of Jane's plot. *This* time, she hasn't married him yet. (And maybe, just this one time, Tess will live.)[66] When reading novels about historical figures, though, that involvement feels a good deal more limited. Stephen Jarvis's 2015 *Death and Mr. Pickwick*, to take one recent example, spends its first five hundred pages or so largely focused on Robert Seymour, *Pickwick*'s original illustrator. I know relatively little about Seymour, but I know he ended his life with a fowling piece, and I know the author knows it. Even if I put the book down, that death has already happened, and the book itself is a reminder of that. The book exists because Seymour died, just as *War and Peace* exists because Napoleon failed.

This feeling of constraint is not an issue in most realist fiction—even in most historical novels. The reason for this is simple: most of the characters we read about are fictional, and so the outcome of their story is not so fenced in by a shared historical narrative. As Lukács famously observed, in the historical novel, "world-historical" figures "can never be central characters in the action" of the historical novel. That role falls to "the 'middling,' merely correct and never 'heroic' hero."[67] These are everyday people, representative of a type. But it is precisely this typicality that allows—or even demands—fictionality. The more fictional the characters are, the more they can be understood as types as well as individuals; the more typical they are, the more the fictional representations will be recognizable. History is necessarily present in all this, but it takes its place in the background, as part of the "real" in realism, and does not take center stage. The result is that history becomes a more or less hidden element of these novels. Lukács, according to Jameson, sees realism as describing a "future of society secretly at work within its present."[68] Implicit in our understanding of realism, then, is the idea that its determining structure is hidden. This results in the paradoxical experience of relative freedom, or character autonomy, that we encounter when reading purely fictional characters: these exist to serve an underlying structure perhaps, but the conventions of realism dictate that this structure cannot be evident. Once we know that a character derives from a specific historical model, on the other hand, even if we don't know the specifics of that history, we can't help but read with awareness that the ending already, immutably, exists.

This helps to account for the historical fate of a novel like *Jack Sheppard*, which shared a moment of extreme popularity with *Oliver Twist* and yet has not only been largely forgotten by literary history but, somehow, *feels* dated. *Oliver*, as I've been discussing, bases its "plot-interest"—using Bain's term—on something withheld: the idea that what we see is not all there is. While we read the events in the narrative, we are also aware that those events are working toward some end—toward a purpose, that is, but also toward a conclusion. This is a condition of intelligibility for most novels in the nineteenth century, a tacit answer to that unspoken question, "Why are you telling me this?" Suspense, in its broader sense, goes beyond the confines of the mystery or the potboiler. Suspense is the indication that a novel has a plan (a *plot*). When we read, then, we understand that we are being told about something more than the scenes and characters that the novel depicts. We are also being promised something about where the narrative is going. This describes an experience of reading that has become deeply familiar as a formal characteristic. What I have been trying to show, through the example of *Oliver*, is that this sort of formal familiarity—this novel that *feels like* a novel—was understood, in its moment, in moral terms.

Jack Sheppard, on the other hand, relies on its readers' understanding of its own historical determining story. It refers back to its source in the confessions of the true Jack Sheppard, hanged at the Tyburn gallows. The book's ending, Jack's death, is the condition of its possibility. In fact, throughout, the novel suggests what its end result will be: a hanging, a confession, and the source of the novel. This circular logic—if we're reading this book, he must have been hanged—calls attention to the fact that, unlike *Oliver, Jack Sheppard* is not underwritten by a separate determining story. Instead, it is determined, through a strange set of operations, by itself. The crime in the novel is a means to an end, but that end is the story itself. This is how its oddly dated feel—an example of an ephemeral subgenre instead of part of the Victorian novel tradition—relates to its narrative form, and the moral understanding of that form. The critics are quite right that *Jack Sheppard* is a novel that is ultimately about crime. This narrative effect comes as the result of the novel's repeated foregrounding of the fact that its narrative is one that is not just being told but also being retold.

Jack Sheppard, we recall, came under attack not only for drawing its interest solely from crime but also for adhering to familiar generic conventions. In Forster's review, the two come to the same thing: as soon as it is clear that the novel is about crime, we know the generic structure, and we know the ending at Tyburn. This connection, though, is not only present in criticism; it is a recurring theme throughout Ainsworth's novel itself. When Jack escapes from prison for the third time in Ainsworth's novel, he finds himself surrounded by his own story. Creeping into town, he comes across a hawker selling "a penny history" of his escapes: "Here's the full, true, and particular account of Jack Sheppard's last astonishing and never-to-be forgotten escape from the Castle of Newgate . . . with a print of him taken from the life."[69] When Jack commits the acts that send him not only to Newgate but also to the *Newgate Calendar*, his story becomes familiar. His name even becomes part of colloquial expressions: "If you don't get back quickly, Lucy, Jack Sheppard will be in the house before you" (313). The dispersal of his story goes on to rather extreme lengths:

> Rounding the corner of a garden wall, he came upon his former place of imprisonment. Some rustic hand had written upon the door 'JACK SHEPPARD'S CAGE'; and upon the wall was affixed a large placard describing his person and offering a reward for his capture. Muffling up his face, Jack turned away; but he had not proceeded many steps when he heard a man reading aloud an account of his escapes from a newspaper. (316)

The prison wall becomes a testimony to Jack's escapes, while on the same wall his name appears again, this time on the placard, and with the goal of returning him to prison. The newspaper, meanwhile, disperses his name and story. Not only hawkers and balladeers, but a generalized anonymous mass seem to be announcing Jack's story.

Such celebrity not only points to the fact that Jack's story is known; it also implies the ending of Jack's story. Forster suggested that one led to the other: when we recognize the story, we know how it will end. For his celebrity consistently threatens him with recapture. His picture is in a broadsheet; his name is written on the wall; his name and picture are together on the wall on "wanted" posters. As much as Jack has previously expressed a desire to be "remembered" for his "bold" escapes (289), his fame now seems to push him toward that final moment at Tyburn. As he tries to avoid the broadsheet hawkers, he hears his name again: "Hurrying down the Haymarket, he was arrested by a crowd who were collected round a street singer. Jack paused for a moment, and found that his own adventures formed the subject of the ballad" (315). The use of the term "arrested" here is telling; Jack's very fame makes it nearly impossible for him to remain incognito. Jack does not remain with the crowd: "Not daring . . . to listen to [the ballad], he ran on" (315).

Such moments demonstrate the way in which the novel itself thematizes the idea of an interest that "hangs upon the gallows." As the story progresses and Jack Sheppard moves steadily toward the fame that would make him such a fixture in the eighteenth- and nineteenth-century imagination, that very fame becomes an agent in his eventual capture. This trajectory becomes even more clear in the novel's most famous staging: that written by J. B. Buckstone and performed at the *Adelphi*. There a hawker is selling Jack's "last dying speech and confession" on the street—an obvious falsehood, since Jack is still alive. Jack, for somewhat unclear reasons, "fells the hawker to the ground." The hawker in turn stops advertising the narrative of Jack Sheppard and instead advertises Jack himself: "There he is—I know him—Jack Sheppard! Escape! escape!"[70] Buckstone's dramatization, when it does not stay true to the letter of Ainsworth's novel, stays true to its spirit, and this scene is no exception. The "dying speech" becomes a self-fulfilling prophecy. Buckstone thus makes explicit what Ainsworth repeatedly suggests: the diffusion of Jack's story into culture takes precedence over the narrative itself. In *Oliver Twist*, as we saw, people will react to Oliver's story in the same way that we are to react to the novel—but first Oliver has to tell them his story. In *Jack Sheppard*, in contrast, there is no need to tell. As with the novel's readers, so with its characters: everyone knows who he is, and everyone knows how he will end.

Readers of Newgate novels would "read and read," in Thackeray's words, though there could be little doubt about the ending. Since these novels dealt with known figures—or characters who resembled known figures— interest would be focused on static characters. In the discussion of *Jack Sheppard* that follows, my claim will be that the novel, by foregrounding the ways in which Jack's story is already part of a larger cultural context, moves away from an end-oriented narrative scheme. The novel does not only have a conclusion that a reader, acquainted with the historical person of Jack Sheppard, would already know; rather, the inevitability of that ending becomes a central element of the novel's method.

Such foregrounded inevitability has a corollary in the novel's other main character: Jonathan Wild. Though the novel ostensibly follows Hogarth's *Industry and Idleness* series by placing Jack, the "idle apprentice," in opposition to Thames Darrell, the "industrious apprentice," the more compelling dyad—and the one that caught the public's imagination to a greater degree—is made up of Jack and Wild. In contemporary reviews, the character of Darrell receives little mention; Wild, on the other hand, is almost always discussed. One reviewer writes, "The real hero of the volume before us is not Jack Sheppard, but Jonathan Wild";[71] for another, "one of the principal heroes—indeed, in everything of importance, *the* principal—is Jonathan Wild."[72] Given that Ainsworth subtitled the first volume of his triple-decker "Jonathan Wild," this hardly seems an unfair assumption on the reviewer's part. As I have discussed earlier, such concentration on Wild brought up a number of unflattering comparisons with Fielding. This concentration on Wild, though, was not simple audacity on Ainsworth's part, as his reviewers seemed to imply. Rather, Wild becomes a sort of embodiment of Jack's gallows destiny. As Jack puts it, "if my career were truly exhibited, it must be one long struggle against destiny in the shape of—." Though he trails off here, his interlocutor completes the sentence for him: "Jonathan Wild" (286).

In order to understand how Wild could play this role, it is necessary to understand the real-life model that influenced Ainsworth's depiction. Wild was not only the most famous "thief-taker"—a private citizen who would capture thieves for hire—of early eighteenth-century London but also the key figure in the underworld of the time. Wild took advantage of the draconian regulations related to theft, which sentenced anyone found receiving stolen goods to death, to enforce obedience. If a thief did not work with Wild in his role of thief, at the price that Wild demanded, then he would most likely be sent to the gallows by Wild, in his role of thief-taker.[73]

In *Jack Sheppard*, Wild's duplicity serves a formal function: from the beginning it makes clear where Jack's story is going, tying the character and the story to its end at Tyburn. Wild, in Ainsworth's rendition, mentors Jack as a criminal with the express purpose of later having him brought to the gallows. Not satisfied with bringing about the execution of Jack's father—for having refused to take part in one of Wild's plots—he tells the widowed Mrs. Sheppard that he will see Jack, still a newborn infant, hanged as well: "I'll hang him upon the same tree as his father. . . . I'll be his evil genius!" (37). With Jack's story, the dual nature of Wild's career takes on a close unity. He will influence Jack toward a life of crime, in order to have him hanged for that self-same crime. Wild, then, becomes the embodied agent of Newgate narrative. He produces the thief but in so doing sends him on a trajectory whose final destination is always the Tyburn gallows. Forster's description of *Jack Sheppard*'s "undeviating" narrative trajectory toward the gallows describes as well the path that Wild sets out for Jack. At times, in fact, it seems as though Wild is directing the novel's very narration. In the final lines of the novel's second volume, Wild takes a twelve-year-old Jack under his wing. Mrs. Sheppard frantically asks how many years he will give her son before bringing his promise to bear: "'NINE!' answered Jonathan, sternly" (164). The next lines are those that open the third volume: "Nearly nine years after the events last recorded . . ." (164). He not only serves the dual purpose of both beginning and ending Jack's criminal career; his character serves to show that, in *Jack Sheppard*, the two are in fact inseparable. Without the gallows, there would be no Newgate hero and thus no novel. The character of Wild has the function of anticipating the gallows—the ending that is already certain, the sine qua non of the novel itself—from the moment of Jack's birth.

The fact that Newgate narrative, as embodied by Wild, assumes its ending as a given is tied to an essential theme of the novels: Newgate novels do not just tell a story, but rather *retell* it. Though Hollingsworth remains justifiably cautious about classifying all Newgate novels as being based on *Newgate Calendar* narratives, he does suggest that even the imaginary stories, such as Bulwer's *Paul Clifford*, were written as if they "might have come" from the *Newgate Calendar*. In this principle, he is supported by what is perhaps a more accurate judge of essential characteristics than academic criticism: contemporary parody—a form that relies for its effect on the recognizability of the generic qualities it mocks.

In the 1830s, *Fraser's* offered two different parodies of the Newgate genre. The first of these, the 1832 *Elizabeth Brownrigge*, took aim at Bulwer's extremely popular *Eugene Aram*. Bulwer's novel purported to tell the story of a small-town schoolteacher and brilliant self-taught linguist who had committed a murder earlier in his life. The murder is eventually discovered and, after an impassioned speech in his own defense, Aram is hanged. The real-life Aram had in fact made some significant contributions to the study of comparative etymology, and the speech in the novel is in large part taken verbatim from eighteenth-century historical record. But Bulwer goes well beyond this, making of Aram "a man, certainly among the most eminent in his day for various and profound learning," who, though a recluse, "would feed the birds from his window . . . and tread aside to avoid the worm on his path."[74] It is on this point that the *Fraser's* parody seized. Like Aram, Elizabeth Brownrigg was a real-life criminal who held some sway over the popular imagination. Unlike Aram, however, Brownrigg's appeal did not derive from any intellectual achievements, but only a surpassing barbarity: she, along with her husband and her son, tortured and whipped a number of serving girls, leading to the death of one. Her entries in the various Newgate collections perhaps gathered special attention due to their frequent descriptions—accompanying almost every description of a beating—of the "poor girls . . . tied up naked."[75] The point of the parody is easy enough to see; just as Bulwer gave Aram "more learning and virtue than he possessed," so the ostensible young author of *Elizabeth Brownrigge* makes his "heroine"—now possessing a more classy silent "e"—into a "young gentlewoman of independent fortune, a paragon of beauty, a severe and learned moral philosopher."[76] All of this, the author assures Bulwer in a prefatory epistle, is an effort to "pursue the same path" as the author of *Eugene Aram* who, "being in search of . . . [a] hero of romance, . . . turned to the pages of *The Newgate Calendar*, and looked for him in the list of men who have cut throats for money." The author's chooses Brownrigg for his own tale, he says, because "she is a classic personage—her name has been already been 'linked to immortal verse.'" To hold Bulwer's novel up to ridicule, pains are taken to imitate it as closely as possible; and the fact that the main character of the tale is already well known from her Newgate narratives is an indispensable generic element.

Five years later, after the success of *Oliver Twist* and during the publication of *Jack Sheppard*, *Fraser's* offered another parody, this time in the form of a complete novel. Thackeray's *Catherine*—written under the name of "Ikey Solomons, Jr.," a reference to the London fence upon whom Dickens had based the character of Fagin—was designed, in the author's words, to present a Newgate novel that would be make it impossible for the reader to "mistake virtue for vice" or "allow a single sentiment of pity or admiration to enter his bosom for any character in the piece" (133). Knowing what the "public likes" in its novels, Thackeray writes, "[we] have chosen rogues for our characters, and have taken a story from the *Newgate Calendar*" (19). The story that Thackeray chose, about Catherine Hayes's murder and dismemberment of her husband, is calculated to be as unappealing as possible. Of interest here, though, is not so much the particular qualities of Hayes's story, but the fact that Thackeray saw the necessity of choosing a Newgate biography as the basis for his work. Whether or not it was explicitly stated, it seems to have been implicitly understood that the way to make something *look* like a Newgate novel was to draw inspiration from pre-existing stories.

In *Jack Sheppard*, however, we see a concern not only with the story's sources, but also with the way in which the story itself feeds back into culture. The broadsheets lead to the capture, which leads to the gallows, which leads to more broadsheets. This cultural feedback loop was clearly familiar to Ainsworth, whose invention of Dick Turpin's ride from London to York in *Rookwood* had already become part of the highwayman's unofficial biography. The choice of Turpin as a subject for that novel, furthermore, had come from listening "by the hour to [highwaymen's] exploits, as narrated by my father, and especially to those of 'Dauntless Dick.'"[77] The sort of story that Ainsworth tells in *Jack Sheppard* is thus closer to Paul Veyne's definition of myth: "an anonymous tale that can be collected and repeated but that can have no author."[78] Perhaps it is not quite accurate to say that there was "no author" of the criminal biographies that characterize Newgate novels; it is generally easy enough to search through the various *Newgate Calendars*, newspaper reports, and eighteenth-century representations to find source material. But it is precisely this very profusion of source material that makes the authority over criminal biographies anonymous, a sort of shared cultural property. Ainsworth's description of those who are spreading and repeating Jack Sheppard's story are notable in their generality: "a hawker," "a crowd," "a bystander," "a street singer," "some rustic hand," "a man." If one crowd on the Haymarket is hearing a ballad about Jack Sheppard, then most likely, or so the implication goes, some other crowd somewhere else is hearing it as well.

In addition to these popular forms, Ainsworth also drew a good deal of his inspiration from more canonical eighteenth-century sources. The parallel of Jack with his endlessly virtuous fellow apprentice Thames Darrell comes from Hogarth's *Industry and Idleness* series. No small element of inspiration also came from John Gay's *Beggar's Opera*, whose Macheath and Peachum are based loosely on the historical figures of Jack Sheppard and Jonathan Wild, respectively. Beyond just drawing from these sources, though, Ainsworth also makes their assumption of Jack's story an element of the novel. While Jack is in Newgate prior to his third escape, he is visited by Hogarth and Gay, along with the painter Sir James Thornhill, described as "the greatest artist of the day." (279). As Thornhill paints Jack's portrait, Gay and Hogarth discuss plans for their upcoming works:

> "Egad, Jack," said Gay, "you should write your adventures. They would be quite as entertaining as the histories of . . . any of my favorite rogues—and far more instructive."
>
> "You had better write them for me, Mr. Gay," rejoined Jack.
>
> "If you write them, I'll illustrate them," observed Hogarth.
>
> "An idea has just occurred to me," said Gay, "which Jack's narrative has suggested. I'll write an opera, the scene of which shall be laid altogether in Newgate, and the principal character shall be a highwayman. I'll not forget your two mistresses, Jack."
>
> "Nor Jonathan Wild, I hope," interposed Sheppard.
>
> "Certainly not," replied Gay. "I'll gibbet the rascal. . . ."
>
> . . .
>
> [Hogarth:] "I've an idea as well as you, grounded in some measure upon Sheppard's story. I'll take two apprentices, and depict their career." (285–86)

In such passages, Ainsworth calls attention to the more respectable sources for his story, placing his novel in more dignified company than that of street ballads and Newgate biographies. At the same time, however, these passages function to remove some of the authority that Hogarth and Gay might have over Jack's story. For in both cases, they base their work on the story as told in the novel: "Jack's narrative has suggested," "grounded in some measure upon Sheppard's story." The order of attribution is thus reversed; the sources upon which Ainsworth drew for his novel are here presented as drawing, themselves, upon Ainsworth. There was, of course, no "Thames Darrell" for Hogarth to draw upon for his "industrious apprentice"; Ainsworth drew the idea from Hogarth. But through his depiction of the story as presented in his novel, Ainsworth insists that his story is not only a retelling of other influential accounts. The novel thematizes its own capacity to influence future retellings.

This knotting-up of influence becomes even more striking in the Cruikshank illustration that accompanies the prison visit. The painting that it shows Thornhill working on was an influential element of the Jack Sheppard story in its own right. One anonymous poet in the *British Journal*, frequently quoted in *Newgate Calendars*, went so far as to attribute Jack's fame to the painting: "Thornhill, 'tis thine to gild with fame / Th' obscure, and raise the humble Name; / To make the form elude the Grave, / And Sheppard from oblivion save."[79] Since it depicts the moment of painting, Cruikshank's illustration of Jack in this scene is modeled on Thornhill's painting. As he had done with Gay and Hogarth, though, Ainsworth refuses to let the ultimate authority for the image rest with the original source. First, Jack's gently smiling expression in the painting is attributed to the rendition of his adventures:

> Sir James Thornhill commenced operations; and while he rapidly transferred his lineaments to the canvas, engaged him in conversation, in the course of which he artfully contrived to draw him into a recital of his adventures. . . . During the narration Jack's features lighted up, and an expression, which would have been in vain looked for in repose, was instantly caught and depicted by the skillful artist. (284)

The painting is unquestionably the source for the illustration, and it may be in part, if *British Journal* doggerel is to be believed, the source of the fame that informs the novel as a whole. But here Ainsworth again insists that the source for the painting lies in the "narration" of Jack's adventures. There is no need for the author to go into the details of this "rendition of his adventures," since the novel itself is precisely that rendition. In addition to his expression, the novel also offers an explanation for Jack's *contrapposto*. As his narration turns to Jonathan Wild, Jack begins to frown, and Thornhill decides it will be necessary to change the subject: "Here Hogarth received a private signal from Thornhill to attract Sheppard's attention" (284). Turning his head across the room toward Hogarth—at the precise moment that

George Cruikshank, *The Portrait*. Left to right: Austin, the turnkey; Sir James Thornhill; Figg, the prizefighter; Jack Sheppard; John Gay; William Hogarth. (Ainsworth, *Jack Sheppard*, facing page 281).

Cruikshank illustrates—produces the pose, and the portrait. Gay praises it as "the very face . . . with all the escapes written in it" (285). Not "pictured" or "figured," but "written"; the escapes can only be figuratively written in the portrait because they have been literally written in the novel.

Ainsworth's lack of subtlety no doubt adds some comedy to these proceedings. So it seemed, in any event, to Thackeray. In *Catherine*, after the murder of Catherine's husband and a waterborne battle referred to as the "Thames at midnight"—clearly modeled on a similar scene in *Jack Sheppard*—Thackeray finishes his chapter with a narrative non sequitur:

> After this follows another episode. Two masked ladies quarrel at the door of a tavern overlooking the Thames: they turn out to be Stella and Vanessa, who have followed Swift thither; who is in the act of reading *Gulliver's Travels* to Gay, Arbuthnot, Bolingbroke, and Pope. Two fellows are sitting, shuddering, under a doorway; to one of them Tom Billings flung a sixpence. He little knew that the names of those two young men were—*Samuel Johnson* and *Richard Savage*. (121)

Before this scene, oddly, while Catherine's husband is being murdered, Thackeray fills the page with asterisks. Thackeray's parodic focus is perhaps less than sharp here, but the implication would seem to be that Ainsworth takes attention away from the more vice-ridden parts of his narrative by flattering the reader and himself with nearly arbitrary literary name-dropping.

It seems, though, that Thackeray—not surprisingly—is rather ungenerous here. Ainsworth goes beyond a simple list of historical figures or a blunt attempt at historical context. Instead, while calling attention to his novel's source material, Ainsworth also offers its own narrative as the source material *for* the source material. Ainsworth is not only concerned with Jack's notoriety; he is concerned with the relation of his own novel to that notoriety, and to the way it both draws from and feeds into the story of Jack Sheppard. Beyond simply highlighting the fact that his story is a retelling of an old story, he seems to suggest that previous tellings—which informed the novel—were retellings themselves. The effect is ultimately to remove any one site of authority for Jack's story, to make its source, in Veyne's words, "anonymous."

Telling and retelling, narrative cause and effect, become once again intertwined as a result of one more odd touch in Cruikshank's illustration: an issue of the *Daily Journal*, conspicuously dated October 15, 1724, lying in the corner. This detail corresponds, as does nearly all of Cruikshank's clutter, to an element from Ainsworth's text.[80] Hogarth reads aloud an item from the paper, saying that Jack's mother has disappeared; realizing that she has fallen into Jonathan Wild's power, Jack resolves to escape from Newgate that night. Of course, since the plot surrounding Jack's mother is Ainsworth's invention, the actual issue of the *Daily Journal* bearing that date has no such information. It does, however, have a mention of "Joseph Blake alias Blewskin," who, being brought to trial "along with John Sheppard and William Field," attacked Jonathan Wild "and with a small clasp Knife cut his throat even to the Windpipe in a very dangerous Manner."[81] While these events do occur in the novel, the chronology is somewhat off. The novel's Blueskin—in Ainsworth's updated spelling—attacks Wild only after Jack escapes and is recaptured, some days later (324). This incongruity is rather surprising, given Ainsworth's consistently meticulous—though often clumsy—correlation of his novel with historical dates and events. Yet, if this seeming aside to the reader is out of character for the novel, it is nonetheless the case that the newspaper does play a significant narrative role, since it spurs Jack on to his greatest, and most famous, escape. The very newspaper that moves Jack to escape tells the story of his recapture. And the plate that shows Jack being recorded for posterity refers back to a piece of the historical record itself. This confusion of source and conclusion, ultimately, suggests the way in which *Jack Sheppard* displays little concern for the question of narrative closure. As Paul Ricoeur puts it well:

> As soon as a story is well-known—and such is the case with most traditional and popular narratives . . .—retelling takes the place of

telling. Then following the story is less important than apprehending the well-known end as implied in the beginning and the well-known episodes as leading to this end.[82]

The interest of the story may hang upon the gallows, but that does not mean that it stops with the gallows. Rather, the novel continually recalls Tyburn to the reader specifically because it does not only end at Tyburn; it also begins there.

By explicitly placing itself in an economy of telling and retelling, *Jack Sheppard* stands—to rephrase Shklovsky's comment about *Tristram Shandy*—as the most typical of Newgate novels. Bulwer's novels and *Rookwood* relied on readers' familiarity with the stories they were telling, or at least with the sort of stories they were telling. They relied, in other words, on the fact that people understood the ways in which they were retellings. *Jack Sheppard*, I think, goes further; beyond simply engaging in the act of retelling, beyond foregrounding its own ending, it consistently thematizes the fact that it does so. Furthermore, as the cultural phenomenon that followed it would attest, it invited further retellings itself. The novel thus stands as an unexpected example of what Roland Barthes would call the "writerly text": a text that, as Barthes puts it, "I would consent to write (to re-write), to desire, to put forth as a force in this world of mine."[83] Barthes's parenthetical equivocation between writing and rewriting describes the forceful ambivalence upon which Ainsworth seems to insist throughout the novel. By writing, he is rewriting. Yet as he seems to suggest throughout the novel, the story he is writing will itself cause other stories to be written—a notion that ended up being quite accurate.

Jack Sheppard thus helps us understand what the Newgate novel was— that is, what it meant for a novel to be about crime. The Newgate novel, by foregrounding the ending and treating the ending as a source, ends up being a strange creature. Temporally, the Newgate novel is like Barthes's writerly text that both engages in and invites retelling: "a perpetual present, upon which no *consequent* language . . . can be superimposed" (5). At the same time, though, the genre does have a determining story—just as much as the later parts of *Oliver Twist*, or *Jane Eyre*, do. The difference here is that this story is not hidden from us. The novel makes the events that it describes into the "law of the text." For that reason, it exerts a power over the reader's interest, in the active way that Forster and Thackeray have characterized. But that interest is not motivated by anything but the story itself. With *Oliver Twist*, we have a crime novel that might not be about crime; with *Jack Sheppard*, we see what it means for the events described to be the focus of the reader's interest. And, through the circularity of end and beginning implied in this, *Jack Sheppard*—and the Newgate novel in general, insofar as it is like *Jack Sheppard*—seems to grant the criminal hero the possibility of perpetual, unpunished, life.

CHAPTER 3

GETTING *DAVID COPPERFIELD*: HUMOR, *SENSUS COMMUNIS*, AND MORAL AGREEMENT

The discussion, in the previous chapter, of the differences between the moral reception of *Oliver Twist* and that of the larger Newgate novel subgenre was firmly rooted in a specific formal technique: suspense. Suspense, after all, offers a way of describing the structuring elements that a novel does *not* reveal to its reader but nonetheless determine the novel's narrative trajectory. In this way, it offers a relatively straightforward model for moral intuition—that is, a felt principle directing the reader's orientation toward the unfolding of events. But what about novels that are not particularly suspenseful?

David Copperfield offers, a decade later, one answer to these questions. The novel, at a narrative level, is not all that concerned with suspense. A few elements are held back from the reader, but they do not particularly matter to the direction of the story. We do not necessarily know, for example, that Uriah Heep has been stealing from Mr. Wickfield; but neither reception history nor anecdote indicates that many readers are likely to be overly curious about this one way or the other. Unlike Fagin and Monks's backroom deals in *Oliver Twist*, the question of "What is Heep up to?" is hardly asked until the moment it is answered. Even the one significant narrative effect of Heep's machinations—David and his Aunt Betsey's loss of their savings—seems to be brought about more by Dickens's autobiographical urge, as David shifts seamlessly from his life as a lawyer to a trajectory of journalism, stenography, and fiction writing. The interest in the financial ruin derives from how David removes himself from it, not from how he got into it. *Copperfield*, then, does not rely on withholding information; what the narrator does not say is hardly worth knowing. The same is true at the level of character psychology as well: almost nothing is withheld. As D. A. Miller puts it, "The secret subject [in *David Copperfield*] is always an open secret."[1] Keeping with the example of Uriah: the novel does not reveal the character's malevolence, but it certainly does not hide it either. It is difficult to imagine a reader too surprised by Uriah's true nature, once he appears with his "mask off."[2] Unlike a good number of Dickens's other novels—whose narratives, as Viktor Shklovsky points out, tend toward suspense[3]—*David Copperfield* maintains a level of openness with its readers: no unexpected familial connections, no unexplained plot twists later explained by a secret plan, no mysterious benefactors, not even a false name. As the narrator writes toward the end of the novel, "I have made it thus far, with no purpose of suppressing any of my thoughts" (796).[4] We understand what the narrator knows, and in most cases—Steerforth's character, Agnes's more-than-sisterly love—we understand a few things more as well.

And it is this *understanding*, as I will argue in this chapter, that is central to the way that *David Copperfield* produces its sense of narrative necessity. Unlike *Oliver Twist*—or, for that matter, *Jane Eyre*, or *Little Dorrit*—*David Copperfield* does not rely on an inaccessible back-story. Instead it relies on a shared understanding, but one so implicit that it seems to be more of an intuitive sense than any sort of rational knowledge. It relies, in other words, on the idea of *sensus communis*: what Kant describes as "a faculty for judging that in its reflection takes account (*a priori*) of everyone else's way of representing in thought."[5] *David Copperfield*'s narrative is structured around an awareness of, and agreement with, a larger collective judgment—"everyone else's" judgment—even though it cannot say what, exactly, this judgment contains. The narrative's forward trajectory, in other words, does not come from a hidden "law," present only in its phenomenal manifestations; instead it comes from something that is present, and shared, at all times, while still remaining obscured. Characters, and the reader, "get it" while not being quite sure what "it" is.

Of course, we also "get it" because Dickens is a humorist: the "greatest humourist whom England ever produced," according to one obituary notice.[6] The double valence of the term is not incidental; I will argue that humor, properly understood, is essential to Dickens's narrative strategy, and to the sort of formal intuitions that he requires from his readers. Humor, in other words, plays the role in *David Copperfield* that suspense plays in *Oliver Twist*. While suspense is the formal technique that produces an affective narrative response to withheld knowledge, humor produces that response to an implicit shared knowledge. This may seem rather distinct from our modern conception of humor; and, indeed, a good deal of my argument will be based on the fact that, for Dickens and his contemporaries, the idea of humor was not at all confined to things that might make an audience laugh. In fact, as we'll see, the Romantic and Victorian conceptions of "true humor" often shied away from laughter, and Dickens himself shows some distrust for the response. Humor, I will argue, was understood rather as a sense of implicit community—not so much laughing when we get the joke, as the experience of "getting it" itself. As Henri Bergson puts it, a precondition for laughter is that the "intelligence . . . must always remain in touch with other intelligences"; it would not be possible if "you felt yourself isolated from others."[7] My focus will be on how Victorian humor—and particularly that of its "greatest" practitioner—produces this "felt" connection of "intelligences."

Even though this discussion will require a bit of hermeneutic excavation—the genealogy of affective responses to wit and humor from the eighteenth century through the *fin de siècle*—the central affective response that I will be discussing should not be foreign to Dickens's modern readers. As I will suggest, a certain critical fondness for affective responses in general—and laughter in particular—has led many unintentionally to misrepresent the experience of reading Dickens. He is a humorist, to be sure, but if this led to as much laughter as certain critics seemed to indicate, reading him would be a physical endurance test, and university seminar rooms would produce a deafening din. My argument will be that our understanding of the novel's narrative trajectory actually suggests that we still understand Victorian humor, though we perhaps misapply the term.

The use of humor, in the novel, further combines the act of reading with moral intuition. Everyone in the novel has an implicit understanding of the way things should be—even if they don't know it, or can't quite put it into words. According to the decidedly non-humorous intuitionist William Whewell, the business of the moral philosophy lay in producing the system that would move society toward this ethics it already implicitly knew: not "inventing a new system of the world, but analyzing the actual system, which exists, and always has existed."[8] The work of the moralist, then, is not to create a moral system but to find the language for one that we already have. In a somewhat Hegelian fashion—though he himself had little respect for Hegel—Whewell's work sees a gradual unfolding of human awareness of what "always has existed." The result, paraphrasing Alexander Pope, is that the moralist "must give us back the image of our mind. He must show us the connections of moral truths which had governed our thoughts, though we had not unfolded them into reasonings" (20). The point is that the intuitions that direct us are the still-folded—but shared—moral truths. Dickens certainly does not make any claims toward being a moral philosopher, of any persuasion, but what I will try to argue is that the narrative trajectory of *David Copperfield* works along similar lines to those that Whewell describes. Victorian humor is the style that allows a novel to be motivated by something both shared and unspoken.

Making this all quite tricky, though, is the line that the novel draws between "everyone" and "someone," between its anonymous social backdrop and its named characters. Though there may be a knowledge that everyone possesses, an individual character—a David or a Dora or an Emily—remains excluded from any explicit knowledge. At the same time, they themselves, when they are out in the novelistic world and not onstage, are part of this "everyone." Characters thus possess an implicit knowledge of what everyone thinks, since they themselves, when they are not before us as characters, think it as well.

What persists, as an underlying axiom, is the sense that this larger common knowledge is correct. As an example, consider the following scene from near the novel's beginning, as David describes his everyday life after Mr. Murdstone has married his mother:

> Yes, and again, as we walk home, I note some neighbours looking at my mother and at me, and whispering. Again, as the three go on arm-in-arm, and I linger behind alone, I follow some of those looks, and wonder if my mother's step be really not so light as I have seen it, and if the gaiety of her beauty be really almost worried away. Again, I wonder whether any of the neighbours call to mind, as I do, how we used to walk home together, she and I; and I wonder stupidly about that, all the dreary dismal day. (50)

In the passage's first sentence, David is an object, along with his mother, of the neighbors' gaze. In the second sentence, though, he separates himself from that position. Though he says he is "alone," he has actually joined the neighbors: not only because his gaze "follow[s]" their "looks" but also because, through his separation from his family, he has gained the knowledge that they seem to share. That is, the language of the passage implies that his immersion among the whispering neighbors has informed him that Clara's step is "not so light," and that "the gaiety of her beauty be . . . almost worried away." Reading between the lines, we might imagine that he had overheard whispers, but the important thing is that no whisper is actually present in the text. David is not *told* the truth; by a shift of narrative perspective, it becomes evident that he *knows* the truth. And, even more to the point, he has already known it. His rhythmic return to the word "again," along with his use of the present progressive, suggests that this was either a repeated instance or, perhaps more likely, an event that rises before the narrating David with an imminent strength. Either way, the narrative style makes it hard to locate this in time, as a specific incident with a before and an after. The effect of the movement in this passage, then, is not a sudden rush of enlightenment—like, say, the perspective shift at the end of a James novel, or the epiphany at the end of a *Dubliners* story. Rather, the emphasized repetition makes it seem a return to some experience that has already been accessed before. There is no shock or surprise in the immersion in the crowd; rather it seems a return to something that David already is, one of the whispering townspeople himself.

Another word for this sort of unknowing assent is "convention," and it is here that *David Copperfield* makes perhaps an even greater claim to producing moral intuition in its readers than a suspenseful novel like *Oliver Twist*.[9] With *Oliver Twist*, the narrative motion of the character away from crime, and the reader's sense that that movement was what the character was *about*, framed the relationship between morality and novel structure. In *David Copperfield*, the connection between narrative and moral intuition is both more abstract and more powerful; the key term here is "providence." In *Oliver Twist*, everything worked according to a plan we had no access to; in a providential plot, though, everything is working according to *the* plan.[10] The most familiar moment of providence in the plot occurs with the death of David's first wife: the childlike Dora. Like so many other Victorian protagonists—Mr. Rochester and Dorothea Brooke come to mind—David finds himself in a marriage that produces not only unhappiness but also a narrative impediment. The novel does not end with the marriage; but, at the same time, the marriage blocks the moment that will allow the novel to end. Barbara Hardy notes the way out of this: "Many a marital problem in Victorian function has to be solved by the Providential death."[11] Abstractly, this seems a rather clumsy bit of deus ex machina, but readers are generally willing to excuse it—in fact, hope for it—in order to work past the narrative impediment. In other words, most of us are willing to overlook a bit of blunt functionality, even unto death, in the name of narrative satisfaction. In this way, most readers are not that different from Eliot, who, in her 1856 "Silly Novels by Lady Novelists," subjected these conventions to her most withering scorn: "[The heroine] as often as not marries the wrong person to begin with, and she suffers terribly from the plots and intrigues of the vicious baronet; but even death has a soft place in his heart for such a paragon, and remedies all mistakes for her just at the right moment."[12] Yet this scorn did not stop her from using these identical conventions, almost to the letter, fifteen years later in *Middlemarch* and *Daniel Deronda* (though the latter does not quite offer the remedy that Gwendolen, or we, expect). We can assume that she had not forgotten herself in that decade and a half; the hackneyed conventions must not have seemed so hackneyed when she wrote them. Indulging in biography for a moment, it is safe to assume that Eliot had come, just as Dickens had by 1849, to wish for a providential end to a loveless marriage (in Dickens's case, his own; in Eliot's case, Lewes's). As Hardy puts it, "Convention and personal fantasy meet" in the providential deaths of *Middlemarch* and *David Copperfield* (132).

While a novelist might inscribe his or her "personal fantasy" into providence, though, the case is rather different for a reader. Dickens and Eliot, at least at the significant junctures in these two novels, imagine a world that "works" in accordance with their desires. The reader, on the other hand, is faced with a narrative-ethical world and, if the reader has some level of narrative comprehension, intuits the loose outline of those rules. A reader feels some dread when Dorothea walks toward Casaubon's study to be burdened with his work after his death, or cannot help but wonder with David what might have been, "if Dora and [David] had never known each other" (678); and that same reader might well feel some sort of relief, or narrative satisfaction, when Dorothea finds Casaubon dead, or Dora soon afterward dies of some unidentifiable feminine ailment. That does not mean, though, that the reader has any particular opinion, outside of the novel, about what would be the best, or at least the most natural, outcome for a poorly matched spouse.

To talk so generally about "readers' desires," of course, is to invite argument. But my point is less about reception history and more about generic expectations. In the previous chapter, I offered Thackeray's parodic *Catherine* as a commentary on Newgate conventions, since parody serves to make plain the conventions of ephemeral lower-brow genres. To understand the conventions of a specific moment of novelistic realism, though, we are better served by looking at even more realism. There is a certain parody at the heart of the realist tradition, in which successive generations of writers distinguish themselves from the previous generation by being "realer" than previous convention. As Harry Levin puts it,

> Fiction approximates truth, not by concealing art, but by exposing artifice. The novelist finds it harder to introduce fresh observations than to adopt the conventions of other novelists, easier to imitate literature than to imitate life. But a true novel imitates critically, not conventionally; hence it becomes a parody of other novels, an exception to prove the rule that fiction is untrue.[13]

In other words, to demonstrate that their fiction is "real," realist novelists point out what is conventional in previous attempts at realism. Jameson sees this "systematic undermining and demystification" as the "processing operation variously called narrative mimesis or realistic representation, the secular 'decoding,' of those preexisting inherited traditional or sacred narrative paradigms which are its initial givens."[14] In the latter part of the century, the providential marriage plot was a persistent target for such "decodings." Such canonical creations as Eliot's Gwendolen Harleth, Henry James's Isabel Archer, and Thomas Hardy's Tess Durbeyfield offer repeated negations: God does not step in for any of these unhappily wed characters, forcing them to refigure providence as a maddening exercise of personal agency. Chapter 5 will discuss this theme in *Daniel Deronda*; for our present purposes, though, the important thing about these works is that their narrative effects came about through a denial of previous literary convention. To the extent that they have unhappy—or, at least, ambiguous—endings, they speak not only to narrative conventions, but to the way that those conventions become connected with readers' desires.[15] The assumption of a desire produced by convention allows for these novels' sense of realist moral pedagogy: "you think it works this way, but really that's just a wish-fulfilling convention." So in *Daniel Deronda*, for example, at the very moment that Gwendolen is disappointed by Daniel's rejection, Eliot offers the reader the most direct, and lofty, moral address in the novel, invoking "the great movements of the world, the larger destinies of mankind."[16] The novel's key moment for moral instruction, in other words, comes when things do not work out in the fashion that novelistic convention has told us that they should. What is assumed here—assumed in order to be disappointed—is a certain desire to see conventions enacted.

"Convention" is also an important term for us because it reminds us that formal narrative devices went a long way toward re-inscribing a social status quo. The marriage plot in particular, by bringing together formal resolution with social sanction, seems particularly coercive to many critics. As Moretti puts it, "One either marries or, in one way or another, must leave social life."[17] What I would like to suggest here, though, is that a novel like *David Copperfield* does not just resolve on marriage simply because there is already an existing social agreement about the societal importance of the institution. That is, the novel doesn't draw its sense of what *ought* to happen solely from a pre-existing set of conventions it assumes we all share. Rather, by representing tacit consensus through humor, it models the experience of shared opinion. When the final successful marriage does come, it is no surprise. But that is not just because Victorian readers demanded a marriage; it is also no surprise because the large mass of characters—from Aunt Betsey to an unnamed beggar in the street—know it's coming. We don't just "get it" because we share the social convention; we know the social convention is shared because the novel offers us the experience of "getting it."

Whether or not we feel license to talk about Victorian readers' narrative expectations and desires, we can look to the contemporary authorities on the subject. And from that point of view, it certainly seems that *David Copperfield* makes use of a known convention to move David and the reader forward, even when it means that readers will allow, perhaps even wish for, the death of another character. In what follows, I will show how convention—both literary and social—is emphasized in both the novel's thematics and its style. To read *David Copperfield* is to feel that one "gets it," along with the rest of the anonymous society that David feels at his back. As I will show, David is himself a part of society as well, and it is his unconscious membership that motivates the narrative. And as David moves along, in fits and starts, from house to house, we feel that David is slowly moving toward us.

A SCENE OF READING

To say that *David Copperfield* yields a sense of the larger public group goes against the grain of our received model of novel reading, which presents the act as withdrawn and private. The image of the young David, alone with his novels, has become one of the iconic figures of the solitary reader:

> My father had left in a little room up-stairs, to which I had access (for it adjoined my own) a small collection of books which nobody else in our house ever troubled. From that blessed little room, Roderick Random, Peregrine Pickle, Humphrey Clinker, Tom Jones, The Vicar of Wakefield, Don Quixote, Gil Blas, and Robinson Crusoe, came out, a glorious host, to keep me company. (53)

Like Jane Eyre, holed up in her breakfast room with *Bewick's*, David takes solace from his grim home life in reading. He can share the "company" of literary characters only because he has been left alone, and is not "troubled" by anyone downstairs. This figure of an individual reader narrating himself in the first person to other individual readers—to *us*, in other words—seems tailor-made for new-historicist critics such as D. A. Miller and Mary Poovey, who see here the identity formation of the modern, middle-class reader: psychologized, split between public and private.[18] Such an approach generally emphasizes the solitude of reading; in fact, for Miller, solitude becomes a constitutive quality of the act of novel reading. While discussing the generalized "novel-reading subject," he notes, axiomatically, that "he is reading in private" (208). In this, Miller reiterates a basic assumption of novel theory, the most canonical expression of which is likely due to Ian Watt. For Watt, the novel form, starting with Richardson, was a reflection of modernity's larger transition from "the objective, social, and public orientation of the classical world" to a "subjective, individualist and private orientation of . . . life and literature."[19] Following this critical line of thought, the experience of reading makes any reader into a David or a Jane: apart from others, and focused inward.

The standard approach to David's scene of reading thus reflects the main current of novel criticism, not only by seeing it as an inward-facing and solitary act but by associating this inwardness with the private and the domestic sphere. Miller makes this connection explicit in his discussion of *Bleak House*: "Since the novel counts among the conditions for [its] consumption the consumer's leisured withdrawal to the private, domestic sphere, then every novel-reading subject is constituted—willy-nilly and almost before he has read a word—within the categories of the individual, the inward, the domestic" (82). Whatever we might say about *Bleak House*'s dialogism, in other words, Miller sees the novel as something that one must withdraw *to*, away from external life. Since we cannot finish a novel in a single sitting, it remains, as we do other things, in "the mode of *having to get back to it*" (83). Even if we read it out loud, he further claims, we do it in the form of "family reading"; the desire to return to the novel is a "nostalgic desire to get home." The novel is something distinct from the everyday world *out there*—even as it relies on that world to provide its referent. We might note, in support of this claim, that the family life that David and Jane are escaping is not *their* family life; the Murdstones are outsiders in the Rookery, and Jane is treated like an outsider in the Reeds' home.

My argument in what follows, though, will be that this model of reading is insufficient for describing the sort of intersubjective affect that *David Copperfield*'s narrative structure relies on.[20] As a first step toward making this point, before I talk about the readers of the novel, I would like to point out the insufficiencies of the standard model for talking about the reader *in* the novel. The sort of reading that the novel depicts is not so much a withdrawal from the outside world as it is a form of vague consciousness of that world. Consider what occurs as we continue reading the scene in David's attic, beyond his catalog of novels. David goes on to describe an image that "rises" before him: "When I think of it, the picture always rises in my mind, of a summer evening, the boys at play in the churchyard, and I sitting on my bed, reading as if for life" (53). The picture in David's mind seems to zoom in, in almost cinematic fashion: from the surrounding evening, past the churchyard outside with the "boys at play," and into the attic room. The motion here is inward, to be sure, but something strange happens along the way: those "boys" in the churchyard—where do they come from? Certainly, they are not with David; they are outside and he is inside. Before this moment, though, they have had no textual presence at all. David has mentioned the churchyard a number of times, but there has never been anyone in it. In fact, the narrator has gone out of his way, up until this point, to describe the churchyard as a "quiet" space, not only unpopulated, but dead: "the quiet churchyard out of the bedroom window, with the dead all lying in their graves at rest, below the solemn moon" (14). There is a mention of "other children" a few pages prior, but it comes in a general way, and negatively: "As to recreation with other children of my age, I had very little of that; for the gloomy theology of the Murdstones made all children out to be a swarm of little vipers . . ." (52). So, thanks to Murdstone, David's home life has been separated from the outside world. Reading is neither an escape inward nor a surrender to the private sphere; it is a recuperation, however internalized, of the relation with the world outside. It is only in the act of reading that David is able to imagine himself and these children as somehow being part of the same imagined "picture."

This moment depicts a sort of socialization. The groundwork had been laid by previous moments, following a rough dialectical logic. We have already seen that David is separated from his family, conceptually, by an awareness of the other whispering families in church. But this does not do much to place David within a group, other than perhaps the general group of people who live in Suffolk. A more specific possibility is offered in the "other children of [his] age." Note the "other" here: even though the group is brought up negatively, David is already linguistically part of it. The final image that "rises" before David might not bring him together with these children in any real way, but it does lead to an imagined frame that can hold both David and the boys. In the moment of reading, David has come to see his individual experience as being part of the larger experience of the group that includes him. He is not "at play in the churchyard" with the boys, but he is *with* them. The companion piece to the scene in the attic is the scene of young David at school, "story-telling in the dark" for the entertainment of the other boys in his boarding room, based on the memory of these novels (90). Again he is "up-stairs" (81); again he is in the company of Peregrine Pickle and Gil Blas. Now, though, the other boys whose presence he senses—he cannot see them well, since they are "in shadow," but he is "glad they are all so near" (82)—are in fact present. The repetition of the reading scene literalizes its logic; he is now one of the boys. The scene is usually read in the context of the novel as a *Künstlerroman*, as a moment in the writer's development: retelling and embellishing novels, shifting from the child who reads to the man who writes. But, since *David Copperfield* is quite reticent about the experience of writing, there is no scene of David-as-writer that it particularly resembles. It does, however, resemble the scene of reading, and thus it seems better understood as a literalization of that experience. Or we could look at it from the other side: reading about Peregrine Pickle alone and silently in the attic feels something like the concrete experience of having other fellows near, being one of the boys.

Given this representation of reading, the idea that David offers a template for a novel's reader would take on a different meaning. Specifically, it would mean that reading *David Copperfield* is not a solitary move away from others, and not necessarily a move into the private sphere. The essential historicist insight into the identity emulation that goes on in reading seems accurate, but we have to reconsider just which identity is being formed. Miller's identification with David comes from being bookish and appreciating literature of the previous century. This is a pretty fair description of the reader of *David Copperfield* in the twentieth or twenty-first century. But the representation of reading in the novel, and the mindset that accompanies it, makes a good deal more sense if we are willing to imagine what the experience of reading *David Copperfield* would have been in its moment: the experience in partaking in a cultural experience that was *popular*.

"Popular" can be a slippery term, since it can refer either to work that seems designed for mass consumption or to work that people actually consume. It is one of Raymond Williams's keywords, and his discussion points to this tension:

> Popular culture was not identified by the people but by others, and it still carries two older senses: inferior kinds of work . . . and work deliberately setting out to win favor (popular journalism as distinguished from democratic journalism, or popular entertainment); as well as the more modern sense of well-liked by many people, with which of course, in many cases, the earlier senses overlap.[21]

What I mean by the term here is something closer to the second meaning, of being "well-liked by many people." Pushing the definition a bit further: I mean that form of cultural experience that carries with it the knowledge that others are experiencing it at the same time. Popular fiction, as I am describing it, is similar to the idea of convention, with which I began. It is not enough for everyone to be doing it; everyone must also be aware, at some level, that everyone is doing it. So I am talking less about "popular fiction" like supermarket romances,[22] and more about the sorts of literary phenomena and manias that surrounded, in the eighteenth and nineteenth centuries, the releases of *Pamela*, *Pickwick*, Ainsworth's *Jack Sheppard*, Byron's *Corsair*, and du Maurier's *Trilby*.[23] For a modern publishing example, we can think about a *Harry Potter* novel, in the day or week after its release.[24] Of course, the sort of effect that I am talking about is not limited only to published works. For example, certain episodes of serial television shows—series finales, season premieres—produce similar effects.[25]

In his contemporary context, we can include Dickens's novels—though none ever matched the popularity of *Pickwick*—in this list. Dickens was by this time a known quantity: readers knew of his popularity, they knew that other people were reading him, and he knew what they expected of him. Richard Altick writes that *Dombey and Son*, the novel immediately preceding *David Copperfield*, "reflects the conception of his steady audience that Dickens had formed over a decade of successfully writing for it."[26] The reading of the novels themselves easily exceeds Miller's domestic description. Rather than reading aloud being only an inward-facing activity—doing the police in different voices around the family hearth—it seems to have been a public activity as well. One anecdote has the illiterate charwoman of Dickens's mother-in-law attending "on the first Monday of every month a tea held by subscription at a snuff-shop above which she lodged, where the landlord read the month's number aloud."[27] Dickens's popularity among the reading public—or listening public—of nearly every class was nearly unprecedented. To read a part of a Dickens novel, when it was published, was knowingly to take part in an activity, with the understanding that others were doing the same thing, at the same time.

This discussion recalls Benedict Anderson's famous argument that the explosion of print culture in the eighteenth and nineteenth century was indispensable for the "imagined communities" that underlie nationalism.[28] In particular, the traditional multi-plot novel can be understood as "a complex gloss upon the word 'meanwhile'"—that is, a representation of people who will never meet each other and yet are part of a larger community moving in unison (25–26). This is true even for a first-person novel like *David Copperfield*; one could imagine, say, a useful comparison of failed upward social mobility in the characters of Little Emily and Uriah Heep, even though those two never meet and neither one is aware of the other. At the same time that this form of fictional representation serves an educative purpose, teaching people to imagine in this fashion, Anderson sees the newspaper as actually allowing people to imagine themselves within a community of their own. Reading the newspaper "is performed in silent privacy, in the lair of the skull. Yet each communicant is well aware that the ceremony he performs is being replicated simultaneously by thousands (or millions) of others of whose existence he is confident" (35). The sign of this simultaneity is the date at the top of the page, "the single most important emblem on it" (33). The two most important cultural forms for the maintenance of the imagined community, then, are the novel, which performs communal connection, and the periodical, which allows us to place ourselves into it. Dickens—publishing in parts, a mass phenomenon since the fifth number of *Pickwick*—neatly combines these two textual forms.[29]

In spite of the familiarity of Anderson's argument, though, novel theory and criticism remain ill-suited to describing this sort of literary engagement: the experience of reading something with the knowledge that others are reading it at the same time. Of course, there is a good deal of discussion in narrative theory of the "popular" as opposed to the "serious" or "canonical" or "literary"—meant here as generic terms rather than evaluative ones.[30] But such work usually ends up transferring the notion of popular from a collective activity to either formal characteristics or the relationship between the work and the literary tradition. A Raymond Chandler or Philip K. Dick novel, by most scholarly accounts, would seem to be a better representation of popular fiction than a widespread literary phenomenon such as, say, Dan Brown's *The Da Vinci Code*. At the same time, critics are adept at analyzing the way a novel would be read in a specific cultural context, but how do we approach the analysis when the novel itself is a significant part of that context? Historicist scholarship tends to connect what people were reading *inside* their homes to a certain political and social context outside the home; looking at accumulated discourse, critics point to what people were talking about and thinking about: "hidden links between high cultural texts, apparently detached from any direct engagement with their immediate surroundings, and texts very much in and of their world [i.e., non-literary texts]."[31] In the case of the popular text, though, what we might learn is that the "world" that exists apart from the literary text is actually concerned specifically with that literary text. If we attempt to think about the question of popularity, in other words, we do not see the novel as a necessarily private experience to be held up against a different public experience. Reading certain novels, whether inside or outside the house, becomes a sort of public experience in itself. One knows that others are reading the same thing at the same time. The connection with other people is vague and anonymous, to be sure, but it is a connection all the same.

I have raised, perhaps polemically, more questions here than it is within the scope of this chapter to answer. A full cultural account of the popular novel, as I have described it, would be a project in itself. For the purpose of this chapter, however, it is sufficient to indicate that the model of reading as a form of communal connection—as figured in David's scene of reading in the attic—goes some of the way toward describing the experience of reading a Dickens novel. Still, it does not go all the way. What I have been describing is a sense that other people are *doing* the same thing. The theme of agreement requires that people are somehow in alignment with one another. In fact, Dickens's style does lend itself toward a sort of unspoken agreement at the stylistic level. The method it uses is a familiar one, in discussions of Dickens, but perhaps unexpected in this context: to produce a sense of unspoken moral agreement, Dickens relies on humor.

HUMOR AND *SENSUS COMMUNIS*

If the reader *in* Dickens is linked with the reader *of* Dickens, as I have been suggesting, it is important to have some sense of how Dickens was read as a matter of convention. And this much we know: Victorians considered Dickens a humorist. The *Spectator*, as mentioned above, eulogized him as the "greatest humourist whom England ever produced—Shakespeare certainly not excepted." Two years later, in 1872, John Forster would open his *Life of Charles Dickens* by offering nearly identical praise: "Charles Dickens, the most popular novelist of the century, and one of the greatest humourists that England has produced. . . ."[32] Insight into the experience of reading Dickens—especially when that's mirrored by experience within the novel—would seem to require that we understand the nature of this praise.

Yet though it is clear that Dickens *was* a humorist, it is much less clear now what that term once meant. The most obvious meaning would be that Dickens made people laugh. And, in fact, it is difficult to find modern discussions of Dickens's humor that do not, almost reflexively, seem to define his humor as that quality which will produce laughter in the reader. This assumption is no doubt due in large part to the importance of Henri

Bergson's essay "Laughter," which holds a place of importance in literary discussions of humor matched only by Freud's *The Joke and Its Relation to the Unconscious*.[33] Both of these works—dating from the first years of the twentieth century, but written *about* the nineteenth—focus heavily on the physical act of laughter. Furthermore, this idea, that "the most popular novelist" was popular because he made his readers laugh, fits in well with one of our received Victorian types: readers of *Punch* and patrons of the comic theater, culturally childlike and easy to amuse. In 1877, George Meredith would describe these figures as "hypergelasts": "the excessive laughers, ever-laughing, who are as clappers of a bell, that may be rung by a breeze, a grimace."[34] Meredith, distinguishing his own form of wit from the larger Victorian store of humor, made it clear that these laughing English are not to be relied upon for their discernment or taste: "to laugh at everything is to have no appreciation of the comic of comedy." The only English alternative Meredith offers is the "agelast," or "non-laugher." This is our other Victorian image: black-clad and serious, "men who . . . if you prick them, do not bleed." While Meredith was trying to carve out space for a more cerebral and moral—and continental—form of comedy, the current choice in England seemed to lie between two extremes: be blind to humor and laugh at nothing, or appreciate humor and laugh at everything.

Meredith's binary may seem excessively stark, but it has had a good deal of critical staying power—even if its evaluative valence has shifted. In modern criticism, such thorough laughter—at chosen authors—becomes more often a form of good reading than of bad culture. This is in large part because of its joint association with Freudian release and Bakhtinian carnival.[35] Deleuze is probably the most consistent on this front: "You cannot admire Kafka if you do not laugh frequently while reading him"; "Those who have read Nietzsche without laughing—without laughing often, richly, even hilariously—have, in a sense, not read Nietzsche at all."[36] If you do not laugh "frequently" or "often," you simply are not reading Kafka or Nietzsche correctly. If you don't get it, you won't get it.

The same comes up in discussions of Dickens: to "get" Dickens, to respond to his style, carries with it something like the imperative to laugh, and laugh often. James Kincaid's *Dickens and the Rhetoric of Laughter*—the most complete book-length discussion of the subject in Dickens—focuses exclusively on this affective reaction in the reader: "Every time we laugh at Sam Weller's witty attacks on the law, we are moving a step further from our usual position of commercial safety; laughter at Sam Tappertit implicates us in his final crippling; laughter at Mr. Micawber forces us to."[37] But what if "we" do not laugh at all of these moments—perhaps only at some, perhaps at different ones?[38] Kincaid's implication seems to be that if we do not laugh at such properly humorous moments, then we are somehow missing the full rhetorical power of Dickens's novels. The novel, or so the argument goes, only can be appreciated by those hypergelasts who laugh frequently at Sam Weller, at Sam Tappertit, at Wilkins Micawber.

But, as Thackeray said, "If Humour only meant laughter, you would scarcely feel more interest about humourous writers than about the private life of poor Harlequin."[39] In this section, I will argue for a broader understanding of Victorian humor than as simply the experience that makes us laugh.[40] That is to say, I will be seeking to discuss Dickens's humorous style in a way that does not assume that his readership is necessarily full of hypergelasts now. Even more importantly, as I hope to demonstrate, his readership was not so full of hypergelasts *then*, either. The key affective result of Dickens's humor, particularly in *David Copperfield*, is not so much laughter as it is an experience similar to the one that I described in the previous section: an experience of being in community with a larger group of unknown others. Not so much what happens after we "get it," in other words, as the phenomenological experience of "getting it" itself: the comprehension of an unsaid meaning, and the shared understanding that allows that meaning to remain unsaid.[41] Meredith suggests as much about his conception of "comedy" when he writes that, unlike the forceful laughter of satire, "The laughter of comedy is impersonal and of unrivaled politeness, nearer a smile—often no more than a smile. It laughs through the mind, for the mind directs it; and it might be called the humor of the mind."[42] Meredith's description of this "humor of the mind" moves away from physical manifestation; laughter becomes a mental state. More importantly, it becomes a mental state that implies the social, as indicated by his use of terms like "politeness" and "impersonal." He sums up this concept by linking his concept of humor with a "state of society . . . founded in common sense." As he puts it:

> You must, as I have said, believe that our state of society is founded in common sense, otherwise you will not be struck by the contrasts the Comic Spirit perceives, or have it to look to for your consolation. . . . [T]o feel [the Comic Spirit's] presence, and to see it, is your assurance that many sane and solid minds are with you in what you are experiencing. . . . A perception of the Comic Spirit gives high fellowship. (48–49)

Meredith's description of the Comic Spirit—the "humor of the mind" that need not produce laughter—thus returns to the experience that I have been describing in Dickens: the "assurance that many sane and solid minds are with you in what you are experiencing." This "perception" moves humor from an individual or personal experience to a stylistic one that expresses shared experience, or, as Meredith calls it, "Common Sense."

Meredith likely believed that he was being somewhat heterodox in his idea of comedy, but in what follows, I will suggest that his ideas fit quite well with the main stream of Romantic and Victorian thought on the subject, though the terminology occasionally differed. In particular, I will argue that Victorians, including Dickens, did not immediately associate humor with laughter. In fact, as the large body of Victorian work on the distinction between wit and humor indicates, humor tended to be based on this idea of "Common Sense"—and what I will call, for the sake of both clarity and tradition, "*sensus communis*"—an unspecified intuitive feeling of connection with others. In fact, by many accounts, laughter could actually be detrimental to this experience. This idea, of *sensus communis*, displays a connection between literary Victorian ideas of the style of humor, on the one hand, and an intuitive moral and political tradition extending from Shaftesbury to Hannah Arendt, on the other. The affect produced by humor in other words, tends toward the moral side of the sort of connectedness in reading I have been describing.

At the outset, though, it is worth pointing out the limits that this discussion will run up against. The central question here is a hermeneutic one: how people in another time read a text. In the case of an affective reaction, though, we find ourselves at a double remove, since we only have access to people's re-inscriptions of their reactions into the literary. Jonathan Rose, in an essay on historical reader-response criticism, quotes the memoirist George Acorn's "suspiciously Dickensian" account of reading *David Copperfield* to his family: "And how we all lived it, and eventually, when we got to 'Little Em'ly,' how we all cried together at poor old Peggotty's distress! The tears united us, deep in misery as we were ourselves."[43] Rose concludes that, since "unalloyed truth in autobiography" is elusive, the main significance of a passage like this is to "measure Dickens's influence on working-class readers." That may be so—unless a critic's goal is actually to determine what made working-class readers cry, in which case it would certainly make a difference whether or not this anecdote were true. But since, for the most part, we only have textual accounts of reactions, we must approach them with a certain amount of suspicion. And then there are also the questions of numbers: even if we were to encounter a number of accounts of people laughing or crying at a text, that would not mean that everyone, or even most people, did so. Even if we believe Acorn's account, it would hardly prove that "the Victorian reader" or "the English common reader" by and large cried at "poor old Peggotty." So there's only so much we can say, one way or the other, about whether Victorian fiction actually made people laugh.

That being said, unlike early-modern drama or even eighteenth-century fiction, Victorian fiction owes a good deal of its critical appeal to the fact that it offers a way out of this hermeneutic bind. Whether a critic prefers to tell time by Marxian modes of production or Foucauldian *epistemes*, there is a general agreement that in talking about the mid-nineteenth century, we are to some extent talking about ourselves. Fredric Jameson, for example, would categorize our contemporary moment as postmodern. But he would still see that as the third stage of a realist/modernist/postmodernist triad, determined by the historical progression of capitalism through a classical market stage, a monopoly and imperial stage, and, finally, our current global stage. So, for Jameson, nineteenth-century realism "show[s] the functioning of all those realities of capitalism that have not changed substantially . . . wage slavery, money, exploitation, the profit motive."[44] Miller, meanwhile, sees the "novelistic" as something that has now been "freely scattered across a far greater range of cultural experience." The continuity here does not depend on an economic base, but the ultimate effect is the same as what we see in Jameson: to speak about the Victorian novel is to "to recognize a central episode in the genealogy of our present."[45] If a novel is *too* foreign—if it requires too much hermeneutic investigation—then it will hardly count as a Victorian novel at all.[46] But there is also a flip side to this: critics move almost imperceptibly from projecting their reading habits backwards to the opposite approach. Critics bring what they take to be Victorian reading habits into the present, and treat them almost as critical fact, as when Miller analyzes the form of the sensation novel by referring to *The Woman in White*'s "sensation effects *on us*" (153). Dickens makes many modern readers laugh out loud, I am sure, and *The Woman in White* may well make people physically shudder—of that, I am not so sure—but both reactions, ultimately, seem to be based on the idea that these works had these effects on their Victorian readers, and so, if we are to understand them, we must allow, sometimes perhaps disingenuously, that they have the same effect on us.

My suspicion is that many readers are actually, affectively, closer to their Victorian counterparts than they imagine. If many modern readers rarely laugh aloud while reading Dickens, we should at least be suspicious, absent evidence, that Victorian appreciation of Dickens as a humorist was tied entirely to laughter. There certainly is evidence to the contrary: take, for example, Elizabeth Gaskell's portrayal of a Dickens reader in *Cranford*. While fictional, this representation suggests humor and laughter were not necessarily linked. Captain Brown, who thinks *The Pickwick Papers* "famously good," reads a section of the latest number aloud to the assembled ladies of Cranford—most of whom laugh "heartily."[47] Yet, though *Pickwick* can produce laughter in social situations, we are also shown two scenes of Captain Brown's reading practices: "He was rather ostentatious in his preference of the writings of Mr. Boz; would walk through the streets so absorbed in them that he all but ran against Miss Jenkyns" (14). Later, he meets his demise on his job at the railroad in similar fashion: "The Captain was a-reading some new book as he was deep in, a-waiting for the down train" (16). The nature of the Captain's rapt attention is unclear, but it would at least seem that laughter is confined to the social situation, and reading aloud. No laughter comes from reading the same book to oneself.

A couple of related notes from *Cranford*'s textual history allow us to further generalize from this example. Gaskell's work was published in parts in Dickens's *Household Words*, and the scenes with Captain Brown occur in the first part. Whether or not we assume that Gaskell meant this description to please her editor, the fact that Dickens asked for and happily published more parts suggests that he in no way took this as an affront. More interesting, though, is the fact that Dickens replaced these references in the original publication with references to a collection of Thomas Hood's collection of comic poems, *Hood's Own*.[48] Dickens claimed that the move was motivated by modesty: "with my name on every page of Household Words there would be—or at least I should feel—an impropriety in so mentioning myself."[49] It is difficult to say whether this is an accurate expression of Dickens's motivations, but, in any case, it certainly seems that he felt that the replacement of a collection of humorous poems for a number of *Pickwick* would convey the sense of Gaskell's story. That is, he understood the meaning of these scenes not to depend only on the text being a hit—he did not replace it with the also-popular *Pelham*—or even, necessarily, on being a novel; rather the scenes depended on the fact that *Pickwick* was a work of humor. Furthermore, due to Dickens's clear respect for Hood, we can assume that no insult was intended in showing that even a work subtitled *Laughter from Year to Year* would not necessarily produce laughter in an appreciative reader.[50] So, whether or not we can know how anyone actually read, we would be safe in assuming that Dickens's own understanding of his work, *as* humorous work, was not dependent on consistent laughter.

This characterization of humor is not only the case for Dickens's own work. In the middle of the nineteenth century, and stretching on to the time of Meredith's lecture, very few humorous works were seen to be necessarily dependent on laughter. That is not to say that laughter was unimportant; in fact, the question of laughter was central to the key debate in the theories of comedy that ran through the period. Meredith stressed the distinction between "the laughter of satire" and the "no more than a smile" of comedy. More often, though, the debate focused on the distinction between another couple of key terms: "wit" and "humor." This distinction took a number of subtle, and sometimes contradictory, forms, but it can be summed up as follows: wit is cerebral, based around ideas and their incongruity; humor is more sentimental, based around feelings, and particularly, sympathy. So, Leigh Hunt, for example, would see himself following in the tradition of Locke and Addison by defining wit as "the [a]rbitrary juxtaposition of dissimilar ideas," while defining humor as "a tendency of the mind to run in particular directions of thought or feeling more amusing than accountable."[51] Note that, although he situates humor in the mind, he does not associate it with "ideas" but rather with "thought or feeling."

That "thought" and "feeling" could be used interchangeably helps to indicate the distinction, for Hunt, between "thought" and "idea": the latter
has content, while the former is more a "direction" the mind "run[s] in."[52]
Another metaphorical distinction, following through on the image of flow-
ing water, is that of dry sterile intellect, on the one hand, and some sort of
warm organic and *moist* sentiment—as in the "humours"—on the other.[53]
As the American critic Edwin P. Whipple put it: "Humour originally meant
moisture—a signification it metaphorically retains," while wit was "originally a name for all the intellectual powers."[54] The different origins for the
two terms goes a long way toward explaining the odd distinctions that keep
popping up between them. Wit seemed more due to Locke—Hunt cites
him—while humor seemed to come out of Galen. It was the slow discovery
of the eighteenth century and Romantic era that they fell under the same
rubric of "comedy."[55]

As is so often in the case when the rhetoric of head and heart are brought
to bear, the distinction between wit and humor took on moral connotations as well. As one *Blackwoods* writer put it in 1820:

> [H]umour is a far higher power than wit, and frequently draws its ma-
> terial from far deeper sources in human nature. The *humours* of man-
> kind are not only endless, but in their most interesting exhibitions
> they are inseparably blended with their affections, their happiness,
> and their whole moral as well as natural being.[56]

The split between humor and wit, then, was not only a question of rhetoric
or genre: humor expressed something deeper about human nature, and was
therefore more apt to express the truth of the "whole moral . . . being." Carlyle, in an oft-quoted line, was one of many who made use of the head/heart
binary to describe the distinction: "true humour," as opposed to wit, was
something that "springs not more from the head than from the heart." He
then extends this bodily distinction to what is effectively a Romantic—he
was writing on the German Romantic Jean Paul Richter—moral distinction: "it is not contempt, its essence is love."[57] This quote, when it is introduced today, is more often than not taken to be a distinction between
kind-hearted and mean humor, between laughing *at* and laughing *with*
someone. But while it is true that Carlyle is being evaluative, he is not distinguishing between good and bad humor; rather, he is distinguishing between humor and wit. And he certainly is not comparing two different
sorts of laughing, as the third and final distinction demonstrates: "it issues
not in laughter, but in still smiles, which lie far deeper."[58] Laughter, then,
is the sign of something cerebral and contemptuous, perhaps cruel—while
the lack of laughter is more often the sign of "true humour."

Carlyle's moral distinction, then, is manifested through different sorts
of physical affect. But why such a negative view toward laughter? We might

be tempted to see in this a rigid Victorian-ness, shying away from physical exuberance. In fact, the opposite was more the case; as Robert Bernard Martin puts it, "All the Romantic and Victorian distrust of the intellect is implicit in Carlyle's praise of 'true humour'" (28). A good deal of our current sense of the subversive physicality of laughter is due to the so-called release theory of laughter, now largely associated with Freud. There were Victorian versions of this conservation-of-energy model as well,[59] but the idea that what was being liberated by laughter had been repressed, and was somehow libidinal in nature, was not much present in the nineteenth century. Instead of release, Victorians mainly associated laughter with two other familiar theories: "superiority" and "incongruity." The first had the longer tradition, stretching back to Hobbes's claim that "the passion of laughter is nothing else but a sudden glory arising from sudden conception of some eminency in ourselves, by comparison with the infirmities of others."[60] This formulation was quite popular among Restoration theorists of humor, such as Dryden and James Drake.[61] The latter is most often associated with Kant's discussion in the Third *Critique*: "In everything that is to provoke a lively, uproarious laughter, there must be something nonsensical (in which therefore the understanding can take no satisfaction). Laughter is an affect arising from the sudden transformation of a strained expectation into nothing."[62] Kant's theory quickly gained adherents during the nineteenth century, in no small part because it allowed laughter to be seen as an ethically neutral act.

Henri Bergson's famous essay on laughter brings these two theories together, in a theory of social coercion.[63] According to Bergson, we laugh at the image of a person who is acting in a mechanized, repeatable manner: a living being who is not acting like a living being. As Bergson puts it, we laugh at the image of "something mechanical encrusted on something living," or, in other words, "every time a person gives the impression of being a thing."[64] Now, the reason for this laughter is one part incongruity (it is incongruous for a person to be acting like a mechanical thing) and one part superiority (*we*, at least, are acting like living beings). For Bergson, though, this laughter has a purpose: to act like a repetitive thing "expresses an individual or collective imperfection which calls for an immediate corrective. This corrective is laughter, a social gesture that singles out and represses a special kind of absent-mindedness in men and in events" (117). Leaving aside the specifics about repetition and the mechanical—a distinction that is quite important to Bergson's larger theory about what constitutes "really living life," but which we do not need to take for granted here (82)—we can see Bergson's theory as distinguishing just what it was that made Victorians so uncomfortable with the prevailing theories of laughter. Both "superiority" and "incongruity," when presented in social terms, lend themselves to the exclusion of others: with a shared superiority over a seemingly incongruous butt. "True humor," as we shall see, was quite the opposite; discussions of humor turned repeatedly to a sense of sympathy and kinship with the most eccentric individuals.

Before turning to this "true" English humor, though, let us look at the theme of laughter in *David Copperfield*. We have already seen, in the publication history of *Cranford*, that neither Dickens nor his contemporaries saw laughter as a necessary result of his humor. Beyond presenting it as simply unnecessary, though, *David Copperfield* follows the Victorian tradition I have been discussing by treating laughter with suspicion. We do not need to look far in the novel to find this to be the case. In fact, we do not need to look further than the very first appearance of laughter and the first man who laughs: Mr. Murdstone—who will marry David's mother, send him out into the world to work, and ultimately leave him alone to make his own way.

> "Come! Let us be the best friends in the world!" said the gentleman, laughing. "Shake hands!"
> My right hand was in my mother's left, so I gave him the other.
> "Why that's the wrong hand, Davy!" laughed the gentleman. (18)

The laughter may seem benign, but it comes along with a series of Oedipal mandates: that David be separated (physically, in this case) from his mother; that David learn correct societal conventions, such as which hand to shake with. Note the verb: Murdstone doesn't "order" David to use the right hand or "say" that he must; he "laughs" it. This laughter becomes an accompanying presence as Murdstone moves further into David's life. When David finds himself among Murdstone's friends soon after—including one Quinion, who will later oversee David's employment at Murdstone and Grinby's counting house—the adults start discussing "Brooks of Sheffield": a coded reference to David. The conversation flies over David's head, but he is aware of the laughter: "There seemed to be something very comical in the reputation of Mr. Brooks of Sheffield, for both the gentlemen laughed heartily when he was mentioned" (22). Murdstone's admission that Brooks of Sheffield is "is not generally favorable" about the "projected business" (the marriage to Clara) is met, once again, with laughter:

> There was more laughter at this, and Mr. Quinion said he would ring the bell for some sherry in which to drink to Brooks. This he did; and when the wine came, he made me have a little, with a biscuit, and, before I drank it, stand up and say, "Confusion to Brooks of Sheffield!" The toast was received with great applause and such hearty laughter that it made me laugh too; at which they laughed the more. In short, we quite enjoyed ourselves. (22–23)

The scene can be painful to read—even without any knowledge of what will come of Murdstone's marriage to Clara, or of Quinion's role in David's London degradation. What it portrays is a familiar experience: "confusion" in the face of a joke that everyone else seems to get, laughing along without quite knowing why. As with the scene when Murdstone shakes his hand, laughter again becomes a sign of the baffling behaviors that we conform to.

These early scenes prepare us for the fact that Murdstone—"the gentleman, laughing" —will be the novel's central figure of the horror of trying to bend others to one's will. Murdstone's desire in marrying David's mother is to "[form] her character," which as Betsey Trotwood later puts it, is what "wear[s] her deluded life away" (48, 208). He does not kill her, but as his murderous name indicates, his presence in the house is instrumental in her death. This is a theme that repeats throughout the novel, especially when David finds himself reiterating Murdstone's attempts by trying to "form [Dora's] mind" (676). In fact, one of the novel's central morals would seem to lie in the unquestioning acceptance of the nature of other people. Emma Micawber comes to accept her husband's wastefulness, just as Peggotty comes to accept her husband's miserliness. The novel's most idealized couple along these lines—ingenuous, asexual, and infinitely accepting— would be Aunt Betsey and Mr. Dick.

Laughter, identified with Murdstone, is presented as being opposed to this sort of acceptance of eccentricity and difference. Humor, on the other hand—detached from a crueler laughter—was associated in the eighteenth and nineteenth centuries with a host of eccentric characters who, though flawed, were not expected to change: Parson Adams from *Joseph Andrews*, Uncle Toby from *Tristram Shandy*, Don Quixote, and Falstaff.[65] As Charles Lamb put it, a humorist focuses on "the diversified bents and humours, the blameless peculiarities of men, as they deserve to be called, rather than their 'vices and follies.'"[66] The negative "blameless" is key here; the peculiarities *could* draw blame, if etched by the wrong hand, and therefore be mistaken for vice or folly, which should be either punished or corrected. The humorist, on the other hand, showed people a character who, in his eccentricities, was different from them but further led them to feel an affection for this difference rather than a desire to lessen it. What is most moral in humor, then, is that it is a sort of sympathy that maintains distinctions.

Humor thus becomes a sort of fellow-feeling; taken to its extremes, this feeling could become one of expansive universalism. Carlyle expresses this in his writing on Jean Paul Richter. Humor, he writes, is "the ruling quality with Richter": "He is a humorist from his inmost soul; he thinks as a humorist, he feels, imagines, acts as a humorist."[67] What this means, for Carlyle, is that Richter "is a man of feeling, in the noblest sense of that word; for he loves all living with the heart of a brother; his soul rushes forth, in sympathy with gladness and sorrow, with goodness and grandeur, over all Creation." A full description of why Carlyle thought this to be true about Richter, and to what extent Carlyle's characteristic overstatements should be taken at face value, would take us too far afield. What I wish to point out here is how quickly Carlyle unfolds humorist: from "feeling" to "sympathy"—these we have seen already—and finally to the universal sympathy "over all Creation." If humor allows for sympathy regardless of distinction, then, as Carlyle's argument would have it, it allows for undistinguished sympathy, a fellow-feeling with everyone. This use of the term, furthermore, is not unique to Carlyle, nor to discussions of Richter. Earlier in the same decade, in his *Defense of Poetry*, Shelley drew the distinction between wit and humor along similar universal lines: in "periods of decay" such as the Restoration, Shelley claims, "Comedy loses its ideal universality: wit succeeds to humour; we laugh from self-complacency and triumph instead of pleasure."[68] The "triumph" here recalls Hobbes's "sudden glory," but Shelley also stresses the individual nature of that glory, by linking it with "self-complacency." We have already seen the physical invoked as part of the head/heart binary, but here the physical sensation—"pleasure"—is offered in opposition to the "self." Thus the warm feelings that we have seen associated with humor, as opposed to wit, are now further associated with humor's "universality."

We might be tempted to take these formulations with a grain of salt—Carlyle and Shelley were not known for understatement—but, in fact, they fit in well with a longstanding tradition in English thought. Specifically, the idea that the moral value of humor lies in the sense of connection it creates with others can be found in the early eighteenth century in the work of Anthony Ashley Cooper, Lord Shaftesbury, the source of many of the ideas of the English school of moral intuitionist philosophy.[69] In the case of the *sensus communis*, we can see the belief in a sort of connection that, *pace* Hobbes and Mandeville, could motivate people through their moral interests, not just their self-interest.[70] Shaftesbury's 1709 "Sensus Communis: An Essay on the Freedom of Wit and Humor" seeks to refute Hobbes's account of humor and to defend humor from the accusation that it worked contrary to either reason or sociability. To counter this, Shaftesbury describes a conversation that he recently had taken part in: "A great many fine Schemes, 'tis true, were destroy'd; many grave Reasonings overturn'd: but this being done without offence to the Partys concern'd, and with improvement to the good Humour of the Company, it set the Appetite the keener to such Conversations."[71] The larger theme of the work is that humor can induce men to reason, as a habit, by inviting them to "find pleasure in it" (70). But central to this account is the idea that humor will produce pleasure through a sense of sociability. It is, after all, the basis of a "company" to have "conversations." In other words, it produces a sense of fellow-feeling that reason can follow from. There is, it should be pointed out, a strong elitist current here: Shaftesbury goes on to remind his reader that he is "writing . . . in defence only of the Liberty of the Club and of that sort of Freedom which is taken amongst Gentlemen and Friends" (75). Still, the fact that his notion of the social was inherently limited should not distract from the fact that humor was for Shaftesbury a social experience. If it was only to be defended within the club, then this also meant that the experience of humor, properly conceived, was that of "friends" in a "club."

Extending our discussion from Shaftesbury to the larger tradition around the idea of *sensus communis*, it is important to distinguish between the literal translation of this term, "common sense," and this meaning of intersubjective assent. Kant, in the third *Critique*, offers the best-known distinction of the terms. Kant defines common sense in a relatively straightforward manner as "the common human understanding, which, as merely healthy . . . understanding, is regarded as the least that can be expected from anyone who lays claim to the name of a human being." *Sensus communis*, on the other hand, expresses "the idea of a communal sense, i.e., a faculty for judging that in its reflection takes account (*a priori*) of everyone else's way of representing in thought."[72] He hastens to add that he is referring here "not so much to the actual as to the merely possible judgments of others": that is, not so much how others *do* judge, as how we imagine them to judge. Without getting into the fine points of the third *Critique*, we can see why this *sensus communis* was necessary for his aesthetic project. As he explains it, in looking at "judgments of taste," we are looking at something that has neither an objective necessity nor pure subjective freedom. To say that a painting is beautiful is, for Kant, different than to say that one *likes* that painting. Judgments of taste are subjective, and yet, at the same time, make a distinct claim to being valid for others as well. Such judgments "thus have a subjective principle, which determines what pleases or displeases only through feeling and not through concepts, but yet with universal validity" (5:238). The ground for aesthetic judgments, then, rests in this "feeling." Hannah Arendt offers a good summary: *sensus communis* "for Kant did not mean a sense common to all of us, but strictly that sense which fits us into a community with others, makes us members of it and enables us to communicate things given by our five private senses."[73]

My argument is that this communal feeling offers the ground for understanding humor as well. The aesthetic sense that Kant spells out offers a way of describing the intersubjective experience that Shaftesbury, Carlyle, and Shelley all associate with humor. This feeling, in other words, is more central to the idea of humor—at least in previous centuries—than the physical reaction of laughter. And, furthermore, I would argue that we can see the intuitive relation of humor with this feeling even in arguments that associate humor largely with laughter. Bergson, as I have mentioned, is mainly interested in laughter, in ways that follow the basic distinctions we have laid down. Laughter, he claims, demands "a momentary anaesthesia of the heart," and its appeal "is to intelligence, pure and simple."[74] He follows up these familiar assertions, though, with a paragraph in which he expands on this appeal to the intelligence: "This intelligence, however, must always remain in touch with other intelligences. . . . You would hardly appreciate the comic if you *felt* yourself isolated from others. Laughter appears to stand in need of an echo" (emphasis mine). For Bergson, to "appreciate the comic" means to laugh, so this passage suggests that there is a *feeling* of connection—you must not "[feel] yourself isolated"—that serves as the necessary ground for laughter. This connection, though, is not universal; just as it requires a group, it also implies that there will be outsiders to that group: those who don't get the joke. Thus laughter requires not only a sense of connection but a sense of community, with all the problematics of exclusion and anxiety that this term implies.[75] Bergson seems to sense that he is treading on difficult ground, as his language becomes impressively vague: "laughter always implies a kind of secret freemasonry, or even complicity, with other laughers, real or imagined." A secret society of fellow laughers, who might be themselves imagined: Bergson's thought seems to be circling around the fact that laughter does not require a community of like-minded individuals. Instead, it requires a sense—even if only imagined—of being part of a larger group. To quote Arendt again, "Common sense, by virtue of its imaginative capacity, can have present in itself all those who actually are absent."[76] Bergson's terms remain vague, in large part because he is not discussing laughter itself; instead he is discussing what he takes to be the affective precondition to laughter. Before the intelligence can *know* something to be risible, in other words, it has to *feel* a connection with others—even if the connection is only an imagined one, even if the others are only an Andersonian "imagined community."

We have come full circle. I started off by decoupling humor from wit, and, at the same time, humor from the necessity of laughter. This led to a conception of humor as an accepting sort of sympathy, the form that allowed connection between reading subject and textual object without demanding change. This in, turn, led to the idea of *sensus communis* in moral thought: an idea that began in discussions of humor and that provides a link between humor and notions of moral intuition. This decoupling of the linguistic and the physical is rare in modern discussions of humor, but here is some grounding for it in work on another set of conjunctions of the linguistic with the physical: that is, on the "erotic," the "sexual," the "pornographic." It is no surprise that work on these fields would be rather more advanced than work on humor; it reflects the critical role that Freud, Foucault, and queer theory more generally play in contemporary literary studies. A particularly significant move has been the decoupling of erotic affect from sexual arousal. Sharon Marcus has argued against the modern

critical trend of necessarily linking the two terms together, particularly
when it comes to female desire:

> "Erotic" and "sexual" are not used here as interchangeable terms. The
> erotic and the sexual can and do intersect, but only the sexual refers to
> acts that involve genital arousal. Sexual desires are wishes to perform
> or fantasies about engaging in such acts. . . . Because the erotic has no
> necessary connection to sex acts, to describe a dynamic or relationship
> as erotic requires no evidence of sex.[77]

The erotic, as Marcus goes on to describe it, following Roland Barthes's discussion in *Sade/Fourier/Loyola*, is "an affective valence defined by intensity,
obsessiveness, theatricality, and pleasure." The erotic, then, lies at the nexus
of the sign-system and affective response, and can include many objects—
including, but certainly not limited to, those involving or implying sex. At
the same time, though, erotic involvement is not simply coincidental to sexual arousal. Rather, sexually arousing texts, and particularly pornographic
texts, make use of an "erotic repertoire" that they share with other elements
of mainstream culture. Pornography requires an erotic attachment with
the object, in other words, but not every erotic attachment leads to genital arousal. I am not claiming that humor does the same affective work as
the erotic; I am claiming instead that, like the textual erotic, it is a style of
interaction between a reader and a text that allows for, but is not limited
to, an involuntary physical reaction. Because of the sense of Freudian trans-
gression attached to laughter, the insistence on a physical laughter-based
reading in critics as different as Kincaid and Deleuze seems homologous to
the "incitement to talk about sex" that Foucault analyzes.[78] The absence of
laughter in Carlyle, though, does not necessarily indicate some sort of re-
pression or denial of the body; instead it can open the door for a discussion
of humor as an "affective valence" in its own right.

   At this point, there seem to be two related strains in my discussion of
Victorian humor: the sympathetic relation to the eccentric individual, such
as Falstaff or Uncle Toby; and this larger *sensus communis*, which seems to
make a social act out of the experience of "getting it." What I would like to
suggest is that these two strains coincide in Dickens's work in a specifically
"Dickensian" way: he produces a sense of community around the sight of
the eccentric individual, without holding that individual up to any sort of
ridicule or demand for change. We can think of this as the community of
sense in Bergson without the social correction that follows upon it. An early
example—which should be familiar enough as a sort of Dickensian style—
should help illustrate this. The novel starts with the narration of David's
birth, and the introduction of the character of David's great-aunt Miss Betsey, who will reappear later as his benefactress. Here, when Peggotty and

her nephew Ham arrive with the delivering doctor and nurse, they encounter the formidable figure of Miss Betsey:

> Those allied powers were considerably astonished, when they arrived within a few minutes of each other, to find an unknown lady of portentous appearance, sitting before the fire, with her bonnet tied over her left arm, stopping her ears with jeweller's cotton. Peggotty knowing nothing about her, and my mother saying nothing about her, she was quite a mystery in the parlor; and the fact of her having a magazine of jewellers' cotton in her pocket, and sticking the article in her ears in that way, did not detract from the solemnity of her presence. (9)

For most, I imagine, this will not be laugh-out-loud funny. At the same time, though, it will not allow itself to be taken completely seriously. Some of this can be explained by incongruity: "portentous" and "solemnity" sitting next to the crass physicality of an old woman sticking cotton in her ears. This fits with Hippolyte Taine's tendentious account of English humor: "saying very jocular things in a solemn manner."[79] But reading it as simple incongruity, whether of event or tone, misses the oddness of the scene somewhat. Incongruity relies upon a moment at which an expectation is frustrated—when what looks to be a whole lot turns out to be very little. Here, though, the expectation is not quite deflated: the scene is weird, and not a little bit astonishing given the circumstances. Why is Miss Betsey putting jeweler's cotton in her ears? One mundane possibility is offered by the doctor, that she has a "local irritation" (10). Betsey, though, replies that this is "nonsense." Another explanation may be that Betsey does not wish to hear the pains of Clara Copperfield's labor. This explanation is plausible enough, perhaps, but does not occur to any of the characters. The cotton, in other words, is part of what defines the character of Miss Betsey, but it is also a mark of the character's otherness. It is an unassimilable kernel in the depiction of the character, which keeps us from identifying thoroughly with her.

The plural is important: it keeps *us* from identifying with her. For Miss Betsey is the object of an audience; the subject of the first sentence is "those allied powers." Though the reader is told at the outset that these powers "were considerably astonished," the sentence has to work itself through a series of delays and subordinate clauses until the source of that astonishment reveals itself. Each comma-separated phrase serves only to increase the reader's curiosity. Here, as is so often the case in Dickens's prose, syntax has a noticeably temporal dimension. If phrased in terser terms, the sentence would have allowed the reader to encounter both the viewers (the Peggottys, the doctor, and the midwife) and the viewed (Miss Betsey) in the same tableau. As it is, though, the length of the sentence joins the reader's perspective to that of the characters. The statement that something was astonishing soon becomes a question: "What is so astonishing?" Moving toward the end of the sentence, the reader is also in a position to be astonished. Think of any number of Dickensian tableaus—Sam Weller on the witness stand during Pickwick's trial, Micawber reading aloud his indictment of Heep—where a crowd looks in amazement at one of Dickens's stock eccentrics. Viewing the picture, we are looking at them as much as at their object. But Dickens's style, in the textual example, brings us together with them.

Thus, it is humor, the term that was so frequently associated with Dickens by his contemporaries, which describes the sort of affective readerly reaction to Dickens that I discussed in the previous section. To put it another way, we can say that the frequent insistence on Dickens as a humorist spoke more to his ability to make readers feel a sort of *sensus communis* than to any ability, necessarily, to make readers laugh. Of course, it bears repeating that I am not arguing that Dickensian humor cannot produce laughter; but as with the relation of eroticism and genital arousal that Marcus describes, laughter is just one possible reaction to the experience produced by humor, and, for Victorians, far from the most trustworthy one.

THE COMMUNAL UNCONSCIOUS

Instead of Kincaid's claim that to understand Dickens we need to laugh, then, it would be more appropriate to say that to understand Dickens, we need to feel a vague connection to others. But *do* we feel this connection? At an intuitive, and imprecise, level, I would certainly argue that we do. Dickens's narrative voice cannot quite be taken seriously, even when he is talking about serious matters. Whether it's the expressionist names or the repetitive characters, few readers, I think, would believe that they are getting a straight representation of the world as either they or Dickens would actually perceive it. From Dickens's own time forward, critics have stressed the power of his imagination, rather than his power of observation.[80] The point here is not meant to be a complicated one; Dickens writes with an almost unequaled stamina of tone. While Trollope, for example, may produce effect from letting the authorial voice slip for a moment,[81] Dickens never lets up. To read Dickens, then, is in a sense always to be called upon to "get" something.

This formulation is, as I have said, an imprecise one; what I will argue in the remainder of this chapter is that Dickens's use of *sensus communis* in the novel produces the novel's underlying narrative mechanism. That is, the experience of *sensus communis* underwrites the novel's production of a sense of narrative necessity. This will become clearer once we look more closely at how this necessity functions in the novel. Though *David Copperfield* takes the form of a fictional autobiography, the novel's narrative trajectory is not determined simply by the events in the title character's life. In fact, as many readers of the novel have noted, with some disapproval, the underlying structure of the narrative seems to do a lot of work that David should be doing himself. Alexander Welsh makes this case plainly: "Helpless as a child and passive as an adult—except in his devotion to work—the hero owes his eventual good fortune to an aggressive plot."[82] Welsh's caveat about work is crucial, and I will discuss it at length later in this section. The larger point, though, seems to be that the novel does not require David to *do* things for himself; whatever the force is that moves the novel forward will do it for him. The most representative scene of David's passivity—and one that will likely have caused many readers some discomfort—comes toward the novel's end, when he discovers the location of Emily, thus tying up one of the novel's subplots. An incensed Rosa Dartle has arrived there first, and her abuse of Emily fills half a chapter: "The miserable vanity of these earthworms!"; "Why don't they whip these creatures! If I could order it to be done, I would have the girl whipped to death!"; and so on (700, 701). There is a certain rhetorical charge here, sadistic though it may be. But what accounts for David, standing in the doorway, silently watching this? The reason he gives is confused, and confusing: "I did not know what to do. Much as I desired to put an end to the interview, I felt that I had no right to present myself; that it was for Mr. Peggotty alone to see and recover her. Would he never come? I thought impatiently" (698). One critic has brushed off this explanation, calling David's refusal to interfere "inexplicable."[83] Another has claimed that the reason is, in context, "understandable," but that "his silence as Rosa goes on and on imposes . . . an outrageously unjust penalty on Emily. David should have intervened."[84] The issue here—and a good example of the sort of passivity that readers see in David—is the sense that as a character in the novel, he should have *done* something;[85] but instead he expresses his "impatience" for something to *happen*. Indeed, as the abuse continues on for pages, even his initially stated "desire" to intervene drops out, and we only see him waiting for the episode to end: "Would [Mr. Peggotty] never, never come? How long was I to bear this? How long could I bear it?" (702). David's question is our question; and like us, he is waiting for the story to reach its conclusion.

We can abstract from this scene a basic topography of *David Copperfield's* narrative structure: passivity and stasis are associated with the space inside the house; the forward-moving "aggressive plot" comes from outside the house. Novelistic narrative, in general, can be seen as a form of mediation between two different principles: a descriptive principle that describes how things *are*; and an end-oriented, teleological principle that logically connects the way things are with how they were before, and how they will become.[86] These are, essentially, the synchronic and diachronic axes of the novel.[87] What is interesting about *David Copperfield* is the way that it localizes these general novelistic principles. If some change does not enter from outside, what is going on inside the house could continue indefinitely. The novel would remain in what amounts to a single non-narrative moment, without any teleological progress. In the scene in Emily's room, the novel leaves ambiguous whether Rosa hears, along with David, "a distant foot upon the stairs" (702). But there is no reason to think that his arrival alone would prompt her to stop. Throughout the chapter, Mr. Peggotty's arrival has been defined as the moment that would end the episode; his appearance on the stairs is the sign that the story is ready to move on. Rosa, as a character, does not leave because of his arrival, but as part of the novel, she leaves because of what his arrival indicates: that the scene is over. Had he not arrived, there would have been nothing to prevent the scene from continuing on forever. This claim may sound like overstatement, but recall that, at the novel's end, David describes Rosa alternately berating and comforting Mrs. Steerforth: "Thus I leave them; thus I always find them; thus they wear their time away, from year to year" (853). The dynamic inside a home does not change in *David Copperfield*, without some intrusion from the outside—the entrance of Murdstone into David's home, say, or the entrance of Steerforth into Peggotty's. These examples are negative, certainly, but the change can be a positive one as well, as with Peggotty's belated rescue of Emily. The narrative structure of *David Copperfield*, based on this model, works through a series of fits and starts. To oversimplify only a bit, the novel places David in a house, with the promise that things may remain as they are; this state of affairs grows increasingly unsatisfactory, until some events either allow or force David to leave. From his childhood home with the Murdstones, to the home he shares with the Micawbers in London, through the home he makes with Dora: each time he arrives in a home, the novel makes it increasingly clear that he should move on. If he is passive inside his home, the narrative pressure comes from outside.

Thus, we can see the novel as pushing David, unwillingly, through a series of domestic spaces. The principle, is similar to, but expanded from, the one noted by Alexander Welsh: "the main action of *David Copperfield* is the replacement of one wife by another."[88] The move from Dora to Agnes is certainly one of the most evident examples of a move from dissatisfaction to satisfaction. But it is only one example of what is a much larger pattern in the novel. To add one more rather obvious link in this chain, we have David's mother: Clara. Not only does her relationship with David before Murdstone's arrival present an almost too-perfect portrait of a pre-Oedipal family romance, but she also prefigures Dora: by debilitating ingenuousness and early death, in addition to the slant rhyme of their names. Furthermore, this initial happiness—unsustainable though it might have been—offers the model of happiness that David finally finds in Agnes. The novel's main action, then, is not necessarily from "one wife" to another, so much as it is from one home to another.

Of course, Clara *is* something like a wife—but in the context of *David Copperfield*, this says less about one specific relationship and more about the way the novel blurs the lines between its parent-child relationships and its romances. Numerous central characters—David, Agnes, Steerforth, Dora, Uriah—have no siblings and are raised by only one parent. In each of these cases, the parent in question is of the opposite sex. Beyond the much-discussed Oedipal overtones of David's life with Clara, it seems that in every one of these upbringings, Oedipus or Elektra has some odd presence. Agnes, Mr. Wickfield's "little housekeeper" (217), is the very image of her mother, so much so that David imagines that the portrait of the late Mrs. Wickfield "had grown womanly, and the original remained a child" (217). Steerforth's mother reacts to his flight with Emily much as a jilted lover might: "to take up in a moment with a miserable girl, and avoid me!" (457). Of Mrs. Heep and Uriah, David writes, "I have no doubt she did [love him]; or that he loved her, however strange it might appear; though to be sure, they were a congenial couple" (736). Then there are fatherly husbands with childlike brides: figures such as the elder David Copperfield and Dr. Strong, whom Annie calls "my husband and father" (640). Finally, there is the odd case of Mr. Peggotty and Emily. Though he is neither her father nor her husband, he acts as both. As Philip Weinstein points out, Mr. Peggotty proposes to Emily in Ham's stead; he acts as the one most betrayed by Steerforth; and, finally, he sets sail with her for Australia to "begin a new life over theer" (711) without Ham, "quite alone" (712).[89]

I am not suggesting that the novel contains a blunt incestuous undercurrent. Instead it seems to collapse the difference between parent-child and spousal relationships. None of the couples—at least until the novel's end—is particularly good at filling either role, and the result is that home life is always presented as a binding, limiting relationship. The marriages are broken or threatened when someone comes from the outside: Mr. Murdstone, say, or Jack Maldon. And in each case, no matter how imperfect the relationship, it is always devastating when it is broken.

The plot of the novel moves by fits and starts, as characters align and realign themselves, marriages and deaths occurring in tandem. Peggotty, for example, only marries Barkis after Clara's death, and in large part because of it: "'I shall always be near my pretty's resting-place,' said Peggotty musing, 'and able to see it when I like; and when *I* lay down to rest, I may be laid not far off from my darling girl'" (133). On the other side of the sentimental spectrum is Murdstone, with whom marriage is a death sentence, as is rather bluntly suggested by his acquisition of his second marriage license in Doctors' Commons, just as Peggotty is settling her dead husband's estate. The greatest beneficiary of the link between death and marriage, however, is David. It is only Mr. Spenlow's sudden and convenient death, occurring just days after he had forbidden David to marry his daughter, that allows David to marry Dora in the first place. Dora's death finally allows David to marry Agnes. There is no subtlety here; on her deathbed, she explicitly leaves him to his "good angel," charging Agnes that "only [she] would occupy this vacant place" (844). A neat summary of these interwoven tendencies of marriage, death, and interpersonal relationship can be seen in Mr. Wickfield's story of Agnes's mother:

> "She married me in opposition to her father's wishes, and he re-nounced her. . . . He was a very hard man, and her mother had long been dead. . . . He broke her heart. . . . She loved me dearly, but was never happy. She was always laboring away under this distress. . . . She left me Agnes, two weeks old." (820)

A woman with a single father breaks their "marriage" to enter another marriage. This marriage brings about her death both indirectly, through her grief over her father's renunciation of her, and directly, through childbirth. Just as she exits though, Agnes enters, forming yet another pseudo-marital relation.

Static inside the house; change—and the plot—pushing in from outside. Recall the scene in the attic, though, or the scene walking home from church: even inside, David has a connection with the outside world. The motivating force from outside is something that even the most passive inside-the-house character has access to. An example occurs in the one overt exception to the novel's passive presentation of David: his decision to escape from his life of child labor in London.[90] The titles of the novel's twelfth and thirteenth chapters put this agency at center stage: "Liking life on my own Account no better, I form a great Resolution" and "The sequel of my Resolution." In the text, David further makes it clear how unique the resolution was, while also suggesting that its source was unclear:

> I had resolved to run away.—To go, by some means or other, down into the country, to the only relation I had in the world, and tell my story to my aunt, Miss Betsey.
>
> I have already observed that I don't know how this desperate idea came into my brain. But once there, it remained there; and hardened into a purpose than which I have never entertained a more determined purpose in my life. I am far from sure that I believed there was anything hopeful in it, but my mind was thoroughly made up that it must be carried into execution.

At the moment he explains his resolution, then, it is already in place: a "hardened purpose." The decision has already been made before this account takes place: the relevant language here is all past-perfect. Now, what Dickens is doing here—stressing the unknown origin of an idea or decision, making every decision refer back to a decision that has already been made—is a common piece of narrative sleight of hand, lending some sense of psychological depth to the process of decision-making. Usually, as with Pip's decision in *Great Expectations* to leave for London, the determined close reader can hunt down clues that have been dropped earlier in the text, so every explicit decision recalls an implicit reference to that decision made earlier.[91] In this case, we see David stressing that he does not know "how this desperate idea came into [his] brain." The implication, at least, is that this moment of decision grew out of, or at least reflects, a narrative necessity in the novel. Barthes claims that decision making is just a cosmetic cover for the narrative's drive forward: the freedom of a character to choose, as portrayed by a sort of psychological overdetermination, exists ultimately to mask "by superposition the implacable constraint of the discourse."[92] The agency, in other words, is like Mr. Peggotty's entrance: a nudge forward from some unknown place out there, moving David from one house (the Micawbers', in London) to another (his aunt's, in Dover).

The difference in this case, though, is that the David who moves the narrative along and the David who is moved along are the same person. Yet this figure is also split: the decision-making David is outside the house, while the passive David is inside. This becomes clearer if we trace back to the moment that David decides that he must leave London. It occurs when the Micawbers announce that, due to Mr. Micawber's financial and legal woes, they will be leaving London, and that David will have to find a new place to live:

> I had grown to be so accustomed to the Micawbers, and had been so intimate with them in their distresses, and was so utterly friendless without them, that the prospect of being thrown upon some new shift for a lodging, and going once more among unknown people, was like being that moment turned adrift into my present life, with such a knowledge of it ready made, as experience had given me. All the sensitive feelings it wounded so cruelly, all the shame and misery it kept alive within my breast, became more poignant as I thought of this; and I determined that the life was unendurable. (167)

It is not particularly surprising, of course, that he should want to leave this life that was "fraught with . . . pain, . . . mental suffering and want of hope" (210). But what this passage shows is that it did not necessarily *seem* that painful while David was living with the Micawbers. It is only with the threat of the loss of this domestic life that he determines that "the life was unendurable." To be more precise, he has already known that it was unendurable: "like being that moment turned adrift into my present life, with such a knowledge of it ready made, as experience had given me." In other words, the David that is living this present life—going about his life outdoors, "among unknown people"—already has the knowledge. But that David is, for the David that is narrating the novel, himself an "unknown person." In order to make the decision that moves him and the novel forward, it is this understanding that David accesses. We can think of this as an inversion of existential anxiety: instead of falling from an embeddedness in *Das Man* ("what *one* does") into unmoored individuality in order to assert agency, David falls from his individuality into embeddedness. In order to rescue Emily and move the novel along, Mr. Peggotty must intervene from outside the house; in order to move David's story along, David himself must intervene—the David who is part of the everyday life outside.

This idea—that the role of motivation is given over to an "unknown person" that is both part of us and distinct from us—sounds a good deal like the psychoanalytic unconscious. Given the important position of a libidinal Freud in American Dickens criticism,[93] I should stress that by "unconscious" I do not mean much in the way of physical drives. Rather, I am referring to a more broadly Lacanian sense of the unconscious as the shared language and concerns that pre-exist our subjecthood: the "discourse of the Other" that underwrites the self.[94] To access this unconscious is to access the social world that we are already a part of, to draw from "riches already involved in the symbolic system as it has been constituted by the tradition in which we as individuals take up our places."[95] We do not need to subscribe to a fully Lacanian model to see how this idea offers a way of understanding how the novel underwrites its teleological narrative drive. The push forward comes from outside the house, yes, but it also comes from the part of the characters themselves that dwell outside the house. The motivating drive of the novel exists in a communal unconscious,[96] in which an ultimate agency resides in a sort of shared understanding, which is for the most part forgotten.

The difference between the inside and the outside of the house, of course, is not simply topological; it is also the split between private and public, personal and professional. The "present life" that David is "turned adrift into," after all, is a life in which he is forced to work for a living. That is, the part of his life that is part of the novel's communal unconscious is also part of its professional world. This echoes George Orwell's famous observation that "[i]n Dickens's novels anything in the nature of work happens off-stage."[97] This exclusion, for Orwell, is not just thematic; it leads to a formal quality of Dickens's fiction: "Dickens sees human beings with the most intense vividness, but sees them always in private life, as 'characters,' not as functional members of society; that is to say, he sees them statically."[98] Orwell links private life together with Dickens's famously static representation of characters. In other words, to be a character in a Dickens novel is, almost by the very nature of Dickens's art, to be static—that is, not to *do* anything. For Orwell, the nature of action is to take part in "functional" social life. To be presented a character absent from work, then, is to get a representation of what that character "is" at the expense of what a character "does." Being a character in Dickens is something you do on your own time—when you are off the clock.

Perhaps the best way to formulate the particularly Dickensian form this communal unconscious takes, then, is as a form of forgetting: the leaving behind of the working world when a character returns home. This forgetting is not specific to Dickens: "Don't talk about work at the dinner table" is one of the fundamental principles of middle-class life. But it's a specific sort of forgetting, where the outside world passes out of sight, perhaps out of consciousness, but never out of mind. Just as no middle-class worker ever actually forgets her job—she will still get up in the morning—so David doesn't actually let work go. When David describes his courtship of Dora, for example, a thorough working discipline seems to coexist with complete absorption in his domestic life: "I loved her, and I went on loving her, most absorbingly, entirely, and completely. But going on too, working pretty hard, and busily keeping all the irons I now had in the fire" (529). The next chapter begins with a series of paragraphs that describe this absorption, describing step by step David's disciplined approach to learning stenography, which seems to belie the "absorbingly, entirely, and completely" in the previous paragraph. The two trajectories—passive domestic David, disciplined public David—go on at the same time. But here the form of Welsh's description is as important as its content: "Helpless as a child and passive as an adult—except in his devotion to work—the hero owes his eventual good fortune to an aggressive plot." Work is an aside, an interruption that does not derail the syntax of the larger sentence. In the same way, while the novel occasionally reminds us that David is constantly working, it is easy to forget that backdrop—easy to forget the public David that underwrites the private one that we read.

Indeed, part of the experience of reading *David Copperfield* is an experience of forgetting its well-populated public world. Earlier, I mentioned the similarity in the scenes of reading between David and his literary twin Jane Eyre.[99] The difference is that while David's consciousness expands to take in the boys in the churchyard, Jane remains only aware of John Reed and the others inside the house. This is not so much a limitation of Jane's imagination, though, as it is a statement of Brontë's imagination of the outside; who, in the fog outside Gateshead, could Jane be aware of in the first place? Put simply, there are more people outside in *David Copperfield* than there are in *Jane Eyre*. When the London novelist imagines an outside, it is populated; for the Yorkshire novelist, less so. For Brontë, the space between private spaces is cold, hostile, barren. We can see this in the journeys they both take to run away from home—David heading to Aunt Betsey's in Canterbury, Jane to the Rivers' at Moor House. Again, the settings have some structural similarity: running away from a home and occupation they find unlivable, they set out on the road; both lose their parcel in a carriage; both walk almost to the point of starvation before reaching a home that will take them in. In Jane's case, this voyage takes place in unpopulated space:

> The population here must be thin, and I see no passengers on these roads: they stretch out east, west, north, and south—white, broad, lonely. . . . Not a tie holds me to human society at this moment—not a charm or hope calls me where my fellow-creatures are—none that saw me would have a kind thought or a good wish for me. I have no relative but the universal mother, Nature.[100]

Brontë seems to invoke a certain tautology here: the space between habitations is uninhabited. Or, to put it another way, there is no public in the public space in *Jane Eyre*.

I bring this up to highlight just how different the case is in Dickens. If *Jane Eyre* surprises by its lack of people outside the house, *David Copperfield* surprises by the density of its population—more, I would imagine, than most readers can remember, and certainly more than they *need* to remember. Turning to the scene that parallels Jane's solitary escape, we find any number of figures on the road to Canterbury. First, David comes across Mr. Dolloby, who underpays him for his waistcoat; then he meets an old drunkard named Charley, who has a set of Dickensian exclamations—"Oh, my eyes and limbs, what do you want? Oh, my lungs and liver, what do you want? Oh, goroo!" (178)—all his own. Following this, a gang of boys, who run around Charley's shop, chase after David. Finally, after hiding from "ferocious looking ruffians," he comes across a tinker, who tries to rob him, and he is rescued by the tinker's female companion, whom David sees— over his shoulder, as he runs—being beaten as a result (181). Now, it would be a stretch to say that any of these portraits actually rises to the level of character; they do, however, definitely have their own distinctive characteristics.[101] They are "memorable" in that particularly Dickensian way.[102] Even David thinks so; while the novel, made up of retrospective narration, is all memory, the narrator makes sure to point out the lasting impression of these characters. On meeting Charley: "I never was so frightened in my life, before or since" (179); on the tinker's abused companion: "I never shall forget seeing her fall backward on the hard road" (181). The claim, then, is that these characters between houses will stay present in David's consciousness. Yet, for all that, they are never mentioned again. The public space between the Micawbers' and Betsey's has an asserted presence, but functionally—and, for most readers, I would imagine, even practically—it slips away.

But what persists as a reminder of this outside world, and of the working world, is the language of the novel. David, though we never see him at work on his writing, is a novelist. More to the point, he is the author of *David Copperfield*—even if he "never meant [it] to be published on any account." His labor, in other words, is present throughout the novel. Of course, this could be said of nearly any Dickens's novel: the overwhelming, rather intimidating energy of the prose both reminds you of the novelist's labor while, at the same time, effacing that labor through its consistency. Trollope and Thackeray occasionally affect some degree of weariness, reminding the reader of the hard work of writing but, at the same time, presenting a more natural, private, voice. Dickens, though, maintains such a strong consistency of tone that, just like David's, his work is at once always present and always hidden. The working world is the space of the novel's communal unconscious, because the novel is, quite literally, a record of the working world. And at the same time, it is in this tone that people found Dickens's humor. Because he never breaks tone, there is something beyond the page, waiting there for the reader to "get it."

BLIND, BLIND, BLIND

In the remainder of this chapter, I will offer a reading of the narrative structure of *David Copperfield*, in terms of the categories that I have brought up so far: the source of motivation in a sensed, but rationally unknown, social sphere, the felt necessity from the everyday world of convention weighing on character and reader alike. This structure offers an excellent example of an intuited narrative necessity that does not rely on suspense. Instead, it relies on formal mechanics produced by the sort of Victorian humor that I have been outlining: not only describing David's motivation in a communal unconscious but implying the reader's membership in the community as well.

One of the most oft-quoted moments of *David Copperfield* occurs when David, returning from boarding school, finds his young mother alone, nursing his new half-brother. As he recalls laying his head on her breast, he writes, "I wish I had died. I wish I had died then, with that feeling in my heart! I should have been more fit for Heaven than I ever have been since" (104). This is, to be sure, an odd sentiment, for it would seem to suggest that for all the trials and successes, tragedies and ultimate bliss with Agnes, none has in the end been truly worth it. If David could have avoided all this *Bildung* in the first place, it would have all been for the better. The same sentiment appears again, as he recollects Agnes's self-sacrificing praise about Dora: "Oh, Agnes, sister of my boyhood, if I had known then, what

I knew long afterwards!—" (504). It is perhaps best that David allows this sentence to trail off, as its implied completion would be an admission that the hard-won experience of the novel is something that he would rather do without.

Such moments seem indicative of a larger aspect of the novel: it is a reluctant *Bildungsroman*, with an implicit preference for innocence over experience. Consider, for example, the judgment that David passes upon learning of Steerforth's seduction of Emily: "In the keen distress of the discovery of his unworthiness, I thought more of all that was brilliant in him, I softened more towards all that was good in him. . . . I believe that if I had been brought face to face with him, I could not have uttered one reproach" (443). Franco Moretti, writing on the English *Bildungsroman*, sees this moment as exemplary: "If then, as with Steerforth, innocence proves to be mistaken— too bad for experience. What has been learned will be disavowed and forgotten, rather than revise the initial judgement."[103] David's essence remains what it was in childhood. The novel's happy ending, David's marriage to Agnes, is a fitting tribute to this sacred childhood, as Agnes tells him, "I have loved you all my life!" (842). David, in turn, calls Agnes "the source of every worthy aspiration I had ever had" (844). The final bliss that the novel presents, in other words, is not so much the fruit of a lifetime of experience as it is a return—a final coming into being for the protagonist of what he has always been. Critics as distinct as Moretti, Alexander Welsh, and Harry Stone have all pointed out the novel's similarity to a "fairy tale": a form whose essential element is the return to the place of origin.[104]

But there is a basic difference between *David Copperfield* and a fairy tale: the personification of the happy ending that the narrative is working toward, Agnes, is with David throughout most of the novel. There is nothing to travel toward; David must instead realize something that is already true, but that is hidden from him: namely, that Agnes is the correct mate for him, and that his brotherly feelings for her are in fact the correct form of love. In other words, the novel has to perform an odd narrative maneuver: move toward an ending that seems natural because it is something that has always been inside of David while at the same time never presenting that knowledge.

I said at the opening that David makes a point of being as open as possible with the reader about all things. There is, however, one significant exception, and it relates to this conclusion with Agnes:

> I have now recalled all that I think it needful to recall here . . . with one reservation. I have made it, thus far, with no purpose of suppressing any of my thoughts; for, as I have elsewhere said, this narrative is my written memory. I have desired to keep the most secret current of my mind apart, and to the last. I enter on it now. I cannot so

completely penetrate the mystery of my own heart, as to know when I began to think that I might have set its earliest and brightest hopes on Agnes. I cannot say at what stage of my grief it first became associated with the reflection, that, in my wayward boyhood, I had thrown away the treasure of her love. I believe I may have heard some whisper of that distant thought, in the old unhappy loss or want of something never to be realized, of which I had been sensible. But the thought came into my mind as a new reproach and new regret, when I was left so sad and lonely in the world.

The "secret current of [David's] mind"—his love for Agnes—is presented here as something that has been held back from the reader. At the same time, though, David offers that the reason it had been held back is that his consciousness of it had grown so slowly that he was not sure when he first became aware of it. In other words, the only part of the novel that has been withheld from the reader is one that has been withheld from David as well.

It is hard to imagine, though, that any reader would be as surprised by this revelation as David seems to imagine. This is not suspense, in the sense that we saw it in *Oliver Twist*, nor is it a succession of events whose meanings inhere in themselves, as in *Jack Sheppard*. Rather, it seems closer to what we saw in Newman's *Apologia*: a controlling internal motivation whose presence can be felt, and is known by the reader, before it is known by the character itself. It is certainly clear that Agnes loves David, and it becomes increasingly clear that David loves Agnes in return. Agnes channels many readers when she asks David, right before declaring her love for him, "Do you know, *yet* . . . ?" It seems that she cannot quite believe that he has not yet figured out that their love—which, as they both attest, stands as the motivation for nearly everything they do—has been there all along.

The novel has a specific figure for this relationship with knowledge: *blindness*. Specifically, the novel introduces this term, through the voice of Aunt Betsey, to refer to David's inability to see his correct trajectory. As David speaks about his budding love for Dora, Betsey replies with, "Blind, blind, blind" (489). The statement is a blunt enigma: blind to what? But David does not ask his aunt what she means. And, even more notably, the older narrating David lets it pass without comment. Instead, the novel suggests a pause in Betsey's speech, by closing her quote, and then, in the next paragraph, opening her quote again:

"Ah, Trot!" said my aunt, shaking her head, and smiling gravely; "blind, blind, blind!"

"Someone that I know, Trot," my aunt pursued, after a pause, "though of a very pliant disposition, has an earnestness of affection in him that reminds me of [Clara]." (489)

So, in between the enigmatic statement and its continuation, there is no reaction, no question, no attempt at narrative interpretation. The narrator opens a grammatological space here for a response but leaves it blank. It draws our attention, in other words, to what it does not say. Punctuation here takes the form of a sort of audible silence, or narrative pause. The question, if asked, would have a rather obvious answer; but it would be an answer that is also the book's conclusion. Consider again, the way in which David trails off while admitting that he had *some* knowledge: "Oh, Agnes, sister of my boyhood, if I had known then, what I knew long afterwards!—" (504). The real meat of the sentence is covered over by a punctuated pause, almost as if the em-dash were crossing out the counterfactual result. Even by the looser standards of Victorians in general, and Dickens in particular, the exclamation/dash combination is an odd one.[105] The exclamation gives the apostrophic statement the appearance of a declaration, but what it declares is something missing. It is not the case that there is no knowledge there, in other words; we are told that there is, and that David has no conscious access to it.

So "blindness," as it appears here in the novel, refers to a presence, the knowledge of which is never made explicit in the novel. That is to say, it does not mean that David is simply unaware; instead it refers to the specific awareness of something that cannot, or will not, be put into words.[106] The novel makes this meaning explicit as it again invokes the figure of blindness. Betsey continues to try to direct David toward Agnes by saying that someone as "earnest" as David needs someone who is also "earnest" to "sustain him and improve him." When he does not pick up on the hint, mistakenly believing she is referring to Dora, she repeats herself: "'Oh, Trot!' she said again; 'blind, blind!' and without knowing why, I felt a vague unhappy loss or want of something overshadow me like a cloud" (490). This moment offers an example of a standard form of narrative expression: a communication of meaning to the reader which, by its very nature, demands that it remain somehow distinct from the surface level of the narrative. We understand it, even if it is not explicitly stated, and even if the characters in the novel do not consciously understand it themselves.

When I say "consciously," though, I do not mean to suggest only that the characters have a subconscious understanding, after the fashion of Freudian psychoanalysis. Rather, the understanding is what I have referred to as the "communal unconscious" produced by *sensus communis*. Recall that the novel validates the judgments of the anonymous world outside the house. A particularly clear moment of this occurs as the scene with Agnes continues. Immediately after David trails off in his apostrophe, he narrates heading down to the street: "There was a beggar in the street, when I went down; and as I turned my head towards the window, thinking of her calm seraphic eyes, he made me start by muttering, as if he were an echo of the morning:

'Blind! Blind! Blind!'" (505). The joke here is clear enough; the blind beggar's self-description appears to David as an echo of Betsey's words. But this
does not only appear as a coincidence. Betsey knows; the reader knows;
and now it seems that everyone outside knows as well. The fact that David
thinks this particular beggar's speech is worth transcribing, without, again,
bothering to interpret or even explain his interest, makes it clear that he
himself knows as well. The very end toward which the novel is moving,
then, is one that David understands at some level, and that the anonymous
group of "everyone" around him—readers and characters—understands as
well. David, as a character, is moving toward the communal understanding
he already has, but to which he is blind.

Here we have the essential narrative mechanism of *David Copperfield*,
a pressure coming from the outside which, because it is not explicit, is
only understood as an internal intuition. David knows there is something
wrong—a "vague unhappy loss"—while at the same time being unable to
understand what exactly it is. I have already described, in the last section,
how the novel's alternation between stasis and change is associated with
the spaces inside and outside of the house. What we see now, though, is
that the space outside the house, where the beggar is standing, or where
the townspeople watch David and Clara walk home from church with the
Murdstones, is also associated with David's unrepresentable internality:
what I have been calling his unconscious, but what we could also call, to go
back to the Kantian-ethical language of my first chapter, his noumenal self.
In other words, the change that comes from outside the house can also be
understood as the change that comes from David himself. The move toward
anonymous agreement is a move toward what David has always been.

This reading fits in well with the observation that the characters in *David
Copperfield* are fixed, static entities. While it is not quite the case they are
the sum of their tics—Rosa Dartle's "isn't it, though?", Uriah Heep's "um-
bleness," Betsey Trotwood's "eccentric and somewhat masculine" nature
(581)—the true characters are not far beneath the exterior. As D. A. Miller
puts it, "The secret subject [in *David Copperfield*] is always an open secret"[107]
This is rather clear; it is hard to imagine a reader surprised by Uriah's true
nature, once he appears with his "mask off" (730). There is very little distance from the surface to the true character beneath, and the truth is usually not hard to spot. As for Betsey, as Miller points out, "Though David
knows [her] only as a legendary dragon, . . . he nonetheless risks throw-
ing himself on her mercy sight unseen" (205); he cannot forget "how [his]
mother had thought that she felt her touch her pretty hair with no ungentle
hand" (171). Of course, something happened to make each character who
he or she is, whether it be Betsey's failed marriage, Uriah's education, or
Rosa's emotional and physical scarring at the hands of Steerforth. In each
case, however, the event took place before the action of the novel, or at

least before the entrance into David's life. Once these characters become *characters*—that is, figures in the novel—they are doomed to be creatures defined by a fixed quantity of characteristics. Any change that might occur is only in the degree to which they mask these characteristics. Miss Murdstone, in admitting that she is "not the creature of circumstance or change" (382), is exceptional only for her self-awareness.

Rosa Dartle, whose magnificent rage makes for some of the novel's strongest moments, offers perhaps the best glimpse of this mechanism. Upon their first encounter, David comes to understand that her telltale scar provides a direct conduit for her buried anger: "It was not long before I observed that it was the most susceptible part of her face, and that, when she turned pale, that mark altered first. . . . I thought her, for one moment, in a storm of rage; and then I saw it start forth like the old writing on the wall" (288). As far as Rosa's character goes, David sees the writing on the wall quite plainly. Her explosion, when it comes, is something to behold: "If I could hunt her to her grave, I would. If there was any word of comfort that would be a solace to her in her dying hour, and only I possessed it, I wouldn't part with it for Life itself" (459). It is not, however, a surprise. Indeed, as David himself makes clear, the real force is not in her words—so different from her wont—but in her body: "The mere vehemence of her words can convey, I am sensible, but a weak impression of the passion by which she was possessed, and which made itself articulate in her whole figure, though her voice, instead of being raised, was lower than usual" (459). However much her words might be a departure from her habitual passive aggression, this true "passion," residing in her body, has always been visible. It has, in a nearly literal fashion, slipped through the cracks. Her rage shows on her scar, and her "wasting fire" finds "a vent in her gaunt eyes" (285). The writing is not only on the wall; it is written all over her face. Even change as violent as Rosa's outburst, then, is practically static, as it only makes explicit that which was already quite apparent.

The result, in *David Copperfield*, is a certain iterative quality, but it is one perhaps best understood as a sort of "reflective equilibrium."[108] The term is from Rawls, and represents a process by which successive approximations at an idea removes increasing difficulties and confusions. Generally speaking, the propriety of such an equilibrium can be judged by whether an approximation expresses the idea in a way that seems to get it across. Of course, in *David Copperfield*, there is not an idea, just a "vague . . . want of something" that indicates that the external reality does not match David's internal state. Equivalently, this could be taken to say that the external reality does not match the dictates of the shared communal unconscious. This resembles in some way the *fort-da* game that René Girard sees as central to the novel form's narration of "triangular desire": the structural desire for that which another desires. This "imitative desire," Girard claims, "is always the desire to be Another."[109] Such desire, furthermore, can never be satisfied by the object it sees itself as pursuing. The moment of possession of the object of desire, as Girard sees it, may be summed up in "the famous Stendhalian exclamation: 'Is that all it is?!'" (88). This idea of a repeated dissatisfaction works well to describe *David Copperfield*, and what I located in the previous discussion as the narrative dynamic motivating the main character's progress from home to home.

Such dissatisfaction is an integral part of the novel. As Kelly Hager notes, in examining such marriages as the Micawbers, the Strongs, David and Dora, and Betsey and her estranged husband, "the novel is more about desertion than unity, more about separation than marriage."[110] Hager is not speaking of actual separation, for outside of Betsey Trotwood, whose separation occurs before the novel, and Emily, who leaves her fiancé but is eventually reunited with her pseudo-husband in Mr. Peggotty, no one actively ends their marriage. I would perhaps add to this list Steerforth, who leaves his mother/wife, and in the process destroys both himself and her. For characters with less destructive tastes, however, there is only dissatisfaction and a good deal of wishful thinking, as exemplified by Emma Micawber's insistent declaration, "I never will desert Mr. Micawber," repeated so often that it is difficult not to read the opposite desire into it. David, meanwhile, "in the innermost recesses of [his] mind," wonders what might have been, "if Dora and I had never known each other" (678).

Such a sense of dissatisfaction, a sense that there has to be *something* else, points strongly to the presence of a world beyond the limiting interpersonal relationships of the novel. Indeed, moments of consciousness of such a world do take place. Consider, for example, David's arrival at Salem House, when he is required, as punishment for biting Mr. Murdstone, to wear a placard bearing the words, "Take care of him. He bites":

> What I suffered from that placard, nobody can imagine. Whether it was possible for people to see me or not, I always fancied that somebody was reading it. It was no relief to turn around and find nobody; for wherever my back was, there I imagined someone always to be. . . . The playground was a bare gravelled yard, open to all the back of the house and the offices; and I knew that the servants read it, and the butcher read it, and the baker read it; that everybody, in a word, who came backwards and forwards to the house, of a morning when I was ordered to walk there, read that I was to be taken care of, for I bit. I recollect that I positively began to have a dread of myself, as a kind of wild boy who did bite. (75)

Three important points arise here. First, David is alone, without the comfort of other characters and their reassuring characteristics. In their stead, he is conscious of an anonymous "everybody." This consciousness, then, is not of a world beyond people, but of a world beyond knowable characters. Solitude, paradoxically, comes as a result of a widening of social perspective. This leads to the second point: David is acutely aware of being seen. The shame that pervades this passage arises from the mute judgment he is sure that the world, uncountable and unknowable, is passing on him. Third, David feels the force of this judgment, wrong though it may be, is to make him the very thing he is seen to be: "a kind of wild boy who did bite." This perfect helplessness in the face of the unknown is figured in the placard placed on his back; no matter which way he turns, he is always being seen, and judged, by those he cannot see in turn.

The sort of close, and closed, relationships between recognizable characters fostered in *David Copperfield*, then, acts as a blockade of sorts against the consciousness of a larger world, and the helplessness that comes with its judgment. Without such a relationship, the outside world intrudes. Recall the scene, discussed at the outset, of David walking back from church with his mother and the Murdstones: "I note some neighbours looking at my mother, and at me, and whispering. Again as the three go on arm-in-arm, and I linger behind alone, I follow some of those looks and wonder if my mother's step be really not so light as I have seen it . . ." (50). Excluded from his relationship with his mother, "linger[ing] behind alone," he becomes conscious of the world's judgment. Emily, as well, when she leaves her circle of relationships, opens herself up to the judgment of the world, as "the news of what had happened soon spread[s] throughout the town" and David "overhear[s] people speaking of it at their doors" (444). Even Uriah Heep, when he is finally unmasked, opts for an informal resolution, among those he knows, rather than face the external judgment of the law.

The novel thus offers two means of engagement with the external world. Both are unsatisfactory, but both tend toward the other. Relationships with other characters, unmodifiable as they are, lead to a desire for dissolution. A consciousness of the larger world of "everybody," with its isolating effect, leads to a desire for interpersonal relationships. The pivotal moment in David and Dora's marriage comes when David realizes the simultaneous presence of both of these modes. Dora's incompetence at housekeeping leads to their swindling at the hands of their page. As the page continues to reveal the extent of the thefts, David becomes "so ashamed of being a victim, that I would have given [the page] any money to hold his tongue, or would have offered a round bribe for his being permitted to run away" (673). It as a result of this shame that David is forced to become again conscious of the outside world: "'My love,' said I, 'it is very painful to me to think that our want of system and management, involves not only ourselves (which we have got used to), but other people.'" (673). As forming Dora's mind is an impossibility, David is ultimately left solitary, even in the midst of his

marriage: "I could not endure my own solitary wisdom; I could not recon-
cile it with her former appeal to me as my child-wife. I resolved to do what I
could, in a quiet way, to improve our proceedings myself" (677).

It is at this point, in one of the novel's central passages, that David proceeds to a moment of dialectical self-realization:

> What I missed, I still regarded—I always regarded—as something that
> had been a dream of my youthful fancy; that was incapable of reali-
> sation; that I was now discovering to be so, with some natural pain,
> as all men did. But, that it would have been better for me if my wife
> could have helped me more, and shared the many thoughts in which
> I had no partner; and that this might have been; I knew.
>
> Between these two irreconcileable conclusions: the one, that what
> I felt, was general and unavoidable; the other that it was particular
> to me, and might have been different: I balanced curiously, with no
> distinct sense of their opposition to each other. When I thought of
> the airy dreams of youth that are incapable of realisation, I thought
> of the better state preceding manhood that I had outgrown; and then
> the contented days with Agnes, in the dear old house, arose before
> me, like spectres of the dead, that might have some renewal in an-
> other world, but never never more could be reanimated here. (678)

David vacillates between two impulses here. On one side is a consciousness
of the larger world. Here the emphasis is on rules applied from without,
over which he has no control. His language—"as all men did," "general
and unavoidable"—is here that of an external set of conventions, the law
of "everybody," which he helplessly feels forced on himself. At the same
time, however, he feels a sense that there should be something he could
do about it. This takes the form of an interpersonal relationship: "my wife
could have helped me more." He is thus simultaneously conscious of the
external world of law and judgment, over which he has no control, and
the interpersonal world, in which he feels he should have some control but
has none. Seemingly lost beneath these antitheses is the kernel of his innocence, the "dream of [his] youthful fancy," seemingly unrealizable. Yet
here something remarkable occurs; the two antitheses cease to oppose one
another. David balances both, "with no distinct sense of their opposition to
one another." It would seem that perhaps some synthesis between the two
was being reached. And indeed, in an almost mystical fashion, the figure of
Agnes rises before David, like a "spectre."

Why Agnes? How does she somehow offer a resolution to the dissatisfaction experienced in both interpersonal relationships and solitude? Agnes,
notably, is David's "good angel," a quiet and forgiving, but watchful, eye.
When David goes drunkenly into the London night, it is Agnes who sees

him, as he remembers her face "with its indelible look of regret and won-der" (354). If it is hard to imagine a more benevolent judge, it is nonetheless the case that Agnes is the only character able to stand in the stead of the anonymous world. Thus, when David is alone in Switzerland, it is Agnes's letters that he receives, and they guide him: "she urged no duty on me; she only told me, in her own fervent manner, what her trust in me was" (794). Taking the place of shame, then, is a kinder figure, one whose judgments are not an imposition from an outside, but rather based in David's own self: "She knew (she said) how such a nature as mine would turn affliction to good" (794). The external gaze that Agnes represents is one that tells David to be what he always has been, "the source of every worthy aspiration [he has] ever had." In this, she offers an interpersonal relationship—a relation-ship inside the house, with another character—that is at the same time a relationship with the outside world. If her character, as such, is largely an absent quantity, it is because her character expands to fill David's world; if she is lacking in personality, it is because she stands in for a larger anony-mous external reality. At the moment of their final joining, Agnes comes to embody David's past as well, as he sees "the spirit of my child-wife" looking "even out of [her] own true eyes" (842). In the novel's final words, Agnes's unity with the external world becomes absolute:

> And now, as I close my task, subduing my desire to linger yet, these faces fade away. But, one face, shining on me like a Heavenly light by which I see all other objects, is above them and beyond them all. And that remains.
>
> I turn my head, and see it, in its beautiful serenity, beside me. My lamp burns low, and I have written far into the night; but the dear presence, without which I were nothing, bears me company.
>
> O Agnes, O my soul, so may thy face be by me when I close my life indeed; so may I when realities, when realities are melting from me like the shadows which I now dismiss, still find thee near me, point-ing upward! (855)

All of the characters of the novel fade away, then, and there is Agnes. She of-fers a final mystical synthesis: a figure inside the house who contains within her the world "above" and "beyond" the house as well. That is, she brings the space in which David lives—as David, the character—together with the anonymous outside world. She is *someone* who, at novel's end, becomes *everyone*. In this, she allows David to achieve his conclusion, as his inter-nal yearnings—which have always been outside the walls, and beyond the world of characters—rise to the level of textual representation.

CHAPTER 4

BACK IN TIME: THE *BILDUNGSROMAN* AND THE SOURCE OF MORAL AGENCY

There is a quietly haunting line toward the end of Margaret Oliphant's 1866 *Miss Marjoribanks*. In announcing its main character's unmarried status in its title, the novel tells us what it will be working to undo. "I don't mean to be Lucilla Marjoribanks for ever and ever," the title character insists, suggesting a trajectory toward the moment at which she will be neither a Miss nor a Marjoribanks.[1] Readers of Austen or Eliot will not be surprised by the general contours the novel takes:[2] an independent, intelligent domineering young heroine, Lucilla Marjoribanks, is spoiled by her father; busy with her position in town and flirting with "a wit and a man of fashion," she brushes off the more prudent proposals of her cousin, Tom Marjoribanks.[3] The novel's end, though, finds her wiser and a bit chastened, and she accepts marriage to Tom, taking his name—Marjoribanks, the name that has always been hers:

> [A]ll Carlingford interested itself, as has been said, in the details of the marriage, as if it had been a daughter of its own. "And yet it is odd to think that, after all, I shall never be anything but Lucilla Marjoribanks!" she said, in the midst of all her triumphs, with a certain pensiveness. (496)

Whatever it is that Lucilla had been preparing for, it turns out, will never come: what she has already been is what she shall remain. The "pensiveness" here recalls Roland Barthes's conclusion that the "the classic text is pensive . . . , keeping in reserve some ultimate meaning."[4] That is, while Lucilla's narrative works its way toward her fulfilled development, that development will remain tacitly held back—a narrative promise that cannot be kept. *Middlemarch* ends on a similar note: "Many who knew [Dorothea], thought it a pity that so substantive and rare a creature should have been absorbed into the life of another, and be only known in a certain circle as a wife and mother. But no one stated exactly what else that was in her power she ought rather to have done."[5] Lucilla and Dorothea's narrative conclusions foreground what Andrew Miller has called the "optative" mode in realist fiction: the tendency to dwell in counterfactuals of "lives unled."[6] Miller invokes the image, from Kierkegaard, of Victorian characters "nailed to themselves."[7] Lucilla, in this scene, is nailed to herself; try though she might—try though she *did*, for the whole of the novel—she "shall never be anything but Lucilla Marjoribanks."

This all might seem like making much of a technicality; she *has* gotten married, after all, and even though her name hasn't changed, the legal source of the name has. But it is precisely this shift—something remaining the same while its source changes—that I want to focus on here. "Marjoribanks" had previously been a name that signified Lucilla's relation to her father; now, it is the name that signifies her relation to Tom. But just as importantly, with her father having died rather late in the novel, and not there to give her away at the wedding, it is "all Carlingford" that acts as her father, as if she were "a daughter" of the town itself. In other words, at the marriage ceremony, "Marjoribanks" ceases to be the name that she had received from her father, and now becomes a name that she receives from the community. It is true that, as numerous critics have noted, the resolution of the female *Bildungsroman* is almost always a scene of loss.[8] But unlike Emma Woodhouse before her or Dorothea Brooke after, we are able to see something of what Lucilla gains in her (regretful, necessary) exchange: not the negation of the person she has been, but a redefinition of the foundation of that person in terms of her community.

In this chapter, I will argue is that such communal redefinition is reliant on a temporal dynamic: characters come to be able to recognize themselves in a community when they are able recognize themselves in the past. Lucilla's final stage of narrative development comes when she understands differently the prior conditions that determine the person she is. By redefining the source of Lucilla Marjoribanks in terms of her community, she effectively changes the stakes of the game. Instead of Lucilla's integration into her community being an event that still needs to happen in the novel, Lucilla discovers that, through a redefinition of the past, she has already been integrated. What this resembles, ultimately, is nothing so much as the recuperative time-travel plots of late twentieth-century, in which the secret to future resolution lies in changing the past.[9] Recalling the Rawlsian conception of ethics, discussed in the introduction, as "acting in accordance with a law that we give to ourselves,"[10] I would like to suggest that the *Bildungsroman*, as a narrative form, depends on unifying oneself with that law-giving self in the past.

We have already seen a form of this unification in the previous chapter. There, I argued that narrative development in *David Copperfield* depends on finding the communal bases for one's intuition. This experience, which I called, after Shaftesbury and Kant, *sensus communis*, was mobilized by the experience of humor: the sort of "getting it" that requires a tacit understanding of the judgment of others. In this chapter, I will take that argument one step further and argue that the notion of *sensus communis*—dating back to the moral-sense philosophy of Shaftesbury—becomes fundamental for the structure of the *Bildungsroman*. Indeed, as we shall see, the very concept of *Bildung* traces back to Shaftesbury, through the German importation of his works. In tracing this history, we will also be able to see how the *Bildungs-roman* went from being just one story among others to being the central story of the novel form. Such a claim, of course, is one part history and one part historiography: not just what happened but also what we choose to emphasize in our retelling of events. Yet, here the two are oddly intermixed. We focus on, and find meaning in, certain stories from the past—the ones that seem still to be *about us*—for the same reason that the characters in those stories identify with their past selves. In the moral form of the Victorian novel, in other words, we find the ethical basis for the study of the Victorian novel.

A THOUGHT EXPERIMENT

Suppose I tell you that I have a Victorian novel for you to read. I have not yet told you who wrote it or what it's about. But if you have some familiarity with the field, with the meanings attached to the "Victorian novel," then you likely know quite a bit about it. It will be long—probably five hundred pages or more in a modern Penguin edition. It will not offer much in the way of sex scenes. Its hero will probably be young and not yet set in life. There will be some maturation, most likely some carriages or a railroad, a career for a hero or a marriage for a heroine, and a polite degree of anxiety about industrialization and commodity culture.

But here's something else you will probably know: the novel that I'm going to give you will not be particularly difficult to read. It may take you a while—but it will seem more familiar, more like a *novel* than the work of the eighteenth and early nineteenth century (Austen, as always, conspicuously excepted); and it will require a good deal less aesthetic sophistication and effort against the grain than a modernist novel. When we talk about the "Victorian novel," one of the principal things we are referring to is a certain sweet spot in relation to the post–World War II reader: modern enough to be recognizable; not so modern as to be obscure. And for this reason, it does not need to be *taught* to competent contemporary readers—at least not at the level of basic textual comprehension. More precisely, we can say that Victorian novels are those novels that do not need to be *mediated* by historians or interpreters. They might benefit from such mediation, as those who have taught them know, but that is only because students are only too eager to find themselves in them. Teachers and critics have to assert the need for historical or formal mediation precisely because the novels do not seem like they need it: because they seem *im*mediate. Neither dated nor obscure, they are *readable*.

Theories of the realist novel, more generally, take this sort of experiential proximity as a given. José Ortega y Gasset, in his *Meditations on Quixote*, addresses this question directly. In discussing *Don Quixote*'s famous categorization as the first novel, he moves quickly to an interpretation that stresses readerly familiarity. *Quixote*, he says,

> is said to be a novel; it is also said, and perhaps rightly, that it is the first novel in point of time and in merit. Much of the satisfaction that the contemporary reader finds in it comes from what it has in common with the kind of literature favored in our times. As we peruse its old pages, we find in them a modern note which is bound to draw the venerable book closer to our hearts: we feel it to be at least as close to our innermost sensibility as are the builders of the contemporary novel—Balzac, Dickens, Flaubert, or Dostoievski.[11]

This provides Ortega with the jumping-off point for his "Short Treatise on the Novel": "But what is a novel?" begins the next paragraph. But it is worth lingering over the claims already made. First: to be a "novel" is to have, in some way, a "modern note" that brings a book "closer" to its twentieth-century readers. And second: to be "close to our innermost sensibility" is to be like Balzac, Dickens, Flaubert, or Dostoevsky—in other words, like a nineteenth-century realist.

In Victorian studies, the emphasis on immediacy might be less explicit, but it is fundamental all the same. In fact, it does not seem too much a stretch to say that *readability* is the operative defining principle of the Victorian novel. It is not a quality that we happen to find in the works we study but rather the means by which we decide which works to study in the first place.[12] Usually, critics of the nineteenth-century novel frame this selection as a sort of descriptive analysis: making implicit use of the familiarity of the object of study. I have already had cause to cite Jameson's claim that nineteenth-century realism "show[s] the functioning of all those realities of capitalism that have not changed substantially . . . wage slavery, money, exploitation, the profit motive."[13] But surely that is not a claim about every text from the nineteenth century. What we see is not so much an act of description as one of *prescription*. A novel that does not align with present-day "realities of capitalism" or "cultural experience" will not disprove the claims; it will just fall, like *Jack Sheppard*, outside the field of study.

A quick look back makes it clear how limited this collection of readable novels is. David Masson, in his 1859 *British Novelists and Their Styles*, probably the earliest engagement with the Victorian novel as a serious object of study, lists "thirteen distinct varieties of the British novel, as in existence during the quarter of a century after Scott's influence had begun, and as in existence still." They are: (1) "the novel of Scottish life and manners"; (2) "the novel of Irish life and manners"; (3) "the novel of English life and manners"; (4) "the fashionable novel" (what we would now call the "Silver-Fork novel"); (5) "the illustrious criminal novel" (now the "Newgate novel"); (6) "the traveller's novel"; (7) "the novel of American manners and society" (a subset of the traveller's novel, which, like the next one is "worthy of being separately classed"); (8) "the Oriental novel, or novel of Eastern manners and society"; (9) "the military novel"; (10) "the naval novel"; (11) "the novel of supernatural phantasy"; (12) "the art and culture novel"; and (13) "the historical novel."[14] While we can certainly recognize some examples of the Silver-Fork novel and the Newgate novel, this odd hodgepodge of classificatory schemes takes the form more as a contextual background for a set of chosen works: *Oliver Twist* is not notable as an example of the Newgate novel subgenre, but rather the Newgate novel subgenre is notable because it gave us *Oliver Twist*.

Masson, though, seems to sense that the seriousness of the novel enterprise rests in his twelfth category: "the growth and education of an individual character of the more thoughtful order" (225). This is the "art and culture novel," what we would now call the *Bildungsroman*. What is particularly striking in Masson's description, though, is that even while he admits that the "art and culture novel" is not particularly common in England—"I do not know that we have yet, or, at all events, that we have had till very recently, any very pure specimen of the novel so designated" (225)—he still seems to see it not so much as its own category but rather as an elevation of the tendencies inherent in the other categories he has discussed. So, for example, he suggests that the "most characteristic product of the time was, and is, the Fashionable Novel" (229); yet he suggests at the same time that "what is best in our fashionable novels seems to have arisen from an occasional desire on the part of those who practise such a style of fiction to make it subserve some such purpose [of growth and education]" (225). One form, then, can seem to by subsumed by another. Or, to look at it from the other side, one form—the *Bildungsroman*—can transcend and elevate other forms.

It is not simply the fashionable novel that Masson finds the *Bildungsroman* to elevate. In fact, in looking at more serious "novels of purpose"—"Novels," Masson explains, "made in the service not of 'contemporary fun' merely, but also of contemporary earnest"—he emphasizes that it is the themes of the *Bildungsroman* that make them into something more than topical "pamphlets" (265, 266):

By far the highest class of recent novels of purpose have been some which might be recognized by themselves . . . under the name of Art and Culture Novel. . . . The novels I mean are those which, concerning themselves or not, in a dogmatic manner, with the specialties of present political or ecclesiastical controversy . . . address themselves rather to that deeper question of fundamental faith as against fundamental skepticism, which is proclaimed everywhere as the one paramount fact of the age—embodying certain views on this question in the supposed education of an imaginary hero, or of several imaginary personages together, who pass through various intellectual stages to attain one that is final. In all novels whatsoever, of course, the hero passes through a series of mental stages, the usual goal or consummation being an all-consoling, all-illuminating marriage. But in the Art and Culture novel, as I consider it, the design is to represent a mind of the thoughtful order, struggling through doubt and error toward certainty and truth. . . . (266)

As this passage proceeds, Masson's focus shifts from social-problem novels to *Bildungsromane* to "all novels whatsoever." By refocusing the specific political agendas of a given "novel of purpose" onto what he sees to be a "deeper," and certainly more abstract, question, Masson depoliticizes them. But as his reference to "pamphlets" suggests, he believes that in doing so, he is also arguing that the best of these novels should be less ephemeral, both in the themes they cover and the fates they meet. The reference to the nuptial conclusion of "all novels" may seem a bit of a non sequitur here, but the rhetorical thrust is clear enough: when novels of purpose make that purpose into something related to development, they not only transcend what we would now call the "social-problem" novel, or the "industrial novel"; they produce something representative of the "deepest" possibilities of the form as a whole. As an example, it is interesting to consider the case of *Mary Barton*: if Elizabeth Gaskell had had her way, and had named the novel *John Barton*, would it have produced the same reaction? While it is impossible to say with any certainty, the absence of any novels in the Victorian canon centered on middle-aged men driven to desperate crime would seem to suggest not. Ruth Bernard Yeazell, in an essay titled "Why Political Novels Have Heroines," ties the political argument of British political novels to their heroines' "development": the relatively chaste possibilities for a Victorian novel heroine, Yeazell argues, shapes the political imaginary around a limited erotic imaginary, with the effect that "social and political anxieties are contained."[15] Political novels, of course, had both male and female protagonists; but Yeazell's essay points to the fact that those with heroines have continued to be central to our understanding of the subgenre.[16] As with *Oliver Twist*, a narrative trajectory of development seems to be the vehicle that has carried these novels from their containment in subgenre.

The special pride of place granted the *Bildungsroman* has continued to this day. As one undergraduate textbook of Victorian literature puts it, "A German form—the Bildungsroman—is often viewed as *the* model of realist fiction."[17] Indeed, in the most influential strands of novel theory, the *Bildungsroman* is either the model for the realist novel or practically synonymous with it. M. M. Bakhtin, though he is best remembered for stressing the "novelistic" as a process that could be present in a wide variety of forms, still allows that to understand "the forms of the novel in the nineteenth century, and above all the realist novel (Stendhal, Balzac, Flaubert, Dickens, and Thackeray)," the *Bildungsroman* is of "special importance."[18] Georg Lukács, of course, placed the *Bildungsroman* in such a central position in his *Theory of the Novel* that the work—and those, like Moretti's *Way of the World*, that follow from it—is essentially a *Theory of the Bildungsroman*. In each of these cases, the key characteristic of the *Bildungsroman* is its goal of mediating between individual development, something that requires some separation from the social sphere, and a reintegration back into that the social sphere. As Joseph Slaughter puts it, "The *Bildungsroman* is a unique and vital variant of the modern novel because it is especially equipped to normalize the conditions of inclusion in and exclusion from the public sphere. . . . The *Bildungsroman* purposes to bridge the gap between exclusion and inclusion."[19] Those who propose the special place for the *Bildungsroman* in the theory and history of the novel would seem to be largely invested in this sort of mediation between an individual and her social context. Even a critic like Ian Watt, who shows no particular interest in the *Bildungsroman* as a form, will suggest that we only reach the "full maturity of the genre" with Austen, and her "harmonious reconcil[iation]" of Richardson and Fielding's styles: one the artist of the private and the internal, the other the artist of the public and external.[20] Even when the *Bildungsroman* is not a key term in the argument, the essential synthesizing characteristic of the *Bildungsroman* is offered as the defining feature of the novel form—and that feature is presented as only fully emerging in the nineteenth-century tradition.

How does this specific narrative trajectory come to stand in for novel narrative in general? The answer, it will turn out, comes from the implicit preference Victorian studies has for novels that seem to offer an immediate connection with the past: novels, that is, in which we can recognize ourselves. It is this principle of selection that ultimately privileges the *Bildungsroman*. Hans-Georg Gadamer, whose hermeneutic approach is specifically concerned with the question of how an aesthetic connection across a temporal divide is possible, sees the theme of development, or *Bildung*, as central to this experience. In *Truth and Method*, Gadamer proposes *Bildung* as that concept which differentiates between works that seem familiar and works that do not: "The concept of *Bildung* most clearly indicates the profound intellectual change that still causes us to experience the century of Goethe as contemporary, whereas the baroque era appears historically remote."[21] "*Bildung*" here refers to the larger concept of what he calls "self-formation, education, or cultivation" (8). Gadamer draws the term from the German hermeneutic tradition of Herder and Dilthey, but, for our purposes it is worth noting that it actually comes into German use from England, in a translation of Shaftesbury's ethical works. We will return to the question of the lineage of the term later in this chapter; for now, it suffices to say that Gadamer argues that works of art which describe an individual's inter-action with tradition will become, themselves, *part* of a tradition. People who cultivate themselves—become part of a culture—become recognizable to others as part of others' cultivation. For the purposes of the argument in this chapter, we could reformulate this as follows: those works that show people recognizing themselves in the past will be the works from the past in which we recognize ourselves.

CHOICES ALREADY MADE

The representative example of the *Bildungsroman* has long been Goethe's *Wilhelm Meister's Apprenticeship*. For Lukács, among others, Goethe's novel depends upon its protagonist's ability to recognize himself in the social world.[22] This recognition is the essential move that makes "reconciliation between interiority and reality" possible.[23] The key moment of such recog-nition occurs when a mentor explains to Wilhelm that

> when [a man's] development has reached a certain stage, it is advanta-geous for him to lose himself in a larger whole, learn to live for others, and forget himself in dutiful activity for others. Only then will he come to know himself . . . (301)

He will "come to know himself" when he "forget[s] himself" in a larger social whole. The principal English instantiation would be Dorothea's "in-calculable diffusion" into public life at the end of *Middlemarch*. What these texts posit is the notion that, in order to find yourself, you must look to your membership in something larger.

Such a connection is different from resigned acceptance of the past. The classic account of this sort of resignation comes in Moretti's *Way of the World*, in which he points to the resolution of the *Bildungsroman* as a final reconsideration and redefinition of what has come before: "the facts have not changed, but their value . . . has. On second reading, the past is perme-ated with a new meaning, its aim the well-being of the individual."[24] The model here for Moretti is the sort of reordering of past events that occurs with the "solution of a mystery": a determination of an underlying *fabula* (story) from a finally complete *sjuzhet* (narration of those events) (70). The oddly genre-bending supernaturalism of *Wilhelm Meister's* mysterious secret society at the Tower underlines this claim. Ultimately, for Moretti, the end of the narration fixes past events into place. *Meaning* is the reparation for the foreclosure of *possibility*. The fixity of narrative conclusion speaks to the fact that Moretti sees this sort of "second reading" as an attempt to make the best of what you are given. Given an unchangeable state of affairs, freedom giving way to necessity, Moretti suggests, the only alternative left is the "*valorization* of necessity, the 'positive' side of . . . the escape from freedom" (69). This is a result of the fact that the *Bildungsroman*, which requires the move toward freedom and individuality, and ends with absorption into community, is "of necessity . . . *intrinsically contradictory*" (6).

This claim is based, at least in part, on the notion that the individual and the communal represent contradictory impulses. What I would like to suggest instead is that the *Bildungsroman*, instead of attempting a narrative resolution to the contradictory demands of individual and community, can instead be understood to offer a representation of the communal basis of moral intuition. Simply put, what I will argue in this section is that the formal principles of narrative in the *Bildungsroman*, the production of the drive forward in the text, develops out of an interplay between seemingly autonomous free choice on the part of its central character and a pre-existing basis for those choices. The sense of "rightness" in a developmental narrative arises from the form's suggestion that a character's choices are always, already, founded in a communal context. The reconsideration of the past in terms of the present is not a final resignation, but, instead, a consistent element of the narrative form of the *Bildungsroman*.

First, though, let us start by considering a choice of some significance in the larger history of the nineteenth-century novel: Wilhelm Meister's decision to leave the world of the theater and devote himself to family and state—that is, to replace his youthful dreams with mature responsibility. If *Wilhelm Meister's Apprenticeship* functions in literary history as the exemplary *Bildungsroman*, then in this choice, we have the locus classicus of nineteenth-century character development. For all its importance, though, the moment, when it comes, passes quickly by: "Wilhelm was about to take a formal leave of the theatre, when he felt that in reality he had already taken leave, and needed but to go."[25] This moment will probably not come as a surprise to anyone reading the novel. The plot has been taking Wilhelm away from the theater for some time. In deciding to go, he just follows along with the trajectory of the plot. At the same time, by projecting this decision into his past, the novel suggests that this narrative trajectory was itself a act of Wilhelm's own will, albeit an act of will that we never see at the level of narrative. This probably makes some intuitive sense—many people have had the experience of making a tough decision and having it not take because it felt like it had not already been made at a deeper level. What this means formally, though, is that the novel works to suggest that Wilhelm's choice, as fictional character, takes hold here because he has already made the choice at a level that redirected the narrative itself.

This is a small—if significant—moment in Goethe's novel, but it is hard to overstate how prevalent this pattern is in nineteenth-century fiction. In what follows, I will look at a number of examples from Dickens's *Great Expectations*, in which the moment of apparent decision constantly refers back to an earlier decision. By the time we see textual evidence of one of Pip's choices, it seems his mind has already been made up. The actual moment of choice remains elusive. This fits in well, perhaps, with our notion of character: it would not do for Pip, or any other character, to make each decision ex nihilo. There must be some consistency; each choice must seem based in what we already know. At the same time, though, for the character to appear as character, the choice must seem somehow free. There is a reason that undergraduates frequently resort to the counterfactual notion that characters are somehow autonomous, that they could have done otherwise. This is part of the illusion that novel narrative creates, and it is, as I will now show, an important determining factor in the sense of narrative necessity.

The first of Pip's choices occurs at the novel's opening, with Magwitch accosting Pip in a graveyard and demanding that Pip steal food for him. This has frequently been identified as the novel's primal scene. It starts the narrative machinery in motion, certainly, and without it there would be no expectations, no trip to London, no dreams of marriage to Estella. Magwitch, though, does not leave Pip a legacy solely because he had threatened him years earlier. He does so because Pip brings him the food. It may seem slightly off-key to refer to this as a choice, given the duress under which Pip committed the theft. All the same, Magwitch later sees it as one, claiming Pip "acted noble,"[26] an evaluation Pip does not deny. Let us address this question first, then. Does Pip have a choice? Not to have a choice means, quite literally, for there to be no alternative; only one course of action presents itself. Pip's situation, on the other hand, provides two very clear alternatives: he may either steal food and a file, and stay silent about it, or he may have his heart and liver torn out. If following a rather obvious pragmatic logic in this case seems like the only sensible way to go, this should not obscure the fact that a choice after all has been made, under a certain set of circumstances.

In his description of his torturous night carrying out Magwitch's order, Pip makes clear that these different options are indeed available to him. The night plays out as an ongoing tug-of-war of these different inclinations. Pip has a clear conscience of his theft being wrong—here figured physically as the piece of bread he must keep hidden in the leg of his trousers (12–13)—but immediately after the mention of that conscience, Pip's mind again turns to a fear of Magwitch and the young man (13). The two leanings seem to pull Pip between them. On the one hand, he says, "The guilty knowledge that I was going to rob Mrs. Joe . . . united to the necessity of always keeping one hand on my bread-and-butter . . . almost drove me out of my mind." On the other hand, as he thinks of the convicts outside, he writes, "If ever anybody's hair stood on end with terror, mine must have done so then" (13). To complicate matters further, his thought of the convicts is not thoroughly one of fear; he already shows some empathy with Magwitch when he imagines him "declaring that he couldn't and wouldn't starve until tomorrow" (13), insofar as he imagines his suffering. The novel repeats this process of conscience overridden by ambivalent fear and sympathy in brief in the following paragraph, in which Pip describes trying to stir the Christmas pudding: "I tried it with the load upon my leg (and that made me think afresh of the man with the load on *his* leg)" (13). Again, we see around the act of theft these three mixed sensations—guilt, fear, and sympathy—with their three contrary, though overlapping, imperatives: I ought not to do this; I ought to do this; I must do this.

Yet nowhere do we see a deliberation between these contrary imperatives actually taking place. At the end of the paragraph described above, as Pip stirs the Christmas pudding, he adds a neat conclusion to his difficulties: "Happily, I slipped away, and deposited that part of my conscience in my garret bedroom" (13). This passage nearly begs for interpretation of Pip's ability to deposit his conscience elsewhere, but we should not overlook its simple denotative import: Pip is going to steal the bread. All of Pip's musings on the matter lend to the difficulty—the "burden" (12)—of stealing the bread. But the actual theft of the bread, the theft as an act, appears as a foregone conclusion.

Even if it is a foregone conclusion, though, the important thing to notice here is that Dickens spends pages on Pip's warring conscience and desire for self-preservation. Rather than present the theft as a matter of simple necessity, the foregone conclusion is still subject to the appearance of deliberation. In other words, Dickens makes it clear that there is a choice to be made, just as he makes it clear that the choice is predetermined. Hearing the guns of the prison ships firing, and feeling the smart of a reproach from Mrs. Joe for asking too many questions, he states: "I felt fearfully sensible of the great convenience that the Hulks were handy for me. I was clearly on my way there. I had begun by asking questions, and *I was going to rob Mrs. Joe*" (15, emphasis mine). The final statement, with its expression of the future tense embedded in the imperfect—"was going to"—could potentially be read as a proleptic statement of fact by the older, narrating Pip, along the lines of "But I would soon find out." However, the childlike guilt of the first prediction that he was on his way to the Hulks—and, just as importantly, the fact that this statement is not true—would suggest that it is the young Pip who makes the statement about the theft, who already feels destined to this act. Rigorously speaking, there is a certain undecidability between these two readings, but it is a productive one for our purposes. For it points to the strong sense of predetermination in this statement, as a choice already in the past and unable to be altered. Such awareness is present throughout the night: "I knew that at the first faint dawn of morning I must rob the pantry" (15). What is not present in the description that led up to this point, however, is a stated reason for *why* Pip knows this to be the case. At every point up to and including the theft, regardless of which position Pip takes toward it, the theft itself has the quality of an act that had already been firmly decided upon in advance. This is not to say that there was no choice; Pip's entire narration of the night refutes that. There is a choice, but that choice had already been made.

The night leading up to the theft, then, presents a compelling formal paradox. On the one hand, by continually stressing Pip's conscience, the novel implies that the act was one that Pip could have chosen not to commit. The option, at least, is always explicitly present. On the other hand, the act is at every point a necessary one. It should be stressed, though, that this necessity does not take the form of Pip's fear of having his liver eaten. That fear is present, of course, but largely irrelevant, since the choice is always presented as having been made, already, in the past.

This would seem to be an example of the sense of felt necessity, already mentioned, that Barthes refers to as "the discourse's instinct for preservation." Barthes's analysis, remember, was specifically about the freedom, or lack of freedom, of a character to choose: Sarrasine's choice of whether or not to visit La Zambinella. For Barthes, the seeming choice is depicted, through a sort of psychological overdetermination, in order to mask "by superposition the implacable constraint of the discourse."[27] The moment *seems* to be one of free alternative, then, but this is only the surface phenomenon of a determining narrative direction.

And yet this would seem to be taking the underlying narrative structure, the determining law that the reader feels, as somehow pre-existing the novel itself. Seen structurally, there is no reason why *Great Expectations* would have necessarily ended without beginning had Pip not brought Magwitch the food. The threat of retaliation would have hung over the narrative every bit as "unbounded," to use a term of Brooks', as that "energy" produced by Pip's actual choice. The structure that Barthes sees as directing the novel is produced, as I discussed in the previous section, through the process of reading.

Of course, the choice is determined by the narrative. Insofar as Pip is an actant in *Great Expectations*, he could not have done otherwise. But at the same time, *this* narrative, *Great Expectations*, only comes into existence with the narration of these choices. To claim that the choice is only the surface appearance of an underlying narrative seems to overlook the equally true fact that the underlying narrative is determined by a seemingly free choice. Pip's choices, as Brooks seems to suggest, are moments of transition in the narrative, dictating the direction it will go. On the other hand, as actual moments of decision, they are oddly undetectable, always seeming to refer back to a decision already made. They dictate the narrative, and yet they are dictated by the causal necessity of the narrative. The former (choice as moments of transition) perhaps fits better with an intuitive reading of the novel; the latter (choice as dictated by the narrative), with an analytic reading. Kant, in his *Groundwork of the Metaphysics of Morals*, makes a similar point:[28] "reason *for speculative purposes* finds the road of natural necessity much more traveled and more usable than that of freedom; yet *for practical purposes* the footpath of freedom is the only one on which it is possible to make use of our reason in our conduct."[29]

The utility of Kant's ethical thought in this reading is the intense scrutiny under which he puts the relation of autonomous choice and constraint; his ethics as a whole can be productively read as being less about right and wrong or good and bad, and more about freedom and necessity. In fact, he refers to his ethics at one point as his "science of freedom" (4:387). The best-known element of this theory is Kant's "Categorical Imperative": "act only in accordance with that maxim through which you can at the same time will that it become a universal law." The received wisdom on this formulation makes it into a procedure for making moral decisions: a situation comes to an agent, the agent tests to see if a reaction would be permissible as a universal law, decides for or against that action. This interpretation is not quite accurate—it seems to overstate the extent to which the process is conscious[30]—but at times in the *Groundwork*, Kant seems to encourage it, particularly in the four concrete examples he offers as illustration. Whatever the case may be, though, this particular aspect of Kant's theory, actually occupies only the first two parts of his *Groundwork*: analytic sections that argue that *if* there is a moral law, *this* is what it would look like. By far the greater part of Kant's ethics, which extends from the third section of the *Groundwork* through the *Critique of Practical Reason*, his *Religion within the Boundaries of Mere Reason*, and finally his *Metaphysics of Morals*, is more concerned with the murkier topics of autonomy and free will—not so much what a moral decision is by definition, but how we can make a free decision at all.

What we are really looking for in the notion of free will, according to Kant, is a cause that is "unconditioned." In other words, there must be something spontaneous, not caused by something else. And *that*, as far as we are able to cognize, is quite impossible to find. In the second *Critique*, Kant makes the unlikely concession that, looked at temporally, free will seemingly cannot exist:

[E]very event, and consequently every action that takes place at a point of time, is necessary under the condition of what was in the preceding time. Now, since time past is no longer within my control, every action that I perform must be necessary by determining grounds *that are not within my control*, that is, I am never free at the point of time in which I act.[31]

Theoretical reason thus finds it impossible to imagine freedom. At the same time, as mentioned above, he believes that in our practical reason—our normal decision-making intuition—we must still consider ourselves free in order to make use of our reason. Furthermore, he asserts the existence of a "moral feeling," which commonly takes the form of guilt. A human being, he writes, may see an act as something "in which he was carried away by the stream of natural necessity" and yet, all the same, "he nevertheless finds that the advocate who speaks in his favor can by no means reduce to silence the prosecutor within him" (5:98). We can feel guilt, in other words, even for an act that seems beyond our control. This serves as a good description of Pip's attacks of conscience—culminating in his sentencing himself to the Hulks—over an action that seemed from the start a foregone conclusion. Not only do we act as if we had free will, but we also feel as if we must have somehow been responsible for acts that, viewed analytically, appear inescapably determined. The reason for this, Kant argues, is that though necessity is indeed the cause of our actions, we have *chosen* to allow necessity to be the cause: "A rational being can . . . say of every unlawful action he performed that he could have omitted it even though as appearance it is sufficiently determined in the past and, so far, is inevitably necessary" (5:98). Kant comes to this conclusion through some finessing of the distinction he makes in the first *Critique* between the appearance of consciousness (which we have access to) and consciousness as thing-in-itself (which we do not).[32] The upshot of these technicalities, though, is that we end up in the odd position of having a subject whose actions are shaped by a maxim—a guiding principle—which the subject chooses to follow "antecedent to every use of freedom in experience."[33] This is one of the strangest points in Kant's ethics; it seems as if he is saying that what appears to be natural necessity actually comes about through our own choice—but through a choice that does not occur in time.[34]

This choice is often read as being purely atemporal after a rather mystical fashion—a reading Kant's own language would seem to encourage. But we need not concede entirely to transcendental idealism. Henry E. Allison, a particularly incisive commentator on Kant, offers the following:

[T]his does not mean that we are to regard fundamental maxims as adopted either in some mysterious pre- or nontemporal manner or by means of a self-conscious, deliberative process. It is rather that through reflection we find that we have been committed all along to such a maxim, understood as a fundamental orientation of the will towards moral requirements.[35]

The ultimate Kantian notion of freedom is founded, first, in the acceptance that we could have done no other and, then, in the understanding that we chose to be able to do no other. To rephrase: every choice that we can sense comes about through the temporal stream of natural necessity, so there must be free will at the level that we cannot sense, and that is itself outside of time. But precisely because we cannot sense this, it would be mystification to imagine actually making this choice. Instead, we must just *take responsibility* for the fact that we must have made a choice, and that this oriented us. As Alenka Zupančič puts it, freedom for Kant demands that *"one has to discover the point where the subject itself plays an (active) part in lawful, causal necessity*, the point where the subject itself is already inscribed in advance in what appear to be laws of causality independent of the subject."[36] In other words, Kantian freedom takes the form—one that we have already seen in Dickens—of a choice that has already been made.

The projects of Dickens in *Great Expectations* and Kant in his ethical work are actually quite similar: the effort to present autonomous decision making in a way that remains true to both the idea of freedom and an intuition of temporal causality. Each moment of decision points back in time to something prior, and seems an effect of necessity at the moment it is made. In this way, each character choice seems—and here we recall Barthes—utterly determined by the constraint of narrative. At the same time, though, the moments of character choice are indispensable to the narrative insofar as they determine its direction. Remember Kant's claim that just as speculative reason cannot conceive freedom, practical reason cannot do without it. The same seems to hold true for the experience of reading *Great Expectations*. We cannot imagine how the narrative would assume its direction without Pip's seemingly free character choices. Where are Pip's choices? Already made. But by locating freedom in decisions already made, we come to see the narrative as something that *ought* to go in a certain direction. From the reader's naive belief in the freedom of Pip's choices comes—returning again to Brooks's usage—the "desire that carries us forward, onward, through the text," that is, narrative desire.

These ethical-narrative dynamics are at play in what is probably the most famous moment of choice in *Great Expectations*: Pip's decision to accept his expectations and go to London. The first question that Jaggers asks Pip is about whether he would be willing to go always by his nickname in order to receive his expectations. Pip's response, since it is his first response, and in the affirmative, must also count as an acceptance of sorts: "My heart was beating so fast, and there was such a singing in my ears, that I could hardly stammer that I had no objection" (136). The moment of Pip's acceptance is

thus actually buried in a comparative phrase. It is only the obvious inevitability of the answer that serves syntactically to highlight the deafening
noise of his excitement. This moment of acceptance is repeated again, with
more impact, when it becomes clear that his expectations will force Pip
to leave Joe for London. Yet his response again shows something less than
deliberation: "I said (glancing at Joe, who stood looking on, motionless),
that I supposed I could come directly" (138). The parenthetical glance serves
notice of Pip's at least implicit awareness that, in accepting, he is also part-
ing, perhaps forever, from Joe. Yet Pip has already begun to answer in the
affirmative—"I said . . ."—before the parenthetical pause. He has already
made the decision to accept.

So when does he make this decision? He has told Biddy earlier that he
wants to be a gentleman. His desire here is forceful: "I never shall or can be
comfortable—or anything but miserable—there, Biddy!—unless I can lead
a very different sort of life from the life I lead now" (125). Forceful though
it may be, however, this sentiment is not in itself a decision. As Pip himself
states, it occupies only one side in a debate ongoing within himself, the
other being occupied by Biddy's sentiment that leaving his comfortable life
would be a "pity": "Now, I too had so often thought it a pity, that, in the singular kind of quarrel with myself which I was always carrying on, I was half
inclined to shed tears of vexation and distress when Biddy gave utterance to
her sentiment and my own" (125). Pip's "quarrel with himself" does not lack
a resolution. Rather, by the time it has been phrased as a quarrel, in a move
that should be familiar by this point, it is already too late; the decision has
been made. "I told her she was right, and I knew it was much to be regret-
ted, but still it was not to be helped" (125).

The portrayal of Pip's decision to go to London, then, follows as necessity
from his decision that he will do whatever it takes to become a gentleman.
Indeed, by the time Jaggers appears, this decision is so implicitly understood that the Barthesian imperative that the "story must go on" appears to
have gained a definite content and direction: the story must go on, toward
London and Pip's expectations. And it is because of Pip's decision, already
made, that we know and expect this. The choice will be made; it must be
made; it has already been made. The fundamental decision that determines
the decision to leave home is itself presented in the language of necessity,
while at the same time being within the domain of free will. It is a "quarrel
with oneself" whose final result, all the same, is "not to be helped."

FAMILIAR STORIES

Pip's narrative of development, then, proceeds as both necessary and self-
determined. It is precisely here that we can locate the freedom of a character:
not in a radical independence from the plot's chain of causation but rather

in the consistent presentation of a strict determination that is nonetheless based on a prior choice. Rather than privileging either character autonomy or the constraint of plot, a reading in these terms focuses on the necessary reciprocity of the two positions. In the *Bildungsroman*, though, where the plot works toward the reintegration of an individual and community, the constraint of plot is a formal representation of the sense of "necessity"—to use Moretti's term—exercised by that individual's social context. So, the sort of autonomy that we saw in our discussion of *Great Expectations* can offer a model as well for understanding how the *Bildungsroman*, more generally, produces a narrative that works toward both development and social inclusion.

The trick here is that these novels do not just present our choices as already having been made; they present them as already having been made by ourselves *as social beings*. Remember, at the level of narration, Pip's choices took the form of backward-projected grammatical sleights of hand. At the level of the underlying, inaccessible story, though, we had to assume these choices had already been made. This is a narratological restatement of Kant's noumenal and phenomenal, but we could also give it a more psychological spin: the choices exist at the level of a subtextual unconscious, which directs Pip's trajectory, and when his textual choices come, they simply follow along. When we look at the way this plays out in the larger body of *Bildungsromane*, what we see is that this essential model of time and narrative holds, but the nature of the choices already made becomes more social in nature. We become a member of a community, in other words, by recognizing that we were already—in the *fabula*, the noumena, or the unconscious—making choices rooted in our communal belonging.

The claim that *Bildungsromane* make, then, is that we do not only come to discover ourselves as part of a social whole; we come to discover instead that we have always been part of a social whole, and that our development lies in recognizing this fact. So, to take one central example from *Wilhelm Meister*, Wilhelm's apprenticeship—his development, broadly speaking— begins to come to an end with his discovery that he is a father: "His apprenticeship was therefore completed in one sense, for along with the feeling of a father, he had acquired the virtues of a solid citizen."[37] From paternity, then, comes citizenship, and the resolution of development. What makes this moment particularly notable though, is that the son that Wilhelm discovers, Felix, is not a stranger; Wilhelm has been caring for him for some time. So the moment that that Goethe highlights as the culmination of Wilhelm's development is one in which, practically, very little changes. He had been taking care of Felix before, and would, presumably, continue to take care of him after. What changes is not the practical arrangement but rather the character's disposition toward it. As Joseph Slaughter has pointed out, Wilhelm does not become a citizen automatically as a result of paternity; he has to claim it: "In Goethe's novel, citizenship names the categorical distinction between ignorant subjection (the father as hapless sperm donor) and the conscious affirmation of social relations (the father as willing foster to his own child)."[38] The key difference here is one of will: Wilhelm is a biological father either way, just as Lucilla is a "Lucilla Marjoribanks" either way. The distinction is not between being one thing and being something else. Instead, it is a choice between, on the one hand, being something unknowingly and passively and, on the other hand, asserting it as an act of will.

We see this active, willing dimension of development emphasized in a debate between Wilhelm's mentor Lothario, and his petit-bourgeois friend Werner. Where Wilhelm and Werner's disagreements had previously revolved around the role of art in society, or Wilhelm's desire to "develop [him]self fully" (174), this conversation centers on the quite practical issue of paying taxes:

> "I can assure you," said Werner, "that in all my life I have never thought about the State, and only paid my dues and taxes because that was customary."
>
> "Well," said Lothario, "I hope to be able to make a good patriot out of you. A good father is one who at mealtimes serves his children first; and a good citizen is one who pays what he owes to the State before dealing with everything else." (311)

The exchange not only hammers home the citizen-as-father figure but underlines one of its trickier implications. If choosing to care for one's children corresponds to choosing citizenship, then, carrying the metaphor in the opposite direction, civic society would seem to play the role not of a protector, disciplinarian, or enabler—it would instead play the role of a dependent. As if to ward off any confusion, Goethe has Lothario connect paying the state taxes to serving food to one's children. Now, the question here is not whether Werner *will* pay his taxes, or even *should* pay his taxes. He already does so, and does so without complaint. By choosing actively to pay his taxes, though—by choosing to do what he already does—he would switch the order of the parental metaphor around. No longer just a child of his community, he would come to see the community as his own child: something that he has made as much as it has made him.

This sort of reciprocity between individual and community is actually a better description of how moral intuition worked, at its more refined levels, than references to physical sensation. We have already seen William Whewell's claim that "The moralist, as well as the poet, must give us back the image of our mind. He must show us the connections of moral truths which had governed our thoughts, though we had not unfolded them into reasonings."[39] In Chapter 3, I discussed how this led to a sense of shared, unconscious, experience: *sensus communis*. Here, I'd like to emphasize the "community" in *"communis."* Moral philosophy, by Whewell's understanding of the term, serves to emphasize a communal belonging—one that already exists, but that we are not yet aware of.

The root for this particular strain of intuitionist thought goes back, as many of them do, to Lord Shaftesbury.[40] So too does the idea of *"Bildung"* that we have seen in Gadamer and others. *"Bildung"*—often presented is as a particularly autochthonous German concept—is a translation of Shaftesbury's description of the "formation of a genteel and liberal character"[41] in his 1711 *Characteristicks of Men, Manners, Opinions, Times*.[42] The *Characteristicks*, a collection of his mature works, argued in various ways for the existence of a harmonious cosmic order: a position that led him to believe that the happiness of an individual, properly cultivated, would coincide with the larger happiness of the species. If properly educated to understand our own intuitions, we can thus follow our own motivations while at the same time working for the betterment of society. Shaftesbury's influence was quite strong in Germany—stronger, in fact, than it was in England, according to Leslie Stephen: "In Germany, where sentimentalism is more congenial to the national temperament, [Shaftesbury] found a warmer reception than amongst his own countrymen."[43] Herder, for example, called Shaftesbury "the beloved Plato of Europe": a "virtuoso of humanity that has had a marked influence on the best minds of our century, on men who have striven with sincere determination for the true, the beautiful, and the good."[44] The same figure who would generate many of the ideas that continued into nineteenth-century intuitionism was, as Herder describes, a specific influence on the German idea of development as well.

If Shaftesbury's presence in this tradition is strangely underplayed by Anglo-American critics discussing British *Bildungsromane*, it is at least partly because of how much his reputation suffered over the nineteenth century and into the twentieth. Stephen, for example, saw in Shaftesbury's work an early example of how, "in England, attempts at *a priori* philosophy have taken the form of an appeal to common sense."[45] This tradition "which thus tries to convert the *vox populi* into the *vox Dei* . . . seems to have been first made popular in the eighteenth century by Shaftesbury." Stephen is critical here because he sees Shaftesbury as elevating conventional wisdom—perhaps even prejudice—into an eternal moral law.[46]

Shaftesbury, though, does not believe that this *vox* rings true from the start; it is more akin to an aesthetic faculty, and it thus requires cultivation. Agents do have a natural and innate "Sense of Right and Wrong," Shaftesbury argued, but this is not an innate ability for judging the morality of acts. Rather, it is a reaction to the motives underlying the actions of others. When those motives are virtuous, or loving, we feel a reflected love for them, what Shaftesbury calls a "reflected Sense": "an Affection towards those very Affections themselves."[47] This affection toward an affection, what Stephen Darwall has called "second-order approval,"[48] thus makes it clear that Shaftesbury's view of the moral sense is something shared, a morality based on certain analogies drawn between different intelligences. This notion is drawn from Lockean epistemology; what Shaftesbury adds to it, though, is the idea that this sort of reflection has the immediacy of sensory perception: he specifically connects it to the "Eye and the Ear" (28–29). As justification for his discussion of affections-toward-affections, Shaftesbury writes,

> The Case is the same in mental or moral Subjects, as in ordinary Bodys, or the common Subjects of Sense. The Shapes, Motions, Colours, and Proportions of these latter being presented to our Eye; there necessarily results a Beauty or Deformity, according to the different Measure, Arrangement and Disposition of their several Parts. (28–29)

The fundamental language here, then, is that of aesthetics. And as a language of aesthetics and taste, it required cultivation. He quotes approvingly from a translation of Persius's *Satires* on the necessity of a moral education:

> Doubtless the seeds of moral goodness and honor which, although we had received them from nature but nevertheless surrounded by vices and very nearly obscured, lie hidden in our minds just as if remotely buried in a deep ditch, unless a better cultivation should occur so that they might stir us in our night labors to excavate them and present them in public actions. (216n)

Tangled metaphor aside—why "excavate" the seeds rather than cultivate them to grow?—Shaftesbury introduces with this passage the idea that our moral education should be that which enables us to recognize ourselves in harmonious connection to others. It should allow us to recognize the essential communal moral agreement that lies hidden in our minds. This requires, according to Shaftesbury, the "formation of a genteel and liberal character"[49]—that is, it requires what, after its translation into German, we come to know as *"Bildung."*

"Bildung," then, as the term comes into German from Shaftesbury, denotes the cultivation of what Shaftesbury would call *"sensus communis"*—"common sense," or shared understanding. This was a key term in my discussion of humor in Dickens in the previous chapter, and it is worth recalling Hannah Arendt's account of the term: "[not] a sense common to all of us, but strictly that sense which fits us into a community with others, makes us members of it and enables us to communicate things given

by our five private senses."[50] Arendt was interested in the possibilities of using Kant's aesthetics as the basis for a political philosophy. In Shaftesbury, though, as Gadamer has pointed out, *sensus communis* already had a "political and social" dimension: it was "an element of social and moral being."[51]

Now, none of this is to suggest that the *Bildungsroman* is properly an English genre.[52] The term itself does not come into common critical usage in German until the end of the nineteenth century, in the work of Wilhelm Dilthey.[53] It is not until the 1930s, with the publication of Susanne Howe's *Wilhelm Meister and His English Kinsmen*, that the term came to be intimately associated with the British novel of the nineteenth century.[54] But even Masson's discussion of the "art and culture novel," and its growing importance for English novelists, sees it as having a foreign root: "By far the greatest example of this species of fiction in modern literature is the 'Wilhelm Meister' of Goethe; and there can be no doubt that that work, since it was translated, has had some influence on the aims of British novel-writing" (225). Now, while Goethe did indeed have some influence—particularly on Coleridge, Carlyle, Lewes, and Eliot[55]—that influence can be easily overstated. There was a fair amount of interest in German works in England around the turn of the nineteenth century—ranging from *The Sorrows of Young Werther* to the multiple adaptations and translations of Schiller's drama *Die Räuber*—but this interest quickly cooled, and during the early decades of the century, the English opinion of German literature was quite low.[56] The point here is not to claim a national proprietorship,[57] but rather to suggest that the philosophical strains that we see in the European *Bildungsroman* map on to the tradition of intuitionist thought.

In brief, then: the operating principle in the narrative structure of the *Bildungsroman* is the discovery that we are all already a member of a community, and that our decisions can be understood as stemming from that community. Proper cultivation—of the sort that Shaftesbury advocates—means the development of a character that can understand and respond to the pre-existing, yet unconscious, shared consensus: the *sensus communis*.

At the beginning of this chapter, I suggested that the concept of readability that seems to underlie the object selection of Victorian studies—the preference shown for texts that seem immanent and familiar—is at least partially due to the ethos of *Bildung* represented in them. Now we can be a bit more precise in this formulation. *Bildung* depends on a cultivation of liberal individuals that allows them to understand themselves as being already part of a community and tradition. The mechanism for doing so is the recognition of the self in the past. This describes the object analyzed by Victorian studies, which, as we have seen, tends to elide the difference between the terms *Bildungsroman*, "realism," and "novel." But it also describes the principle of selection that leads to such elision. The novels, in other words, teach an ethical lesson, the practical implementation of which is the study of those novels.

It is, again, Gadamer who presents the most thorough account of this mutually enforcing circle of object and analysis, or, as he would have it, tradition and interpretation. Gadamer sees, as the basis of all understanding, the "interplay of the movement of tradition and the movement of the interpreter":

> The anticipation of meaning that governs our understanding of a text is not an act of subjectivity, but proceeds from the commonality that binds us to the tradition. But this commonality is constantly being formed in our relation to the tradition. Tradition is not simply a permanent precondition; rather we produce it ourselves inasmuch as we understand, participate in the evolution of tradition, and hence further determine it ourselves.[58]

Again, we have something that sounds like Rawls's formulation of the law that we give to ourselves. Here, though, it is not quite a law that we give to ourselves, but rather a law that we are given by tradition—and which we then, through, an analysis of that tradition, re-inscribe. In terms of Victorian readability, we could understand this field of literary study to be defined by an experience of the recognition of the self in the past. Those books that do not fit this mold, remember, will simply not be taken to be Victorian novels. And, in fact, the field is not just defined by this experience; it is supported by the implied ethical gain of recognizing ourselves in the past. The value of this interpretive practice, though, is itself based on the implicit value of the works that it chooses to study. Georgia Warnke offers a useful gloss on the play of these themes in Gadamer's work:

> The interpretations we project onto these texts are not our own autonomous creations . . . but are rather bequeathed to us as part of the narratives themselves. These already possess specific vocabularies, plots, and sets of issues and insofar as we are "thrown" into the narratives, their languages and trajectories necessarily provide the contours for our understanding of them. . . . As historical beings, we find ourselves in historical and cultural traditions that hand down to us the projections or hypotheses . . . of that which we are trying to understand.[59]

Whether or not we want to take on the complications of the entire Gadamerian concept of tradition and prejudice as a model of understanding, it seems to describe at least *this* particular field: a set of interpretations that reiterate the form of the narratives they analyze; a set of narratives that produce, in their moral form, the ethos of the field that isolates and studies them.

"PROPERLY CULTIVATED MORAL NATURE": MILL'S *AUTOBIOGRAPHY*

The "moral feeling" Kant describes—what he colorfully refers to as "prosecutor," watching over an agents' actions, and acting as an "incentive" to moral action (5:79)—finds an odd echo in the British ethics of the nineteenth century. Though I have been concentrating in this chapter and elsewhere largely on Victorian intuitionists, it is in the writing of the intuitionists' greatest interlocutor that we most clearly find this sort of guilt-based internal acting as moral incentive. John Stuart Mill, in *Utilitarianism*, describes the internal sanction of duty as "a feeling in our mind; a pain, more or less intense, attendant on violation of duty, which, in properly cultivated moral natures rises . . . into shrinking from it as an impossibility."[60] If our moral nature is properly developed, Mill seems to suggest, we will be able to *feel* a wrong state of affairs, and thereby be drawn toward right action.

It is this connection between a moral feeling and the "cultivation" of moral nature that I wish to discuss in this section. I do not mean to suggest that Mill's particular brand of internalism was the same as that of Shaftesbury or, in Mill's own time, Whewell.[61] What I am interested in, though, is the fact that Mill turns, in his posthumously published *Autobiography*, to a narrative account of personal development to explain the connection of his own mental progress and growth with the development of his mature philosophical thought. If, as I have suggested, developmental narrative brings with it a whole host of ethical presuppositions—particularly about a communally founded *sensus communis*—then we should expect to find those in Mill's writing as well. As we saw with Cardinal Newman, the act of writing narrative can bring with it the implicit ideas of the form. By explaining the growth of his thought in terms of a narrative of personal development, Mill ends up making use of the *formal* ethical conceit that the validity of his philosophical positions derives from their basis in a shared ethical sense.

While Mill's work might have depended on a felt internal motivation, he was careful to distinguish it from the sort of innate intuition that he thought undermined the work of Whewell and others like him. Mill remains fairly consistent in his take on this sort of intuitionism throughout his career. To take just one example, from the *Autobiography*:

> The notion that truths external to the mind may be known by intuition or consciousness, independently of observation and experience, is, I am persuaded, in these times, the great intellectual support of

false doctrines and bad intuitions. By the aid of this theory, every inveterate belief and every intense feeling, of which the origin is not remembered, is enabled to dispense with the obligation of justifying itself by reason, and is erected into its own all-sufficient voucher and justification.[62]

The key objection here lies in the reference to intuition arising "independently of observation and experience." Mill, over the course of his work, would attempt to develop instead an account of how we can work with something that *feels* and functions like intuition but derives instead from accumulated experience. Intuition, as Mill sees it, will allow prejudice, superstition, or conventional wisdom to act as the final court of moral appeal. The result, in his mind, would be conservatism disguised as moral law.

The distinction between Mill's account of moral feeling and the one that he criticized in intuitionist philosophers comes down to this question of experience. In his discussion of Adam Sedgwick's *Discourse* and its championing of the "moral sense,"[63] he stresses the importance of developing an innate feeling in order to give it moral content. He begins from a "natural" standpoint:

> The idea of the pain of another is naturally painful; the idea of the pleasure of another is naturally pleasurable. . . . In this, the unselfish part of our nature, lies a foundation, even independently of inculcation from without, for the generation of moral feelings.[64]

If he offers the possibility for a morality "independent" of the external world, he is careful to emphasize that it is at least two steps beneath a functioning ethics: a "foundation" for the "generation" of "moral feelings." Plenty can go wrong in those steps, he suggests, offering the case of children as an example. Sedgwick, following in a tradition common to much moral-sense philosophy, had offered children as an example of strong natural moral feelings. Mill counters: "There is no selfishness equal to that of children, as every one who is acquainted with children well knows." Children, though they might possess affection and sympathy, have not yet been taught how to consider something other than pleasure. We must look instead to morality as the result of education: "The time of life at which moral feelings are apt to be strongest, is the age when we cease to be merely members of our own families, and begin to have intercourse with the world" (61). So, even given the foundation of a natural symmetry between an agent's own pleasure or pain, and that of another, it will require a good deal of cultivation to move from that foundation to developed morality.

The way that Mill's story of cultivation is usually told is in terms of his famous discovery of Wordsworth, and his acceptance of the importance of poetic feeling in a deliberative philosophy. This reading has become something of a stock argument for the importance of aesthetic, apolitical culture, along the lines of the triumph of imagination over philosophy in Dickens's *Hard Times*. The basic account of this reading is certainly suggested by the text, which uses the language of religious conversion to move from proposed social action to poetic reflection. Mill, famously, explains the genesis of his depression as both insipid and soul-shaking: "I was in a dull state of nerves . . . one of those moods when what is pleasure at other times, becomes insipid or indifferent; the state, I should think, in which converts to Methodism usually are, when smitten by their first 'conviction of sin'" (80–81). Questioning himself in a moment of near-Wesleyan self-examination,[65] he considers whether, should his political and philosophical goals be realized, he would be happy: "an irrepressible self-consciousness distinctly answered, 'No!'" (81). If he cannot find guaranteed happiness in the happiness of others, though, he does eventually find them in Wordsworth's poetry. This poetry "seemed to be the very culture of feelings, which I was in quest of. . . . From them I seemed to learn what would be the perennial sources of happiness, when all the greater evils of life shall be removed" (89). Raymond Williams sums up the seeming moral of this account: "These paragraphs are now the classical point of reference for those who decide that the desire for social reform is ultimately inadequate, and that art, the 'source of inward joy,' is fortunately always there as an alternative."[66]

Mill's poetic awakening has been frequently rehearsed, but I would argue that its totemic importance in Mill's developmental narrative has had a tendency to be overstated.[67] To be clear, I am not making a diagnostic claim here about what specific readings or moments assisted Mill in his recovery from depression. What is evident, though, in the account he gives of that recovery, is that the reading of Wordsworth represented neither the first stage nor the last. His depression clearly recurs, and it is not poetry alone that helps to lift it. After his discussion of Wordsworth, Mill turns to an account of his developing philosophical and political thought, and then mentions that these intellectual concerns played a large part in his ongoing depression: "during the later returns of my dejection, the doctrine of what is called Philosophical Necessity weighed on my existence like an incubus" (101). I will say more about the meaning of this "philosophical necessity" below, but the first important point to take away is simply that his dejection continued long past his poetic epiphanies. Indeed, he mentions that the experience with Wordsworth, as well as the moment in which he weeps over Marmontel, are offered because they appear to Mill to be "a kind of turning points, marking a definite progress in my mode of thought." Yet such points, he goes on to say, actually give "a very insufficient idea of the quantity of thinking which I carried on respecting a host of subjects during these years." The implication seems to be, then, that these moments of epiphany acted as a sort of surfacing of a much longer process that continued to be ongoing for Mill. And, in fact, the pacing of the chapter seems to back this up. He makes some attempt at dating his mental progress when describing his first grim moment of self-examination (winter of 1826), and his eventual rehabilitation through literary culture (Marmontel in spring or summer of 1827, Wordsworth in autumn of 1828). Yet when he turns to the thinking that seems to underlie all this, he leaves it floating indefinitely out of time: it was something that has been going on "during these years." It is understandable that critical discussions of Mill's recovery have concerned themselves much more with Mill's aesthetic awakening, and said little about the ongoing intellectual progress, since Mill himself seems to push it into the background of his narrative. But it is this vaguely paced development—ongoing, in the background—that Mill offers as primary, with the more specific moments only being surface phenomena of the larger process.

This sort of background process, as we have seen in Goethe and Dickens, is the stuff of developmental narrative, even if it only becomes accessible through its occasional conscious surfacings, in the form of choices already made. In the case of Mill's development, it seems that this sort of "thinking" is actually a re-establishment of Mill's prior thought in terms of communal consensus. What informs his transformation and recovery, in other words, is an account of a rediscovery, not of poetry, but of a sort of conventional wisdom:

> Much of this, it is true, consisted in rediscovering things known to all the world, which I had previously disbelieved or disregarded. But the rediscovery was to me a discovery, giving me plenary possession of the truths, not as traditional platitudes, but fresh from their source; and it seldom failed to place them in some new light, by which they were reconciled with, and seemed to confirm while they modified, the truths less generally known which lay in my early opinions, and in no essential part of which I at any time wavered. All my new thinking only laid the foundation of these more deeply and strongly, while it often removed misapprehension and confusion of ideas which had perverted their effect. (101)

Mill's intellectual development takes the form of returning to certain commonly held ideas that he had once rejected. At the same time, he wants to emphasize that even though others might believe the same truths, they likely only do so out of convention, whereas *he*—by virtue of "truths less generally known," and because he had to discover the conventions for himself—can possess them more completely. And, finally, these newly rediscovered truths—conventional for others, original for Mill—do not contradict the newer truths, but instead more powerfully affirm them. What Mill is narrating here, then, is a moment not only in which one set of ideas is "reconciled" with another but one in which his own education is reconciled with the conventional wisdom of others. And yet, in this moment of reconciliation, Mill does not have to change the essentials of his already existing beliefs, which had, up until this point, kept him separate from others.

It is not his beliefs that shift, then, so much as the foundation for them. The teachings of his father and Bentham were a rejection of conventional wisdom, but in his recovery from despair, Mill comes to discover that he finds greater, and more permanent, truth in those teachings when they are based *on* commonly held notions. The model here is one that we have already seen in the opening discussion of *Miss Marjoribanks*: just as Lucilla Marjoribanks stays Lucilla Marjoribanks but transfers the authority for that identity from her father to her larger community, so Mill keeps the "essential part" of his earlier opinions but transfers the *proving* source of those beliefs to a shared, communal source: "things known to all the world." His development is not so much a change in orientation as it is a rewriting of the past, a refiguring of origin. By choosing to view our past in a certain way, we choose the present set of conditions that have determined us, and thus achieve, if not freedom from all determination, at least some measure of agency in necessity.

This developmental structure, of rewriting past determination in order to find agency in the present, does not just describe the form of Mill's intellectual progress; it also describes the content. Mill chooses only one example of a truth "known to all the world" to illustrate his point: the question of "Philosophical Necessity," and whether he was "scientifically proved to be the helpless slave of antecedent circumstances: as if [his] character and that of all others had been formed for us by agencies beyond our control, and was wholly out of our own power" (101). The conventional wisdom in this case would be some form of naive free will, set against the associationist model of the character that Mill had been educated with.[68] The conflict that Mill faces here is not that he wishes to believes one or the other but rather that he wishes to believe both:

> I often said to myself, what a relief it would be if I could disbelieve the doctrine of the formation of character by circumstances. . . . I said that it would be a blessing if the doctrine of necessity could be believed by all *quoad* the character of others, and disbelieved in regard to their own. (101–2)

Here we see the concerns that we have been discussing thus far in this chapter, the seeming antinomy between the experience of free will and the theoretical strength of a determinism position. Mill's phrasing is similar to

Kant's: "reason *for speculative purposes* finds the road of natural necessity much more traveled and more usable than that of freedom; yet *for practical purposes* the footpath of freedom is the only one on which it is possible to make use of our reason in our conduct."[69] And his solution is similar as well. We recall that Kant attempted to solve this problem by suggesting a form of willing against time, in which our own agency becomes part of the cause of our determination. Without resorting to the language of idealism, Mill suggests something similar: "what is really inspiriting and ennobling in the doctrine of free will, is the conviction that we have real power over the formation of our own character; that our will, by influencing some of our circumstances, can modify our future habits or capabilities of willing" (102). In other words, while we might be shaped by determining circumstances, we have the ability to ourselves become one of those circumstances.

Much of the discussion of these philosophical points in the *Autobiography* is a gloss of a work that he had already written—written before the composition of the *Autobiography*, that is, but after the experiences he is narrating.[70] In his 1843 *System of Logic*, Mill argues that in spite of his rational conviction in the character being formed by circumstances, it is still the case that anyone has the "power to alter his character":

> Its being, in the ultimate resort formed, for him, is not inconsistent with its being formed *by* him as one of the intermediate agents. His character is formed by his circumstances (including among these his particular organization); but his own desire to mould it in a particular way is one of those circumstances, and by no means one of the least influential.[71]

The intellectual solution that Mill offers for his depression, then, is not so much a turn away from social progress to art as it is a turn away from the sense of determination being something that was done *to* him, and toward the idea that he also had the power to take part in his own determination. It is in this possibility that he is able to locate a feeling that he classifies as freedom: "This feeling, of being able to modify our own character, *if we wish*, is itself the feeling of moral freedom which we are conscious of" (841).

This is all dependent, of course, on having the "will" or the "wish"—Mill emphasizes the conditional in both cases—to change. Mill brings up the question of whether or not such a will is itself determined, and answers the question in rather unsatisfying fashion: "A person who does not wish to alter his character, cannot be the person who is supposed to feel discouraged or paralysed by thinking himself unable to do it" (840). The desire to change oneself and the ability to change oneself come out to the same thing. And while this is still subject to a certain amount of determinism, at least it is not the case for everyone; at least, we might infer, it is not the case for John Stuart Mill. The proof that someone has the capacity for "moral freedom," as Mill calls it—and remember, not everyone does—is that he might feel "discouraged or paralysed": "the depressing effect of the fatalist doctrine can only be felt where there *is* a wish to do what the doctrine represents as impossible" (841). He would use these same terms, in describing the doctrine's effects on him, when he drafted the first six chapters of the *Autobiography* a decade or so later: a "depressing and paralysing influence" which "ceased altogether to be discouraging" (101). The order of influence here is a bit convoluted, so it is worth specifying that the language of the *Autobiography* quotes that of the textually prior *Logic*, even if the *Logic* describes the lived experience that inspired the *Autobiography*. In any event, what is certainly clear is that Mill conflates his own depression with the very condition of possibility for "moral freedom."

From this perspective, then, Mill's account of his depression in the *Autobiography* takes on a rather different dimension. It is not only an indictment of his father and Bentham's philosophy, one that will be healed with a proper dose of literary culture. Instead, it is a mark of freedom: a redefinition of the grounds of one's circumstantial determination. It is through the narration of his mental crisis, in other words, that Mill is able to assert his own role as one of the "circumstances" that formed his own character. To understand how he might be able to do so, furthermore, requires that he rediscover "things known to all the world." The process of achieving a "properly cultivated moral nature," lies in recognizing that agents have the potential to become fully developed individuals only when they realize—or, rather, actively, willfully recognize—that the community that shapes them also includes them as a member.

CHAPTER 5

THE LARGE NOVEL AND THE LAW OF LARGE NUMBERS: *DANIEL DERONDA* AND THE COUNTERINTUITIVE

R
ealist novel narrative, then, works to bridge the space between the internal and the external, the individual and the social, by suggesting that there never really was a gap in the first place. The force experienced as driving the novel forward becomes something associated with the reader: the production of the absent backstory leading toward Oliver's transcendence, or the membership in the sensed community that motivates David. Novels' narrative processes "feel right," in other words, because they work toward an identification of the external world of realist depiction and the internal sensible world. They work, in other words, through ratification of the intuitive: making what *ought* to happen into what *does* happen. As the previous two chapters, on *David Copperfield* and the *Bildungsroman*, demonstrate, the means by which this intuition is implied is often through the suggestion of belonging in a community of tacit consensus.

But what if you cannot rejoin a community? This chapter deals with the counterintuitive: the ending that "feels wrong," or that does not work out as it seems it should. Certainly, this could mean many things, from a poorly constructed novel to the (often banal) pedagogy implied by naturalist accident. The form of the counterintuitive that structures much of George Eliot's *Daniel Deronda*, though, and which enacts the novel's stern moral lesson, develops from Eliot's more social concerns. Eliot, throughout her writing career, worked with an idea of narrative intuition, and formal morality, connected with the model I sketched out above: a working out of the identity between an individual and the larger group. In *Deronda*, though, with its consistent concentration on ideas of probability and statistical significance, we see a conceptual shift in Eliot's thinking about the relation of the one and the many.[1] In short: though the larger workings of human interaction indicate that a certain state of affairs shall certainly come about at the largest levels, this offers no indication of how or when this might resolve in the individual case.

Deronda does, of course resolve, after a fashion—but it famously defers its resolution to the future: "It is better—it shall be better because I have known you."[2] Here, after seventy chapters of arduous moral education, *Daniel Deronda*'s narrator seems content to let Gwendolen Harleth's final line speak for itself. The novel reproduces Gwendolen's letter to Daniel verbatim, and moves on without comment to a description of his preparations for leaving England. But given this line's status as the final testament of Eliot's fraught portrayal of her heroine, its meaning remains rather opaque. The dash in the middle of the sentence: does Gwendolen catch herself overstating the case and rephrase? Or is she saying that it—whatever "it" may be—is now better, and that is because "it" will be better with her in the future? Either way, any satisfaction that the reader may take in these lines is predicated on the belief that things will, in fact, be better for Gwendolen in the future. Gwendolen herself shall become a better person, as Daniel has assured her she would: "one of the best of women, who make others glad that they were born." The indecision over tenses in this line mirrors an ambiguity in the novel's resolution, which takes out a sort of narrative loan against its own indefinite future. At some point, though we do not know when, it *shall* be better for Gwendolen, she *shall* make us happy we were born. And from that, we can find resolution in the novel now.

It is not uncommon, of course, for novels to have forward-looking conclusions. What is notable about *Deronda*'s ending, though, is how little excitement, even interest, Gwendolen seems to show for this future. This does makes some narrative sense; after all, her husband has died, her wealth is gone, and she has been rejected by the man that she thought she would marry. There is a sense of inevitability to this future, emphasized by Gwendolen's recurrent use of the word "shall" in novel's final chapters. "I shall live," she tells her mother, "I shall be better" (807). Compare these lines to her earlier "self-confident" statement: "I will do something. I will be something. Things will come right" (226). At the novel's end, the verb "will," which in proper Victorian usage had the meaning of "wish," is replaced by "shall," which carried the meaning of a "command or obligation."[3] The novel's conclusion relies on a necessary future for Gwendolen—but it is one that will come about regardless of Gwendolen's agency or desire. This neutrality finds a corollary in the reader's experience. On the one hand, the reference to a better future is necessary for the novel's conclusion. On the other hand, the ending does not seem to prompt a desire to see this future realized, better though it may be. The novel's resolution, that is, rests on a sense that even though things are not yet as they should be, it is enough simply to say that they will be. Narrative resolution does not require literary realization of this future better state.

In this chapter, I will argue that Eliot's developing view of the relation between the individual and the larger social group forced her, in *Deronda*, to reconsider the desire to see a better state of affairs realized, and thus to reconsider the connection between moral feeling and narrative structure. The novel's depiction of Gwendolen in particular moves away from the structure common to much of nineteenth-century fiction—*David Copperfield* offered a good example, as does much of Eliot's earlier work—in which the narrative impulse is toward a resolution of internal moral intuition and external reality. *Deronda* instead imagines two nearly separate realms: in one, we find individual characters and actions; in the other, the large-scale movements of social aggregates.

As this last term might indicate, I will be arguing that *Deronda* shows an increasing interest and unease in the counterintuitive explanatory power of statistics and probability, and particularly in one of their key concepts: the so-called law of large numbers. The precise meaning of the term, introduced by the French mathematician Siméon-Denis Poisson in 1835 is the subject of philosophical and mathematical debate, but its intuitive meaning is clear enough. Given a sufficient number of trials, events will conform to their probabilities, even if every event is itself random. If we flip a coin enough times, in other words, eventually the results will end up fifty-fifty—but that does not tell us anything about the outcome of any individual toss. Critics such as Douglas Lane Patey, Neil Hertz, and Leland Monk have shown the ways in which understandings of chance influenced the novel form throughout the eighteenth and nineteenth centuries;[4] what is distinctive about Eliot's work in *Deronda*, though, is that it sees laws that operate at the large scale coexisting with unconditioned autonomy at the individual scale—yet with an insurmountable breach between them. Contemporary thought on this issue affected Victorian understandings of a host of concerns that reads like a list of *Deronda*'s motifs: gambling, physics, population, the progress of history. Eliot's examination of these themes throughout the novel shows a radical departure from her earlier work, with its emphasis on the interdependence between individual elements and the larger group.

Perhaps the most telling way in which Eliot examines the law of large numbers, though, is through the large novel, *Deronda* itself. For the novel presents us with a wide variety of individuals, seemingly detached from one another, and yet together moving under the sway of the narrative itself. *Deronda* has produced debate between critics who believed the novel's separate plots could be easily pulled apart[5] and those who followed George Eliot's insistence on the necessary unity of a novel in which "everything . . . is related to everything else."[6] In this chapter, I will suggest that Eliot's statistical interests offer the means for seeing a novel in which these two impulses are unified. One spin of the roulette wheel is utterly independent of the next, and yet both, together with a suitably large number of subsequent spins, will tend toward a unified outcome. The larger narrative structure of the novel can offer a unity that is not apparent, or even particularly meaningful, as a way of describing the novel's individual subplots and characters. Such a rethinking of the relationship between narrative and its elements also requires a reconsideration of narrative's moral sensibility. For if an individual's moral intuitions describe a different sort of experience than that described by the large novel as a whole, we cannot expect the novel to realize those intuitions. The "ought" of the individual will not become the final "is" of the large novel.

These are difficult ideas to work with, for Eliot and for readers both. For that reason, I will follow Eliot through the different models that she offers—almost experimentally, it seems—to help illustrate these ideas: statistical laws, populations, thermodynamics, and, most importantly, gambling. I will argue that each of these ideas offers Eliot new ways of explaining the relation between part and whole in her fiction. I will hold these against Eliot's conception of the Jews in her novel, which I take to be a holdover of ideas of community more familiar from her previous novels. Even in this case, it will turn out that Eliot's imagining of the Jews is based just as much on ideas of large and small numbers as it is on culture or religion. To set the stage for this argument, though, it will be useful first to look briefly at more familiar novelistic trajectories and their means of representing the relation between the individual and the larger group.

CALCULUS OF THE *BILDUNGSROMAN*: DIFFERENTIATION AND INTEGRATION

Gwendolen ends the novel "forsaken" and alone (805). The hope that the novel offers for the future is not simply that she will become better, but what this means: that she will improve the lives of "others" (810). The actual moment of this resolution is suspended in the novel's future, but even the promise of a resolution of the lonely self with others enacts the conventions that underlies so much of the novel: those of the *Bildungsroman*. *Deronda*, as a novel of moral education, follows the conventions of the *Bildungsroman*—until the conclusion, which defers the resolution typical of the form. In this section, I will discuss the form of the *Bildungsroman*, and particularly Eliot's own *Middlemarch*, to show that the methods usually employed for narrative resolution rely implicitly on a method of *induction*, building up from a single character to represent the larger social group. Such an inductive connection between the individual and the large number is, ultimately, the sort of resolution that *Deronda* refuses to offer to Gwendolen.

Traditionally, the resolution of the *Bildungsroman* depends on the protagonist's ability to recognize herself in the social world. For Georg Lukács, in *The Theory of the Novel*, this recognition is the essential move that makes "reconciliation between interiority and reality" possible.[7] Lukács's argument proceeds along straightforward dialectical lines. First step: the individual—let us call her Dorothea—realizes that she is separate from the larger world. Second step: the individual is set in opposition the external world. Third step: the individual realizes that the external world is social in nature, made of other individuals who are each in a similar state of opposition. What started out as difference, then, becomes similarity and, ultimately, the means of what Lukács calls "reconciliation." He describes this last step, in which we realize that reality is in fact "society," a mass "community" of similar souls:

> Such community is not the result of people being naïvely and naturally rooted in a specific social structure, not of any solidarity of kinship (as in the ancient epics), nor is it a mystical experience of community, a sudden illumination which rejects the lonely individuality as something ephemeral, static and sinful; it is achieved by personalities, previously lonely and confined within their own selves, adapting and accustoming themselves to one another; it is the fruit of a rich and enriching resignation, the crowning of a process of education, a maturity attained by struggle and effort. (133)

Lukács's assumption, then, is that a resolution between internal and external can only come about if the external is itself a collection of other human beings, all with the same goal. The world may be external, but the protagonist is already part of it; successful development lies in realizing this. A final reconciliation with the world, when it comes, is compromise on a grand scale, for it involves not only the protagonist but also all of the other characters who make up her world.

Whether Lukács describes the English *Bildungsroman* accurately in the general case, his formulation seems tailor-made to describe Eliot, and *Middlemarch* in particular.[8] The novel starts off with Dorothea seeing her moral and intellectual ambitions thwarted by rural opinions and limited possibilities. Though she might have the potential to be a modern Saint Theresa, we are led to wonder, as she does, "How can one ever do anything nobly Christian, living among people with such petty thoughts?"[9] She is not just any person, or just any woman—as the novel's protagonist, she steps forward from the general type and becomes an individual. For a description of the rest of the novel's process, I defer to Catherine Gallagher's concise account:

> As Dorothea herself is realized by departures from type, so too does she learn to realize others by imagining their particularity instead of pressing them into categories. From a dark night of the soul that all

readers of the novel will recall, the heroine awakens to a sympathetic understanding of errancy itself. She finds what heroism is left over for women in the modern world by an empathetic envisioning of the suffering of the very people who have just wounded her, Rosamond and Will Ladislaw. In short, realizing in others what the narrator calls "equivalent centers of self" is the supreme ethical act in Eliot's novels.[10]

The drive toward an undefined heroism that particularized Dorothea at the novel's beginning, then, reaches its goal through the realization that others—even those others who were seen as the oppositional forces that the heroism had to overcome—are particularized in their own right.[11] Gallagher's reference to Rosamond and Will is particularly useful here, since it is through her rapprochements, amiable and amatory respectively, with Rosamond and Will that Dorothea is able to fulfill some form of her heroic ambitions.[12] She does this, of course, by marrying Will, and moving to the city as a politician's wife. This conclusion, with its assertion of nuclear-familial roles as narrative conclusion, is famously unsatisfying for many critics. It is no more satisfying for many of the inhabitants of Middlemarch, who think it "a pity that so substantive and rare a creature should have been absorbed into the life of another, and be only known in a certain circle as a wife and mother" (836). But this is the nature of reconciliation in the *Bildungsroman*: resignation in the face of a world of other people or, as *Middlemarch*'s narrator describes it, "the mixed result of a young and noble impulse struggling amidst the conditions of an imperfect social state" (838).

Satisfying or not, *Middlemarch*'s conclusion demonstrates not only an ethics of individuation but also a narrative drive toward reintegration. This, as Lukács describes it, is central to the genre. The marriage plot offers the most obvious example: the protagonist, having removed him- or herself from the nuclear family for the sake of particularization (not just a Bennet, but *Elizabeth*) ultimately returns to and reasserts that structure. *Middlemarch* takes the larger step of integrating Dorothea into that unrepresentable collection of individuals: the city, London. The language is first that of personal disintegration: her "full nature" breaks into "channels"; her effect is "incalculably diffusive" (838). Yet that disintegration only leads to greater reintegration. We lose Dorothea, but we gain a society that is full of Dorotheas—"the number who have lived faithfully a hidden life"—and shows traces of Dorothea's influence throughout.

What I want to stress here is that a novel like *Middlemarch* solves the problem of the unrepresentability of a society of individuals through a process of induction.[13] Dorothea learned from her own example that other people had equivalent internal lives, but we do not see those. We just assume—as Dorothea must as well—that they are *like* her. The extreme case of this comes in a redemption of the anonymity of the city through the claim that, in some sense, everyone there *is* Dorothea. The narrative drive toward reintegration proceeds along inductive lines: we can represent society through the individual case. But this is not just an expedient means to represent something that is difficult to put into words; it is also the novel's narrative resolution. That is to say, the plot that follows Dorothea's desires to balance her ideals with the possibilities of the world is resolved by the realization of the similarity of Dorothea to others. For that reason, society is no longer a mysterious exterior presence, because we know what it looks like; it looks like Dorothea. The novel's final "reconciliation between interiority and reality" thus requires a society that we can understand the same way that the novel's protagonist understands it: as built up from the individual case. The traditional *Bildungsroman*, as exemplified by *Middlemarch*, thus shows an implicit reliance on the ability to represent society as compiled inductively from individual units. This is not the case in *Deronda*; there is little sense at the end of *Deronda* of an England that can in any way be understood inductively through the figure of Gwendolen. Hence her interiority remains at a divide from the social reality of others. Deronda, on the other hand, certainly does succeed in his reintegration back into the Jewish community, to an almost hyperbolic extent. But this successful resolution is not simply a result of Deronda's moral character or Eliot's romantic beliefs in his messianic potential. It also offers an example of how reintegration and its attendant narrative resolution require the novel to build groups up from their individual elements—a representational strategy, we shall see, that is closely tied to the novel's imagining of large and small numbers.

A COUNTABLE RACE

Reintegration is denied to Gwendolen, as I have said, but not to Daniel. Or rather, it is not denied to Daniel once he discovers that he is Jewish. This discovery of identity leads to an ending similar to Dorothea's, in that they both leave the novels for an unrepresentable place, where acts of heroism are possible. Of course, the endings strike rather different tones. A pre-existing London requires a compromise that tempers Dorothea's conclusion, while Daniel's messianic role as the founder of a new state offers the possibility of an uncompromised heroism.[14] Dorothea is a moderately successful Teresa, while Daniel at least has the capacity to be a wholly successful Moses. In fact, as George Levine has suggested, Daniel and Mordecai are the only characters in Eliot's work that are allowed such heroism: "in all the novels but *Daniel Deronda*, heroism takes the shape of resignation exclusively."[15] Even Mordecai's death, at the novel's end, is presented as a triumphant return to the fold, as Daniel and Mirah embrace him while he utters the *shema*: "the confession of the divine Unity, which for long generations has been on the lips of the dying Israelite" (811). The possibility of reintegration, in the Jewish section of the novel, would seem to be a largely spiritual business.

Yet, at least part of the success of reintegration in the Jewish plot derives from a rather more profane consideration: there are simply not that many Jews. It is much easier to integrate into a society, or conceptually build a society from an individual, if the society is smaller in number. This term, "smaller," is more complicated than it may at first appear; in Eliot's literary imagination, I will argue, *any* conception of a number is in some sense a small number, insofar as it allows for inductive representation. Recall the conclusion of *Middlemarch*, and Eliot's description of society as understood inductively through Dorothea: "the number who have lived faithfully a hidden life." Even though she is not specific about what that "number" might be, the fact that society has been built up from the individual case requires that it be seen as a multiple of the individual. It is thus presented as being made up of discrete units, and not as a continuum.

Eliot consistently imagines Jewish society, diasporic though it might be, in terms of such numbers. Mordecai, at his most messianic, makes repeated numerical reference: "Thousands on thousands of our race . . ." (527); "The heritage of Israel is beating in the pulses of millions" (536); "Ours is an inheritance that has never ceased to quiver in millions of human frames" (536); "that I may keep in mind the spiritual poverty of the Jewish millions" (571). Such lines are understandable enough in light of a Zionist rhetoric which would use population numbers as a way of drawing unity across political borders. Still, what is notable in *Deronda* is how unique such language is to the novel's Jews. With only rare exception, numbers serve three purposes in the novel. First, they mark short, easily conceptualized times and distances, such as "fifty miles" or "seven weeks." Second, and most frequently, numbers are used for monetary amounts: dowries and inheritances. And, finally, numbers are used to count Jews. When Deronda first wanders through London's Jewish quarters in search of Mirah's family and comes across Ezra Cohen's shop, the narrator points out, "There might be a hundred Ezra Cohens lettered above shop-windows, but Deronda had not seen them" (382). Embedded in this line is a reminder of the providence that trails Deronda throughout the novel—what are the odds?—but its quantification also allows for that providence to pass without too much comment. A hundred Ezra Cohens, after all, is not *so* many.

Or, to be more precise: it is not a question of whether "hundred," "thousand," or "million" signify large or small numbers of people, or even whether they signify any specific number at all. Rather they signify a characteristic of a group of people: that it is *countable*. The term comes from the mathematician Georg Cantor, in a series of works written throughout the 1870s—the first published in 1874, the same year *Deronda* began publication—that are considered the point of inception of modern set theory. A set is countable if its elements can be put in one-to-one correspondence with some subset of the integers (one, two, three . . .). This is little more than a rigorous definition of what we already mean by counting. What made Cantor's work a breakthrough is that he showed that a set could be "countably infinite" if its elements could be placed in correspondence with the infinite set of all integers.[16] Such a set can be *counted*, in other words—even if that counting should go on forever. This is to be distinguished from "larger" infinities, such as the "number" of points on a continuous line. This latter sort of infinity, known as the "continuum," is not countable; choose any two points on a line, and you will never be able to count all the points between them. The significance of this distinction for the purposes of our discussion is that it suggests that a group may be understood as countable, even if the actual count of its elements is unknown or unknowably large. Of course, there is not an infinite number of Jews, nor of gentiles. But the point is less about the specific numbers and more about the way that the social body as a whole is imagined. In this sense, there is not just a difference of degree— not just *more* gentiles—but also of kind. The English group is of a different, larger sort; as far as their representation in *Daniel Deronda* is concerned, they cannot be counted at all.[17]

In fact, to be enumerated among the English, even metaphorically, is to be removed from the larger group: "We English are a miscellaneous race, and any chance fifty of us will present many varieties of animal architecture or facial ornament; but it must be admitted that our prevailing expression is not that of a lively, impassioned race" (102). The English are most English, in other words, at the level of "prevailing" societal characteristics. To enumerate—in this case, the number is fifty—is to see the particularities that do not fit the generalization. Eliot's method of imagining what it means to be English seems to be based on going beyond such particularities, through the statistical cancellation of exceptions. Any enumerable group of English individuals will be just that: individuals, possessed of "miscellaneous . . . varieties." Now, fifty is a small number when compared with Mordecai's "Jewish millions." Isn't it possible that given a larger number, of the sort that Mordecai uses, the English could be represented in countable fashion as well? Possible, perhaps—but in *Deronda*, we find that this is not the case. There is no use of enumeration to imply the great number of the English. A countable group, whether fifty English or a thousand Jews, is of a different qualitative type than that which the novel imagines for the English as a whole.

Gwendolen's failure of reintegration at the novel's conclusion, then, can be traced to the noninductive way in which the novel imagines the English, in contrast to the way the English are imagined in *Middlemarch*, or the way the Jews are imagined in *Deronda*. In *Middlemarch*, as we have seen, induction succeeds; a "number" of Dorotheas is built up from the individual case

and, for the sake of representability, can offer that individual case as synecdoche. The same process is evident in Deronda's discovery of his Jewish
identity. The first time he goes into the Jewish quarter, he is in search of one
Ezra Cohen, and discovers two Ezra Cohens, which offers the possibility
of "a hundred Ezra Cohens." When one of those Ezras (Mordecai) explains
why he lives with the other Ezra, he says it so that he "may keep in mind
the spiritual poverty of the Jewish millions." Jewish consciousness, at its
most high-flown, is still built from the individual case. Daniel enters the
Jewish quarter to find Ezra Cohen, and he finds a nation: a nation that can
be expressed as a million Ezra Cohens. No matter how large a number may
be, it can be made up from—or broken down into—smaller numbers. Thus
we have, for example, the almost interchangeable usage of "thousands on
thousands" and "millions."

Mordecai's frequent recourse to numerical language, colloquial though
it may be, reflects Eliot's own method of imagining the Jews. Her notes
for the novel refer on four different occasions to population numbers: how
many Jews in Russia, Poland, Austria, France, Ireland, and other coun-
tries. She revises her own earlier numbers—1,300,000 in Russia instead of
200,000—and even attaches a clipped article titled "Jewish Population of
the World" to the inside front cover of one of her notebooks.[18] Repeatedly,
she notes the world's Jewish population, finally settling on seven million.
We see this number again in her later essay, "The Modern Hep! Hep! Hep!,"
when she refers to "the seven millions scattered from east to west."[19]

This insistence on Jewish enumerability is not unique to Eliot. In fact,
part of the reason that Eliot was able to find so many ready numbers is
that, as Ian Hacking points out, "the number and distribution of Jews was a
regular topic" in nineteenth-century discussion.[20] It would not be going too
far to suggest that this interest mounted almost to a fixation, among anti-
Semites, philo-Semites, and ostensibly neutral social scientists alike. On the
anti-Semitic side, population numbers were being used in Prussia to stir up
fears of mass Jewish immigration.[21] Meanwhile, statistics played a large part
in the emerging "'respectable' scientific racism" of the nineteenth century,
which, after emancipation, frequently focused on classifying, enumerating,
and pointing out the social place of European Jewry.[22] In response to such
social-scientific objectification, European Jews "became *subjects*, or partici-
pants, as well as objects within the social sciences, empowered to construct
their own narratives around the statistics about the Jewish present and future."[23] In Germany, Salomon Neumann published *The Fable of Mass Jewish
Immigration: A Chapter in Prussian Statistics*, to refute the fears of Jews pour-
ing over the German borders. In the Hebrew press, articles were published
with titles such "Counting the Sons of Israel" (in *Ha-Asif*), "The Counting of
the Sons of Israel" (in *Ha-Tsefirah*), and "The Wisdom and Benefits of Num-
bering (Statistics)" (also in *Ha-Tsefirah*).[24] In England, Joseph Jacobs—a great

fan of Eliot, and deeply influenced by *Daniel Deronda*—published papers such as "Studies in Jewish Statistics" and "The Comparative Distribution of Jewish Ability." His work details everything from the relative birthrates of Jews and Christians in Tuscany,[25] to the incidences of "genius" and "lunacy" among Jews.[26] A newspaper article in 1850 suggested "that there are hardly more than from 4,000,000 to 5,000,000 Jews in the whole world," while one in 1885 offered the absurdly specific "6,377,602."[27] Both broke the number down into smaller national populations, and both bore the same name: "Statistics of the Jews."[28]

The evident motivations and countermotivations here make it difficult to assign a single root cause for the Jewish numerical obsession, but Eliot seems to have been particularly drawn to the way in which these discussions allowed for an inductive view of society. These discussions led to an image of a society that could be built from individuals, precisely because they were concerned with literally producing a new society, in the form of a Jewish homeland. As Mitchell Bryan Hart puts it, "Jewish statistics was, conceptually, the child of Jewish nationalism."[29] For Hart, this follows from the observation that "the creation of a vital and viable 'Jewish culture' . . . was an essential condition for, and component of, Jewish national life" (29). The nature of such a "Jewish culture," though, had to be compiled from the nature of the Jews, themselves. One commentator in *Ha-Tsefirah* poses the question: "What will the builder do without materials, without tools? He was not given straw, and was told to make his own bricks! There are no statistics for Israel. There is no one who is is gathering materials for building."[30] This trope, of statistics providing the "bricks" for building a new state, was repeated with only slight variation throughout the period, and into the early twentieth century: "We must know with greater precision about the national material with which we have to work. We need an exact anthropological, biological, economic and intellectual statistic of the Jewish people."[31] For Eliot, and for Mordecai, this "greater precision" is not as necessary as the ability to imagine, in some comprehensive way, the nature of Jewish life, in its various individual facets. For this, the model was Leopold Zunz. Zunz, whose work Eliot quotes in the epigraph to chapter 42,[32] had written his *Outline of Future Statistics of the Jews* (*Grundlinien zu einer küntfigen Statistik der Juden*) in 1823 as part of his attempt to develop a new "Jewish Science." His statistics were not numerical in nature, being instead based on the German notion of the "science of states."[33] As we shall see in the next section, though, this science would soon become numerical. Indeed there was enough of a continuum between Zunz's *Statistik* and later statistics that Neumann would later in the century dedicate his tables of Jewish birthrates to Zunz.

Nineteenth-century discussions of the Jews, then, imagined a culture—especially insofar as it was a nascent *national* culture—that had the

characteristic of countability. Zunz, whom Eliot cites, is an important example of this, in his belief that a *Wissenschaft des Judentums* must contain a
Statistik der Juden. For Eliot, as for Zunz, the two are joined together. This is
perhaps best encapsulated in one of the many notes Eliot makes on population in her notebooks: "7,000,000 יהודים."[34] Here Eliot departs from the tool
of her trade, Roman letters, to write out "seven million *yehudim*" ("Jews") in
Arabic numbers and Hebrew script. These appended symbols of countability and culture serve as a concise statement of Eliot's imagining of the Jews.
The ability to imagine a Jewish community, after the fashion of the rural
communities from her earlier novels, depends on the ability to imagine the
community as built up from its individual elements.

Surprisingly, then, it is precisely in the novel's plot of foreignness that
we find ourselves on native Eliotic ground. That is to say, it is in the Jewish
part of the novel that we find the organic principles of society that have
been consistently associated—and rightly so—with Eliot. Drawn from the
social theory of Comte and Spencer and the physiological theory of Lewes,
Eliot's organicism is based on a strong interdependence between individual
and society.[35] As Eliot puts it in one essay, "society stands before us like that
wonderful piece of life, the human body, with all its various parts depending on one another."[36] The organism in question need not always be the
human body, but the essential idea of society as a powerful system of mutual dependencies provides one of the most characteristic markers of Eliot's
work. As Steven Marcus puts it:

> Society, in [Eliot's] novels, is represented as a living whole, composed
> or articulated of differentiated members, each of which fulfills or pos-
> sesses a special function. As a consequence, the individual person is
> not separable from the human whole; and in turn the social whole
> is equally dependent on each individual person, since each contrib-
> utes to the common life. Society and individual persons, then, are not
> separable or distinct phenomena, but are in reality the collective and
> distributive aspects of the same circumstance or thing; one expresses
> the group as a whole, the other the members that compose it.[37]

The organic metaphor requires, then, not only that we understand the individual in terms of the social whole but also that we understand the social
whole in terms of the individual. Marcus's phrasing lingers on this essential
reversibility; the particular and the whole are the "collective and distribu-
tive aspects of the same . . . thing" only when we can work from one to the
other. The metaphor obtains, in other words, only when society is seen to
be a collection—even a seemingly infinite collection—of individuals. The
"pulses of millions" are each separate, and yet together they produce community: "the heritage of Israel."

As I have been arguing, though, Eliot's conception of the English in *Daniel Deronda* is of a quite different sort, with the result that the commonplace of the organic seems a good deal less apt. While the organic in Eliot is based on the mutual reference of the part and the whole to one another, we have in the case of the English, a part that, in being removed from the whole, is contrary to it. Recall that it was not a specific fifty that would disprove the general case, but "any chance fifty." In the case of Grandcourt, one is enough. Upon Grandcourt's first appearance in the novel, the narrator offers far more minute physical description of him—height, hairline, hair color, even the angle of his whiskers—than of any other characters in the novel, save the central two. She then launches on a long sentence that *seems* to be further description but turns out to be quite the opposite:

> The correct Englishman, drawing himself up from his bow into rigidity, assenting severely, and seeming to be in a state of internal drill, suggests a suppressed vivacity, and may be suspected of letting go with some violence when he is released from parade; but Grandcourt's bearing had no rigidity, it inclined rather to the flaccid. (111)

The sentence's conclusion may provoke a giggle—did *Eliot* write that?—but it also likely provokes some semantic surprise. For it is difficult not to read the sentence as opening with a continuation of the steady description of Grandcourt, as if it read "*This* correct Englishman." Grandcourt, after all, is nothing if not "correct," and "rigidity" recalls the word "perpendicular," already used twice in the preceding sentences to describe him; he is in the process of introducing himself to Gwendolen, and no doubt straightening himself from a bow. The sentence, until the semicolon, seems to simply utilize a descriptive noun in place of the male pronoun or proper name: "Grandcourt, drawing himself up from his bow. . . ." Her description thus inherits the dim outlines of character, even though, as we learn at the end of the sentence, she is not talking about any individual at all. She is rather describing the English *homme moyen*, the embodiment of the English "prevailing expression."[38] Thus, to backtrack on my earlier claims a bit, it is not quite correct to say that the English are not conceived as a group made up of individuals. They are so conceived, after a fashion, but the individual in question is not one that exists. He is instead a statistical aggregate, the embodiment of the continuum. Any actual individual, or "any chance fifty" individuals, will become so only by their negation of this figure. Thus, when Grandcourt steps forth from this bowing aggregate, he does not, to use Marcus's terms, express the group as a whole. Instead, by virtue of his individuation, he is separated from it.

Separation through characterization, though, is a necessary part of novelistic narrative; the problem, as Gwendolen will discover, is how difficult it is to reinsert oneself into the group. As much as Eliot might imagine the possibilities that the Jews—and their conceptually smaller number—might offer, she seems to worry over the problem of the English one and many throughout the novel. Take, for example, the young Anna Gascoigne, and her desire to leave England and go with her brother to Canada: a sort of juvenile version of the Deronda impulse, minus the nation-building. The novel suggests that this desire was really an opposition to the trappings of English feminine life: "gloves, and crinoline, and having to talk when I am taken out to dinner—and all that" (88). The narrator then offers a self-conscious attempt to reintegrate Anna back into the general course of English events:

> I like to mark the time, and connect the course of individual lives with the historic stream, for all classes of thinkers. This was the period when the broadening of gauge in crinolines seemed to demand an agitation for the general enlargement of churches, ballrooms, and vehicles. But Anna Gascoigne's figure would only allow the size of skirt manufactured for young ladies of fourteen. (88)

The quote opens with a statement of narratorial predilection. But the narrator is not simply explaining what she likes to do, as if readers have never seen it before. *Deronda*, after all, was released to a public that knew what to expect from an Eliot novel, and this sort of drawing back is a stock Eliotic move.[39] "I like," then, should be read as making reference to what she would normally do in this situation: "connect the course of individual lives with the historic stream." And, indeed, that is what seems to be happening; this is the age not only of large crinolines but also of the very material effects that fashion would have on "churches, ballrooms, and vehicles," that is, the worlds of religion, leisure, and transportation. These lines, at first, read like a primer on Eliot's understanding of the individual in history. We move, in short order, from Anna's peevish comment about crinolines to the nearly world-historical. Or, rather, we would, if it were not for that final "But." That connection of Anna with the historic stream is what the narrator would normally do, and it is what she likes to do. The only problem is that the clothes do not fit the individual.

Eliot's more familiar methods may work with Jews—and, as I have suggested, she may have chosen the Jews in part because they allowed her to imagine some continued existence of the organic in the contemporary world—but they do not work for the relation of the English individual and that larger continuous "stream." Both elements are there for Eliot, but there is now a breach between them. The group is somehow too large to be countable; it cannot be built up from its individual elements. Conversely, the individual elements cannot be extracted from the group, other than as exceptions. The necessary reversibility of the organic model, upon which rests so much of its explanatory utility, does not obtain. How then to describe the English? Eliot's thought requires a new model, one that offers a way of describing the way groups work in the realm of large numbers. That model will prove to be statistics.

ELIOT'S DEMON

When Zunz's words open the novel's chapter 42—the chapter in which Mordecai most explicitly states the novel's Zionist ideals to a pub full of amateur "philosophers"—there is no mention of his *Statistik der Juden*. Yet the very sort of statistical questions that Zunz was himself considering quickly assert themself in the chapter. In fact, the entire evening's discussion occurs under the sign of statistical thought. When Mordecai and Daniel first enter the pub, they are greeted by a man named Miller, who catches them up to speed with the discussion so far:

> This is what I call one of our touch and go nights, sir. . . . Sometimes we stick pretty close to the point. But to-night our friend Pash, there, brought up the law of progress, and we got on statistics; then Lilly, there, saying we knew well enough before counting that in the same state of society the same sort of things would happen, and it was no more wonder that quantities should remain the same than that qualities should remain the same, for in relation to society numbers are qualities—the number of drunkards is a quality in society—the numbers are an index to the qualities, and give us no instruction, only setting us to consider the causes of difference between social states. . . . (524)

This speech is a mouthful, to be sure, and the fact that it is prefaced as a wandering away from "the point"—whatever that might be—seems designed to make Mordecai's single-minded purpose stand out in bas relief. This does not mean, however, that the "statistics" that they had "got on" before Deronda and Mordecai's entrance should be read simply as intellectual riffing. Instead the discussion that precedes Mordecai's pronouncements offers a glimpse of Eliot's understanding of the more intellectually daring elements of European thought at the time. The fact that most readers will forget the specifics of the "phlegmatic discussion" under the weight of Mordecai's "high-pitched solemnity" (538) allows her the possibility, further, of offering these statistical ideas in a tentative fashion. Still, it is these statistical notions, and the different ways that they address the nature of large collective bodies, that will come to offer an alternative model for imagining the English in the novel.

Miller's summary of the statistical discussion actually offers a good introduction to the ideas that were developing at the time. One thing that should be noted here is that statistics are *not* understood in the sense that we today would understand them: as an abstract science of error approximation. Instead, the quantitative content of statistical discussion acts as a means of qualitatively describing society: "in relation to society numbers are qualities—the number of drunkards is a quality in society—the numbers are an index to the qualities." The "numbers," then, are not important, in and of themselves, so much as they are a means to an end, "an index of qualities." In fact, as statistics developed, numbers were a relatively late addition. Statistics, at the end of the eighteenth and well into the nineteenth century, was the province not of statisticians but rather of *statists*: those who investigated the nature of the political state.[40] This was particularly true in Germany, where statistics continued to be taught in this form well into the nineteenth century. The science became more strictly quantitative with the rapid increase—detailed throughout Foucault's work—in census data, medical records, and police reports in the eighteenth and nineteenth centuries. From these developments, the statists had their raw material. Population could indicate the state's power or health, suicide rates could indicate its overall unhappiness or pathology, and so on.[41] Even as the science became numerical, in other words, it was still a science that was first and foremost about the political and social body.

Statistics in nineteenth-century England and France, though, were not just descriptive; they became prescriptive and, often controversially, predictive.[42] John Sinclair, who wrote the twenty-one-volume *Statistical Account of Scotland* at the end of the eighteenth century, offers the following account of the nature of German statistics and how he believed that his work had improved on them:

> Many people were at first surprised at my using the words, *Statistics* and *Statistical* . . . . In the course of a very extensive tour, through the northern parts of Europe, which I happened to take in 1786, I found that in Germany they were engaged in a species of political inquiry to which they had given the name of *Statistics*. By statistical is meant in Germany an inquiry for the purpose of ascertaining the political strength of a country, or questions concerning matters of state; whereas the idea I annexed to this term is an inquiry into the state of a country, for the purpose of ascertaining *the quantum of happiness enjoyed by its inhabitants, and the means of its future improvement.*[43]

Sinclair's work makes use of a good deal of numerical surveys, but it does not employ many of the mathematical methods that would come to be considered statistical in England over the next half-century. What is important here is that already Sinclair suggests that the role of statistics is not only to offer some way of measuring qualities—using numbers to show, in *Deronda*'s terms, society's "qualities"—but also to show how society may be improved.

In Sinclair's account, at the very beginning of the century, statistics could point a way forward. What came to be much more troubling as the discipline developed, however, was the idea that there were "statistical laws." The most famous statement of such laws would come at the end of the century, with Emile Durkheim's 1891 *Suicide*, in which he noted the consistent "collective tendencies" in what is commonly seen as an unpredictable and individual act. Durkheim viewed these tendencies as acting on the individual like a natural law: "Collective tendencies have a reality of their own; they are forces as real as cosmic forces."[44] Others noted the odd regularity of dead letters at post offices, a result that is based not only on an individual choice but on accident. If statisticians took greater care to explain the nature of such laws as the century went on, it did not stop people from believing in, objecting to, and above all, being troubled by the notions of such laws. Percy Fitzgerald, in his biography of Dickens, tells of his concern with the "tyrannical power of the law of averages." When the number of people killed in one year was beneath its annual average, Dickens said, "is it not dreadful to think that before the last day of the year some forty or fifty persons *must* be killed—and killed they will be."[45]

Even more disconcerting to many Victorians was what Miller explains to Deronda as the "law of progress." The idea of such a law was most associated with the historical determinist Henry Buckle, who, in his massive two-volume *History of Civilization in England*, attempted to replace, as the object of historical analysis, the individual with the statistical law. In the introduction to his work, Buckle discusses the regularities of suicides, murders, marriages, and dead letters, finally concluding:

> To those who have a steady conception of the regularity of events, and have firmly seized the great truth that the actions of men, being guided by their antecedents, are in reality never inconsistent, but, however capricious they may appear, only form part of one vast scheme of universal order, of which we in the present state of knowledge can barely see the outline,—to those who understand this, which is at once the key and the basis of history, the facts just adduced [i.e., suicides, etc.], so far from being strange, will be precisely what would have been expected, and ought long since to have been known.[46]

We not only can understand seemingly arbitrary events in terms of necessary statistical laws; we can also understand the very "universal order" of which they are all a part. As Helen Small describes Buckle's project,

"Human actions might wear the appearance of arbitrariness, individuals might assert their free will, but in the aggregate, and across time, they were subject to fixed mathematical laws."[47] To completely disregard the possibility of free will as Buckle did, of course, could not be expected to sit well with Eliot, who confessed in a letter, "he is a writer who inspires in me a personal dislike."[48] Such dislike, though, along with Lewes's scathing reviews,[49] suggests a familiarity with his work and with his idea of statistical laws. Whether or not Eliot agreed with his conclusions, the public-house conversation shows a commitment at least to attempt to work through these distasteful concepts.

A seemingly offhand remark in the pub offers the model for these ideas. One of the speakers, Marrables, who had been conveniently introduced by the narrator as a "laboratory assistant" upon Daniel's entrance, makes the point that ideas may spread "by changing the distribution of gases" (525). Such intrusions of natural science mark Eliot's writing throughout her career—Henry James once criticized *Middlemarch* for being "too often an echo of Messrs Darwin and Huxley"[50]—and have drawn a great deal of critical attention in recent decades, most of the discussion focusing on the scientific bases for Eliot's idea of the organic. Yet the odd tentativeness of this particular scientific interjection should make us take notice. The character of Marrables exists in the novel only to offer this line about gases. In fact, after being introduced with his credentials, and then saying his line, the character is never heard from again. Such blunt functional treatment is out of keeping for Eliot and suggests an idea that she was still attempting to work out. If she forces it in here, though, she does so with good reason; the discussion of gas provides a scientific figure for society that will replace the organic model.

The science of gases, at the time Eliot was writing, was a specifically *statistical* idea. Or, at least, it had recently become so. James Clerk Maxwell had first introduced his kinetic theory of gases—in which the thermal qualities of a gas are due only to molecular motion—in 1865. Eliot had already been somewhat familiar with the basic elements of the discussion about molecular theories, having been introduced to them by her and Lewes's friend, the physicist John Tyndall, and Eliot was familiar with Tyndall's *Heat as a Mode of Motion*.[51] She also had attended Maxwell's lectures and read his articles on gas molecules, and she makes reference to one of these articles in her notes for the novel.[52] Meanwhile, Lewes was making repeated reference to Maxwell's molecular theories in his *Problems of Life and Mind*.[53] Eliot would thus have had some knowledge of Maxwell's refinements of Tyndall's theories.[54]

These refinements made what had previously been a more conventional scientific view of the nature of collective bodies into a statistical one. Maxwell had noted that it was impossible to follow the motion of any one molecule: "the working atomists have therefore adopted a method which is . . .

new in the department of mathematical physics, though it has long been in use in the section of Statistics."[55] This method is the one that Maxwell noted had proved so successful in studies of "age, income-tax, education, religious belief, or criminal convictions"—namely, the application of statistical methods of error approximation.[56] Buckle's writings were a key influence; Maxwell would later write that "Buckle demonstrated statistically that if only a sufficient number of people is taken into account, then not only is the number of natural events like death, illness, etc., perfectly constant, but also the number of so-called voluntary actions—marriages at a given age, crimes, and suicides. It occurs no differently among molecules."[57] Maxwell's breakthrough in his kinetic theory, in other words, was to claim that the methods that had been developed for the study of large groups of people over long stretches of time could also be used to understand the physical world. In this, Maxwell is exemplary, but not unique. As Theodore Porter puts it, "Seemingly without exception, those who applied statistical thinking to any of the sciences during the second half of the nineteenth century thought in terms of analogies with the social sciences."[58] Statistical thinking transformed the social world into a laboratory of sorts, but its introduction into natural sciences required precisely the opposite move: thinking of the laboratory in terms of the social world.

Social theory was thus never too far removed from Maxwell's thought in the development of his statistical theory of gases, even as he introduced the notion that is, thanks to Thomas Pynchon's *Crying of Lot 49*, probably most associated with his name among literary scholars: "Maxwell's demon." Maxwell himself never used the term "demon," but he did imagine "a being whose faculties are so sharpened that he can follow every molecule in its course."[59] Such a being could distinguish faster-moving particles from slower-moving particles in a chamber, and allow only the faster ones to pass to another chamber. The chamber with the faster particles will rise in temperature without, technically, any work being expended, and the second law of thermodynamics would thus be broken. What is the purpose of this thought experiment? The being was in fact little more than an ideal physicist. Existing theories of gas essentially relied on a dynamic billiard-ball model of molecules; statistical approximations of molecules were necessary, but only because of our inability to observe closely enough. If we could overcome such limitations, and could see each individual molecule as we could each billiard ball, there would be no need for statistical method. Maxwell's point in his introduction of the demon is that if we had such observational powers, something so fundamental as the second law of thermodynamics would not apply. As Maxwell goes on to say:

> This is only one of the instances in which conclusions which we have drawn from our experience of bodies consisting of immense numbers

of molecules may be found not to be applicable to the more delicate observations and experiments which we may suppose made by one who can perceive and handle the individual molecules which we deal with only in large masses. (329)

This is the key point at which Maxwell's theory diverges radically from the organic models so familiar in Eliot. To understand the law of the body as a whole, the observer not only must make do with the fact that she cannot observe the individual elements. Instead, even the idea that the individual elements could *ever* be seen, given sufficient observational capacity, must be thrown out. Maxwell reiterates this point: "In dealing with masses of matter, while we do not perceive the individual molecules, we are compelled to adopt what I have described as the statistical method, and to abandon the strict dynamical method, in which we follow every motion by the calculus" (329). The dynamical model, in which the whole is built up of mutually interacting and interdependent elements, has been replaced with the law of "statistical method."[60]

We cannot see every individual element of the whole, and if we could, the whole would no longer make sense. We should remember, of course, that Maxwell developed his statistical theories after reading Buckle, so his molecules always bear some analogical relation to individuals within a social whole. This social corollary will no doubt be familiar to readers of Eliot, because it lies behind *Middlemarch*'s famous evocation of the social sublime: "If we had a keen vision and feeling of all ordinary human life, it would be like hearing the grass grow and the squirrel's heart beat, and we should die of that roar which lies on the other side of silence."[61] This "we" we can take to be Eliot's "demon"—the hypothetical "being whose faculties are so sharpened" that it can see and hear every particle of the social whole. That this demon would necessarily perish can be taken, at the character level, as a statement on the limits of sympathy. We could also read this sentence, though, in the context of the pier-glass metaphor and the other narratorial discourses on the method that occur throughout *Middlemarch*. By this reading, "we" would really be "I," the narrator, expressing her inability to extend her observation to its extreme. This reading gains credence from the shift, occurring right before these lines, from the narrator's usual first-person singular ("Nor can I suppose that when Mrs Casaubon is discovered . . .") to a plural that seems more royal than inclusive ("we do not expect people to be deeply moved by what is not unusual . . ."). The narrator, with the expectation of certain reactions from her readers, fades into a larger group, with expectations of each other. Ultimately, though, it is the narrator who does not expect people to be deeply moved by Dorothea's suffering, and it is the narrator who cannot express the feelings of every character that inhabits her world. The death from the roar that the narrator describes, then, is also the death of the narrator, the ultimate impossibility of narration, if its goal is the description of every motivation and sentiment. Maxwell's demon, if it existed, would break the second law of thermodynamics; Eliot's demon would deny the possibility of narration.

The gas that Marrables introduces into the conversation thus provides a model for the English society that Eliot imagines, which, unlike Jewish society, cannot be described in terms of its individual elements. The gas model helps to move past the paradoxes of the organic, which finds itself up against the narratorial limits of its own claims about the interdependence of the one and the many. Eliot would continue to try to work out this molecular model in later works, such as her essay on the "Political Molecule" in *Theophrastus Such*, though she would never have a chance to realize it fully. Such a model, however, does not mean, as it would for Buckle, that the individual is simply an effect of greater social laws. Maxwell, after all, had explicitly moved away from determinism in the description of the motion of his molecules. He allowed for chance, for some sort of freedom, but not in a way that was reflected in the greater laws of the whole. If Maxwell translated the social into the scientific, the translation into the literary presented Eliot with a rather confusing state of affairs: the individual could be free, the social whole could be bound by laws, and each could seemingly exist independently of each other.

IN MEDIAS DOLORES

Daniel Deronda thus replaces the organic with the statistical, the web network with the gas—at least as far as the novel's gentile characters go. But such societal metaphors are essentially spatial, while the process of reading a novel, and particularly a novel of education, is temporal. As far as the traditional *Bildungsroman* goes, this diachronic dimension is expressed through the accumulation of some sort of life experience. Given the social nature of the *Bildungsroman*, such experience will generally take the form of learning from other people and internalizing the lessons learned, all the while drawing links between one's internal state and an external world made of other people. Franco Moretti describes this process as a series of encounters, each with the potential to add to the protagonist's accumulated experience: the protagonist "prolongs the encounter, he probes into the conversation, he recalls it, he puts his hope in it. . . . The novelistic plot is marked by this curvature towards interiority, which dispenses meaning and thereby creates events."[62] Just as importantly, though, the protagonist must move past the experience "before personality becomes unilaterally and irrevocably modified" (46). The key Continental figure for this process tends to be the youth—think Wilhelm Meister or Eugène de Rastignac—facing the city and its myriad experiences. In its rural English form as well, though, we can see Dorothea grow through and away from Casaubon, through and away from Rosamond, and finally through and away from Middlemarch itself.

The process depends on the accumulation of experience, as represented by other characters. Yet, here too we find a reliance on a certain sort of literary induction. The protagonist meets with a finite number of other characters, and the experiences with these characters come to stand in for the external world. Rastignac not only completes *Père Goriot* on equal ground with Paris, but he himself becomes a synecdoche for Paris over the course of the *Comédie*,[63] as a result of his accumulated experience with the various extremes that make up the city: Goriot, Vautrin, Mme de Beauséant. The underlying axiom here relies on the notion that an understanding of the larger social whole that Paris represents can be built up from a series of individual characters-cum-experiences, over the course of a novel.

Gwendolen's temporal experience is not of this sort. But what sort is it? What is the temporal experience that corresponds to the statistical model that underlies so much of *Deronda*? We are in fact acquainted with this experience at the novel's beginning, from the moment we see Gwendolen at the roulette table. As the remainder of this chapter will argue, the novel's central motif of gambling provides a recurring attempt to think through a way of interacting with the world, in which a procession of individual moments do not coalesce to form a meaningful *experience*, as such.

Gambling—and particularly the gambling hall—may seem a rather grim choice for describing experience, since it is so clearly negative for Eliot. Not to put too fine a point on it: Eliot figures the gambling hall as hell. She never uses the colloquial "gambling hell" in *Deronda*, partially because it referred to lower-class establishments, but also most likely because she feared draining any semblance of subtlety from the thematic pun that opens the novel. In any event, she shows a good deal less discretion in her letters. Referring to the casino at Bad Homburg, the model for the novel's Leubronn, she writes that "Hell is the only right name for such places."[64] In another letter, she pushes the point further: the casino "is a Hell not only for the gambling, but for the light and heat of the gas," which create a scene of "monotonous hideousness" (314). If this is hell to Eliot, then the opening scene certainly qualifies. Seeing it through Deronda's eyes, the narrator describes "dull, gas-poisoned absorption" (9). The hellishness is only hammered home by demonic conjunctions of the elegant and the bestial: "the white bejeweled fingers of an English countess were very near touching a bony, yellow, crab-like hand stretching a bare wrist to clutch a heap of coin" (9). Even Gwendolen, in this context, is demonic: described as a "serpent" with a "Lamia beauty" (12).

What makes the scene hellish, though, is less its imagery and more its dull repetitions. The players are imagined as lotus-eaters: "there was a certain negativeness of expression which had the effect of a mask—as if they had all eaten of some root that for the time compelled the brains of each to the same narrow monotony of action" (9). Yet unlike Odysseus's crew, it is not the case that the gamblers in the casino are doing nothing. They are doing something; it is just the same thing over and over again. It thus becomes almost mechanized; the only voice that can be heard in the casino is the croupier's "occasional monotone in French, such as might be expected to issue from an ingeniously constructed automaton" (7–8). When, after flashing back eleven months, the novel works its way back to its opening scene, Sir Hugo reiterates the point: "I never cared for play. It's monotonous. . . . I suppose one gets poisoned with the bad air" (161). The gas gives the scene its hellish tint and smell, but it is the repetition without completion, the image of gamblers as Sisyphus, that seems so central to Eliot's horror.

For all the critical discussion of Eliot's antipathy to gambling—on which, more later—it seems that it is this structure of repetition, rather than the gaslight and the avarice, that she looks on with the most distaste. For it is far away from the roulette tables that we find the novel's more prolonged vision of hell, in Gwendolen's marriage to Grandcourt. The marriage is shown to be iterative, an ongoing series of "shock[s] of humiliation" (423). After the wedding-night scene in which he forces Gwendolen to take off her pendant of emeralds and wear Lydia Glasher's diamonds, the narrator states, "What had happened between them about her wearing the diamonds was typical" (426). The narrator offers, in support of this claim, the description of a strikingly similar scene in which he again insists that she wear Lydia's diamonds. The nearly identical content of these scenes strengthens the narrator's claim of typicality. Shortly after this, when the novel returns to the present, we are shown another scene, in which Grandcourt castigates Gwendolen for wearing the turquoise necklace, which Deronda had redeemed for her, with such cold cruelty that it produces the "bitterest mortification in her soul" and sends her into a "shuddering fit" that evening (447–48). Read in succession, this series of examples seem almost absurdly specific, as if Grandcourt's cruelty were limited to an insistence that Gwendolen put on diamonds and remove all green gems. This repetition, though, should be taken more to indicate the uselessness of specifics in this context. All of these examples seem the same because Gwendolen's repeated "shocks," no matter what different forms they take, are the same: Grandcourt's assertions of mastery over her. Of course, we are left to assume that each of the shocks must be different—otherwise they would not be shocking—but in their difference, they maintain an essential identity. That is, each one is new, unpredictable, and yet each one remains a repetition. None of this should take away from Grandcourt's cruelty; but Eliot seems less interested in the specifics of that cruelty, and more interested in its iterative quality. The true horror of the situation lies in its monotony of shock.

The description of Gwendolen in her marriage, then, seems to bring Eliot's figure of the Leubronn gambler, as a figure doomed to repetition, out of the casino and into the everyday. Walter Benjamin, in his discussion of Baudelaire, suggests that it is this repetition that makes the gambler, along with the factory worker, particularly emblematic of a developing nineteenth-century mindset in which experience itself becomes impoverished. Gambling, as Benjamin describes it,

> certainly does not lack the futility, the emptiness, the inability to complete something which is inherent in the activity of a wage slave in a factory. . . . The manipulation of the worker at the machine has no connection with the preceding operation for the very reason that it is its exact repetition. Since each operation at the machine is just as screened off from the preceding operation as a *coup* in a game of chance is from the one that preceded it, the drudgery of the laborer is, in its own way, a counterpart to the drudgery of the gambler. The work of both is equally devoid of substance.[65]

Baudelaire, Benjamin admits, "did not have the faintest notion" of the facts of industrial wage labor. Yet that does not change the fact that Benjamin saw in Baudelaire's scenes of gambling, as Richard Wolin puts it, "a parable for the disintegration of coherent experience in modern life."[66] The passer-by jostled on the street, the worker at his machine, the gambler at the table—for each, there is no longer a continuous accumulation of experiences but rather a series of "shock experience[s]" (176). The paradox is that even while the shocks repeat, they never offer a connection between the past and the future; we cannot predict the next, and we cannot use the next to understand the last. Richard Shiff puts it well: "The shock experience tenaciously resists assimilation and may even repeat itself as if timelessly, neither acquiring referential meaning, nor exhibiting meaningful variation, nor assuming the easy familiarity of habit."[67] It is not necessarily clear why, for Benjamin, the assembly-line worker would not be able to fall into a habit; but then, the essay on Baudelaire seems ultimately less concerned with material conditions and more concerned with urban crowds and gambling, the phenomenology of the *flâneur*. And on these topics, Benjamin describes an experience that is at once always the same, and—since there is no arc of accumulated life experience—forever new.

This experience, for Benjamin as for Eliot, is hell. He offers "gambling" as one of his "keywords of hell,"[68] and writes that the experience of gambling is like the experience of "time in hell": "the province of those who are not allowed to complete anything they have started."[69] At the same time, since for him the gambler was a figure of the "modern"—a slippery term that should be taken here to mean Baudelaire's mid-nineteenth-century Paris—the experience of the modern itself became an experience of hell:

The "modern," the time of hell. The punishments of hell are always the newest thing going over in this domain. What is at issue is not that "the same thing happens over and over." . . . It is rather that precisely in that which is newest the face of the world never alters, that this newest remains, in every respect, the same.—This constitutes the eternity of hell.[70]

We should note here the double meaning of the term "modern" for Benjamin. On the one hand, it is the period easily associated with a time, place, means of production. On the other hand, what makes the "modern" modern for Benjamin is the fact that it is always "that which is newest." And it is this latter meaning that seems to have the most resonance. It is for this reason that the odd conjunction of Eliot with Baudelaire—moralist and immoralist together—makes sense. I am less concerned here with the question of whether or not *Daniel Deronda* is in some sense a "modern" or—which term has even less utility here—a "modernist" novel, and more concerned with the way that it portrays the experience of "now-ness." Benjamin I take not only to be a critic of modernity but also an original thinker on this experience. So too is Eliot; Nicholas Dames has described *Deronda*'s effect as "the depiction of characters who live outside of time in a constant 'now.'"[71] In both cases, we have a monotony of shock that disconnects the individual from the past and the future. Again, the gambler at the roulette wheel or the *trente et quarante* table becomes the figure for this disconnected present. In Benjamin, instead of the arc of a lifetime of accumulated experience, all drawn toward fulfillment in the future, there is instead only "the ivory ball that rolls into the *next* compartment, the *next* card which lies on top" (179). In Eliot, this present structures the form of the overdetermined gambling scene that starts the novel, the "now" produced by *in medias res*.

That *Deronda* is remembered, somewhat erroneously, as Eliot's "only novel with a present-day setting"[72] suggests this double effect of the figure of gambling: both a mark of now and of "now-ness." The novel in fact takes place over a stretch of roughly two years starting in October 1864[73]—that is, a period of time roughly a decade before the novel was published. Of course, this is closer to the time of publication than any other of Eliot's novels, but a decade is still a notable length of time, and the impulse to brush over the lag should strike us as a curious one. Eliot explicitly marks her temporal setting by references to the American Civil War (90), and the Austro-Prussian war (622). Perhaps the most interesting marker is the casino itself. Rhine gambling halls were officially closed at the end of 1872.[74] Eliot knew this, and it was presumably why she went out of her way to visit the casino at Homburg, while she still could, in 1872. She writes: "I get some satisfaction in looking on from the sense that the thing is going to be put down."[75] Had Eliot not set her novel in the past, she would have been forced to do without one of her central symbolic motifs. And had she not set it a decade in the past, the tone of ongoing monotony at the casino would have been lost. For though she does not mention it explicitly in her letters, the upcoming closure of the casinos was a significant topic of discussion around the tables.[76] Interestingly enough, it is this central metaphor, available only in the past, that is in large part responsible for the commonplace of the novel's "present-day setting."[77]

One somewhat obvious way that gambling has this effect is through its role as an indictment of wild speculation in late-century England. This appears early in the novel, when Gwendolen returns from losing her money by gambling to learn that the firm of Grapnell and Company has lost her family's money by speculating. This would likely remind readers of the 1866 failure of Overend and Gurney[78]—another marker of the past decade—but it also makes a larger claim about the state of England's economic system. When a specific firm failed is less important than the implication that such imprudence is still going on at this very moment. Recall the title of Trollope's great work on gambling and speculation, written only a year before *Deronda*: *The Way We Live Now*.[79] Much has been written on the analogies between speculation and gambling in late-nineteenth-century England[80]—it comes so easily that Eliot seems almost to want to get it out of the way and move on—but what I wish to point out is how it makes the novel seem a contemporary concern. There is little point, after all, in drawing analogies in order to rail against something ten years in the past.

At the same time that gambling invoked the present thematically, though, it was the *experience* of gambling—what I have been calling its monotony of shock—that produced in the novel a formal "now-ness." This formal quality, I believe, was every bit as important for the novel's claims to contemporaneity. To support this claim, it will be useful to look at a species of rather less rarefied works of the same period: sensation novels, like those Wilkie Collins and Mary Elizabeth Braddon. Discussions of these novels hammered on the fact that, unlike the gothic or the ghost story, they described the present moment. H. L. Mansel characterized the sensation novel as "usually a tale of our own times."[81] Mansel claims that this is essential to the novel's nervous effects: "a tale which aims at electrifying the nerves of the reader is never thoroughly effective unless the scene be laid in our own days." Henry James agreed, suggesting that the true innovation of the sensation novel was that it "introduced into fiction . . . the mysteries which are at our own doors." The "novelty" of Braddon's *Lady Audley*, for example, "lay in the heroine being . . . an English gentlewoman of the present year, familiar with the use of the railway and the telegraph. . . . Modern England—the England of to-day's newspaper—crops up at every step."[82] As with *Deronda*, though, these claims for the contemporaneity of sensation novels often overstate the case. *The Woman in White*, for example, is actually set in 1851, eight years prior to its publication[83]—not ancient history, by any means, but hardly the present moment either.

Such insistence on the immediate contemporaneity of sensation novels is due, I believe, to a combination of two effects. First, there is sensation itself: sensation novels are stocked with nervous characters, and they work to make their readers feel these sensations as well. In D. A. Miller's formulation, the sensation novel "renders our reading bodies, neither fighting nor fleeing, theaters of neurasthenia."[84] The desired effect of the sensation novel, in other words, is to produce the same sensation in its readers that it describes in its character. It may have taken place in the past, but it is playing out in the reader's body—the novel's "theater"—*right now*. Related to this presence of sensation is the second effect: the element of forgetting. Characters in sensation novels tend to forgetfulness or even amnesia, as a result of their repeated shocks and sensations. As Dames puts it, Collins's novels "are often constructed out of momentary amnesias produced by sensation."[85] And just as with the sensation that produces the forgetting, the readers follow the characters' affect: sensation novels were understood to produce forgetfulness in their readers through their rapid appearance and perceived disposability. Sensation novels were seen as a series of immediate, and yet repeated, shocks at the level of both the sentence and the installment. In both cases, the shocks would combine to cancel out the accumulation of experience. Unlike the *Bildungsroman*, whose narrative arc of development is based on such inductive accumulation, the sensation novel does not really *go* anywhere. This was the backdrop for James's and Mansel's insistence on contemporaneity. When time is marked by the repetition of shock, it is always right now.

Deronda, it has been suggested, owes some debt to the sensation novel. Barbara Hardy sees the mark of Collins's *Woman in White* in Gwendolen's "nervous equipment": "she is afraid of being alone, she is afraid of being loved, she is afraid of certain changes in the light, she is afraid of large open spaces."[86] Still, let us not underestimate the presence of Collins-esque sensation throughout the novel. Gwendolen's fear might be a psychological characteristic—she "is" afraid—but it manifests itself in the physical. When she is alone, for example, the fear surfaces as a "tremor" (63); large open spaces do not only terrify her, but also "set her imagination at work in a way that [makes] her tremble" (64). Then, of course, there are her repeated bouts of screaming. Gwendolen's "nervous equipment" has the capacity to assert itself at any time. And it does, in a manner at once regular and unpredictable. Ultimately, though, it is in Gwendolen's marriage to Grandcourt that the hellishness of the monotony of shock becomes evident. As Ann Cvetkovich points out, Gwendolen's interiority becomes contested ground, as Grandcourt seeks to control her.[87] Consider the following passage, which would seem equally at home in *Deronda* or *The Woman in White*:

Why could she not rebel and defy him? She longed to do it. But she might as well have tried to defy the texture of her nerves and the palpitation of her heart. Her husband had a ghostly army at his back, that could close round her wherever she might turn. She sat in her splendid attire, like a white image of helplessness. (447–48)

All the necessary thematic elements are there: the manipulatively cruel husband, the specter of sadism and psychological control, the country house that looks respectable to the world and is, in fact, a prison without bars. Just as important, though, is the fact that Grandcourt's power over Gwendolen is paralleled by "the texture of her nerves and the palpitation of her heart." The horror is made physical, and is communicated to the reader, in terms of nervous sensation.

This domestic horror is also where the novel most insists on the formal "now." The reader does not dive directly into Gwendolen's hell. Like the novel's opening scene, her suffering is first glimpsed through Deronda's eyes, and only then are we given the backstory of the object of his gaze. The result is that when the narrator returns to Gwendolen's interiority, after describing the marriage from Daniel's viewpoint, it is supposed to come as something of a revelation that Gwendolen is, and has been, suffering "miseries" (423). If this claim is not quite as surprising to an actual reader as the narrator might imply—we have, after all, already glimpsed Gwendolen's guilty fits and Grandcourt's cruelty—she makes up for it by employing the rhetoric of surprise.[88] The first use of "miseries" ends a paragraph, and the next paragraph begins with rhetorical affirmation: "Yes—miseries." The break between paragraphs, it seems, was the space in which the implied reader was to have responded with some sort of incredulity. Such insistence on the unexpected fits a basic Eliotic argument: that we cannot know the pain being suffered by others, all around us. The formal move is one that we are familiar with from Eliot's previous novels, and especially her treatment of heroines like Hetty Sorrel and Dorothea Brooke: joining a character, and particularly a female character, in the midst of her ongoing sufferings. In *Deronda*, Eliot breaks new ground by joining Gwendolen *in medias res*, but she has already well accustomed her readers to joining her characters *in medias dolores*. When we enter Hetty's point of view at the full term of her pregnancy,[89] or meet up with Dorothea on her honeymoon to find her "sobbing bitterly,"[90] their stories suddenly extend backward, as it is made clear that the the characters' unhappiness has been going on all this time—in Hetty's case, for months[91]—without our having known about it.

Setting aside for the moment the implications for sympathy and its limitations, we can see that the application of this technique in *Deronda* has a significant effect on the sense of time in the novel. At the time that Daniel comes to visit Gwendolen and Grandcourt, and we learn of her miseries, the two are still newlyweds, having only been married seven weeks before. This at least is how Deronda, who is seeing them for the first time together, experiences the marriage. It is not, however, how Gwendolen experiences it: "Already, in seven short weeks, which seemed half her life, her husband had gained a mastery . . ." (423). These weeks may be "short" for the outside world, certainly for Deronda, who has all but forgotten about Gwendolen. For Gwendolen, though, they seem to take years. At a relatively early point, the marriage seems to extend back for Gwendolen, as if it had been a constant state. The novel's method of joining her mid-suffering emphasizes this point. The starting point becomes irrelevant; the important thing is that her suffering is going on *now*, and that it has been ongoing. And since, like gambling, the marriage offers no arc—Gwendolen is as miserable when we first join her as she will ever be in the marriage—it seems as if it can continue forever. If each "shock of humiliation" is different, and yet each is somehow the same, how can there be any narrative progress?

The answer lies in a certain sort of suspense. This is not to use the term in its usual form, however, in which narrative is carried along by a series of posed and resolved enigmas.[92] This form of suspense plays little role in Eliot's fiction; Caroline Levine goes so far as to suggest that Eliot shows a consistent suspicion of the mechanics of suspense throughout her career.[93] With characters like Hetty, Dorothea, or Gwendolen, we almost seem to have the converse of suspense; as soon as we know that something has been hidden from us, we know what that something is.[94] The suspense that underlies Gwendolen's marriage is of a different sort: a sense that, though we might not know how or when, *something* has to happen. Gwendolen feels the same thing within herself: "When my blood is fired I can do daring things—take any leap; but that makes me frightened at myself"; "if feelings rose—there are some feelings—hatred and anger—how can I be good when they keep rising? And if there came a moment when I felt stifled and could bear it no longer—" (452, 453). She does not finish the latter sentence. Are the "daring things" suicide? Murder? Running away to the Continent? It does not really matter, so long as she knows, and the reader knows, that something will happen. What makes hell ultimately unbearable, in both its classical and Christian presentations, is that its monotony of shock can continue for all eternity. Gwendolen predicts that the moment will come when she can "bear it no longer." At some point, in some form, the monotony will have to break.

If Gwendolen's marriage brings the experience of gambling into the domestic narrative, then the suspense underlying her marriage brings with it the gambler's intuition. This intuition tells us that over the long haul, the odds will even out. Take, for example, the opening scene of Tom Stoppard's *Rosencrantz and Guildenstern Are Dead*. The two are placing wagers on whether a coin will come up heads or tails, and it has come up heads seventy-five times in a row. As Guildenstern describes this seeming denial of the laws of probability: "There is an art to the building up of suspense."[95] At the level of the law of large numbers, where deviations cancel out, there will eventually be a return to some sort of equilibrium. The case, or so the reader senses, must be the same in the large novel.

THE GAMBLER'S FALLACY

The remainder of this chapter will argue that this form of expectation is an essential part of the novel's understanding of experience, but one that the novel ultimately critiques. Before that, though, it will be useful to take a moment to separate the metaphor of gambling, as it plays throughout the novel, and the literal act of gambling, as we see it in Leubronn at the novel's opening. The reason such a distinction is necessary is that Eliot so consistently applies the metaphoric language of gambling in *Daniel Deronda* that it is tempting to think that most every character in the novel is a gambler, and every choice a gamble. Gwendolen is a gambler, of course. The Davilows and Gascoignes are gamblers for investing with Grapnell and Company. Deronda is a gambler of a different, more admirable sort, "invest[ing] his luck" to help Hans Meyrick in school (183), and finally, as Wilfred Stone puts it, "risk[ing] his whole inheritance for a visionary ideal."[96] In fact, one moral conclusion the novel offers is that we are all of us gamblers in our everyday lives: "There are enough inevitable turns of fortune which force us to see that our gain is another's loss:—that is one of the ugly aspects of life" (337). Actually to play at roulette, Deronda suggests, is simply a difference of degree, "exaggerating" this fact of life. Gwendolen's decision to marry Grandcourt, we are told, is "like roulette" (692). But a metaphor tells us little without some sort of literal referent. So, in order to glean some meaning from the blanket application of this metaphor, we need to understand what the novel has to say about gambling itself.

First, let us look at the novel's presentation of an inveterate gambler. There is only one in the novel—and it is not Gwendolen. Lapidoth, the prodigal father of Mirah and Mordecai, is the very embodiment of the gambler. His most human sensibilities have been replaced by a desire for gaming. As Mordecai tells him, "you have become a gambler, and where shame and conscience were, there sits an insatiable desire" (776). The narrator then offers illustration of this. After the "lightning" of Mordecai's admonishments has passed, he falls to thinking about roulette: Mordecai "passed like an insubstantial ghost, and his words had the heart eaten out of them by the numbers and movements that seemed to make the very tissue of Lapidoth's consciousness" (778).[97] Gambling here is not just an action; it is an ontology. Lapidoth *is* a gambler.

No one else is, though. Deronda's antipathy to roulette is made abundantly clear; Sir Hugo has "never cared for it" (161). Grandcourt plays but finds it a "confounded strain" (161), and the narrator makes a point of stating, before he arrives at Diplow, that no one believed him to be a gambler (93). And what about Gwendolen, the "fair gambler, the Leubronn Diana"? She is quite different from Lapidoth, in that the "insatiable desire" that makes up his being remains always external for Gwendolen. In the novel's opening set piece, she is surrounded by other players gripped by the "gambler's passion" (8). Yet Gwendolen plays "not because of passion, but in search of it" (17). More importantly, she never plays again. Even her fantasies of what might have been, while married to Grandcourt, show a separation from the world of the casino: "she had heard stories at Leubronn of fashionable women who gambled in all sorts of ways. It seemed very flat to her at this distance, but perhaps if she began to gamble again, the passion might awake" (429). Gwendolen daydreams herself in the role of the gambler, desiring the "gambler's passion." But desire is a relation with something separate from oneself. Though Gwendolen, like Grandcourt or Sir Hugo, might play at gaming, she lacks the passion that would make it part of "the tissue of her consciousness."

This "passion" is not just some sort of disease, brought on by avarice or, as Sir Hugo would have it, bad air. What differentiates Gwendolen from a real gambler is her intuitive understanding of the role played by chance. After finding out the full extent of her losses, she considers going back to the tables: "With ten louis at her disposal and a return of her former luck, which seemed probable, what could she do better than go on playing for a few days?" (17). Gwendolen had been winning before, after all, and then she began to lose. Judging by the past, the first thought that comes to her mind is that a return to winning—that is, to her "former luck"—would be the probable next step. In deciding against returning to the tables, though, she shows her awareness that she is just as likely to go on losing:

> Gwendolen's imagination dwelt on this course and created agreeable consequences, but not with unbroken confidence and rising certainty as it would have done if she had been touched with the gambler's mania. She had gone to the roulette table not because of passion, but in search of it: her mind was still sanely capable of picturing balanced probabilities, and while the chance of winning allured her, the chance of losing thrust itself on her with an alternate strength. (17)

To be touched by the "gambler's mania," then, is to be unable to see "balanced probabilities." By contrast, what makes Gwendolen "sane" here is that she realizes that nothing that has happened in the past—her earlier winning streak, her later losing streak, her family's crushing loss—will in any way influence the turn of the wheel.

Lapidoth, the novel's figure for the "gambler's mania," takes the opposite approach to the issue of chance as a determining factor. Rather than see balanced future probabilities of good fortune and bad, he believes that fortune is a self-correcting system: "Luck had been against him recently; he expected it to turn" (774). This is known as the "gambler's fallacy," and Eliot understood it to be at the heart of the gambler's mistaken understanding of the nature of chance. In preparation for her work on the novel, she had read an article entitled "Gambling Superstitions," which discussed the paradoxes of gambler's fallacies at length. In particular, the author, Proctor, dwelt on the "the theory of the maturity of chances—'the most elementary of the theories of probability'"[98] This "theory" suggests that the law of probability dictates that a run of bad luck will be followed by a run of good luck: if red comes up ten times in a row, then you should bet on black. Such a belief, the author writes, "might safely be termed the most mischievous of all gambling superstitions." The paradox in this theory, and the reason that it is therefore so mischievous, is that results *do* tend toward their probabilistic outcomes, and yet the gambler can still know nothing about the outcome of the next roll of the die or spin of the wheel. This, it seems, is what fascinated Eliot. She summed it up well in her notebook: "True that results will right themselves but not over any given number of localized chances."[99] The gambler's superstition lies in the belief that he can be systematically able to predict the outcomes of any specific—or as Eliot calls it, "localized"—event based on a probability that only obtains as long-term ratio. The fact that such predictions seem intuitively reasonable make them, for Eliot, no less superstitions. After all, as her narrator rhetorically asks, "Who supposes it is an impossible contradiction to be superstitious and rationalising at the same time?" (19).

Lapidoth exemplifies this superstitious belief in the power of a seemingly rational system to predict future events. The narrator describes him, awake at night, going "back over old Continental hours at *Roulette*, reproducing the method of his play, and the chances that had frustrated it" (778). The phrasing here is precise; chance frustrates the method of play, but chance is not what Lapidoth is concerned with. He is instead dwelling on, and likely refining, the method itself. As Proctor puts it, "There has never been a ruined gambler . . . who has not believed that when ruin overtook him he was on the very point of mastering the secret of success" (704). The specific nature of Lapidoth's method of play is uncertain, but it is safe to assume that it is was one of the numerous gambling systems that English travelers to the Continent so often remarked on.[100] The common thread in these reports was an amazement at Continental gamblers' belief in these systems. Proctor's term—"superstition"—appears with regularity. One traveler to Monte Carlo, for example, described the "truly astonishing" number of systems for sale:

[F]or the man who fancies that superstition has been destroyed by the influences of nineteenth century materialism, there is a great surprise in store at Nice. The extent of shop-window space devoted in that town to the impossible demands of the gambler, will be a revelation to him. The gambler demands a "system," that is, a previously arranged sequence of bets so cunningly devised that the odds which would otherwise be in favour of the bank become by its use in favour of the gambler, and, needless to say, the demand is met.[101]

Nice, Monte Carlo, even Paris—the gambling systems for sale in these towns become a last stronghold of superstition against modern rationality. As the author goes on to say, "A 'system' is the gambler's fetish, and even when the system has ruined him he still believes in it" (487). Such systems represented not only a belief in one's luck, or an uncontrollable mania; rather, they offered the illusion of control over the workings of chance.

Such systems were just as present in German gambling towns, and particularly the one in Homburg, on which Eliot modeled her opening scene. Pamphlets known as *Deutsche-Kalifornien*—so called after the Gold-Rush slang of the day—were available both in and around casinos.[102] The *Kalifornien* offered advice on all facets of gambling, combining techniques for knowing when to bet, how to bet, and in what frame of mind to bet. The popularity of these systems would have been almost impossible to miss. One visitor to the roulette tables at the Kursaal—the tables that would be represented in the novel's opening scene—wrote, "Nearly every gambler had a coloured paper lying before him, or an infallible system, in accordance with which he played. One had a small machine, representing a miniature barrel-organ, the handle of which he turned, thrust a pin several times into the table of figures inside it, and whispered to his companion what he should back."[103] This latter machine appears to be a rather overwrought method for determining which numbers will come up next, based on a record of which have come up in the past.[104] The systems that the author describes as nearly covering the gaming tables were, as we have seen, common all over Europe. Yet they were likely even more common in the casino in Homburg. According to the English traveler quoted above, the casino's owners, the brothers François and Louis Blanc had taken deliberate steps to draw "all the 'players upon a system' to Hambourg" (469). They were the first to introduce the "half *refait*" in *trente et quarante* (or, as it was sometimes called, *rouge et noir*), which lessened the already slight house advantage in this game.[105] This, along with the fact that Homburg roulette wheels had only one zero while those in Baden had two—again halving the house advantage over punters wagering on a color—made the Kursaal at Homburg the most popular casino in Germany among those believing that the odds could be worked in their favor.

This, then, should offer some context for Eliot's 1872 trip to Homburg, often credited with having "supplied the germ" for *Daniel Deronda*.[106] Eliot and Lewes had traveled to the Continent so that she might finish *Middlemarch*. While in Homburg for their health—they were on a strict regime of "drinking the waters and taking the baths" (456)—they were taken to the casino by a Lady Castletown, whose acquaintance they had made in town. As mentioned earlier, their curiosity was no doubt stoked by the fact that the German casinos would be closing forever in little over three months. What is most remembered from this trip, though, are the outraged letters Eliot wrote describing the casinos, which seem to offer us our first hazy sight of the novel's opening. In one we see the figure that would become Gwendolen: "Miss Leigh, Byron's grand niece, who is only 26 years old, and is completely in the grasp of the mean, money-raking demon. It made me cry to see her young fresh face among the hags and brutally stupid men around her."[107] Another presents a description of the cast of characters that surround the gaslit tables:

> I am not fond of denouncing my fellow-sinners, but gambling being a vice I have no mind to, it stirs my disgust even more than my pity. The sight of the full faces bending round the gaming table, the raking-up of the money, and the flinging of the coins towards the winners by the hard-faced croupiers, the hateful, hideous women staring at the board like stupid monomaniacs—all this seems to me the most abject presentation of mortals grasping after something called a good that can be seen on the face of this little earth. Burglary is heroic compared with it. (312)

Eliot, in this letter, shows little interest in understanding what fills her with such disgust. She flings insults—"hateful," "hideous," "stupid"—but makes little effort to describe. Her rhetoric—"this little earth," "burglary is heroic"—strikes a high pitch. Her only effort at analysis is to say that she has so little fellow-feeling for gamblers because she, herself, has no taste for gaming.

Unfortunately, received wisdom has too often taken Eliot at her words in these letters, and held up her largely unexamined condemnation of gambling as axiomatic in reading the novel. Yet, though she began with an instinctive dislike, her interests turned quickly to understanding what delusions lay at the heart of the desire to gamble. Though she does not mention it in her letters, we know that the casino at Homburg would have been literally papered with gambling systems, and filled with punters who believed that they themselves had the secret to beating the odds. And furthermore, we know that upon her arrival back in England, she turned immediately to a study of the nature of these "gambling superstitions" and why they were faulty. We can see this not only in her descriptions of Lapidoth and Gwendolen, but also in her representation of Homburg as Leubronn. In the novel, she describes not only "hideous" or "stupid" gamblers but also the nature of their delusion. One gambler, described at some length, is "probably secure in an infallible system which placed his foot on the neck of chance" (9). To make it clear that such systems are, as her research taught her, "gambling superstitions," she immediately follows this with a description of an older man, who chooses his plays based on "no severity of system, but rather some dream of white crows, or the induction that the eighth of the month was lucky." The term "induction" not only draws the link between the ostensibly rational superstition and the overtly fetishistic one; it also makes clear what it is that is so superstitious about such systems: the belief that an induction from a limited number of examples will be in any way predictive about what will happen next.[108] The proof of this is the fact that both lose: the systematic gambler is forced to prepare a "new pile" of stakes, having just lost the last one, while the older seer is busy "ask[ing] for change."

In other words, though her letters present a rather simple rigidity, her actual preparation for the novel showed that she wanted to understand the nature of the gambler's delusion of control. The manner in which she wrote these lessons back into the character of Lapidoth suggests that her understanding of the "gambler's mania" was far more subtle than simply seeing it as a "mean, money-raking demon." She rather saw it as the failure to understand that though, over long enough time spans, certain statistical certainties will hold sway, such laws are not reducible to the individual case. Her note on probability is worth restating, not only because it refutes Lapidoth but because it describes the breach between the individual and aggregate that lies at the heart of the novel: "True that results will right themselves but not over any given number of localized chances." They will only right themselves at the largest levels.

Gwendolen, until the very last scene with Deronda, expects her story to right itself. The reader has likely expected this as well. Gwendolen's marriage seemed to cry out for some fortunate spin of the wheel, after a seemingly endless succession of losses, and that winning turn came at sea, in the form of Grandcourt's providential death. The only thing left, for Gwendolen and for the reader, would be for the bad marriage to be balanced by the good one and the figure of the "spoiled child" to be replaced with that of the wiser wife. Such, after all, is the narrative equilibrium reached in so many novels of experience: *Vanity Fair, Jane Eyre, David Copperfield, Middlemarch.* Marry imprudently; suffer; be rescued by the spouse's providential death; remarry. One of the novel's most wrenching scenes occurs when Gwendolen discovers that her plot will not tend to such equilibrium, in the form of marriage to Deronda, thanks to his threefold announcement that he is a Jew, marrying Mirah, and leaving for Palestine. This scene is also the occasion for Eliot's most extended, and extensive, use of the long view, as she invokes "the great movements of the world, the larger destinies of mankind" (803). The novel's great moment of moral seriousness, in other word, does not come with Gwendolen's possible sin of omission leading to her husband's death or Deronda's reclamation of his heritage. It comes instead at the moment that a character does not get what it seems—seems to her, and to us—that she is due. And the way that the novel makes sense of this moment is to direct our attention away from the "localized" instance to the level at which things reach their proper balance: the "great," the "larger."

It directs *our* attention to this lesson—but not Gwendolen's. In introducing the "larger destinies," the narrator is carefully vague about where these thoughts are occurring: "There comes a terrible moment to many souls . . ." (803). After escalating this terrible moment through chariots of fire, the "submission of the soul," and the "awful face of duty," the narrator then retreats, back to the first inkling of something larger: "That was the sort of crisis which was at this moment beginning in Gwendolen's small life" (804). Gwendolen, in other words, is refused even the consolation of her place in a larger universe, where things balance out properly. We are given to believe that she might one day reach this understanding, but ultimately the novel does not even allow the character the integration of realizing the larger movements of the "historical stream." The understanding of these workings is so counterintuitive that the best Gwendolen is given is "something spiritual and vaguely tremendous."

The use of the large novel, though, is that it can frustrate what seems to be the correct coming-to-equilibrium of one story, Gwendolen's, while still suggesting that the story as a whole worked out as it should. Eliot's oft-quoted reminder that she "meant everything in the book to be related to everything else"[109] refers to the unity of the interrelations in the book, but it also refers to the narrative. The novel as a whole asserts that the Gwendolen's disappointment makes sense in "the big picture." But it is only as the reader of a novel that there can be such comfort. The logic of large numbers brushes by Gwendolen, leaving her only with a simple, forward-looking moral imperative—"I shall live" (807). She follows this by the final declaration that though she has no internal sense that she will "be the best of women, who make others glad that they are born" (810), she still has faith in Deronda's assertion that this will turn out to be the case. The narrative of the novel, in other words, ultimately divorces moral desire from any sort of intuition. It continues to exist only for those who can see the interrelation of the individual with the large numbers: that is, the reader.

COROLLARY: JULIET FENN

Eliot's lesson thus seems a rather gloomy one for any individuals not fortunate enough to discover, like Deronda, that they are part of an enumerable community. For the rest, there is the lesson of the large novel: things, as a whole, do work out as they should, but that does not mean that they work out that way for individuals. That is to say, when the novel follows its molecular-statistical model, we can only locate progress among the larger group. The difficulty of this for literary representation, though, is an obvious one: as soon as a character is individualized, he or she becomes an exception to the "prevailing expression" of the larger group.

The way that Eliot balances this helpless outlook is through another formal quality of the large novel: its profusion of characters. Even though Eliot insists that we avoid the gambler's fallacy of believing a small sample size of events will come together in a meaningful way, this does not mean that *nothing* will come together in a meaningful way; it only means that it will not come together that way for Gwendolen, or you or me, or any other individual. However, "results will right themselves" for large groups, over time—not because any individual event will tend back toward equilibrium, but because the large numbers will simply outnumber the exceptions. In the novel, though, it is much easier to represent the exceptions than these large numbers. Even though there is a large cast of characters in *Deronda*, their main purpose, it seems, is to stand as a sort of negative space for individualized characters to move through. The cast of characters expresses conventional wisdom in the form of rural gossip, and provides the backdrop from which the central characters "come forward," as Grandcourt does when he approaches Gwendolen from out of a crowd (111). Though these characters are often named, they are often essentially invisible. Such is the case, for example, when Gwendolen sits down to dinner in "the ladies' dining room" after the archery meeting. We are told that there are other women sitting beside her, insofar as we are told that she does not talk with them, but no description or even dialogue is offered. The narrator may be offering as critique her claims that Gwendolen "when left alone in [other women's] company had a sense of empty benches" (116). Gwendolen's sense, though, is the reader's sense as well. The other women, Catherine Arrowpoint excluded, are *there*, in some sense, but only as undifferentiated backdrop in opposition to Gwendolen.

One of these women, though, a certain Juliet Fenn, does get a name, without ever being quite individualized. We might call her the *femme moyenne*, if it were not for the colorful language that is used to describe her unattractiveness: "It was impossible [for Gwendolen] to be jealous of Juliet Fenn, a girl as middling as mid-day market in everything but her archery and plainness, in which last she was noticeable like her father: underhung and with receding brow resembling that of the more intelligent fishes" (114). That fishy appearance, though, is explained away with a parenthetical digression on questions of physical attractiveness and natural selection. Her distinguishing characteristic, in other words, is given as the nearly inevitable result of movements at a vast scale. The inevitability of her appearance, as well as her insignificance for Gwendolen, is reasserted later in the novel: "Miss Juliet Fenn, a young lady whose profile had been so unfavorably decided by circumstances over which she had no control, that Gwendolen some months ago had felt it impossible to be jealous of her" (418). But it is also Juliet Fenn who beats the two individualized, and physically attractive, women at the archery meet. According to one observer: "There's luck even in these games of skill. That's better. It gives the hinder ones a chance" (104). Luck, in the form that assists Juliet in the archery match, is not simply random chance. Rather it functions as a sort of even distribution; it evens things out for "the hinder ones." In the figure of Juliet, we have a marker of the aggregate, which displays the meaning in such large-scale processes as Darwinian evolution and the workings of luck. But this is only because Juliet has never been fully differentiated from the uncountably large social backdrop, and so she never has to be reintegrated into it. Yet, among the English, it is only for the Juliet Fenns, the large group, that we can expect things to "work out" in the end.

AFTERWORD

. . . or, more properly, "After*ward*." Because, after all, the Victorian era does end. And that leaves a book like this in a rather tricky position. My subtitle is "The Ethical Experience of the Victorian Novel"—but *who*, exactly, is having the sort of phenomenological reactions to novel narrative that I am discussing? If it is mainly twentieth- and twenty-first-century readers, then how do we connect them to novels from a very different time? In each of my chapters, I have certainly looked for some record of contemporary mainstream opinion, whether in relation to Oliver's outcome, Dickens's propensity to make us laugh, or a desire to see Gwendolen married and re-integrated back into *Deronda*'s aggregate whole. At the same time, though, it would be disingenuous to deny that this book falls back on concerns of present-day reading. This occurs to some extent because arguments about narrative form function by a principle of recognizability: if my reader does not expect, by the novel's midway point, that Oliver will stay away from crime, or if that same reader does not sense some subdued motivating strength under David Copperfield's evident passivity, then my arguments will be a good deal less successful. The question, ultimately, is one of presentism and historicism: how do we connect our own experience to these objects and experiences which are centuries old?

Before I attempt to address this, it will be useful to sum up. My argument so far has been twofold. First, I have tried to show that an insight into the moral concerns of Victorians would also offer insight into their formal engagement with the novel form. A closer look at the content of Victorian moralizing, in other words, would also show an unexpected formalizing: in terms of suspense, developmental narrative, humor, and even, in *Deronda*, the ultimate insufficiency of the Victorian novel form as a cognate to the failure of socially grounded intuition. The second point that I have tried to make is that, while an approach grounded in Victorian moral philosophy might reveal unexpected dimensions of these formal practices, it would not make them look drastically different. They would still be recognizable—*readable*, to use the term I offered earlier—because their ethical concerns have become embedded in what we consider to be purely formal responses. As I suggested in my introduction, I am not certain that this ethical tradition is one that we should necessarily be striving to emulate. It is, however, one that has become a part of the way we read.

By why the *Victorian* novel? If the moral-formal concerns that I've been discussing are still with us, as I believe that they are, why does this book focus solely on the nineteenth century? To a certain extent, the answer is institutional. I don't mean this only in the drab sense of disciplinary constraint, though there is that; books, especially first books, are written in fields of specialization, and the nineteenth-century novel is mine. But I think there is a more positive version of this idea: disciplinary formations, and the consensus that they produce, go a long way toward describing what a certain period means. I touched on this already in my discussion of the *Bildungsroman*, but it bears emphasis: when we talk about the Victorian novel, we are not talking about all novels written between Victoria's coronation and her Diamond Jubilee. Lots of people wrote books in the nineteenth century, but, if our shared field of reference is any indication, only about twenty-six wrote Victorian novels. Start with a big eleven: all of Austen (not, it bears repeating, a Victorian), all of Charlotte and Emily Brontë, some of Collins, all of Dickens, all of Eliot, most of Gaskell, some of Gissing, all of Hardy, a bit of Thackeray, and as much Trollope as you can bear. Add two more to the count if we include James and Wilde. Then another thirteen, mainly for specialists, bringing us to twenty-six: Ainsworth, Braddon, Anne Brontë, Butler, Bulwer-Lytton, Carlyle (for *Sartor Resartus*), Disraeli, Martineau, Meredith, Oliphant, Schreiner, Stevenson, and Stoker. I'm sure a few are missing, but beyond this set, I think the expectations of shared reference fall off sharply. The point of compiling this list is to show that when we talk about the periodization of a field we are, in very real ways, talking about the ideas that we use to structure our periodization: the principle of selection by which we choose our texts.

"Choose" is probably the wrong word here; we don't freely choose which works make up the field. In part this is because of obvious institutional pressures. But a much more significant reason is that the felt proximity of Victorian novels tends to be a fundamental axiom for the field. In spite of the fact that we're talking about works from another century, and another country, most of the critical apparatus built around the field depend on the notion that, in talking about the nineteenth century, we are talking about ourselves. Most forms of critical historicism—whether they tell time by a Marxist or Foucauldian clock—take this for granted: Victorian novels fall within the bourgeois epoch or the modern *episteme*. They describe a time whose society tells us something about our own society, but with enough temporal distance to allow us to recognize things about our society more effectively. We know ourselves better, or so the story goes, when we can recognize ourselves in the past. If historicism shows a preference for denaturalizing certain texts, then along with this comes a preference for texts that seem natural in the first place. This isn't only a point about historicism; formalism in general, and narratology more specifically, usually takes a certain coherence and legibility as a given. To the extent that nineteenth-century realism becomes a key site for formal narrative analysis, it does so because it most fits the model of a story that makes sense, that works according to a narrative grammar that we understand.

For myself, this presentist heritage is not one that I would be anxious to divorce myself from. It seems to be an open secret among Victorianists that many of us are not primarily invested in either England or the nineteenth century. Speaking personally, I came to the field less because of a deep sense of attachment to either the time or the place, and more out of a desire to work within the closest thing the English language seemed to have to a realist tradition—and to work with the formalist and historical-materialist critical traditions that implies. I wasn't interested, and am still not overwhelmingly interested, in "speak[ing] with the dead," to use Stephen Greenblatt's famous phrase.[1] I am more interested in talking to myself: the way I think about my role in society, the way I encounter the fraught pleasures of reading. Not just talking to myself, actually—the choice of texts is not an individual one, so *we* are talking to *ourselves*.

This is part of the heritage of the Victorian novel. People see value in it because it seems to describe concerns that are still with us. As D. A. Miller puts it, "The 'death of the novel' . . . has really meant the explosion everywhere of the novelistic, no longer bound in three-deckers, but freely scattered across a far greater range of cultural experience."[2] The story of the Victorian novel, according to Miller, is thus the story of "a central episode in the genealogy of the present." Of course, this also means, as I suggested above, that this is partially because we select those novels which will seem to fit into that genealogy. But we also reproduce them: the mechanics I have been associating with the Victorian novel have continued rather unabated across cultural forms: novels, films, cable television prestige drama. The reason, I think, that we can detach the Victorian novel from the Victorian era in this way is two-fold. First of all, it speaks to the fact that the formal qualities we have been looking at are not tied completely to either England or the nineteenth century; rather they are, in many ways, features of realism more generally. If, for whatever reason, realism was associated with one chapter in literary history but not with the next, that does not mean that its position in the market, or in the culture more generally, had diminished greatly. Now, the question of why obscurity became a significant mark of literary style in the twentieth century is one that is beyond the scope of this study.[3] Yet the very notion of difficulty, of a literature that succeeds in no small part because it overturns our sense of how things *should* work in a novel, is always in part dependent on a continued intuitive understanding of those conventions. The underlying intuitions of realist fiction not only continue to exist in popular entertainments; they are also implied, in their absence, by any work that seeks to call them into question.

This idea—the dependence of the unexpected upon a tacit understanding of the expected—has a corollary in literary history. As Fredric Jameson has suggested, authors who wished to consider their work as "modern" or "modernist" required some sort of field to judge their work against. The work in question, as far as prose was concerned, tended to be the Victorian novel. In other words, we can associate Victorian fiction—a body of work that is well over one hundred years old—with the present in some small part because the modern fiction that followed it required something static on which to base the "new." Jameson makes this point:

> [W]e may observe that the division of literature into [realism and modernism] is dictated by the attempt to deal adequately with modernism, rather than the other way around (in this sense, even Lukács' accounts of realism are defensive and reflect his own "conversion" to the earlier artistic style). The concept of realism that thereby emerges is always that with which modernism has had to break, that norm from which modernism is the deviation.[4]

Jameson's goal here is to make modernism dialectically dependent on realism, and thereby to produce a periodization of literature that follows the continuities of capitalism, rather than one that decisively breaks at the turn of the century. But the paradoxical result of this approach is that it sets up the "norm"—the text that seems to obey the rules we implicitly understand—to be located in the past. To the extent that narrative difficulty is a result of defying expectation—or, as countless critical arguments have it, the "calling into question" of those expectations—it is necessary that we define it against some originary set of texts that held those expectations. This sort of static past is, for Jameson, a fiction, albeit one central to a certain sort of literary periodization:

> [W]henever you search for "realism" somewhere it vanishes, for it was nothing but punctuation, a mere marker or a "before" that permitted the phenomenon of modernism to come into focus properly. So as long as the latter holds the center of the field of vision, and the so-called traditional novel or classical novel or realistic novel or whatever constitutes a "ground" or blurred periphery, the illusion of adequate literary history may be maintained.[5]

The idea of a stable realism is something that can only be maintained from a distance; when we look too closely, we see that nothing perfectly fits the mold, and that nothing is, itself, thoroughly readable. There is something here of the old mathematical proof that there are no uninteresting numbers: if there were uninteresting numbers, one of them must be the smallest; and then it would be the smallest uninteresting number, which is interesting. When we draw out realist novels to look at them closely, they become distinctive—interesting to us precisely because of how they break the rules. Literary critics tend to place a good deal of value on novelists who, like cops in movies, play by their own rules.

But it's useful, I think, to understand the rules that we live by. Understanding is not the same as ratifying, of course—but it doesn't seem that any useful critique can occur without that understanding. When we talk about "the Victorian novel," we are talking less about the multiple possibilities of the books themselves and more about the criteria by which we label things familiar, intuitive, and like us. The Victorian novel, a tradition that we have inherited and continue to maintain and produce, is *ours*, in a way that it was not even the Victorians'. As I've said in a few places in this book, I don't think the moral structure of the Victorian novel should provide us with lessons. It's not what we ought to be, but rather what we are. That seems like a good place to start.

NOTES

INTRODUCTION: "MORALISED FABLES"

1. Friedrich Nietzsche, *The Portable Nietzsche*, ed. and trans. Walter Kaufmann (New York: Viking Press, 1964), 515–16.
2. Nietzsche, *Portable Nietzsche*, 515–16.
3. For an application of Nietzsche's ideas to a specific case of Victorian religion, see Donald D. Stone, "Arnold, Nietzsche, and the 'Revaluation of Values,'" *Nineteenth-Century Literature* 43, no. 3 (1988): 289–318. As for women writers, Eliot gets off easy compared with the "fertile writing-cow" George Sand (Nietzsche, *Portable Nietzsche*, 516).
4. Insults aside, there is good evidence to suggest that Nietzsche thought of Eliot first and foremost as a novelist. This came about, it seems, mainly through the reading habits of his mother and infamous sister: "In 1879 a letter from his sister describes an acquaintance by likening her to Maggie Tulliver, or 'Gretelchen' as she becomes in German and she clearly knows that he will understand the comparison. In the following year a letter from his mother mentions *Adam Bede* as one of the books she and his sister have been reading, and in 1887 he reminisces in a letter to his sister about an occasion when she had with her a volume of *Middlemarch* by 'the Good Eliot' ['der braven Eliot']." John Rignall, *George Eliot: European Novelist* (Surrey: Ashgate, 2011), 158.
5. William Makepeace Thackeray, *Catherine: A Story by Ikey Solomons, Esq. Junior*, ed. Sheldon F. Goldfarb (Ann Arbor: University of Michigan Press, 1999), 132.
6. Caroline Levine, *The Serious Pleasures of Suspense: Victorian Realism and Narrative Doubt* (Charlottesville: University of Virginia Press, 2003); Nicholas Dames, *The Physiology of the Novel: Reading, Neural Science, and the Form of Victorian Fiction* (Oxford: Oxford University Press, 2007).
7. "Wenn thatsächlich die Engländer glauben, sie wüssten von sich aus, 'intuitiv', was gut und böse its." It is not a term he uses freely in moral discussions. Though it appears a small number of times in *Beyond Good and Evil*, written two years before *Twilight of the Idols*, he does not use it at all in the *Genealogy*, written only one year before.
8. Bernard Williams, *Ethics and the Limits of Philosophy* (Cambridge, MA: Harvard University Press, 1985), 93–94. It should be noted here that there are two later versions of intuition, sometimes discussed in relation to literature—especially in modernism—in the philosophies of Henri Bergson and G. E. Moore. Both of these have received more attention in both the history of literature and the

history of ideas than the scholars I am discussing here. For discussions of these two thinkers in relation to British fiction, see e.g. Mary Ann Gillies, *Henri Bergson and British Modernism* (Montreal: McGill-Queen's University Press, 1996); Tom Regan, *Bloomsbury's Prophet: G. E. Moore and the Development of His Moral Philosophy* (Philadelphia: Temple University Press, 1986).

9. Henry Longueville Mansel, *Letters, Lectures, and Reviews, Including the Phrontisterion; or, Oxford in the 19th Century*, ed. Henry W. Chandler (London: John Murry, 1873), 135.

10. John Stuart Mill, *Utilitarianism*, ed. Roger Crisp (New York: Oxford University Press, 2003), 50.

11. J. B. Schneewind, "Moral Problems and Moral Philosophy in the Victorian Period," *Victorian Studies* 9 (1965): 30. For some time, Schneewind's work has been unparalleled in its exposition of the importance of intuitionism in nineteenth-century English moral thought, and his discussion of the subject is essential background. See also J. B. Schneewind, "Whewell's Ethics," in *Studies in Moral Philosophy*, ed. Nicholas Rescher, American Philosophical Quarterly Monograph Series (Oxford: Basil Blackwell, 1968), 108–41. Another excellent recent resource is Laura J. Snyder, *Reforming Philosophy: A Victorian Debate on Science and Society* (Chicago: University of Chicago Press, 2006). Though Snyder's book deals more with the scientific and logical side of the debate between Mill and Whewell, it does touch on the moral implications of this debate. See especially chapter 5. Information on the place of religion in the debate between intuitionists and utilitarians, especially as it relates to novels, can be found in Robert Newsom, "Dickens and the Goods," in *Contemporary Dickens*, ed. Deirdre David and Eileen Gillooly (Ohio State University Press, 2009), 35–52. For the prehistory of these debates, from Shaftesbury through Smith and Hume, see D. D. Raphael, *The Moral Sense* (New York: Oxford University Press, 1947); James Bonar, *Moral Sense* (London: George Allen & Unwin, 1930).

12. Discussing "ethical criticism," Jameson makes sure to distinguish his topic from "a moralizing, or moralistic, didactic gesture of the type presumably extinct with the Scrutiny group if not with the Victorian age." Fredric Jameson, *The Political Unconscious: Narrative as a Socially Symbolic Act* (Ithaca: Cornell University Press, 1981), 60.

13. Henry James, "The Life of George Eliot," in *Literary Criticism: Essays on Literature, American Writers, English Writers*, ed. Leon Edel (New York: Library of America, 1984), 1002.

14. F. R. Leavis, *The Great Tradition: George Eliot, Henry James, Joseph Conrad* (New York: New York University Press, 1963).

15. Virginia Woolf, *The Second Common Reader*, ed. Andrew MacNeillie (New York: Harcourt Brace, 1986), 233.

16. See Dominick LaCapra, *Madame Bovary on Trial* (Ithaca: Cornell University Press, 1982), ch. 2.

17. Georg Lukács, *Studies in European Realism: A Sociological Survey of the Writings of Balzac, Stendhal, Zola, Tolstoy, Gorki, and Others*, trans. Edith Bone (London: Merlin Press, 1989), 56; Roland Barthes, *S/Z*, trans. Richard Miller (New York:

Hill and Wang, 1974), 135; Peter Brooks, *Reading for the Plot: Design and Intention in Narrative* (New York: Vintage Books, 1985), 37

18. Marjorie Garber, Beatrice Hanssen, and Rebecca L. Walkowitz, eds., *The Turn to Ethics* (New York: Routledge, 2000).

19. Jameson, *Political*, 59.

20. When Martha Nussbaum, to take an extreme example, describes the morally salutary effects of reading, it sounds more like a prescription for proper reading practices than a description of novels themselves. Novels, she writes, "convey the sense that there are links of possibility, at least on a very general level, between the characters and the reader. The reader's emotions and imagination are highly active as a result." What evidence is there for these claims? How do we diagnose those who do not read in this way? Martha C. Nussbaum, *Poetic Justice: The Literary Imagination and Public Life* (Boston: Beacon Press, 1995), 5.

21. Amanda Anderson, *The Powers of Distance: Cosmopolitanism and the Cultivation of Detachment* (Princeton: Princeton University Press, 2001); Levine, *Suspense*; Andrew Miller, *The Burdens of Perfection: On Ethics and Reading in Nineteenth-Century British Literature* (Ithaca: Cornell University Press, 2008)

22. In highlighting these critics, I am pointing specifically to the influence of their work on reading ethics in the Victorian novel. They are certainly not alone in drawing lessons from their texts. Far from it: Jameson has suggested that ethical criticism, reading in order to draw some sort of lesson, is "still the predominant form of literary and cultural criticism today [1981], in spite of its repudiation by every successive generation of literary theorists (each for a different reason)." Jameson, *Political*, 59

CHAPTER ONE: WHAT FEELS RIGHT

1. Georg Lukács, *Studies in European Realism: A Sociological Survey of the Writings of Balzac, Stendhal, Zola, Tolstoy, Gorki, and Others*, trans. Edith Bone (London: Merlin Press, 1989), 55.

2. Lukács is the exception in popular narrative theory, with his Marxist-Hegelian belief in the great novel's ability to capture the "total picture" of society at a given time. For him, the science that explained the experience of narrative was historical materialism itself. The reader was moved by the experience of history itself. Still, it is worth remembering that Fredric Jameson not only felt compelled to defend Lukács against charges of vulgarity and datedness (especially in his introduction to *The Historical Novel*) but also, in *The Political Unconscious*, to supplement Lukács's project with the techniques of formalism and semiotics: in order to extend Lukács's discussion of Balzac, he turns in the next paragraph to Todorov and Greimas (Jameson, *Political*, 164).

3. Noam Chomsky, *Knowledge of Language: Its Nature, Origin, and Use* (Westport, CT: Greenwood Publishing Group, 1986), 36. This citation, and the one that follows, were both brought to my attention in Michael Devitt, "Intuitions in Linguistics," *British Journal for the Philosophy of Science* 57, no. 3 (2006): 481–513.

4. Quoted in Devitt, "Intuitions," 481–82.

5. See Julia S. Falk, "Saussure and American Linguistics," in *The Cambridge Companion to Saussure*, ed. Carol Sanders (New York: Cambridge University Press, 2004), 119–20. The translation between the two sets of terms is not exact. One particular distinction is that the Saussurean axiom of language as a "social fact" gets replaced by what David McNeill calls "a kind of individual psychology." David McNeill, *Gesture and Thought* (Chicago: University of Chicago Press, 2005), 76–77, also 78–79. This move has certainly not been without its critics. See, e.g., John Hewson, "*Langue* and *Parole* Since Saussure," *Historiographia Linguistica* 3, no. 3 (1976): 329.

6. Jonathan Culler, *Structuralist Poetics: Structuralism, Linguistics, and the Study of Literature* (Ithaca: Cornell University Press, 1975), 9.

7. Seymour Chatman, *Story and Discourse: Narrative Structure in Fiction and Film* (Ithaca: Cornell University Press, 1978), 22.

8. Barthes, *S/Z*, 135.

9. Brooks, *Reading*, 37.

10. Thackeray, *Catherine*, 132.

11. Dames, *Physiology*, 39.

12. Alexander Bain, *Mental and Moral Science: A Compendium of Psychology and Ethics*, 3rd ed. (London: Longman, Green, 1884), 268. For a much more extended discussion of this use of the term "interest" as it relates to narrative, see the following chapter.

13. Dorothy J. Hale, *Social Formalism: The Novel in Theory from Henry James to the Present* (Stanford: Stanford University Press, 1998), 9.

14. Martha C. Nussbaum, *Love's Knowledge: Essays on Philosophy and Literature* (New York: Oxford University Press, 1990), 8.

15. Richard Rorty, *Contingency, Irony, and Solidarity* (Cambridge: Cambridge University Press, 1989), 16.

16. See Hale, *Social Formalism*, chs. 1, 3.

17. Adam Smith, *Theory of Moral Sentiments*, ed. D. D. Raphael and A. L. Macfie (Indianapolis: Liberty Fund, 1982), 10.

18. See, for example, the synthesis of Bakhtinian dialogism and Levinasian ethics in Adam Zachary Newton, *Narrative Ethics* (Cambridge, MA: Harvard University Press, 1995).

19. Gayatri Chakravorty Spivak, "Ethics and Politics in Tagore, Coetzee, and Certain Scenes of Teaching," *Diacritics* 32, nos. 3–4 (2002): 22. Coetzee is a frequent topic of this sort of analysis, and with good reason. His novels—*Disgrace* perhaps most of all—deny both characters and the reader the comfort and reassurance that comes from intersubjective identification with another. In one knowing passage, Lucy tells David that she intends to carry her pregnancy from the rape to term. When he asks why she had not told him, she responds:

> I can't run my life according to whether or not you like what I do. Not any more. You behave as if everything I do is part of the story of your life. You are the main character, I am a minor character that doesn't make an appearance until halfway through. Well, contrary to what you think, people are not divided into major and minor. I am

not minor. I have a life of my own, just as important to me as yours is to you, and in my life I am the one who makes the decisions. (J. M. Coetzee, *Disgrace* [New York: Penguin, 2000], 198)

Coetzee thus points out how the novel tradition uses its ethic of intersubjectivity to solidify its division of major and minor characters: those whose eyes we see the world through, and those whose pain we feel. A book on Coetzee that takes a largely Levinasian approach is Derek Attridge, *J. M. Coetzee and the Ethics of Reading: Literature in the Event* (Chicago: University of Chicago Press, 2005).

20. Luc Boltanski, *Distant Suffering: Morality, Media, and Politics*, trans. Graham D. Burchell (Cambridge: Cambridge University Press, 1999), 38.

21. Audrey Jaffe, *Scenes of Sympathy: Identity and Representation in Victorian Fiction* (Ithaca: Cornell University Press, 2000), 8.

22. Rae Greiner, *Sympathetic Realism in Nineteenth-Century British Fiction* (Baltimore: Johns Hopkins University Press, 2012), 8–9.

23. This example, like many others discussed in this section, was first brought to my attention in J. B. Schneewind, *Sidgwick's Ethics and Victorian Moral Philosophy* (Oxford: Oxford University Press, 1977), 89.

24. Adam Sedgwick, *A Discourse on the Studies of the University*, 5th ed. (London: John W. Parker, 1850), 57.

25. *Times*, January 10, 1834.

26. John Stuart Mill, "Sedgwick's Discourse," in *Essays on Ethics, Religion, and Society*, ed. John M. Robson, vol. 10, *The Collected Works of John Stuart Mill* (Toronto: University of Toronto Press, 1985), 52.

27. "[The *Discourse*] excited great indignation in my fathers and others, which I thought it fully deserved." John Stuart Mill, *Autobiography*, ed. Jack Stillinger (New York: Houghton Mifflin, 1969), 120.

28. Stephen Darwall, *The British Moralists and the Internal "Ought": 1640–1740* (Cambridge: Cambridge University Press, 1995), 13. The reference is to a rather diverse collection of thinkers: "Hobbes, Cudworth, Cumberland, Locke, Shaftesbury, Hutcheson, Butler, and Hume."

29. Mill, for example, uses the two terms interchangeably in *Utilitarianism*, moving from freely from a reference to moral sense theory and utilitarianism to a reference to "the intuitive [and] what may be termed the inductive school of ethics" (50).

30. William Whewell, *Lectures on the History of Moral Philosophy in England* (London: J. W. Parker, 1854), ix.

31. Mansel, *Letters*, 132–33.

32. William Edward Hartpole Lecky, *History of European Morals from Augustus to Charlemagne* (New York: D. Appleton, 1921), 1.

33. "The opposition between 'inductive morality' and 'intuitive morality,' which the contemporary English school so often insists upon." Jean-Marie Guyau, *La morale anglaise contemporaine: Morale de l'utilité et de l'évolution* (Paris: Félix Alcan, 1885), 200.

34. Francis Hutcheson, *An Inquiry into the Original of Our Ideas of Beauty and Virtue*, ed. Wolfgang Leidhold (Indianapolis: Liberty Fund, 2004), 9–10.

35. D. D. Raphael writes that Hutcheson's usage "appears to have been the first" (Raphael, *Moral Sense*, 15).

36. John Locke, *An Essay concerning Human Understanding*, ed. Peter H. Nidditch (New York: Oxford University Press, 1975), 351.

37. Whewell, *Lectures* xx.

38. Mansel, *Letters*, 136–37.

39. Schneewind, "Moral Problems," 34–35.

40. Foucault's claim, in *The Order of Things*, that the end of the eighteenth century, and Kant in particular, marked an epistemic shift to an emphasis on an inaccessible internality—as epitomized by the transcendental subject—describes this change in focus well, though it does not offer much in the way of explanation. Michel Foucault, *The Order of Things: An Archaeology of the Human Sciences* (New York: Vintage Books, 1994), 247–48.

41. Certainly, *Hard Times* is the best known of these, but we can find it in novels throughout the century. Sometimes, an almost hyperbolic expression can appear in rather muted language, as in Disraeli's description in *Sybil* of four-year-old girls being sent to work in the mines. Disraeli writes that the children's labor is a "punishment which philosophical philanthropy has invented for the direst criminals, and which those criminals deem more terrible than the death for which it is substituted." Thus Disraeli not only compares the worst extents of English class oppression to Benthamite prison reform but actually makes the two equivalent. Perhaps striking a more familiar tone is Eliot's mock apology in "Janet's Repentance" for her inability to think in utilitarian terms: "emotion, I fear, is absolutely irrational; it insists on caring for individuals; it absolutely refuses to adopt the quantitative view of human anguish, and to admit that thirteen happy lives are a set-off against twelve miserable lives, which leaves a clear balance on the side of satisfaction. This is the inherent imbecility of feeling, and one must be a great philosopher to have got quite clear of all that." Benjamin Disraeli, *Sybil; or, The Two Nations*, ed. Sheila Smith (New York: Oxford University Press, 1981), 140; George Eliot, *Scenes of Clerical Life*, ed. Jennifer Gribble (New York: Penguin, 1998), 314.

42. Ruth Bernard Yeazell, "Why Political Novels Have Heroines: *Sybil, Mary Barton*, and *Felix Holt*," *Novel* 18, no. 2 (Winter 1985): 126.

43. Elizabeth Gaskell, *Mary Barton*, ed. MacDonald Daly (New York: Penguin, 1996), 385. A clearer statement of the same point comes in *North and South*, when she writes that Margaret Hale "saw less of power in its public effect, and, as it happened, she was thrown with one or two of those who, in all measures affecting masses of people, must be acute sufferers for the good of many." Elizabeth Gaskell, *North and South*, ed. Patricia Ingham (New York: Penguin, 1995), 70.

44. Charles Dickens, *Hard Times*, ed. Kate Flint (New York: Penguin Books, 1995), 60.

45. Quoted in Raymond Williams, *Culture and Society, 1780–1950* (New York: Columbia University Press, 1983), 88.

46. Williams, *Culture*, 89.

47. Williams, *Culture*, 96.

48. Gaskell, *Mary Barton*, 62.

49. Robyn Warhol, *Gendered Interventions: Narrative Discourse in the Victorian Novel* (New Brunswick, NJ: Rutgers University Press, 1989), 64-65. Warhol gives a thorough account of the various forms that Gaskell's references to "you" and "we" take in *Mary Barton*.

50. Carolyn Lesjak, *Working Fictions: A Genealogy of the Victorian Novel* (Durham, NC: Duke University Press, 2006), 37.

51. See Jonathan H. Grossman, *The Art of Alibi: English Law Courts and the Novel* (Baltimore: Johns Hopkins University Press, 2002), 118–25.

52. Tzvetan Todorov, "Narrative Transformations," in *The Poetics of Prose*, trans. Richard Howard (Ithaca: Cornell University Press, 1977), 232.

53. Hutcheson, *Inquiry*, 145.

54. "In every system of morality, which I have hitherto met with . . . of a sudden I am supriz'd to find, that instead of the usual copulations of prepositions, *is* and *is not*, I meet with no proposition that is not connected with an *ought*, or an *ought not* . . . .'Tis necessary . . . that a reason should be given, for what seems altogether inconceivable, how this new relation can be a deduction from others, which are entirely different from it." David Hume, *A Treatise of Human Nature*, ed. Ernest C. Mossner (New York: Penguin, 1985), 520.

55. Geoffrey Galt Harpham, *Getting It Right: Language, Literature, and Ethics* (Chicago: University of Chicago Press, 1992), 183.

56. See, e.g., Harry J. Gensler, *Formal Ethics* (New York: Routledge, 1996), ch. 8.

57. André Gide, *The Counterfeiters*, trans. Dorothy Bussy and Justin O'Brien (New York: Knopf, 1947), 171.

58. John Rawls, *A Theory of Justice* (Cambridge, MA: Belknap Press, 1999), 225.

59. Friedrich Nietzsche, *Thus Spoke Zarathustra: A Book for None and All*, trans. Walter Kaufmann (New York: Penguin, 1978), 139.

60. Friedrich Nietzsche, *The Gay Science*, trans. Walter Kaufmann (New York: Vintage, 1974), 273.

61. G.W.F. Hegel, *Hegel's Philosophy of Right*, trans. T. M. Knox (New York: Oxford University Press, 1967), 32. For insight into the possible similarities between Hegel's project and Rawls's project in a *A Theory of Justice*, see the discussion of *Versöhnung* in John Rawls, *Lectures on the History of Moral Philosophy*, ed. Barbara Herman (Cambridge, MA: Harvard University Press, 2000), 331.

62. Michel Foucault, "The Ethics of the Concern of the Self as a Practice of Freedom," in *Ethics: Subjectivity and Truth*, ed. Paul Rabinow, vol. 1, *Essential Works of Foucault, 1954–1984* (New York: New Press, 1997), 284. For more on Foucault's rhetorical style, in his later works, of disowning theories associated with him, see Amanda Anderson, *The Way We Argue Now: A Study in the Cultures of Theory* (Princeton: Princeton University Press, 2006) ch. 6.

63. Geoffrey Galt Harpham, *Shadows of Ethics: Criticism and the Just Society* (Durham, NC: Duke University Press, 1999), 37.

64. Chatman, *Story*, 108–13.

65. Immanuel Kant, *Groundwork of the Metaphysics of Morals*, ed. and trans. Mary Gregor (Cambridge: Cambridge University Press, 2002), 4:455–56. Page number given in this and future references to Kant are for the German Academy

of Sciences edition of Kant's collected works, given in the margins of most English editions.

66. See, e.g., *Groundwork* 4:452–53: "As a rational being, and thus as a being belonging to the intelligible world, the human being can never think of the causality of his own will otherwise than under the idea of freedom; for, independence from the determining causes of the world of sense (which reason must always ascribe to itself) is freedom."

67. E. M. Forster, *Aspects of the Novel* (New York: Brace & World, 1954), 130.

68. Jonathan Loesberg, *Fictions of Consciousness: Mill, Newman, and the Reading of Victorian Prose* (New Brunswick, NJ: Rutgers University Press, 1986), 1.

69. John Henry Cardinal Newman, *Apologia Pro Vita Sua*, ed. David J. DeLaura (New York: W. W. Norton, 1968), 12.

70. Immanuel Kant, *Critique of Practical Reason*, ed. and trans. Mary Gregor (Cambridge: Cambridge University Press, 2001), 5:98.

71. Jacques Lacan, *The Four Fundamental Concepts of Psychoanalysis*, ed. Jacques-Alain Miller, trans. Alan Sheridan (New York: W. W. Norton, 1998), 275.

72. J. Hillis Miller, *The Ethics of Reading: Kant, de Man, Eliot, Trollope, James, and Benjamin* (New York: Columbia University Press, 1987), 28.

73. Harpham, *Shadows*, 35.

74. J.J.C. Smart and Bernard Williams, *Utilitarianism, For and Against* (New York: Cambridge University Press, 1973), 104.

75. Some distinction has to be drawn between "act-utilitarianism," which would judge by the consequences of the act in itself, and "rule-utilitarianism," which would judge from the consequences of the act universalized as a general rule. So, to use one oft-cited example, an act-utilitarian ethic might support deploying ten United Nations peacekeepers on a dangerous mission that will definitely save fifty lives; a rule-utilitarian might point out that such a deployment could make people much less inclined to sign up for reserve duty, thereby leading to an inability to deploy peacekeepers in even more dangerous catastrophes.

76. Perhaps the most significant way in which ethical examples match our understanding of realism is through their suggestion of an arbitrary main character; it could, in the abstract, be any one of us. This seems to match well with Lukács's view of the *Bildungsroman*, in which the choice of protagonist is "merely accidental": "the hero is picked out of an unlimited number of men who share his aspirations" (Georg Lukács, *The Theory of the Novel: A Historico-Philosophical Essay on the Forms of Great Epic Literature*, trans. Anna Bostock (Cambridge, MA: MIT Press, 1991), 134). A fuller examination of the development of the ethical example as literary genre would be, I believe, profitable for understanding the relation of the literary and the philosophical, especially in the Anglo-American tradition, but it lies outside the scope of this current approach.

77. Williams's necessity, it should be said, is not the same as an intuitionist's, and certainly not the same as Kant's—he is much more concerned here with the question of "moral integrity." My point, though, is less about what he is arguing for, and more about *how* he is arguing *against* utilitarianism.

78. Bernard Williams, *Moral Luck: Philosophical Papers 1973–1980* (Cambridge: Cambridge University Press, 1981), 26–27. This follows his more famous example of

the biography of Paul Gauguin. Of course, since the vast majority of people will have no firsthand account of Gauguin's biography, the trimmed-down version of his life that most of us encounter will also take the form of a literary example of sorts—though one missing an author.

79. Bernard Williams, *Shame and Necessity* (Berkeley: University of California Press, 1994), 12.

CHAPTER TWO: THE SUBJECT OF THE NEWGATE NOVEL

1. Louis James, *The Victorian Novel* (London: Blackwell, 2006), 156.

2. Quoted in Philip Collins, ed., *Charles Dickens: The Critical Heritage* (London: Routledge, 1996), 45. The diary entry is from December 30, 1938. An entry from exactly one week earlier mentions finishing Bulwer-Lytton's *Eugene Aram*—one of the crime novels discussed in this chapter. Suffice it to say that Newgate novels were early Victorian novels in more ways than one.

3. John Forster, "The Literary Examiner," *Examiner*, November 3 1839, 691. For the most complete discussion of the *Jack Sheppard* phenomenon, see Martin Meisel, *Realizations: Narrative, Pictorial, and Theatrical Arts in Nineteenth-Century England* (Princeton: Princeton University Press, 1983), 265–79. For a compelling discussion of the relations between this phenomenon and increasing social alienation, see Matthew Buckley, "Sensations of Celebrity: *Jack Sheppard* and the Mass Audience," *Victorian Studies* 44, no. 3 (Spring 2002): 423–63.

4. Sir Theodore Martin, quoted in Horace Bleackley, *Trial of Jack Sheppard* (Edinburgh: William Hodge, 1933), 99. The chorus of the song means roughly, "Never mind, pals, keep on stealing." It does not appear in the novel *Jack Sheppard* but rather in Ainsworth's 1831 *Rookwood*.

5. William Makepeace Thackeray, *The Letters and Private Papers of William Makepeace Thackeray*, ed. Gordon N. Ray (Cambridge, MA: Harvard University Press, 1945), 1:395.

6. Keith Hollingsworth, *The Newgate Novel, 1830–1847: Bulwer, Ainsworth, Dickens, and Thackeray* (Detroit: Wayne State University Press, 1963), 132. Hollingsworth's book offers the only comprehensive study of the Newgate subgenre that this chapter will address. Though I offer some different interpretations than Hollingsworth, his work is so complete as to offer a fuller discussion of most of the contemporary pieces that I reference.

7. Review, *Athenaeum*, October 26, 1839, 803.

8. Bulwer-Lytton had been Edward Lytton Bulwer until he was created a baronet in 1838. Since he had written the works under consideration prior to lordship and hyphenation, I follow Keith Hollingsworth in using the shorter name to refer to him simply as "Bulwer" henceforth.

9. Some critics include Dickens's 1841 *Barnaby Rudge* and Bulwer's 1846 *Lucretia* on this list as well, largely as postscripts.

10. D. A. Miller, *The Novel and the Police* (Berkeley: University of California Press, 1988), 2.

11. Franco Moretti, *Atlas of the European Novel: 1800–1900* (London: Verso, 1998), 84.

12. John Forster, "The Literary Examiner," *The Examiner*, September 10, 1837, 581.

13. "Recent Novels," *Monthly Chronicle* 5 (February 1840): 221–22.

14. Boris Tomashevsky, "Thematics," in *Russian Formalist Criticism: Four Essays*, trans. Lee T. Lemon and Marion J. Reis (Lincoln: University of Nebraska Press, 1965), 67.

15. See LaCapra, *Bovary*, ch. 2.

16. "Recent Novels," 220, 221.

17. Thackeray, *Catherine*, 132.

18. William Makepeace Thackeray, "Horae Catnachianae: A Dissertation on Ballads, with a Few Unnecessary Remarks on Jonathan Wild, John Sheppard, Paul Clifford, and — Fagin, Esqrs." *Fraser's Magazine* 19 (April 1839): 409.

19. Steven Marcus, *Dickens: From Pickwick to Dombey* (New York: Basic Books, 1965), 67–68.

20. Burton M. Wheeler, "The Text and Plan of *Oliver Twist*," *Dickens Studies Annual* 12 (1984): 41.

21. A particularly notable moment comes at the conclusion of chapter 7, as Oliver runs away to London. When he visits the orphanage to see his dying friend, the original version reads: "The blessing was from a young child's lips but it was the first that Oliver had ever heard invoked upon his head; and through all the struggles and sufferings of his after life, through the trouble and changes *of many weary years* he never once forgot it." When Dickens revised this passage for the 1838 version, he removed the italicized passage.

22. Charles Dickens, *Oliver Twist*, ed. Kathleen Tillotson (Oxford: Oxford University Press, 1999), 12.

23. Hollingsworth, *Newgate*, 65.

24. Edward Bulwer-Lytton, *Paul Clifford* (Boston: Little, Brown, 1897), 1:xv.

25. Perhaps not wanting to have *Oliver* aligned *too* closely with a novel about a highwayman, he goes on to say, in impressively evasive and ambiguous prose, that Bulwer's novel "cannot be fairly considered as having, or being intended to have, any bearing on this part of the subject, one way or other."

26. Through a number of Bulwerian convolutions of plot, nearly impossible to summarize, the lawyer in question will turn out both to be Paul's real father and the judge who sentences him to death. The lawyer's niece, beside him at the time of the theft, will become Paul's wife after he escapes hanging (Wheeler, "Text and Plan," 50).

27. "Literary Recipes," *Punch*, August 7, 1841, 39. The charity boy likely refers to Paul Clifford. The factory boy is a reference to the main character of Frances Trollope's 1840 *Life and Adventures of Michael Armstrong, Factory Boy*. The carpenter's apprentice is, of course, Jack Sheppard.

28. Miller, *Police*, 6.

29. We might take this as the moment where *Oliver Twist* parts company permanently with *Paul Clifford*. William Brandon, the man who is robbed by Paul's companion, is a lawyer, who insists that Paul be arrested. He also turns out to be not only Paul's father but also the judge in Paul's final trial. Paul, unlike

Oliver, is unable to escape the world of delinquency, through either the novel's criminal story, its love story (she is Brandon's niece), or its genealogical story.

30. Miller, *Police*, 9.

31. Other names that critics have used for the complex of motivations surrounding Monks, the locket, and Mrs. Corney include the "inheritance story," the "rescue story," and the "mystery story." I have chosen to refer to it as "genealogical" largely because that fits with the network of connections I see it producing between the disparate elements of the novel.

32. Caroline Levine, *The Serious Pleasures of Suspense: Victorian Realism and Narrative Doubt* (Charlottesville: University of Virginia Press, 2003), 2.

33. See, e.g., Jameson, *Political Unconscious*, 152–54.

34. Hitchcock's description of the MacGuffin: "It is the mechanical element that usually crops up in any story. In crook stories it is most always the necklace and in spy stories it is most always the papers" (1939 speech at Columbia University, cited in the definition of the term). The majority of the revelation in chapter 49 centers on the locket and a destroyed will.

35. Charles Dickens, *The Letters of Charles Dickens*, ed. Graham Storey, Kathleen Tillotson, and Nina Burgis (New York: Oxford University Press, 1965), 1:388.

36. Harpham, *Shadows*, 37.

37. *Times*, June 25, 1840, 14.

38. *Times*, July 7, 1840, 7.

39. J. R. Stephens, "Jack Sheppard and the Licensers: The Case against Newgate Plays," *Nineteenth-Century Theatre Research* 1 (1973): 1–13.

40. William Makepeace Thackeray, "Going to See a Man Hanged," *Fraser's Magazine* 22 (July 1840): 154.

41. J. H. Reynolds's reaction is particularly memorable: "'Whom are you depicting, Mr. William Harrison Ainsworth?' asked we; and his novel answered for him, 'Jonathan Wild.' . . . 'What! Jonathan Wild the Great? After Fielding, *that's* much—ay, *very* much, indeed.'" The contrast with Gay, according to Reynolds, is "still more woful." John Hamilton Reynolds, "William Ainsworth and Jack Sheppard," *Fraser's Magazine* 21 (February 1840): 232, 236.

42. Fielding's work is titled, in full, *The Life of Mr. Jonathan Wild the Great*. Fielding's use of Wild was intended to satirize the Whig party in power at the time, and especially the "Great Man" Walpole, on the grounds that "Greatness consists in bringing all Manner of Mischief on Mankind, and Goodness in removing it from them." Henry Fielding, *The Life of Mr. Jonathan Wild the Great*, ed. Hugh Armory (Oxford: Oxford University Press, 2003), 9.

43. Tomashevsky, "Thematics," 65.

44. Tomashevsky, "Thematics," 66.

45. Jaffe, *Scenes*, 9.

46. Of course, in some cases, a sort of sympathetic identification was a key element of the novels. In his discussion of Bulwer's *Eugene Aram*, Jonathan Grossman offers a compelling reading of the narrative mechanics that an author could use to produce such sympathy for criminals, particularly through an emphasis on the internal in his characters. Grossman, *Alibi*, 143ff.

47. Thackeray, *Catherine*, 133.

48. Bulwer's *Eugene Aram* offers perhaps the best-known example of a novel about the crimes of a "virtuous philosopher." Though Thackeray does not refer to it explicitly here, he, and the rest of the *Fraser's* staff, made the novel the object of frequent ridicule. See also the discussion later in this chapter of the epistle opening to *Elizabeth Brownrigge*.

49. William Makepeace Thackeray, "Thieves' Literature of France," *Foreign Quarterly Review* 31 (April 1843): 233.

50. William Harrison Ainsworth, *Rookwood* (London: J. M. Dent & Sons, 1931), 3.

51. *Examiner* (London), November 3, 1839, 691.

52. The most famous collection, and the source of the generic name, was Andrew Knapp and William Baldwin's *Newgate Calendar; or, Malefactor's Bloody Register*, published in 1773. Of nearly equal popularity was the 1780 *Annals of Newgate*, by the Rev. John Villette, chaplain of Newgate Prison. Other collections include *Select Trials of Murder, Robbery, Rape . . .* (1734–35); *The Lives of the Most Remarkable Criminals* (1735); *The Tyburn Chronicle* (1768); and *The Old Bailey Chronicle* (1788). When I refer to *Newgate Calendars*, I am referring generically to this collection of texts.

53. Dickens, *Letters*, 1:114.

54. *Church of England Quarterly Review* 27 (1850), 25.

55. Brooks, *Reading*, 37.

56. See Nicholas Dames, "Wave-Theories and Affective Physiologies: The Cognitive Strain in Victorian Novel Theories," *Victorian Studies* 46, no. 2 (Winter 2004): 206–16.

57. Bain, *Mental*, 268.

58. Albert O. Hirschman, *The Passions and the Interests: Political Arguments for Capitalism before Its Triumph*, 20th anniv. ed. (Princeton: Princeton University Press, 1997), 20ff.

59. Francis Hutcheson, *A System of Moral Philosophy* (Glasgow: R. and A. Foulis, 1755), 1:9–10. Hutcheson's use of this term is discussed in Hirschman, *Passions*, 65–66.

60. Thackeray's disposition to ironic detachment, of course, should prevent us from taking his commitment to calmness as typical. He felt, for example, that Charlotte Brontë's unhappiness made her unjust toward her characters.: "Novel writers should not be in a passion with their characters as I imagine, but describe them, good or bad, with a like calm." My aim, however, is not to argue that Thackeray's outlook is typical of *all* novel readers. Rather it is to suggest that in the particular discussion of novelistic depictions of crime, Thackeray's language and opinions seem to have held the day. Thackeray, *Letters*, 3:67.

61. From the "Advertisement" to *Catherine*. Goldfarb notes that this is not in the copy text and may have been a posthumous addition. If so, it nonetheless stands as an accurate statement of Thackeray's views. Thackeray, *Catherine*, 190.

62. Thackeray, "Hanged," 155.

63. Thackeray, "Horae," 408.

64. Quoted in Gordon N. Ray, *Thackeray: The Uses of Adversity, 1811–1846* (New York: McGraw-Hill, 1955), 231.

65. William Makepeace Thackeray, *The History of Pendennis*, ed. John Sutherland (Oxford: Oxford University Press, 1994), lvi.

66. The inability to affect what we are reading is a feature of all realist novels: those texts that Barthes labeled as "classic" or "readerly" and leave the reader "with no more than the poor freedom to accept or reject the text." Barthes, *S/Z*, 4. Andrew Miller has pointed to Austen's novels, in particular, as deriving "their peculiarly powerful aesthetic effect for our helplessness before the events about which we read." Miller, *Burdens*, 128.

67. Georg Lukács, *The Historical Novel*, trans. Hannah Mitchell and Stanley Mitchell (Lincoln: University of Nebraska Press, 1983), 39, 33.

68. Fredric Jameson, *The Antinomies of Realism* (London: Verso, 2013), 262.

69. William Harrison Ainsworth, *Jack Sheppard: A Romance* (London: George Routledge & Sons, 1900[?]), 313.

70. J. B. Buckstone, "Jack Sheppard," in *Trilby and Other Plays*, ed. George Taylor (Oxford: Oxford University Press, 1996), 79–80. This scene is also discussed in Buckley, "Sensations."

71. Review, *Athenaeum*, October 26, 1839, 803.

72. Reynolds, "Sheppard," 232.

73. For a thorough discussion of Wild's criminal operation, see Gerald Howson, *Thief-Taker General: The Rise and Fall of Jonathan Wild* (New York: St. Martin's Press, 1971).

74. Edward Bulwer-Lytton, *Eugene Aram* (Boston: Little, Brown, 1897), 32, 43.

75. [Anon.], *The Malefactor's Register; or, New Newgate and Tyburn Calendar* (London: Alex Hogg, 1779), 4:310.

76. "Elizabeth Brownrigge: A Tale," *Fraser's Magazine* 32 (1832): 68. The authorship of this parody remains a matter of some dispute. Critics have come increasingly to agree, however, that the late nineteenth- and early twentieth-century attribution of the piece to Thackeray was mistaken. Miriam Thrall suggests that the piece was most likely written by Maginn, with the assistance of J. G. Lockhart. Whoever the author may be, however, the influence of the piece on *Catherine* seems clear. See Miriam Thrall, *Rebellious Fraser's: Nol Yorke's Magazine in the Days of Maginn, Thackeray, and Carlyle* (New York: AMS Press, 1966), 62–64. For a discussion of articles wrongly attributed to Thackeray, including but not limited to "Elizabeth Brownrigge," see Edward M. White, "Thackeray's Contributions to *Fraser's Magazine*," *Studies in Bibliography* 19 (1966): 68–65.

77. Ainsworth, *Rookwood*, 6.

78. Paul Veyne, *Did the Greeks Believe Their Myths?: An Essay on the Constitutive Imagination*, trans. Paula Wissig (Chicago: University of Chicago Press, 1988), 22–23. The term "myth" is precarious, since it can have so many meanings, often opposed to each other. Rather than risk confusing my usage with that of Frye, Durkheim, or Lévi-Strauss, I will try to avoid the term. For a Lévi-Straussian reading of eighteenth-century criminal narratives such as those of Sheppard and Turpin—which embraces the term "myth"—see Lincoln B. Faller, *Turned to Account: The Forms and Functions of Criminal Biography in Seventeenth- and Early Eighteenth-Century England* (Cambridge: Cambridge University Press, 1987).

79. Quoted in John Hamilton Reynolds, "Hints for a History of Highwaymen," *Fraser's Magazine* 9 (March 1834): 284.

80. Anthony Burton makes this point: "Most of the *Jack Sheppard* plates . . . are heavily loaded with accessories; the reader is intended to miss none of them, and Ainsworth conscientiously details them in the text." Anthony Burton, "Cruikshank as an Illustrator of Fiction," in *George Cruikshank: A Reevaluation*, ed. Robert L. Patten (Princeton: Princeton University Press, 1974), 110.

81. *Daily Journal*, November 15, 1724.

82. Paul Ricoeur, "Narrative Time," *Critical Inquiry* 7, no. 1, Autumn (1980): 179.

83. Barthes, *S/Z*, 4.

CHAPTER THREE: GETTING *DAVID COPPERFIELD*

1. Miller, *Police*, 205.

2. Charles Dickens, *David Copperfield*, ed. Nina Burgis (New York: Oxford University Press, 1981), 630.

3. In "Dickens and the Mystery Novel," Shklovsky refers to Dickensian parallel plots as the "device of several simultaneous planes of action, the relationship among which is not immediately given by the author"; such a device is "a peculiar continuation of the technique of the mystery." Though Shklovsky is focusing on *Little Dorrit*, he implies that his analysis carries through to the "Dickensian device" as it pertains to the corpus as whole. Viktor Shklovsky, *Theory of Prose*, trans. Benjamin Sher (Normal, IL: Dalkey Archive Press, 1998), 137, 146.

4. For the sake of brevity, I have suppressed part of this complicated passage. Though the phrasing in this sentence is absolute, David also says that there is "one reservation," the "most secret current of his mind" which he held back. He is referring here to his love for Agnes, which itself can hardly be a surprise to most readers. The way the novel deals with the presentation of this one withheld piece of knowledge, though, is complicated, and will be the subject of extended discussion later in the chapter. For the moment, suffice it to say that this is the "*one* reservation," in contrast to his larger narratorial intention, and therefore can be taken as the exception that proves the rule.

5. Immanuel Kant, *Critique of the Power of Judgment*, ed. Paul Guyer, trans. Paul Guyer and Eric Matthews (Cambridge: Cambridge University Press, 2000), 5:293.

6. Quoted in James R. Kincaid, *Dickens and the Rhetoric of Laughter* (London: Oxford University Press, 1971), 3.

7. Henri Bergson, "Laughter," in *Comedy*, ed. Wylie Sypher (Baltimore: Johns Hopkins University Press, 1956), 61–190.

8. William Whewell, *Lectures on Systematic Morality* (London: John W. Parker, 1846), 81.

9. David Lewis, in his seminal analytic approach to the subject, emphasizes that any definition of convention must include "tacit convention not created by agreement." David K. Lewis, *Convention: A Philosophical Study*, New York (Blackwell, 2002), 3.

10. See, e.g., Thomas Vargish, *The Providential Aesthetic in Victorian Fiction* (Charlottesville: University of Virginia Press, 1985).

11. Barbara Hardy, *The Moral Art of Dickens* (New York: Oxford University Press, 1970), 131.

12. George Eliot, "Silly Novels by Lady Novelists," *Westminster Review* 66 (1856): 244.

13. Harry Levin, *The Gates of Horn: A Study of Five French Realists* (New York: Oxford University Press, 1963), 51.

14. Jameson, *Political*, 152. This position, it should be pointed out, was first and foremost a formalist one. See Tomashevsky, "Thematics," 80–84; Roman Jakobson, "On Realism in Art," in *Language and Literature*, ed. Krystyna Pomorska and Stephen Rudy (Cambridge, MA: Belknap Press of Harvard Univ. Press, 1987), 19–27.

15. Wayne Booth describes the experience of reading *Tess*: "desiring Tess's happiness, fearing and increasingly expecting her tragic doom." Since for Booth, to desire Tess's happiness is to desire something that she does not receive—"a man who unlike Angel Clare or Alec . . . would appreciate her true quality"— the implication is that the novel somehow leads the reader down a counterfactual path, the possibility of which it then denies. Wayne C. Booth, *The Company We Keep: An Ethics of Fiction* (Berkeley: University of California Press, 1988), 205–6.

16. George Eliot, *Daniel Deronda*, ed. Terence Cave (New York: Penguin, 1995), 803.

17. Franco Moretti, *The Way of the World: The Bildungsroman in European Culture* (New York: Verso, 2000), 23.

18. As Poovey puts it, *Copperfield* is "a psychological narrative of individual development, which both provided individual readers with an imaginative image of what identity was and created a subject position that reproduced this kind of identity in the individual reader." Mary Poovey, *Uneven Developments: The Ideological Work of Gender in Mid-Victorian England* (Chicago: University of Chicago Press, 1988), 89. Miller, memorably, reflects on how the David (Miller) reading Dickens became for him the David reading *in* Dickens. Miller, *Police*, 192.

19. Ian Watt, *The Rise of the Novel: Studies in Defoe, Richardson, and Fielding*, 2nd ed. (Berkeley: University of California Press, 2001), 176.

20. In this I follow David Kurnick's recent reading of the theatrical undercurrent of the Victorian novel: "the novel's interior spaces are lined with longing references to the public worlds they would seem to have left behind." David Kurnick, *Empty Houses: Theatrical Failure and the Novel* (Princeton: Princeton University Press, 2012), 3.

21. Raymond Williams, *Keywords: A Vocabulary of Culture and Society* (New York: Oxford University Press, 1983), 236.

22. Janice Radway notes that the romance readers she interviewed had been for the most part isolated from each other. Janice A. Radway, *Reading the Romance: Women, Patriarchy, and Popular Literature* (Chapel Hill: University of North Carolina Press, 1991), 96. Interestingly, when she returned to the topic in a later article, she moved away from the term "popular" altogether, preferring instead the term "mass-produced literature." See Janice A. Radway, "Reading Is Not Eating: Mass-Produced Literature and the Theoretical, Methodological, and Political Consequences of a Metaphor," *Book Research Quarterly* 2, no. 3 (1986): 7–29.

23. For a discussion of the popular reception, bordering on manias, that these works received, see, e.g., Thomas Keymer and Peter Sabor, *Pamela in the Marketplace: Literary Controversy and Print Culture in Eighteenth-Century Britain and Ireland* (Cambridge: Cambridge University Press, 2005); Ghislaine McDayter, "Conjuring Byron: Byromania, Literary Commodification and the Birth of Celebrity," in *Byromania: Portraits of the Artist in Nineteenth- and Twentieth-Century Culture,* ed. Frances Wilson (New York: St. Martin's, 1999), 43–62; L. Edward Purcell, *"Trilby* and Trilby-Mania: The Beginning of the Best-Seller System," *Journal of Popular Culture* 11, no. 1 (2004): 62–76.

24. The comparison is frequently used, but no less true for it. Terry Eagleton makes the point while discussing Richardson: "To measure the astonishing social impact of these novels, we would have to compare them to the most popular films or TV soap operas of our time. The modern equivalent of Pamela or Clarissa would not be Mrs. Dalloway but Harry Potter." Terry Eagleton, *The English Novel: An Introduction* (New York: Blackwell, 2005), 76.

25. Examples can be embarrassing, since they so quickly become dated. With that in mind, Americans, depending on their generation, might consider including the "Who Shot J. R.?" episode of *Dallas,* or the final episode of *The Sopranos.*

26. Richard D. Altick, "Varieties of Readers' Response: The Case of *Dombey and Son," Yearbook of English Studies* 10 (1980): 70.

27. Edgar Johnson, *Charles Dickens: His Tragedy and Triumph* (New York: Simon & Schuster, 1952), 2:613. This quote is mentioned in Altick, "Varieties," 72. Altick is equivocal about the veracity of the anecdote, but seems ultimately to think that it seems likely, if not particularly meaningful: "Anecdotes are not necessarily reliable history, and while there may have been a number of such clubs, for *Dombey and Son* as well as the other early novels, their existence does not by itself prove very much." It does not prove much, that is, about the class distribution of Dickens's readership. But the existence of such clubs, or even the claim that such clubs existed, strongly suggests that reading a Dickens novel was associated with doing what others around oneself were doing, on a monthly basis.

28. By which Anderson means "all communities larger than primordial villages of face-to-face contact." Benedict Anderson, *Imagined Communities: Reflections on the Origin and Species of Nationalism* (New York: Verso, 1995), 6.

29. Roddey Reid, discussing France, brings the popular novel together with the newspaper as a way of imagining a "national community," claiming the importance of the performance of "identical rituals" among different classes in "the reading of best sellers and the daily consumption of newspapers." Jonathan Culler, discussing Reid and Anderson, brings us one step closer to Dickens, noting that Reid's insight is "especially true of serial novels, such as Eugène Sue's *Le mystères de Paris* of 1842–43 and *Le juif errant* of 1844, which were initially consumed in newspapers." Roddey Reid, *Families in Jeopardy: Regulating the Social Body in France, 1750–1910* (Stanford: Stanford University Press, 1993), 139; Jonathan Culler, "Anderson and the Novel," *Diacritics* 29, no. 4 (1999): 26.

30. The principal example would likely be Todorov's *The Fantastic,* in which he defines "popular" literature—"detective stories, serialized novels, science fiction,

etc."—as those works which do not change our notions of the rules of literature. Only such "popular" literature, for Todorov, qualifies as a genre. But this definition, important though it may be, is more a statement of literary history than actual market or cultural popularity. Tzvetan Todorov, *The Fantastic: A Structural Approach to a Literary Genre*, trans. Richard Howard (Ithaca, NY: Cornell University Press, 1975), 6. See also "Popular Fiction as a Genre" in Peter J. Rabinowitz, *Before Reading: Narrative Conventions and the Politics of Interpretation* (Columbus: Ohio State University Press, 1998), 183–93. Rabinowitz here focuses on the formal generic qualities of a work's popularity. In both cases, a single critic, with a suitably large body of literary reference, can pinpoint the "popularity" of a work without particular concern for whether anyone actually read it.

31. Catherine Gallagher and Stephen Greenblatt, *Practicing New Historicism* (Chicago: University of Chicago Press, 2000), 10.

32. John Forster, *The Life of Charles Dickens* (C. Scribner's Sons, 1907), 1:3.

33. Sigmund Freud, *The Joke and Its Relation to the Unconscious*, trans. Joyce Crick (New York: Penguin, 2002).

34. George Meredith, "An Essay on Comedy," in *Comedy*, ed. Wylie Sypher (Baltimore: Johns Hopkins University Press, 1956), 4.

35. One notable exception to this trend: Žižek has taken a consistent stance against a "belief in the liberating anti-totalitarian force of laughter," believing instead that the pleasure of cynical laughter is "part of the game" in both democratic and totalitarian societies. Slavoj Žižek, *The Sublime Object of Ideology* (London: Verso, 1989), 28

36. Gilles Deleuze, "Jean-Jacques Rousseau: Precursor of Kafka, Celine, and Ponge," in *Desert Islands and Other Texts, 1953–1974*, ed. David Lapoujade, trans. Michael Taormina (Los Angeles: Semiotext(e), 2004), 74; Gilles Deleuze, "Nomad Thought," in *New Nietzsche: Contemporary Styles of Interpretation*, ed. David B. Allison (Cambridge, MA: MIT Press, 1985), 147.

37. Kincaid, *Laughter*, 2.

38. The difficulty in any discussion of affective reactions is that they risk building too much on one's own reaction. As Moretti says, in defending his use of novels that have made him cry as the basis for his discussion of the tearjerker, "There is no other way." Franco Moretti, *Signs Taken for Wonders* (London: Verso, 1988), 158. While I am arguing against any universalizing of the experience of laughter, I have to admit that I am building on my own reaction—and the one I have witnessed in others—of not laughing at every recognizably humorous moment in a Dickens novel. Full disclosure: Sam rarely gets more than a smile out of me, and Micawber not even that. I do laugh, quite a bit, at Mrs. F's aunt in *Little Dorrit*.

39. William Makepeace Thackeray, "The English Humourists of the Eighteenth Century," in *The Works of William Makepeace Thackeray* (New York: Pollard & Moss, 1881), 1:61.

40. Because the argument that follows is generally confined to Victorian ideas of humor, I have excluded all but the most germane findings in twentieth- and twenty-first-century humor research. Suffice it to say that no ultimately satisfactory conclusions seem to have yet been drawn on the relation between

humor and laughter. Salvatore Attardo's comprehensive survey of the literature, with a marked emphasis on linguistics, offers a useful account of recent
attempts to explain the relation. See Salvatore Attardo, *Linguistic Theories of
Humor* (Berlin: Mouton de Gruyter, 1994), 10–13. For a more comprehensive
attempt to apply results from humor research in psychology, linguistics, and
sociology, see Paul Lewis, *Comic Effects: Interdisciplinary Approaches to Humor
in Literature* (Albany: State University of New York Press, 1989).

41. Often we *prefer* that meaning to remain unsaid—one of the first rules of
humor is that you never explain a joke.

42. Meredith, "Comedy," 47.

43. Jonathan Rose, "How Historians Study Reader Response: Or, What Did Jo
Think of *Bleak House?*" in *Literature in the Marketplace*, ed. John O. Jordan and
Robert L. Patten (Cambridge: Cambridge University Press, 1995), 206. The
quote is from Acorn's *One of the Multitude*.

44. Fredric Jameson, "The Ideology of the Text," in *The Ideologies of Theory: Essays
1971–1986*, vol. 1, *Situations of Theory* (Minneapolis: University of Minnesota
Press, 1988), 68.

45. Miller, *Police*, x.

46. As was the case, for example, with the previous chapter's discussion of *Jack
Sheppard*.

47. Elizabeth Gaskell, *Cranford*, ed. Elizabeth Porges Watson (New York: Oxford
University Press, 1998), 9.

48. See Elizabeth Gaskell, "Our Society at Cranford," *Household Words, Conducted
by Charles Dickens* 4, no. 90 (December 1851): 268, 270. The changes are limited to replacing "Boz" with "Hood" and "Pickwick" with "Hood's Own."

49. Letter to Gaskell, 4 December 1851, in Charles Dickens, *The Letters of Charles
Dickens*, ed. Graham Storey, Kathleen Tillotson, and Nina Burgis (New York:
Oxford University Press, 1988), 6:549.

50. See Alvin Whitley, "Hood and Dickens: Some New Letters," *Huntington Library Quarterly* 14, no. 4 (August 1951): 385–413.

51. Leigh Hunt, *Wit and Humor: Selected from the English Poets, with an Illustrative
Essay, and Critical Comments* (London: Wiley & Putnam, 1846), 6, 8.

52. Later, he discusses Chaucer, one of the classical examples of a "humorous"
author, who, as he puts it, combines "the most indelicate with the utmost
refinements of thought and feeling" (51). Nowhere in the work is "idea" used
in conjunction with "feeling."

53. Hunt writes that humor "derives its name from the prevailing quality of *moisture* in the bodily temperament" (8).

54. Quoted in Robert Bernard Martin, *The Triumph of Wit: A Study of Victorian
Comic Theory* (Oxford: Clarendon Press, 1974), 30.

55. The classic work on the transformation in terms from the Restoration to the
Romantics is Stuart M. Tave, *The Amiable Humourist: A Study in the Comic Theory of the Eighteenth and Early Nineteenth Centuries* (Chicago: University of Chicago Press, 1960). For the continuation of this trajectory into the nineteenth
century, Robert Bernard Martin's *The Triumph of Wit* is extremely helpful.
Though I disagree with Martin's conclusion about the superiority of wit, and

thus with the teleology implicit in his title, his reading of the literature is complete enough that the majority of our citations are shared, and I came across many of them for the first time in his book. For readings of specific Victorian works, see Robert Polhemus, *Comic Faith: The Great Tradition from Austen to Joyce* (Chicago: University of Chicago Press, 1980); Roger B. Henkle, *Comedy and Culture: England 1820–1900* (Princeton: Princeton University Press, 1980).

56. Quoted in Tave, *Amiable*, 220.

57. Thomas Carlyle, "Jean Paul Friedrich Richter," in *Critical and Miscellaneous Essays*, ed. Ralph Waldo Emerson (Philadelphia: Carey & Hart, 1852), 12.

58. In *Sartor Resartus*, it is true, Carlyle does say that "no man who has once heartily and wholly laughed can be altogether irreclaimably bad" (26). Perhaps not altogether bad, but, if this and other quotes are to be believed, there might still be room for improvement. Thomas Carlyle, *Sartor Resartus*, ed. Kerry McSweeney (New York: Oxford University Press, 1987).

59. The most notable being Herbert Spencer, "The Physiology of Laughter," in *Essays: Scientific, Political, & Speculative* (London: Williams & Norgate, n.d.), 2:452–66.

60. Thomas Hobbes, *Elements of Law, Natural and Politic*, ed. J. C. A. Gaskin (New York: Oxford University Press, 1999), 55.

61. Tave, *Amiable*, 46. For more on the lesser known Drake, see Edwin E. Williams, "Dr. James Drake and Restoration Theory of Comedy," *Review of English Studies*, 1939, 180–91.

62. Kant, *Judgment*, 5:332.

63. Bergson is "coupling the superiority theory with the incongruity theory." Bernard G. Prusak, "*Le Rire* à Nouveau: Rereading Bergson," *Journal of Aesthetics and Art Criticism* 62, no. 4 (Autumn 2004): 380.

64. Bergson, "Laughter," 97.

65. Martin writes: "The eighteenth century had been quite as perplexed as their descendants about the scorn, degradation, and condescension implicit in the superiority theory of comedy. Briefly, their solution to the problem had been to concentrate on personal aspects of humour, then to exaggerate the sympathy that one must feel in order to have total perception of individuality or eccentricity, so that the object of humour provoked laughter *with* it, not *at* it, finally to make sympathy and love the really distinguishing aspects of humour, as laughter dropped away from it. (Indeed, it almost seemed as if the provocation of laughter was proof that writing was *not* humourous.) The standard examples advanced were those of Sterne's Uncle Toby and (improbable as it may seem to the twentieth century) his story of Le Fever; Don Quixote; and Falstaff in his more amiable aspects." Martin, *Triumph*, 26. Also see Tave, *Amiable*, ch. 7: "Humor and Sweet Philanthropy: Parson Adams, my uncle Toby, Don Quixote."

66. Charles Lamb, *Life, Letters, and Writing*, ed. Percy Fitzgerald (London: John Slark, 1822), 4:312. Lamb is speaking here specifically about Hogarth.

67. Carlyle, "Richter," 11. For more on this connection, and particularly the influence of Richter on *Sartor*, see J. W. Smeed, "Thomas Carlyle and Jean Paul Richter," *Comparative Literature* 16, no. 3 (1964): 226–53.

68. Percy Bysshe Shelley, "Defense of Poetry," in *Shelley's Poetry and Prose*, ed. Donald H. Reiman and Sharon B. Powers (New York: W. W. Norton, 1977), 491. I must admit that, quite unfortunately for my argument, Shelley seems to reverse the association of laughter. In such times, Shelley also argues, "we hardly laugh but we smile." For now, I can only say that on this point, Shelley seems to be out of keeping with many other Romantics and Victorians.

69. Though Hutcheson certainly refined his terms, to the extent that Shaftesbury's own formulations are often difficult to place in the context of nineteenth-century thought.

70. Any full account of *sensus communis* would have to include, in addition to Shaftesbury, Vico. Because neither Kant nor nineteenth-century English thought shows the influence of Vico's work, I have chosen to exclude it in the interest of space and focus. For a book-length explication of the subject, see John D. Schaeffer, *Sensus Communis: Vico, Rhetoric, and the Limits of Relativism* (Durham, NC: Duke University Press, 1990). In Hans-Georg Gadamer's account, Vico's thought seems to be of more interest than that of Shaftesbury, because it displays the Roman classical tradition in its purest form: "Vico lived in an unbroken tradition of rhetorical and humanist culture, and had only to reassert anew its ageless claim." Hans-Georg Gadamer, *Truth and Method*, trans. Joel Weinsheimer and Donald G. Marshall, 2nd ed. (London: Continuum Books, 2004), 21. Benedetto Croce has shown that there was some social interaction between Vico and Shaftesbury—Vico visited Shaftesbury in Naples—which, at least, suggests the possibility of some English moral-sense influence in Vico's work. Benedetto Croce, *Shaftesbury in Italy* (Cambridge: Cambridge University Press, 1923), 8.

71. Anthony Ashley Cooper, Earl of Shaftesbury, *Characteristicks of Men, Manners, Opinions, Times*, ed. Douglas den Uyl (Indianapolis: Liberty Fund, 2001), 1:69. For discussions of Shaftesbury's essay that influenced my account, see Simon Critchley, *On Humour* (London: Routledge, 2002), 80–85; Bo Patterson, "Exploring the Common Ground: *Sensus Communis*, Humor, and the Interpretation of Comic Poetry," *Journal of Literary Semantics* 33 (2004): 155–67; Lawrence Klein, *Shaftesbury and the Culture of Politeness: Moral Discourse and the Cultural Politics of Early Eighteenth-Century England* (Cambridge: Cambridge University Press, 1994), 9.

72. Kant, *Judgment*, 5:293.

73. Hannah Arendt, "Some Questions of Moral Philosophy," in *Responsibility and Judgment*, ed. Jerome Kohn (New York: Schocken Books, 2003), 139.

74. Bergson, "Laughter," 64.

75. The most useful recent attempt in literary criticism to sketch out the difficult interactions between the comic and the community is James F. English, *Comic Transactions: Literature, Humor, and the Politics of Community in Twentieth-Century Britain* (Ithaca: Cornell University Press, 1994). English's book focuses on modernist British literature, and its intention is "less to raise questions for humor theory than to raise questions for cultural politics" (18).

76. Arendt, "Questions," 140. Laughter can take place alone, of course, but it often requires the imagined presence of others. As anecdotal evidence, consider concert films of stand-up comedy, in which the viewer is placed in the position

of an audience member, with the laughter of other audience members clearly audible. It is difficult to imagine a concert film with the comedian simply performing for the camera, and thus for the viewer alone.

77. Sharon Marcus, *Between Women: Friendship, Desire, and Marriage in Victorian England* (Princeton: Princeton University Press, 2007), 113–14.

78. Michel Foucault, *The History of Sexuality*, vol. 1, *An Introduction* (New York: Vintage, 1990), 23. The version of the "repressive hypothesis" at play here would likely be the frequent, and to me mystifying, bit of critical self-castigation surrounding the fact that critics writing on humor are so rarely funny.

79. Hippolyte Taine, *History of English Literature*, trans. H. Van Laun (Philadelphia: Henry Altemus, 1908), 4:4.

80. E.g., Lewes's claim: "in no other perfectly sane mind . . . have I observed vividness of imagination approaching so closely to hallucination." George Henry Lewes, "Dickens in Relation to Criticism," *Fortnightly Review* 11 (1872): 144.

81. Most notably the famous scenes in *Barchester Towers*, in which Trollope admits that he does not like Mr. Slope, or reassures the reader that Eleanor would never marry him. Anthony Trollope, *Barchester Towers* (New York: Oxford University Press, 1996), 64, 146.

82. Alexander Welsh, *From Copyright to Copperfield: The Identity of Dickens* (Cambridge, MA: Harvard University Press, 1987), 140.

83. Philip M. Weinstein, *The Semantics of Desire: Changing Models of Identity from Dickens to Joyce* (Princeton: Princeton University Press, 1984), 41.

84. Janet H. Brown, "The Narrator's Role in *David Copperfield*," *Dickens Studies Annual* 2 (1972): 201.

85. This is a relatively commonsensical way to describe what most people mean by character: for a character to exist at the level of narrative, within the narrative, means that the character should be able to effect change in the world of the narrative. Note, though, that this intuitive definition is actually the flip side of a more rigorously argued actantial, or functional model, in semiotics. Associated mainly with Propp and Greimas, this model claims, essentially, that characters are largely the properly named hosts of a number of narrative functions: subject and object, helper and opponent, sender and receiver. What seems to underlie the model is an essential belief that a character is necessary to manifest an actant. But that also means that a character who does not or cannot act is somehow not worthy of the name.

86. Thomas Leitch labels these the "discursive principle" and the "teleological principle." See Thomas Leitch, *What Stories Are: Narrative Theory and Interpretation* (University Park: Pennsylvania State University Press, 1986), 42, 63. The teleological side has gotten the majority of the attention in formal discussions of the novel (though, as I discussed in the introduction, the discursive has gotten the majority of attention in ethical discussions). For the contrary argument, pointing to the importance of the descriptive, see Amanpal Garcha, *From Sketch to Novel: The Development of Victorian Fiction* (Cambridge: Cambridge University Press, 2009). Ultimately, it is an underlying claim of this book that ethical thought, as the logic connecting "is" and "ought," can offer a useful way of describing the interrelation of these two principles. See the discussion of the theoretical argument in chapter 1.

87. Or, if we prefer, the paradigmatic and syntagmatic axes of a narrative "language."
88. Welsh, *Copyright*, 125.
89. Weinstein, *Semantics*, 38–43.
90. From a biographical point of view, it's worth noting that the one point where Dickens stresses David's agency and control is one in which he, himself, was saved largely by a series of circumstances that were, as Fred Kaplan puts it, "unpredictable and bewildering." Fred Kaplan, *Dickens: A Biography* (Baltimore: John Hopkins University Press, 1988), 43.
91. This narrative mechanism in *Great Expectations* will be discussed at greater length in chapter 4.
92. Barthes, *S/Z*, 135.
93. Which is to say, mainly, Lionel Trilling, Steven Marcus, and Edmund Wilson. See Deborah Epstein Nord, "The Making of Dickens Criticism," in *Contemporary Dickens*, ed. Eileen Gilloly and Deirdre David (Columbus: Ohio State University Press, 2009), 262–85
94. Lacan, *Psychoanalysis*, 131.
95. Jacques Lacan, *Freud's Papers on Technique, 1953–1954 (the Seminar of Jacques Lacan)*, ed. Jacques-Alain Miller, trans. John Forrester (New York: W. W. Norton, 1991), 54.
96. Because the similarity in language might confuse, I should stress that this is not the same as a Jungian collective unconscious. It need not be the unconscious mapped to the group, so much as the assertion that the experience of the group—of the city street and the workday—is difficult to express in the language of character. The communal unconscious owes a great deal to Jameson's idea of the political unconscious as a sort of inexpressible shared experience. The communal unconscious, though, is a good deal more modest; I'm not talking about the realities of shared experience so much as the way the novel depends on *a* shared experience, and furthermore bases its narrative upon that. See, e.g., Jameson, *Political*, 34–35.
97. George Orwell, "Charles Dickens," in *All Art Is Propaganda: Critical Essays*, ed. George Packer (New York: Houghton Mifflin Harcourt, 2008), 37.
98. Orwell, "Dickens," 39. There is one case in which Orwell's claim falls glaringly short: lawyers. The list is extensive: Dodson and Fogg in *The Pickwick Papers*, Jaggers—whose in-court affect is memorably described—in *Great Expectations*, Tulkinghorn in *Bleak House*. As each of these three cases indicate, Dickens saw a danger in the legal profession of the public impinging on, and damaging, the private. Still, the precise reasons not only for Dickens's willingness to show lawyers at work, but his insistence on it, and how that reflects on Orwell's point, falls outside the scope of this current discussion.
99. As an aside, the structural similarities are more striking than I can offer an explanation for here. Both read to hide from cold-hearted guardians; following the scene of reading, both are beaten; both fight back for the first time; both are locked in an attic room; both are then sent off to school. The relation of reading to forced confinement seems worth following up on.
100. Charlotte Brontë, *Jane Eyre*, ed. Q. D. Leavis (New York: Penguin, 1985), 349.

101. Brian Phillips offers Mr. Dolloby, and the way he turns his pipe upside down on his doorpost before entering his shop, as an example of "the easy largesse of detail" with which Dickens writes. Brian Phillips, "Reality and Virginia Woolf," *Hudson Review* 56, no. 3 (2003): 415–30.

102. As an unnamed writer in *Blackwood's* puts it, "Every reader will tell you that he has made acquaintance with Sam Weller and several other remarkable persons, and that he shall never forget them as long as he lives." "Debt and Credit," *Blackwood's Edinburgh Magazine* 83 (1858): 60.

103. Moretti, *Way of the World*, 183.

104. See Moretti, *Way of the World*; Welsh, *Copyright*; Harry Stone, *Dickens and the Invisible World: Fairy Tales, Fantasy, and Novel-Making* (Bloomington: Indiana University Press, 1979).

105. When it is used in the novel, it is almost always the conclusion of an exclamatory aside enclosed in dashes.

106. There are a number of parallels here to the most famous modern discussion of the figure of blindness: Paul de Man's "Rhetoric of Blindness." De Man argues that the insights of the major modern literary critics—Lukács, Poulet, Blanchot—could "only be gained because the critics were in the grip of this particular blindness: their language could grope toward a certain degree of insight only because their method remained oblivious to the perception of this insight." Paul de Man, "The Rhetoric of Blindness: Jacques Derrida's Reading of Rousseau," in *Blindness and Insight: Essays in the Rhetoric of Contemporary Criticism*, by Paul de Man, 2nd ed. (Minneapolis: University of Minnesota Press, 1983), 106.

107. Miller, *Police*, 205.

108. Rawls, *Justice*, 96.

109. René Girard, *Deceit, Desire, and the Novel: Self and Other in Literary Structure*, trans. Yvonne Freccero (Baltimore: Johns Hopkins University Press, 1976), 83.

110. Kelly Hager, "Estranging *David Copperfield*: Reading the Novel of Divorce," *ELH* 63, no. 4 (1996): 991.

CHAPTER FOUR: BACK IN TIME

1. Margaret Oliphant, *Miss Marjoribanks*, ed. Elisabeth Jay (New York: Penguin, 1998), 420.

2. Recall the original title of *Middlemarch*, and the title of its first book: "Miss Brooke."

3. Oliphant, *Miss Marjoribanks*, 21.

4. Barthes, *S/Z*, 216.

5. George Eliot, *Middlemarch*, ed. Rosemary Ashton (New York: Penguin, 1994), 836.

6. Andrew Miller, "Lives Unled in Realist Fiction," *Representations* 98, no. 1 (2007): 123.

7. Miller, "Lives Unled," 118.

8. Cf. Lorna Ellis, *Appearing to Diminish: Female Development and the British Bildungsroman, 1750–1850* (Lewisburg, PA: Bucknell University Press, 1999), 30.

9. The comparison of classical narrative techniques and time-travel stories is similar to that offered in David Wittenberg, *Time Travel: The Popular Philosophy of Narrative* (New York: Fordham University Press, 2013). Wittenberg, though, is primarily interested in the ways in which time-travel stories encourage "even the naive reader" to become a "practicing narrative theorist." I wish to look at the verso side of the argument and point to the way that narratological structures already imply time-travel narrative.

10. Rawls, *Justice*, 225.

11. José Ortega y Gasset, *Meditations on Quixote*, trans. Evelyn Rugg and Diego Marín (Champaign: University of Illinois Press, 2000), 111.

12. I am referring to the assumptions and practices of the field as it stands now. When I presented a preliminary version of these ideas at Princeton University, Deborah Epstein Nord pointed out that the field of "Victorian studies" has gone through a number of changes over the decades, centering around a move away from poetry and prose and toward the novel as its signature form. The field, it seems, became easier to read. For a long view on the history of Victorian studies in United States academia, see Richard D. Altick, "Victorians on the Move, or, 'Tis Forty Years Hence," in *Writers, Readers, and Occasions: Selected Essays on Victorian Literature and Life* (Columbus: Ohio State University Press, 1989), 309–28.

13. Jameson, "Ideology," 68. Jameson is speaking of nineteenth-century European realism more generally, but confining our discussion to the English language brings us back to the Victorian novel. For this reason, in what follows, I will sometimes blur the lines between theoretical discussions of nineteenth-century realism and Victorian novels, unless the author insists on national specificity.

14. David Masson, *British Novelists and Their Styles* (London: Macmillan, 1859), 215–27.

15. Ruth Bernard Yeazell, "Why Political Novels Have Heroines: *Sybil, Mary Barton*, and *Felix Holt*," *Novel* 18, no. 2 (Winter 1985): 127.

16. Pearl Brown echoes this reading in her discussion of Gaskell's novels: "Structurally, both [*Mary Barton* and *North and South*] use not only the convention of the novel of social purpose or the industrial novel but also those of the female bildungsroman to present the maturation of young women in an urban setting." Pearl L. Brown, "From Elizabeth Gaskell's *Mary Barton* to Her *North and South*: Progress or Decline for Women?" *Victorian Literature and Culture* 28, no. 2 (2000): 346.

17. Maureen Moran, *Victorian Literature and Culture* (London: Continuum Books, 2006), 81.

18. M. M. Bakhtin, "The *Bildungsroman* and Its Significance in the History of Realism (Toward a Historical Typology of the Novel)," in *Speech Genres and Other Late Essays*, ed. Caryl Emerson and Michael Holquist, trans. Vern W. McGee (Austin: University of Texas Press, 2004), 19.

19. Joseph R. Slaughter, *Human Rights, Inc.* (New York: Fordham University Press, 2007), 157.

20. Watt, *Rise*, 296.

21. Gadamer, *Truth*, 8–9.
22. This account of the *Bildungsroman* that has received a good deal of excellent analysis. The exemplary analysis is in Moretti, *Way of the World*. For discussions that go beyond the boundaries of the European nineteenth-century, see Slaughter, *Human Rights, Inc.*; Jed Esty, *Unseasonable Youth: Modernism, Colonialism, and the Fiction of Development* (Oxford: Oxford University Press, 2011).
23. Lukács, *Theory*, 132.
24. Moretti, *Way of the World*, 70.
25. From Carlyle's translation. Johann Wolfgang von Goethe, *Wilhelm Meister's Apprenticeship and Travels*, trans. Thomas Carlyle, vol. 2 (London: Chapman and Hall, 1824), 182.
26. Charles Dickens, *Great Expectations*, ed. Margaret Cardwell (Oxford: Oxford University Press, 1994), 312.
27. Barthes, *S/Z*, 135.
28. See previous discussion in the introduction.
29. Kant, *Groundwork*, 4:455–56. Page numbers given in all citations to Kant are for the German Academy of Sciences edition of Kant's collected works, provided in the margins of most English editions.
30. Rawls: "The [categorical imperative] procedure is a schema to characterize the framework of deliberation that [rational and sincere] agents use implicitly in their moral thought." John Rawls, "Themes in Kant's Moral Philosophy," in *John Rawls: Selected Papers*, ed. Samuel Freeman (Cambridge, MA: Harvard University Press, 1999), 498.
31. Kant, *Practical Reason*, 5:94.
32. See, e.g., *Groundwork* 4:452–53: "As a rational being, and thus as a being belonging to the intelligible world, the human being can never think of the causality of his own will otherwise than under the idea of freedom; for, independence from the determining causes of the world of sense (which reason must always ascribe to itself) is freedom."
33. Immanuel Kant, *Religion within the Boundaries of Mere Reason*, ed. and trans. Allen Wood and George di Giovanni (Cambridge: Cambridge University Press, 1998), 6:22.
34. The argument that follows is in large part drawn from Henry E. Allison, *Kant's Theory of Freedom* (New York: Cambridge University Press, 1990), 201ff.; and Alenka Zupančič, *Ethics of the Real: Kant, Lacan* (London: Verso, 2000), 21–42. It is most notably dependent on Allison's conception of the "incorporation thesis," in which Kant suggests that an incentive can determine the will only if an agent has incorporated it into his maxim. That argument, in the interests of focus, has been omitted.
35. Allison, *Kant's Theory*, 208.
36. Zupančič, *Ethics*, 33.
37. Johann Wolfgang von Goethe, *Wilhelm Meister's Apprenticeship*, trans. Eric A. Blackall (Princeton: Princeton University Press, 1989), 307.
38. Slaughter, *Human Rights, Inc.*, 99.
39. William Whewell, *Lectures on Systematic Morality* (London: John W. Parker, 1846), 20.

40. As D. D. Raphael points out, "The expression 'moral sense' was first used by Shaftesbury, but in a loose and vague way." Raphael, *Moral*, 2. Francis Hutcheson certainly refined his terms.

41. Shaftesbury, *Characteristicks of Men, Manners, Opinions, Times*, 1:205n.

42. Susan L. Cocalis, "The Transformation of 'Bildung' from an Image to an Ideal," *Monatshefte* 70, no. 4 (1978): 401.

43. Leslie Stephen, *History of English Thought in the Eighteenth Century*, vol. 2 (London: Smith, Elder, & Co., 1876), 33.

44. Ernest Boyer Jr., "'What Is Religion?': Shaftesbury, the German Enlightenment, and Schleiermacher" (PhD diss., Harvard Divinity School, 2002), 188.

45. Leslie Stephen, *History of English Thought in the Eighteenth Century* (London: Smith, Elder, 1876), 1:61.

46. Certainly, that's what critics of Shaftesbury's intellectual descendants would argue. Mill, in particular, famously categorized the moral sense as a theory by which "every inveterate belief and every intense feeling, of which the origin is not remembered, is enabled to dispense with the obligation of justifying itself by reason, and is erected into its own all-sufficient voucher and justification." Mill, *Autobiography*, 135.

47. Anthony Ashley Cooper, Earl of Shaftesbury, *Characteristicks of Men, Manners, Opinions, Times*, ed. Douglas den Uyl (Indianapolis: Liberty Fund, 2001), 2:28.

48. Stephen Darwall, *The British Moralists and the Internal "Ought": 1640–1740* (Cambridge: Cambridge University Press, 1995), 179.

49. Shaftesbury, *Characteristicks*, 1:205n.

50. Arendt, "Questions," 139.

51. Gadamer, *Truth*, 29.

52. It might not be properly a German genre, either. Jeffrey Sammons has made the point that, given the term's prominence in discussions of the novel, there have been surprisingly few studies of the German *Bildungsromane*, and that discussions of the form—Lukács is a notable offender—often omit the most important specifics: "It is quite astonishing how often in discussions of the subject no actual novels are mentioned. Often such discussions appear to be primarily commentaries on *Wilhelm Meister*. One can scour the secondary literature and still not come up with a very long list of candidates." Jeffrey L. Sammons, "The Mystery of the Missing *Bildungsroman*, or What Happened to Wilhelm Meister's Legacy," *Genre* 14, no. 2 (1981): 233. Sammons ultimately questions the specific importance granted the *Bildungsroman* in discussions of German culture and literature: "This is a genre, and a predominant one at that—a category into which we can, on inspection, admit only *Wilhelm Meister* and maybe two and a half other examples?" (237).

53. The term was first suggested by Friedrich von Blanckenburg in his 1774 "Essay on the Novel," and coined in 1820 by Karl von Morgenstern, but is little used until Dilthey's 1870 biography of Friedrich Schleiermacher. See Susan Fraiman, *Unbecoming Women: British Women Writers and the Novel of Development* (New York: Columbia University Press, 1993), 3.

54. The arguments of Howe's book were further developed in Jerome H. Buckley, *Season of Youth: The Bildungsroman from Dickens to Golding* (Cambridge, MA: Harvard University Press, 1974).

55. Cf. Rosemary Ashton, *The German Idea: Four English Writers and the Reception of German Thought* (Cambridge: Cambridge University Press, 1980). Cf. the discussion of Carlyle's reading of Jean Paul in chapter 3.

56. Ashton, *German Idea*, 4–5. Carlyle, the great proponent of German thought in general and Goethe in particular, characterized English opinion: "[W]e disdain to be assisted by the Germans, whom by a species of second-sight, we have discovered, before knowing anything about them, to be a timid, dream, extravagant, insane race of mortals." Johann Wolfgang von Goethe, *Wilhelm Meister's Apprenticeship and Travels*, trans. Thomas Carlyle (London: Chapman & Hall, 1824), 1:5 (Translator's Preface).

57. Marianne Hirsch makes the point that the generic classification, though it might take different forms in France, England, and Germany, also displays compelling similarities among those traditions: "The definition of a historical genre of the novel of formation not only provides a useful critical tool for the reading of individual works, but also accounts for the different orientations of German, as opposed to French and English realistic fiction" (Marianne Hirsch, "The Novel of Formation as Genre: Between Great Expectations and Lost Illusions," *Genre* 12, no. 3 [1979]: 294). Note that Hirsch groups French and English together in opposition to German, while Moretti famously groups French and German together, and excludes the English *Bildungsroman* as a "fairy-tale novel." Moretti, *Way of the World*, 189

58. Gadamer, *Truth*, 293.

59. Georgia Warnke, "Hermeneutics, Ethics, and Politics," in *Cambridge Companion to Gadamer*, ed. Robert J. Dostal (Cambridge: Cambridge University Press, 2006), 80–81.

60. Mill, *Utilitarianism*, 74.

61. In this, ethics was just one part of a much larger debate, encompassing science and math, between Mill and Whewell. As Laura J. Snyder explains, "Mill's view . . . was . . . deliberately presented in opposition to Whewell's work. . . . [Mill's] overriding desire was to expel the intuitionist philosophy from its 'stronghold' in physical science and mathematics, because he saw this as being the crucial precondition for reforming moral and political philosophy. . . . If he could demonstrate that knowledge of physical science and mathematics did not require any a priori axioms, Mill hoped, then he would have proved the superfluity of a priori elements in morality and political philosophy." Snyder, *Reforming*, 27.

62. Mill, *Autobiography*, 135.

63. See the discussion of Sidgwick's *Discourse* in chapter 1.

64. Mill, "Sedgwick's Discourse," 60.

65. Cf. "A Method of Self Examination" in John Wesley, *The Works of the Rev. John Wesley, A.M.*, 4th ed. (London: John Mason, 1841), 11:499–500.

66. Williams, *Culture*, 66.

67. For a compelling discussion of the odd fact that Mill seems fairly uninterested in Wordsworth's actual poetry, see Clifford Siskin, *The Work of Writing: Literature and Social Change in Britain, 1700–1830* (Baltimore: Johns Hopkins University Press, 1999), 98–99. Siskin has suggested that, for Mill, the mere act of making literary discriminations—Wordsworth is better than Byron; some Wordsworth

poems are better than others—gave Mill access to a different field of knowledge, the "literary," with its attendant reward: "the self- and class-authorizing
ideology of the aesthetic (the taste by which one knows great authors and thus
one's greatness)." A convincing argument for the importance of Wordsworth
in terms of the Hartleyan associationist orthodoxy of the day can be found in
Robert Scott Stewart, "Utilitarianism Meets Romanticism: J. S. Mill's Theory
of Imagination," *History of Philosophy Quarterly* 10, no. 4 (1993): 369–88.

68. "My course of study had led me to believe, that all mental and moral feelings
and qualities, whether of a good or of a bad kind, were the results of association; that we love one thing, and hate another, take pleasure in one sort of
action or contemplation, and pain in another sort, through the clinging of
pleasurable or painful ideas to those things, from the effect of education or of
experience." Mill, *Autobiography*, 82.

69. Kant, *Groundwork*, 4:455–56.

70. The actual composition of the *Autobiography*, published posthumously in
1873, has been the subject of some academic sleuthing and debate. Albert William Levi offers convincing evidence that a good deal of the composition took
place in 1853 and 1854. Albert William Levi, "The Writing of Mill's *Autobiography*," *Ethics* 61, no. 1 (1951): 293.

71. John Stuart Mill, *A System of Logic, Ratiocinative and Inductive: Books IV–VI,
Appendices*, ed. John M. Robson (Indianapolis: Liberty Fund, 2006), 840.

CHAPTER FIVE: THE LARGE NOVEL AND THE LAW OF LARGE NUMBERS

1. This term will call to mind Alex Woloch's *The One vs. the Many*. As I will argue
in this chapter, a good deal of Eliot's inventiveness comes from her attempt to
offer a different solution from that found in most nineteenth-century realism
to what Woloch phrases as the question of how "the discrete representation
of any specific individual is intertwined with the narrative's continual appor-
tioning of attention to different characters who jostle for limited space within
the same fictive universe." Eliot, I will suggest, sees the "fictive universe" not
as containing "limited space" but rather as existing at a level of magnitude
greater than that which can be produced by simply summing up all the characters, major or minor. See Alex Woloch, *The One vs. the Many* (Princeton:
Princeton University Press, 2003), 13.

2. Eliot, *Deronda*, 810.

3. H. W. Fowler, *The King's English*, 2nd ed. (Oxford: Clarendon Press, 1908), 142.

4. See Douglas Lane Patey, *Probability and Literary Form: Philosophic Theory and
Literary Practice in the Augustan Age* (Cambridge: Cambridge University Press,
1984); Neil Hertz, *George Eliot's Pulse* (Stanford: Stanford University Press,
2003); Leland Monk, *Standard Deviations: Chance and the Modern British Novel*
(Stanford: Stanford University Press, 1993).

5. The most famous being Leavis's desire to cut out the Deronda sections and
leave only a novel titled *Gwendolen Harleth*. Leavis, *Great Tradition*, 122.

6. Eliot, *Letters*, 6:290.

7. Lukács, *Theory*, 132.
8. This might just be to say that Eliot was the most Continental of the Victorian novelists. Franco Moretti: "Together with Jane Austen, she was the only novelist to dismiss the judicial-fairy-tale model and deal with the issues characteristic of the continental *Bildungsroman*." Moretti, *Way of the World*, 214.
9. Eliot, *Middlemarch*, 37.
10. Catherine Gallagher, "George Eliot: Immanent Victorian," *Representations* 90, no. 1 (Spring 2005): 70.
11. The strong form of this claim would be that, since every individual is particularized, the novel could be about any one of them. Lukács, in *Theory of the Novel*, makes this argument: the protagonist of the *Bildungsroman* is "merely accidental . . . picked out of an unlimited number of men who share his aspirations" (134). Many of *Middlemarch's* self-conscious discourses on authorial attention—the pier-glass metaphor, "Why always Dorothea?"—can be seen as an attempt to phrase some version of this claim while, at the same time, avoiding the disingenuous assertion that the novel could be about Rosamond or, say, Sir James Chettam.
12. As Sharon Marcus has shown, Dorothea's moments of intense sympathy with Rosamond and Will are *both* essential to the dynamics of the heterosexual marriage plot: "Dorothea and Rosamond come together only because of their shared entanglement with Will, and Dorothea and Will tie the knot only because of the electric decisive affinity Dorothea experiences with Rosamond. Weak as it is, the bond between the two women is the only force powerful enough to tie up the marriage plot's loose ends." Marcus, *Between Women*, 78–79.
13. For more on the problem of induction in the larger philosophical discussions of the period, see Mary Poovey, *A History of the Modern Fact: Problems of Knowledge in the Sciences of Wealth and Society* (Chicago: University of Chicago Press, 1998), ch. 7; and Snyder, *Reforming*.
14. Edward Said offers a strong version of this comparison: "Dorothea emerges at the end of *Middlemarch* as a chastened woman, forced to concede her grand visions of a 'fulfilled' life in return for a relatively modest domestic success as a wife and mother. It is this considerably diminished view that *Daniel Deronda*, and Zionism in particular, revise upward: toward a genuinely hopeful socio-religious project in which individual energies can be merged and identified with a collective national vision, the whole emanating out of Zionism." This more successful heroism, though, relies on the imagining of a place quite different from the crowded cities where *Middlemarch* reaches its conclusion; it requires the myth of an empty Palestine. Edward Said, *The Question of Palestine* (New York: Vintage Books, 1992), 61.
15. George Levine, "Determinism and Responsibility in the Works of George Eliot," *PMLA* 77, no. 3 (June 1962): 271.
16. More technically, a countably infinite set is said to be "denumerable." Unfortunately for my argument, no responsible scholarly conclusions about Eliot's Jews can be drawn from the fact that Cantor denoted the ordinality—that is to say, the "size"—of a denumerable set with a Hebrew letter and a number: $\aleph_0$ (read "aleph null").

17. Of course, when it came to the census, they *could* be counted. There were, literally, a finite number of English. What is important here, though, is the way in which Eliot figures the English as a continuum, while identifying Jews with their numerical representation. See note 18.

18. George Eliot, *George Eliot's Daniel Deronda Notebooks*, ed. Jane Irwin (Cambridge: Cambridge University Press, 1996), 84, 209, 265, 431, 436. The source of the newspaper article is uncertain—Irwin suggests it may have come from the *Jewish Chronicle*. There are no references in her notebook to specifically English populations, and the only general, non-Jewish note avoids the actual numerical size of the population in question: "Population now augmented 14 per ct. in 10 years" (234).

19. George Eliot, *Impressions of Theophrastus Such*, ed. Nancy Henry (Iowa City: University of Iowa Press, 1994), 162.

20. Ian Hacking, *The Taming of Chance* (New York: Cambridge University Press, 1990), 194.

21. Hacking, *Chance*, 180–99.

22. John M. Efron, *Defenders of the Race: Jewish Doctors and Race Science in Fin-de-Siècle Europe* (New Haven: Yale University Press, 1994), 5.

23. Mitchell Bryan Hart, *Social Science and the Politics of Modern Jewish Identity* (Stanford: Stanford University Press, 2000), 8.

24. Oren Soffer, "Antisemitism, Statistics, and the Scientization of Hebrew Political Discourse: The Case Study of *Ha-Tsefirah*," *Jewish Social Studies* 10, no. 2 (2004): 55–79.

25. Joseph Jacobs, *Studies in Jewish Statistics, Social, Vital, and Anthropometric* (London: D. Nutt, 1891), 54. The epigraph to this volume is a quote from *Deronda*: "In relation to society, numbers are qualities." This quote will be discussed at greater length in the next section.

26. Joseph Jacobs, "The Comparative Distribution of Jewish Ability," *Journal of the Anthropological Institute of Great Britain and Ireland* 15 (1886): 351–79. Jacobs's desire is to build on Galton's *Hereditary Genius* in order to show the statistical preponderance of "genius" and "lunacy" among Jews, and the relative low incidence of "mediocrity." Though in no way consciously anti-Semitic—Jacobs was himself Jewish—the discussion of the human elements of the bell-shaped normal curve does produce some rather chilling moments, including a fanciful description that replaces the balls and pins of Galton's quincunx—which showed that randomly dropped balls would fall into a normal curve—with people and "pens": "I have said that our method consists in estimating the number of eminent men among a million Englishmen or Jews, as the case may be. Suppose that we had these million men collected together on Salisbury Plain, and suppose further that we were gifted with the insight of a recording angel and could arrange them in sixteen classes according to their ability, ranging from the greatest genius to the most degraded idiot. A long wall with fifteen projecting walls perpendicular to it would give us, as it were, sixteen pens, in which we could place our various classes" (352).

27. *Times*, January 7, 1850; *New York Times*, October 17, 1885, 3.

28. A problematic aside: it is difficult to watch these accumulating enumerations without feeling pulled backwards, like Benjamin's angel of history, toward

the twentieth century, and its totemic enumeration of Jewish millions. Is it possible that the historical focus on the six million, instead of the over ten million total, is in some part a continuation of this nineteenth-century discursive tradition?

29. Hart, *Social Science*, 28.

30. Quoted in Soffer, *"Ha-Tsefirah,"* 62.

31. Max Nordau, speaking in December 1901, at the Fifth Zionist Conference in Basil. Quoted in Hart, *Social Science*, 29–30. As we saw with Jacobs, though, such insistence on precision need not always be Zionist in nature.

32. The translation that follows this epigraph in the text is, as far as I can tell, the longest existing translation of Zunz into English. Hacking notes that "English readers' most direct knowledge of Zunz will come from George Eliot's *Daniel Deronda*." Hacking, *Chance*, 194n.

33. Luitpold Wallach, *Liberty and Letters: The Thoughts of Leopold Zunz* (London: East & West Library, 1959), 21. For a list of the specific topics these "statistics" would cover, see Fritz Bamberger, "Zunz's Conception of History: A Study of the Philosophic Elements in Early Science of Judaism," *Proceedings of the American Academy for Jewish Research* 11 (1941): 15–16.

34. Eliot, *Notebooks*, 436.

35. For a comprehensive account of the important cross-disciplinary influences in Eliot's organic thought, see Sally Shuttleworth, *George Eliot and Nineteenth-Century Science: The Make-Believe of a Beginning* (Cambridge: Cambridge University Press, 1984), ch. 1.

36. George Eliot, "Address to the Working Men, by Felix Holt," in *Felix Holt, the Radical*, ed. Lynda Mugglestone (New York: Penguin, 1995), 489. It should be noted that this quote proceeds rather ominously ". . . and with a terrible liability to get wrong because of that delicate dependence." This self-conscious fragility is essential to Eliot's organic metaphor, but it would take my discussion too far afield. For a good discussion of this problematic in Eliot's work, see David Carroll, "'Janet's Repentance' and the Myth of the Organic," *Nineteenth-Century Fiction* 35, no. 3 (December 1980): 331–48.

37. Steven Marcus, "Literature and Social Theory: George Eliot," in *Representations: Essays on Literature and Society* (New York: Columbia University Press, 1975), 197.

38. The term was introduced by Adolphe Quetelet in his 1835 *Treatise on Man*. For the intellectual debates surrounding this "character" in Victorian literature and social theory, see Christopher Kent, "The Average Victorian: Constructing and Contesting Reality," *Browning Institute Studies* 17 (1989): 41–52.

39. Gallagher discusses the anxiety that Eliot felt about becoming, in the writing of *Deronda*, "an insistent echo of [her]self." This passage suggests the extent to which her knowledge of readerly expectations of Eliotic maneuvers surfaced in the novel's text. See Catherine Gallagher, *The Body Economic: Life, Death, and Sensation in Political Economy and the Victorian Novel* (Princeton: Princeton University Press, 2006), ch. 5.

40. A good deal of the information here is drawn from the rich and accessible discussions in Theodore M. Porter, *The Rise of Statistical Thinking: 1820–1900* (Princeton: Princeton University Press, 1986); Hacking, *Chance*; and Poovey,

Modern Fact. See also Stephen M. Stigler, *The History of Statistics: The Measurement of Uncertainty Before 1900* (Cambridge, MA: Belknap Press of Harvard University Press, 1986); Alain Desrosières, *The Politics of Large Numbers: A History of Statistical Reasoning*, trans. Camille Naish (Cambridge, MA: Harvard University Press, 1998). For the prehistory of these topics, see Ian Hacking, *The Emergence of Probability: A Philosophical Study of Early Ideas about Probability, Induction, and Statistical Inference*, 2nd ed. (New York: Cambridge University Press, 2006); Lorraine Daston, *Classical Probability in the Enlightenment* (Princeton: Princeton University Press, 1988).

41. Hume offered the most famous statement of the relation between quantity and quality: "it seems natural to expect that wherever there are most happiness and virtue, and the wisest institutions: there will also be most people." David Hume, "Of the Populousness of Ancient Nations," in *Essays: Moral, Political, and Literary*, ed. Eugene F. Miller (Indianapolis: Liberty Fund, 1985), 382. An 1815 article in the *London Medical Repository* analyzed the reason for the comparatively higher suicide rates in Paris than in London after Napoleon's defeat. Hacking points to this as the beginning of numerical sociology, because "(a) there were numbers, and (b) the numbers of suicide were seen as a moral indicator of the quality of life." Hacking, *Chance*, 64.

42. Hacking suggests a "gross but convenient" binary between the development of "Eastern" statistics, focused in conservative Berlin, and "Western" statistics, focused in liberal London and Paris. Eastern statistics, according to Hacking, rejected the idea of "statistical laws," which not only described society but also governed it; Western statistics embraced it. Hacking's explanation:

> Why, if you are a conservative, who regards law as a social product, are you disinclined to think that statistical laws can be read into the printed tables of numerical data, or obtained from summaries of facts about individuals? Because laws are not the sort of thing to be inferred from individuals, already there and counted. Laws of society, if such there be, are facts about the culture, not distillations of individual behaviour.
>
> Why, if you are a liberal who regards law (in the political sphere) as a product of the will of individuals, are you content to find statistical laws in facts about crime and conviction published by the ministry of justice? Because social laws are constituted by individuals.

This would seem, at the very least, to fit with Sinclair's understanding of his importation of German work. Hacking, *Chance*, 37.

43. Quoted in Hacking, *Chance*, 16.
44. Quoted in Hacking, *Chance*, 177.
45. Percy Fitzgerald, *The Life of Charles Dickens as Revealed in His Writings* (London: Chatto & Windus, 1905), 1:207. I was made aware of this reference by its citation in Kent, "Average," 49. Kent, in turn, gives credit to Philip Collins.
46. Henry Thomas Buckle, *History of Civilization in England* (London: John W. Parker & Son, 1857), 1:30–31.
47. Helen Small, "Chances Are: Henry Buckle, Thomas Hardy, and the Individual at Risk," in *Literature, Science, Psychoanalysis, 1830–1970: Essays in Honor of*

Gillian Beer, ed. Helen Small and Trudi Tate (Oxford: Oxford University Press, 2003), 67–68. Small's essay offers an excellent account of the relation between Buckle's specific ideas and the use of the individual in late-Victorian literature.

48. Eliot, *Letters*, 2:485–86.

49. See George Henry Lewes, "Mr. Buckle's Scientific Errors," *Blackwood's Edinburgh Magazine* 90 (November 1861): 582–96.

50. Henry James, "Middlemarch," in *Literary Criticism: Essays on Literature, American Writers, English Writers*, ed. Leon Edel (New York: Library of America, 1984), 965.

51. For a discussion of this friendship see Selma B. Brody, "Physics in *Middlemarch*: Gas Molecules and Ethereal Atoms," *Modern Philology* 85, no. 1 (August 1987): 42–53.

52. Eliot, *Notebooks*, 21.

53. George Henry Lewes, *Problems of Life and Mind: First Series, the Foundations of a Creed* (Boston: J. R. Osgood, 1874), 1:295, 297–98.

54. And Maxwell would have had some knowledge of Eliot, as well. After seeing a discussion of solar myths at the Cambridge Philosophical Society, he wrote a letter to Lewis Campbell, analyzing all of *Middlemarch*'s major characters in "astronomical or meteorological" terms. Lewis Campbell and William Garnett, *The Life of James Clerk Maxwell* (London: Macmillan, 1882), 386.

55. Quoted in Porter, *Statistical Thinking*, 111.

56. Maxwell, of course, was not the first to notice that it was impossible to follow individual molecules. In this he was influenced by Rudolf Clausius's work in the late 1850s. What was new was his application of methods acquired from Laplace, Quetelet, and Buckle. "Clausius had recognized that there would be considerable variation in the velocity of the molecules; but in his mathematical analysis of molecular encounters, he simply used the average molecular velocity. Maxwell, however, maintained that a statistical analysis, analagous in form to Laplace's distribution of errors, was required: he suggested that the velocities were distributed among the molecules in accordance with a statistical distribution function." P. M. Harman, *The Natural Philosophy of James Clerk Maxwell* (Cambridge: Cambridge University Press, 1998), 124. Interestingly, the Austrian Ludwig Boltzmann independently produced not only similar theories, in what would eventually be called the "Maxwell-Boltzmann distribution," but also similar social analogies to explain those theories.

57. Quoted in Porter, *Statistical Thinking*, 113–14.

58. Porter, *Statistical Thinking*, 136. An interesting corollary to this is the fact that quantitative discussions of evolution were from the very beginning "social Darwinism." For such work could only come about through the applications of statistical methods. And that required drawing analogies between Darwin's theories and the proper social domain of statistical research. As anecdotal demonstration, we have the fact that first person to present a statistical refinement of Darwin's theories was his cousin, Francis Galton—the father of modern eugenics.

59. James Clerk Maxwell, *Theory of Heat*, 7th ed. (New York: D. Appleton, 1883), 328.

60. For a more technically precise but still highly readable account, see Harman, *Maxwell*, 124–44.

61. Eliot, *Middlemarch*, 194.

62. Moretti, *Way of the World*, 45–46.

63. As, for example, when Lucien sees him at the opera in *Lost Illusions*.

64. Eliot, *Letters*, 5:312.

65. Walter Benjamin, *Illuminations*, ed. Hannah Arendt; trans. Harry Zohn (New York: Schocken Books, 1968), 177.

66. Richard Wolin, *Walter Benjamin: An Aesthetic of Redemption*, 2nd ed. (Berkeley: University of California Press, 1994), 232.

67. Richard Shiff, "Handling Shocks: On the Representation of Experience in Walter Benjamin's Analogies," *Oxford Art Journal* 15, no. 2 (1992): 90.

68. Walter Benjamin, *The Arcades Project*, ed. Rolf Tiedemann; trans. Howard Eiland and Kevin McLaughlin (Cambridge, MA: Belknap Press of Harvard University Press, 1999), 906.

69. Benjamin, *Illuminations*, 179.

70. Benjamin, *Arcades*, 544.

71. Nicholas Dames, *The Physiology of the Novel: Reading, Neural Science, and the Form of Victorian Fiction* (Oxford: Oxford University Press, 2007), 156.

72. Richard D. Altick, *The Presence of the Present: Topics of the Day in the Victorian Novel* (Columbus: Ohio State University Press, 1991), 182.

73. F. B. Pinion, *A George Eliot Companion: Literary Achievement and Modern Significance* (London: Macmillan, 1991), 203.

74. See E. J. Carter, "The Green Table: Gambling Casinos, Capitalist Culture, and Modernity in Nineteenth-Century Germany" (PhD diss., University of Illinois at Urbana-Champaign, 2002).

75. Eliot, *Letters*, 5:312.

76. Carter shows how the proprietors of the casinos, and in particular of the casino at Bad Homburg, used this excitement as a means of boosting business in the casinos' final days. E. J. Carter, "Breaking the Bank: Gambling Casinos, Finance Capitalism, and German Unification," *Central European History* 39, no. 2 (2006): 201.

77. Not *completely* responsible, of course—we might also look at the presence of railway travel. Interestingly enough, though, Nicholas Daly has argued that the railways had a similar effect as that which I have been ascribing to gambling, and he makes similar connections with the sensation novel. See Nicholas Daly, "Railway Novels: Sensation Fiction and Modernization of the Senses," *ELH* 66, no. 2 (1999): 461–87.

78. Wilfred Stone, "The Play of Chance and Ego in *Daniel Deronda*," *Nineteenth-Century Literature* 53, no. 1 (July 1998): 31.

79. As Stone points out, across the Atlantic we would also find Mark Twain's 1873 *The Gilded Age*—subtitled *A Tale of To-day*.

80. See, for example, the discussion of the triangulated relationship between the terms "investment," "speculation," and "gambling" in David C. Itzkowitz, "Fair Enterprise or Extravagant Speculation: Investment, Speculation, and Gambling in Victorian England," *Victorian Studies* 44, no. 1 (Autumn 2002): 121–47.

81. Henry Longueville Mansel, "Sensation Novels," in *Letters, Lectures, and Reviews, Including the Phrontisterion; or, Oxford in the 19th Century*, ed. Henry W. Chandler (London: John Murry, 1873), 222.

82. Henry James, "Mary Elizabeth Braddon," in *Literary Criticism: Essays on Literature, American Writers, English Writers*, ed. Leon Edel (New York: Library of America, 1984), 742, 744.

83. See Dehn Gilmore, *The Victorian Novel and the Space of Art: Fictional Form on Display* (Cambridge: Cambridge University Press, 2013), 106–11.

84. Miller, *Police*, 146.

85. Nicholas Dames, *Amnesiac Selves: Nostalgia, Forgetting, and British Fiction, 1810–1870* (New York: Oxford University Press, 2001), 169. Dames discusses the actual medical understandings of amnesia not only lying behind the work of the sensation novel but also developing from it. Gilmore also usefully relates forgetfulness occasioned by repeated shocks to the culture surrounding large-scale exhibitions.

86. Barbara Hardy, "Introduction," in *Daniel Deronda* (Harmondsworth: Penguin, 1987), 27.

87. Ann Cvetkovich, *Mixed Feelings: Feminism, Mass Culture, and Victorian Sensationalism* (New Brunswick, NJ: Rutgers University Press, 1992), 136.

88. Since the similarity of terms may mislead, I should point out that I'm not claiming this revelation as a shock experience—first, because it is not repeated, and second, because, contrary to Eliot's claims, it is not particularly surprising.

89. George Eliot, *Adam Bede*, ed. Valentine Cunningham (New York: Oxford University Press, 1996), ch. 34.

90. Eliot, *Middlemarch*, 192.

91. John Sutherland has done the math: "by the time she runs away from Hall Farm . . . Hetty must be six to seven months pregnant." John Sutherland, *Is Heathcliff a Murderer? Puzzles in Nineteenth-Century Literature* (Oxford: Oxford University Press, 1996), 114.

92. In other words, Barthes's hermeneutic code.

93. Levine, *Suspense*, 101ff.

94. Narrative enigmas are often centered around questions of origin. Eliot usually shows little interest in them, but when she does engage them, as with Daniel, her interest is much more in asking the question than in finding out the answer. Cynthia Chase, in an influential deconstructive reading of the novel, makes the point that the novel tends to reverse the temporality of cause and effect. Looking specifically at the question of Daniel's origin, Chase writes, "What the reader feels, on the basis of the narrative presentation, is that it is *because* Deronda has developed a strong affinity for Judaism that he turns out to be of Jewish parentage." Cynthia Chase, "The Decomposition of the Elephants: Double-Reading *Daniel Deronda*," *PMLA* 93, no. 2 (March 1978): 217.

95. Tom Stoppard, *Rosencrantz and Guildenstern Are Dead*, ed. Henry Popkin (New York: Grove Press, 1967), 12.

96. Stone, "Play of Chance," 27.

97. Neil Hertz suggests that the "numerical" consciousness here is a form of "neutral" repetition that runs throughout *Deronda*, countering the novel's commitment to moral involvement (as it does here with Mordecai's lecture). Hertz, *Pulse*, ch. 8.

98. Richard Anthony Proctor, "Gambling Superstitions," *Cornhill Magazine* 25 (1872): 708.

99. Eliot, *Notebooks*, 283. The fact that Eliot was drawn to the mathematical questions inherent in these issues is further evidenced by her jotting down the following mathematical oddity in her notebook: "If a rod be tossed over a grating of parallel bars, the number of times it will fall through will depend on the length & thickness of the rod, the distance between the bars, & the proportion in which the circumference of a circle exceeds the diameter" (283). This is a rather awkward phrasing of the elementary probability result known as "Buffon's needle." It can be shown that, given lines spaced a unit apart, the chance of a needle of unit length landing on one of those lines is $^2/_\pi$. Therefore, if we repeat this experiment, we should be able to get an ever more accurate estimation of π. As Proctor puts it, "we can estimate the proportion in which the circumference of a circle exceeds the diameter, by merely tossing a rod over a grating several thousand times, and counting how often it falls through" (710). That random tosses, repeated often enough, should give us π is often used as an impressive demonstration of the law of large numbers. It certainly seems to have made an impression on Eliot.

100. A hodgepodge of progressive betting schemes—the "Martingale," in which bets are doubled after a loss, and the "Paroli," in which they are doubled after a win—and prediction schemes based on the maturity of chances.

101. Norwood Young, "Gambling at Monte Carlo," *National Review* 16 (1890): 487.

102. Carter, "Breaking," 193ff.

103. Lascelles Wrexall, "Gambling-Houses in Germany," *Dublin University Magazine* 77 (April 1871): 468. This article was originally published in *St. James Magazine* in 1865. It was presumably reprinted due to the imminent 1872 closure of the German casinos.

104. An American visitor helpfully offers this explanation: "A stranger to the spas wonders why most of the players pore so intently over the little printed cards they hold in their hands, sticking metallic pins here and there as the last result of the game is announced. They are keeping the run of the game, marking the numbers and cards which have won, and drawing deductions therefrom for future bets. In this way they are slowly but steadily evolving systems which will prove their bane." Junius Henri Browne, "The German Gambling Spas," *Harper's New Monthly Magazine* 45, no. 265 (June 1872): 9.

105. The details: the sole house advantage in *trente et quarante* occurs when the two rows of cards—the first labeled *noir*, the second *rouge*—both add up to thirty-one. In Homburg, a further rule was added that the final card of the *rouge* row must be black, thus cutting the house advantage in half, to roughly one and one-third percent. See Carter, "Green Table," 36–38.

106. Gordon S. Haight, *George Eliot: A Biography* (New York: Oxford University Press, 1968), 457.

107. Eliot, *Letters*, 5:314.

108. The haughty tone of the travel articles notwithstanding, such intuitive beliefs persist rather unabated. For a psychological discussion of the conflicts between intuition over small sample sizes and the larger laws of probability, see

Amos Tversky and Daniel Kahneman, "Belief in the Law of Small Numbers," *Psychological Bulletin* 76, no. 2 (1971): 105–10.
109. Eliot, *Letters*.

AFTERWORD

1. Stephen Greenblatt, *Shakespearean Negotiations* (Berkeley: University of California Press, 1989), 1.
2. Miller, *Police*, x.
3. Difficulty and ease of reading are centrally important notions in literary studies that are quite, yes, difficult to discuss with any precision. One admirable recent account of modernist difficulty that I found quite helpful was Leornar Diepeveen, *The Difficulties of Modernism* (New York: Routledge, 2003).
4. Jameson, "Ideology," 57.
5. Jameson, "Ideology," 57.

BIBLIOGRAPHY

Ainsworth, William Harrison. *Jack Sheppard: A Romance*. London: George Rout-ledge & Sons, 1900(?).

———. *Rookwood*. London: J. M. Dent & Sons, 1931.

Allison, Henry E. *Kant's Theory of Freedom*. New York: Cambridge University Press, 1990.

Altick, Richard D. *The Presence of the Present: Topics of the Day in the Victorian Novel*. Columbus: Ohio State University Press, 1991.

———. "Varieties of Readers' Response: The Case of *Dombey and Son*." *Yearbook of English Studies* 10 (1980): 70–94.

———. "Victorians on the Move, or, 'Tis Forty Years Hence." In *Writers, Readers, and Occasions: Selected Essays on Victorian Literature and Life*, 309–28. Columbus: Ohio State University Press, 1989.

Anderson, Amanda. *The Powers of Distance: Cosmopolitanism and the Cultivation of Detachment*. Princeton: Princeton University Press, 2001.

———. *The Way We Argue Now: A Study in the Cultures of Theory*. Princeton: Princeton University Press, 2006.

Anderson, Benedict. *Imagined Communities: Reflections on the Origin and Species of Nationalism*. New York: Verso, 1995.

Arendt, Hannah. "Some Questions of Moral Philosophy." In *Responsibility and Judgment*, edited by Jerome Kohn, 49–146. New York: Schocken Books, 2003.

Ashton, Rosemary. *The German Idea: Four English Writers and the Reception of German Thought*. Cambridge: Cambridge University Press, 1980.

Attardo, Salvatore. *Linguistic Theories of Humor*. Berlin: Mouton de Gruyter, 1994.

Attridge, Derek. *J. M. Coetzee and the Ethics of Reading: Literature in the Event*. Chicago: University of Chicago Press, 2005.

Bain, Alexander. *Mental and Moral Science: A Compendium of Psychology and Ethics*. 3rd ed. London: Longman, Green, 1884.

Bakhtin, M. M. "The *Bildungsroman* and Its Significance in the History of Realism (Toward a Historical Typology of the Novel)." In *Speech Genres and Other Late Essays*, edited by Caryl Emerson and Michael Holquist, translated by Vern W. McGee, 10–59. Austin: University of Texas Press, 2004.

Bamberger, Fritz. "Zunz's Conception of History: A Study in the Philosophic Elements in Early Science of Judaism." *Proceedings of the American Academy for Jewish Research* 11 (1941): 1–25.

Barthes, Roland. *S/Z*. Translated by Richard Miller. New York: Hill & Wang, 1974.

Benjamin, Walter. *The Arcades Project*. Edited by Rolf Tiedemann. Translated by Howard Eiland and Kevin McLaughlin. Cambridge: Belknap Press of Harvard University Press, 1999.

———. *Illuminations*. Edited by Hannah Arendt. Translated by Harry Zohn. New York: Schocken Books, 1968.

Bergson, Henri. "Laughter." In *Comedy*, edited by Wylie Sypher, 61–190. Baltimore: Johns Hopkins University Press, 1956.

Bleackley, Horace. *Trial of Jack Sheppard*. Edinburgh: William Hodge, 1933.

Boltanski, Luc. *Distant Suffering: Morality, Media, and Politics*. Translated by Graham D. Burchell. Cambridge: Cambridge University Press, 1999.

Bonar, James. *Moral Sense*. London: George Allen & Unwin, 1930.

Booth, Wayne C. *The Company We Keep: An Ethics of Fiction*. Berkeley: University of California Press, 1988.

Boyer, Ernest, Jr. "'What Is Religion?': Shaftesbury, the German Enlightenment, and Schleiermacher." PhD diss., Harvard Divinity School, 2002.

Brody, Selma B. "Physics in *Middlemarch*: Gas Molecules and Ethereal Atoms." *Modern Philology* 85, no. 1 (August 1987): 42–53.

Brontë, Charlotte. *Jane Eyre*. Edited by Q. D. Leavis. New York: Penguin, 1985.

Brooks, Peter. *Reading for the Plot: Design and Intention in Narrative*. New York: Vintage Books, 1985.

Brown, Janet H. "The Narrator's Role in *David Copperfield*." *Dickens Studies Annual* 2 (1972): 197–207.

Brown, Pearl L. "From Elizabeth Gaskell's *Mary Barton* to Her *North and South*: Progress or Decline for Women?" *Victorian Literature and Culture* 28, no. 2 (2000): 345–58.

Browne, Junius Henri. "The German Gambling Spas." *Harper's New Monthly Magazine* 45, no. 265 (June 1872): 1–21.

Buckle, Henry Thomas. *History of Civilization in England*. Vol. 1. London: John W. Parker & Son, 1857.

Buckley, Jerome H. *Season of Youth: The Bildungsroman from Dickens to Golding*. Cambridge, MA: Harvard University Press, 1974.

Buckley, Matthew. "Sensations of Celebrity: *Jack Sheppard* and the Mass Audience." *Victorian Studies* 44, no. 3 (Spring 2002): 423–63.

Buckstone, J. B. "Jack Sheppard." In *Trilby and Other Plays*, edited by George Taylor, 1–83. Oxford: Oxford University Press, 1996.

Bulwer-Lytton, Edward. *Eugene Aram*. Boston: Little, Brown, 1897.

———. *Paul Clifford*. Vol. 1. Boston: Little, Brown, 1897.

Burton, Anthony. "Cruikshank as an Illustrator of Fiction." In *George Cruikshank: A Reevaluation*, edited by Robert L. Patten. Princeton: Princeton University Press, 1974.

Campbell, Lewis, and William Garnett. *The Life of James Clerk Maxwell*. London: Macmillan, 1882.

Carlyle, Thomas. "Jean Paul Friedrich Richter." In *Critical and Miscellaneous Essays*, edited by Ralph Waldo Emerson, 7–15. Philadelphia: Carey & Hart, 1852.

———. *Sartor Resartus*. Edited by Kerry McSweeney. New York: Oxford University Press, 1987.

Carroll, David. "'Janet's Repentance' and the Myth of the Organic." *Nineteenth-Century Fiction* 35, no. 3 (December 1980): 331–48.

Carter, E. J. "Breaking the Bank: Gambling Casinos, Finance Capitalism, and German Unification." *Central European History* 39, no. 2 (2006): 185–213.

———. "The Green Table: Gambling Casinos, Capitalist Culture, and Modernity in Nineteenth-Century Germany." PhD diss., University of Illinois at Urbana-Champaign, 2002.

Chase, Cynthia. "The Decomposition of the Elephants: Double-Reading *Daniel Deronda*." *PMLA* 93, no. 2 (March 1978): 215–27.

Chatman, Seymour. *Story and Discourse: Narrative Structure in Fiction and Film.* Ithaca, NY: Cornell University Press, 1978.

Chomsky, Noam. *Knowledge of Language: Its Nature, Origin, and Use.* Westport, CT: Greenwood, 1986.

Cocalis, Susan L. "The Transformation of 'Bildung' from an Image to an Ideal." *Monatshefte* 70, no. 4 (1978): 399–414.

Coetzee, J. M. *Disgrace.* New York: Penguin, 2000.

Collins, Philip, ed. *Charles Dickens: The Critical Heritage.* London: Routledge, 1996.

Critchley, Simon. *On Humour.* London: Routledge, 2002.

Croce, Benedetto. *Shaftesbury in Italy.* Cambridge: Cambridge University Press, 1923.

Culler, Jonathan. "Anderson and the Novel." *Diacritics* 29, no. 4 (1999): 19–39.

———. *Structuralist Poetics: Structuralism, Linguistics, and the Study of Literature.* Ithaca: Cornell University Press, 1975.

Cvetkovich, Ann. *Mixed Feelings: Feminism, Mass Culture, and Victorian Sensationalism.* New Brunswick, NJ: Rutgers University Press, 1992.

Daly, Nicholas. "Railway Novels: Sensation Fiction and Modernization of the Senses." *ELH* 66, no. 2 (1999): 461–87.

Dames, Nicholas. *Amnesiac Selves: Nostalgia, Forgetting, and British Fiction, 1810–1870.* New York: Oxford University Press, 2001.

———. *The Physiology of the Novel: Reading, Neural Science, and the Form of Victorian Fiction.* Oxford: Oxford University Press, 2007.

———. "Wave-Theories and Affective Physiologies: The Cognitive Strain in Victorian Novel Theories." *Victorian Studies* 46, no. 2 (Winter 2004): 206–16.

Darwall, Stephen. *The British Moralists and the Internal "Ought": 1640–1740.* Cambridge: Cambridge University Press, 1995.

Daston, Lorraine. *Classical Probability in the Enlightenment.* Princeton: Princeton University Press, 1988.

"Debt and Credit." *Blackwood's Edinburgh Magazine* 83 (1858): 57–74.Deleuze, Gilles. "Jean-Jacques Rousseau: Precursor of Kafka, Celine, and Ponge." In *Desert Islands and Other Texts, 1953–1974*, edited by David Lapoujade, translated by Michael Taormina, 52–55. Los Angeles: Semiotext(e), 2004.

———. "Nomad Thought." In *New Nietzsche: Contemporary Styles of Interpretation*, edited by David B. Allison, 142–49. Cambridge, MA: MIT Press, 1985.

de Man, Paul. "The Rhetoric of Blindness: Jacques Derrida's Reading of Rousseau." In *Blindness and Insight: Essays in the Rhetoric of Contemporary Criticism*, 102–41. 2nd ed. Minneapolis: University of Minnesota Press, 1983.

Desrosières, Alain. *The Politics of Large Numbers: A History of Statistical Reasoning.* Translated by Camille Naish. Cambridge, MA: Harvard University Press, 1998.

Devitt, Michael. "Intuitions in Linguistics." *British Journal for the Philosophy of Science* 57, no. 3 (2006): 481–513.

Dickens, Charles. *David Copperfield.* Edited by Nina Burgis. New York: Oxford University Press, 1981.

———. *Great Expectations.* Edited by Margaret Cardwell. Oxford: Oxford University Press, 1994.

———. *Hard Times.* Edited by Kate Flint. New York: Penguin Books, 1995.

———. *The Letters of Charles Dickens.* Edited by Graham Storey, Kathleen Tillotson, and Nina Burgis. Vol. 1. New York: Oxford University Press, 1965.

———. *The Letters of Charles Dickens.* Edited by Graham Storey, Kathleen Tillotson, and Nina Burgis. Vol. 6. New York: Oxford University Press, 1988.

———. *Oliver Twist.* Edited by Kathleen Tillotson. Oxford: Oxford University Press, 1999.

Diepeveen, Leornar. *The Difficulties of Modernism.* New York: Routledge, 2003.

Disraeli, Benjamin. *Sybil; or, The Two Nations.* Edited by Sheila Smith. New York: Oxford University Press, 1981.

Eagleton, Terry. *The English Novel: An Introduction.* New York: Blackwell, 2005.

Efron, John M. *Defenders of the Race: Jewish Doctors and Race Science in Fin-de-Siècle Europe.* New Haven: Yale University Press, 1994.

Eliot, George. *Adam Bede.* Edited by Valentine Cunningham. New York: Oxford University Press, 1996.

———. "Address to the Working Men, by Felix Holt." In *Felix Holt, the Radical,* edited by Lynda Mugglestone, 483–99. New York: Penguin, 1995.

———. *Daniel Deronda.* Edited by Terence Cave. New York: Penguin, 1995.

———. *George Eliot's Daniel Deronda Notebooks.* Edited by Jane Irwin. Cambridge: Cambridge University Press, 1996.

———. *The George Eliot Letters.* Edited by Gordon S. Haight. Vol. 2. New Haven: Yale University Press, 1954.

———. *The George Eliot Letters.* Edited by Gordon S. Haight. Vol. 5. New Haven: Yale University Press, 1955.

———. *The George Eliot Letters.* Edited by Gordon S. Haight. Vol. 6. New Haven: Yale University Press, 1978.

———. *Impressions of Theophrastus Such.* Edited by Nancy Henry. Iowa City: University of Iowa Press, 1994.

———. *Middlemarch.* Edited by Rosemary Ashton. New York: Penguin, 1994.

———. *Scenes of Clerical Life.* Edited by Jennifer Gribble. New York: Penguin, 1998.

———. "Silly Novels by Lady Novelists." *Westminster Review* 66 (1856): 243–54.

"Elizabeth Brownrigge: A Tale." *Fraser's Magazine* 32 (1832): 67–88, 127–48.

Ellis, Lorna. *Appearing to Diminish: Female Development and the British Bildungsroman, 1750–1850.* Lewisburg, PA: Bucknell University Press, 1999.

English, James F. *Comic Transactions: Literature, Humor, and the Politics of Community in Twentieth-Century Britain.* Ithaca, NY: Cornell University Press, 1994.

Esty, Jed. *Unseasonable Youth: Modernism, Colonialism, and the Fiction of Development.* Oxford: Oxford University Press, 2011.

Falk, Julia S. "Saussure and American Linguistics." In *The Cambridge Companion to Saussure*, edited by Carol Sanders, 107–24. New York: Cambridge University Press, 2004.

Faller, Lincoln B. *Turned to Account: The Forms and Functions of Criminal Biography in Seventeenth- and Early Eighteenth-Century England*. Cambridge: Cambridge University Press, 1987.

Fielding, Henry. *The Life of Mr. Jonathan Wild the Great*. Edited by Hugh Armory. Oxford: Oxford University Press, 2003.

Fitzgerald, Percy. *The Life of Charles Dickens as Revealed in His Writings*. Vol. 1. London: Chatto & Windus, 1905.

Forster, E. M. *Aspects of the Novel*. New York: Brace & World, 1954.

Forster, John. *The Life of Charles Dickens*. Vol. 1. C. Scribner's Sons, 1907.

———. "The Literary Examiner." *Examiner*, September 10, 1839.

———. "The Literary Examiner." *Examiner*, November 3, 1839.

Foucault, Michel. "The Ethics of the Concern of the Self as a Practice of Freedom." In *Ethics: Subjectivity and Truth*, edited by Paul Rabinow, 1:280–301. Essential Works of Foucault, 1954–1984. New York: New Press, 1997.

———. *The History of Sexuality*. Vol. 1, *An Introduction*. New York: Vintage Books, 1990.

———. *The Order of Things: An Archaeology of the Human Sciences*. New York: Vintage Books, 1994.

Fowler, H. W. *The King's English*. 2nd ed. Oxford: Clarendon Press, 1908.

Fraiman, Susan. *Unbecoming Women: British Women Writers and the Novel of Development*. New York: Columbia University Press, 1993.

Freud, Sigmund. *The Joke and Its Relation to the Unconscious*. Translated by Joyce Crick. New York: Penguin, 2002.

Gadamer, Hans-Georg. *Truth and Method*. Translated by Joel Weinsheimer and Donald G. Marshall. 2nd ed. London: Continuum Books, 2004.

Gallagher, Catherine. *The Body Economic: Life, Death, and Sensation in Political Economy and the Victorian Novel*. Princeton: Princeton University Press, 2006.

———. "George Eliot: Immanent Victorian." *Representations* 90, no. 1 (Spring 2005): 61–74.

Gallagher, Catherine, and Stephen Greenblatt. *Practicing New Historicism*. Chicago: University of Chicago Press, 2000.

Garber, Marjorie, Beatrice Hanssen, and Rebecca L. Walkowitz, eds. *The Turn to Ethics*. New York: Routledge, 2000.

Garcha, Amanpal. *From Sketch to Novel: The Development of Victorian Fiction*. Cambridge: Cambridge University Press, 2009.

Gaskell, Elizabeth. *Cranford*. Edited by Elizabeth Porges Watson. New York: Oxford University Press, 1998.

———. *North and South*. Edited by Patricia Ingham. New York: Penguin, 1995.

———. *Mary Barton*. Edited by MacDonald Daly. New York: Penguin, 1996.

———. "Our Society at Cranford." *Household Words, Conducted by Charles Dickens* 4, no. 90 (December 1851): 265–74.

Gensler, Harry J. *Formal Ethics*. New York: Routledge, 1996.

Gide, André. *The Counterfeiters*. Translated by Dorothy Bussy and Justin O'Brien. New York: Knopf, 1947.

Gillies, Mary Ann. *Henri Bergson and British Modernism*. Montreal: McGill-Queen's University Press, 1996.

Gilmore, Dehn. *The Victorian Novel and the Space of Art: Fictional Form on Display*. Cambridge: Cambridge University Press, 2013.

Girard, René. *Deceit, Desire, and the Novel: Self and Other in Literary Structure*. Translated by Yvonne Freccero. Baltimore: Johns Hopkins University Press, 1976.

Goethe, Johann Wolfgang von. *Wilhelm Meister's Apprenticeship*. Translated by Eric A. Blackall. Princeton: Princeton University Press, 1989.

———. *Wilhelm Meister's Apprenticeship and Travels*. Translated by Thomas Carlyle. Vol. 1. London: Chapman and Hall, 1824.

———. *Wilhelm Meister's Apprenticeship and Travels*. Translated by Thomas Carlyle. Vol. 2. London: Chapman and Hall, 1824.

Greenblatt, Stephen. *Shakespearean Negotiations*. Berkeley: University of California Press, 1989.

Greiner, Rae. *Sympathetic Realism in Nineteenth-Century British Fiction*. Baltimore: Johns Hopkins University Press, 2012.

Grossman, Jonathan H. *The Art of Alibi: English Law Courts and the Novel*. Baltimore: Johns Hopkins University Press, 2002.

Guyau, Jean-Marie. *La morale anglaise contemporaine: Morale de l'utilité et de l'évolution*. Paris: Félix Alcan, 1885.

Hacking, Ian. *The Emergence of Probability: A Philosophical Study of Early Ideas about Probability, Induction, and Statistical Inference*. 2nd ed. New York: Cambridge University Press, 2006.

———. *The Taming of Chance*. New York: Cambridge University Press, 1990.

Hager, Kelly. "Estranging *David Copperfield*: Reading the Novel of Divorce." *ELH* 63, no. 4 (1996): 989–1019.

Haight, Gordon S. *George Eliot: A Biography*. New York: Oxford University Press, 1968.

Hale, Dorothy J. *Social Formalism: The Novel in Theory from Henry James to the Present*. Stanford: Stanford University Press, 1998.

Hardy, Barbara. "Introduction." In *Daniel Deronda*, 7–30. Harmondsworth: Penguin, 1987.

———. *The Moral Art of Dickens*. New York: Oxford University Press, 1970.

Harman, P. M. *The Natural Philosophy of James Clerk Maxwell*. Cambridge: Cambridge University Press, 1998.

Harpham, Geoffrey Galt. *Getting It Right: Language, Literature, and Ethics*. Chicago: University of Chicago Press, 1992.

———. *Shadows of Ethics: Criticism and the Just Society*. Durham, NC: Duke University Press, 1999.

Hart, Mitchell Bryan. *Social Science and the Politics of Modern Jewish Identity*. Stanford: Stanford University Press, 2000.

Hegel, G. W. F. *Hegel's Philosophy of Right*. Translated by T. M. Knox. New York: Oxford University Press, 1967.

Henkle, Roger B. *Comedy and Culture: England 1820–1900*. Princeton: Princeton University Press, 1980.

Hertz, Neil. *George Eliot's Pulse*. Stanford: Stanford University Press, 2003.

Hewson, John. "*Langue* and *Parole* since Saussure." *Historiographia Linguistica* 3, no. 3 (1976): 315–48.

Hirsch, Marianne. "The Novel of Formation as Genre: Between Great Expectations and Lost Illusions." *Genre* 12, no. 3 (1979): 293–311.

Hirschman, Albert O. *The Passions and the Interests: Political Arguments for Capitalism before Its Triumph*. 20th anniv. ed. Princeton: Princeton University Press, 1997.

Hobbes, Thomas. *Elements of Law, Natural and Politic*. Edited by J. C. A. Gaskin. New York: Oxford University Press, 1999.

Hollingsworth, Keith. *The Newgate Novel, 1830–1847: Bulwer, Ainsworth, Dickens, and Thackeray*. Detroit: Wayne State University Press, 1963.

Howson, Gerald. *Thief-Taker General: The Rise and Fall of Jonathan Wild*. New York: St. Martin's Press, 1971.

Hume, David. "Of the Populousness of Ancient Nations." In *Essays: Moral, Political, and Literary*, edited by Eugene F. Miller, 377–464. Indianapolis: Liberty Fund, 1985.

———. *A Treatise of Human Nature*. Edited by Ernest C. Mossner. New York: Penguin, 1985.

Hunt, Leigh. *Wit and Humor: Selected from the English Poets, with an Illustrative Essay, and Critical Comments*. London: Wiley & Putnam, 1846.

Hutcheson, Francis. *An Inquiry into the Original of Our Ideas of Beauty and Virtue*. Edited by Wolfgang Leidhold. Indianapolis: Liberty Fund, 2004.

———. *A System of Moral Philosophy*. Vol. 1. Glasgow: R. and A. Foulis, 1755.

Itzkowitz, David C. "Fair Enterprise or Extravagant Speculation: Investment, Speculation, and Gambling in Victorian England." *Victorian Studies* 44, no. 1 (Autumn 2002): 121–47.

Jacobs, Joseph. "The Comparative Distribution of Jewish Ability." *Journal of the Anthropological Institute of Great Britain and Ireland* 15 (1886): 351–79.

———. *Studies in Jewish Statistics, Social, Vital, and Anthropometric*. London: D. Nutt, 1891.

Jaffe, Audrey. *Scenes of Sympathy: Identity and Representation in Victorian Fiction*. Ithaca, NY: Cornell University Press, 2000.

Jakobson, Roman. "On Realism in Art." In *Language and Literature*, edited by Krystyna Pomorska and Stephen Rudy, 19–27. Cambridge: Belknap Press of Harvard University Press, 1987.

James, Henry. "Mary Elizabeth Braddon." In *Literary Criticism: Essays on Literature, American Writers, English Writers*, edited by Leon Edel, 741–46. New York: Library of America, 1984.

———. "The Life of George Eliot." In *Literary Criticism: Essays on Literature, American Writers, English Writers*, edited by Leon Edel, 994–1010. New York: Library of America, 1984.

———. "Middlemarch." In *Literary Criticism: Essays on Literature, American Writers, English Writers*, edited by Leon Edel, 958–66. New York: Library of America, 1984.

James, Louis. *The Victorian Novel*. London: Blackwell, 2006.

Jameson, Fredric. *The Antinomies of Realism*. London: Verso, 2013.

———. "The Ideology of the Text." In *The Ideologies of Theory: Essays 1971–1986*, Vol. 1, *Situations of Theory*, 17–71. Minneapolis: University of Minnesota Press, 1988.

————. *The Political Unconscious: Narrative as a Socially Symbolic Act*. Ithaca, NY: Cornell University Press, 1981.

Johnson, Edgar. *Charles Dickens: His Tragedy and Triumph*. Vol. 2. New York: Simon & Schuster, 1952.

Kant, Immanuel. *Critique of Practical Reason*. Edited and translated by Mary Gregor. Cambridge: Cambridge University Press, 2001.

————. *Critique of the Power of Judgment*. Edited by Paul Guyer. Translated by Paul Guyer and Eric Matthews. Cambridge: Cambridge University Press, 2000.

————. *Groundwork of the Metaphysics of Morals*. Edited and translated by Mary Gregor; introduction by Christine M. Korsgaard. Cambridge: Cambridge University Press, 2002.

————. *Religion within the Boundaries of Mere Reason*. Edited and translated by Allen Wood and George di Giovanni. Cambridge: Cambridge University Press, 1998.

Kaplan, Fred. *Dickens: A Biography*. Baltimore: John Hopkins University Press, 1988.

Kent, Christopher. "The Average Victorian: Constructing and Contesting Reality." *Browning Institute Studies* 17 (1989): 41–52.

Keymer, Thomas, and Peter Sabor. *Pamela in the Marketplace: Literary Controversy and Print Culture in Eighteenth-Century Britain and Ireland*. Cambridge: Cambridge University Press, 2005.

Kincaid, James R. *Dickens and the Rhetoric of Laughter*. London: Oxford University Press, 1971.

Klein, Lawrence. *Shaftesbury and the Culture of Politeness: Moral Discourse and the Cultural Politics of Early Eighteenth-Century England*. Cambridge: Cambridge University Press, 1994.

Kurnick, David. *Empty Houses: Theatrical Failure and the Novel*. Princeton: Princeton University Press, 2012.

Lacan, Jacques. *The Four Fundamental Concepts of Psychoanalysis*. Edited by Jacques-Alain Miller; translated by Alan Sheridan. New York: W. W. Norton, 1998.

————. *Freud's Papers on Technique, 1953–1954 (the Seminar of Jacques Lacan)*. Edited by Jacques-Alain Miller. Translated by John Forrester. New York: W. W. Norton, 1991.

LaCapra, Dominick. *Madame Bovary on Trial*. Ithaca, NY: Cornell University Press, 1982.

Lamb, Charles. *Life, Letters, and Writing*. Edited by Percy Fitzgerald. Vol. 4. London: John Slark, 1822.

Leavis, F. R. *The Great Tradition: George Eliot, Henry James, Joseph Conrad*. New York: New York University Press, 1963.

Lecky, William Edward Hartpole. *History of European Morals from Augustus to Charlemagne*. New York: D. Appleton, 1921.

Leitch, Thomas. *What Stories Are: Narrative Theory and Interpretation*. University Park: Pennsylvania State University Press, 1986.

Lesjak, Carolyn. *Working Fictions: A Genealogy of the Victorian Novel*. Durham, NC: Duke University Press, 2006.

Levi, Albert William. "The Writing of Mill's *Autobiography*." *Ethics* 61, no. 1 (1951): 284–96.

Levin, Harry. *The Gates of Horn: A Study of Five French Realists*. New York: Oxford University Press, 1963.

Levine, Caroline. *The Serious Pleasures of Suspense: Victorian Realism and Narrative Doubt.* Charlottesville: University of Virginia Press, 2003.

Levine, George. "Determinism and Responsibility in the Works of George Eliot." *PMLA* 77, no. 3 (June 1962): 268–79.

Lewes, George Henry. "Dickens in Relation to Criticism." *Fortnightly Review* 11 (1872): 141–54.

———. "Mr. Buckle's Scientific Errors." *Blackwood's Edinburgh Magazine* 90 (November 1861): 582–96.

———. *Problems of Life and Mind: First Series, the Foundations of a Creed.* Vol. 1. Boston: J. R. Osgood, 1874.

Lewis, David K. *Convention: A Philosophical Study.* New York: Blackwell, 2002.

Lewis, Paul. *Comic Effects: Interdisciplinary Approaches to Humor in Literature.* Albany: State University of New York Press, 1989.

"Literary Recipes." *Punch,* August 7 1841, 39.

Locke, John. *An Essay Concerning Human Understanding.* Edited by Peter H. Nidditch. New York: Oxford University Press, 1975.

Loesberg, Jonathan. *Fictions of Consciousness: Mill, Newman, and the Reading of Victorian Prose.* New Brunswick: Rutgers University Press, 1986.

Lukács, Georg. *The Historical Novel.* Translated by Hannah Mitchell and Stanley Mitchell. Lincoln: University of Nebraska Press, 1983.

———. *Studies in European Realism: A Sociological Survey of the Writings of Balzac, Stendhal, Zola, Tolstoy, Gorki, and Others.* Translated by Edith Bone. London: Merlin Press, 1989.

———. *The Theory of the Novel: A Historico-Philosophical Essay on the Forms of Great Epic Literature.* Translated by Anna Bostock. Cambridge, MA: MIT Press, 1991.

The Malefactor's Register; or, New Newgate and Tyburn Calendar. Vol. 4. London: Alex Hogg, 1779.

Mansel, Henry Longueville. *Letters, Lectures, and Reviews, Including the Phrontisterion; Or, Oxford in the 19th Century.* Edited by Henry W. Chandler. London: John Murry, 1873.

———. "Sensation Novels." In *Letters, Lectures, and Reviews, Including the Phrontisterion; or, Oxford in the 19th Century,* edited by Henry W. Chandler. London: John Murry, 1873.

Marcus, Sharon. *Between Women: Friendship, Desire, and Marriage in Victorian England.* Princeton: Princeton University Press, 2007.

Marcus, Steven. *Dickens: From Pickwick to Dombey.* New York: Basic Books, 1965.

———. "Literature and Social Theory: George Eliot." In *Representations: Essays on Literature and Society,* 183–213. New York: Columbia University Press, 1975.

Martin, Robert Bernard. *The Triumph of Wit: A Study of Victorian Comic Theory.* Oxford: Clarendon Press, 1974.

Masson, David. *British Novelists and Their Styles.* London: Macmillan, 1859.

Maxwell, James Clerk. *Theory of Heat.* 7th ed. New York: D. Appleton, 1883.

McDayter, Ghislaine. "Conjuring Byron: Byromania, Literary Commodification and the Birth of Celebrity." In *Byromania: Portraits of the Artist in Nineteenth- and Twentieth-Century Culture,* edited by Frances Wilson, 43–62. New York: St. Martin's, 1999.

McNeill, David. *Gesture and Thought.* Chicago: University of Chicago Press, 2005.

Meisel, Martin. *Realizations: Narrative, Pictorial, and Theatrical Arts in Nineteenth-Century England.* Princeton: Princeton University Press, 1983.

Meredith, George. "An Essay on Comedy." In *Comedy*, edited by Wylie Sypher, 3–57. Baltimore: Johns Hopkins University Press, 1956.

Mill, John Stuart. *Autobiography.* Edited by Jack Stillinger. New York: Houghton Mifflin, 1969.

———. "Sedgwick's Discourse." In *Essays on Ethics, Religion, and Society*, edited by John M. Robson. Collected Works of John Stuart Mill, vol. 10. Toronto: University of Toronto Press, 1985.

———. *A System of Logic, Ratiocinative and Inductive: Books IV–VI, Appendices.* Edited by John M. Robson. Indianapolis: Liberty Fund, 2006.

———. *Utilitarianism.* Edited by Roger Crisp. New York: Oxford University Press, 2003.

Miller, Andrew. *The Burdens of Perfection: On Ethics and Reading in Nineteenth-Century British Literature.* Ithaca, NY: Cornell University Press, 2008.

———. "Lives Unled in Realist Fiction." *Representations* 98, no. 1 (2007): 118–34.

Miller, D. A. *The Novel and the Police.* Berkeley: University of California Press, 1988.

Miller, J. Hillis. *The Ethics of Reading: Kant, de Man, Eliot, Trollope, James, and Benjamin.* New York: Columbia University Press, 1987.

Monk, Leland. *Standard Deviations: Chance and the Modern British Novel.* Stanford: Stanford University Press, 1993.

Moran, Maureen. *Victorian Literature and Culture.* London: Continuum Books, 2006.

Moretti, Franco. *Atlas of the European Novel: 1800–1900.* London: Verso, 1998.

———. *Signs Taken for Wonders.* London: Verso, 1988.

———. *The Way of the World: The Bildungsroman in European Culture.* New York: Verso, 2000.

Newman, John Henry. *Apologia Pro Vita Sua.* Edited by David J. DeLaura. New York: W. W. Norton, 1968.

Newsom, Robert. "Dickens and the Goods." In *Contemporary Dickens*, edited by Eileen Gillooly and Deirdre David, 35–52. Columbus: Ohio State University Press, 2009.

Newton, Adam Zachary. *Narrative Ethics.* Cambridge, MA: Harvard University Press, 1995.

Nietzsche, Friedrich. *The Gay Science.* Translated by Walter Kaufmann. New York: Vintage, 1974.

———. *The Portable Nietzsche.* Edited and translated by Walter Kaufmann. New York: Viking Press, 1964.

———. *Thus Spoke Zarathustra: A Book for None and All.* Translated by Walter Kaufmann. New York: Penguin, 1978.

Nord, Deborah Epstein. "The Making of Dickens Criticism." In *Contemporary Dickens*, edited by Eileen Gillooly and Deirdre David, 262–85. Columbus: Ohio State University Press, 2009.

Nussbaum, Martha C. *Love's Knowledge: Essays on Philosophy and Literature.* New York: Oxford University Press, 1990.

———. *Poetic Justice: The Literary Imagination and Public Life.* Boston: Beacon Press, 1995.

Oliphant, Margaret. *Miss Marjoribanks*. Edited by Elisabeth Jay. New York: Penguin, 1998.

Ortega y Gasset, José. *Meditations on Quixote*. Translated by Evelyn Rugg and Diego Marin. Champaign: University of Illinois Press, 2000.

Orwell, George. "Charles Dickens." In *All Art Is Propaganda: Critical Essays*, edited by George Packer, 1–62. New York: Houghton Mifflin Harcourt, 2008.

Patey, Douglas Lane. *Probability and Literary Form: Philosophic Theory and Literary Practice in the Augustan Age*. Cambridge: Cambridge University Press, 1984.

Patterson, Bo. "Exploring the Common Ground: *Sensus Communis*, Humor, and the Interpretation of Comic Poetry." *Journal of Literary Semantics* 33 (2004): 155–67.

Phillips, Brian. "Reality and Virginia Woolf." *Hudson Review* 56, no. 3 (2003): 415–30.

Pinion, F. B. *A George Eliot Companion: Literary Achievement and Modern Significance*. London: Macmillan, 1991.

Polhemus, Robert. *Comic Faith: The Great Tradition from Austen to Joyce*. Chicago: University of Chicago Press, 1980.

Poovey, Mary. *A History of the Modern Fact: Problems of Knowledge in the Sciences of Wealth and Society*. Chicago: University of Chicago Press, 1998.

———. *Uneven Developments: The Ideological Work of Gender in Mid-Victorian England*. Chicago: University of Chicago Press, 1988.

Pope, Alexander. *An Essay on Criticism*. In *The Norton Anthology of English Literature*, 6th ed., vol. 1, 2217–34. Edited by M. H. Abrams. New York: W. W. Norton, 1993.

Porter, Theodore M. *The Rise of Statistical Thinking: 1820–1900*. Princeton: Princeton University Press, 1986.

Proctor, Richard Anthony. "Gambling Superstitions." *Cornhill Magazine* 25 (1872): 704–17.

Prusak, Bernard G. "*Le Rire* à Nouveau: Rereading Bergson." *Journal of Aesthetics and Art Criticism* 62, no. 4 (Autumn 2004): 377–88.

Purcell, L. Edward. "*Trilby* and Trilby-Mania: The Beginning of the Best-Seller System." *Journal of Popular Culture* 11, no. 1 (2004): 62–76.

Rabinowitz, Peter J. *Before Reading: Narrative Conventions and the Politics of Interpretation*. Columbus: Ohio State University Press, 1998.

Radway, Janice A. "Reading Is Not Eating: Mass-Produced Literature and the Theoretical, Methodological, and Political Consequences of a Metaphor." *Book Research Quarterly* 2, no. 3 (1986): 7–29.

———. *Reading the Romance: Women, Patriarchy, and Popular Literature*. Chapel Hill: University of North Carolina Press, 1991.

Raphael, D. D. *The Moral Sense*. New York: Oxford University Press, 1947.

Rawls, John. *Lectures on the History of Moral Philosophy*. Edited by Barbara Herman. Cambridge, MA: Harvard University Press, 2000.

———. "Themes in Kant's Moral Philosophy." In *John Rawls: Selected Papers*, edited by Samuel Freeman, 497–528. Cambridge, MA: Harvard University Press, 1999.

———. *A Theory of Justice*. Cambridge: Belknap Press, 1999.

Ray, Gordon N. *Thackeray: The Uses of Adversity, 1811–1846*. New York: McGraw-Hill, 1955.

"Recent Novels." *Monthly Chronicle* 5 (February 1840): 219–31.

Regan, Tom. *Bloomsbury's Prophet: G. E. Moore and the Development of His Moral Philosophy*. Philadelphia: Temple University Press, 1986.

Reid, Roddey. *Families in Jeopardy: Regulating the Social Body in France, 1750–1910*. Stanford: Stanford University Press, 1993.

Review of *Jack Sheppard*, *Athenaeum*, October 26, 1839.

Reynolds, John Hamilton. "Hints for a History of Highwaymen." *Fraser's Magazine* 9 (March 1834): 279–87.

———. "William Ainsworth and Jack Sheppard." *Fraser's Magazine* 21 (February 1840): 227–45.

Ricoeur, Paul. "Narrative Time." *Critical Inquiry* 7, no. 1, Autumn (1980): 169–90.

Rignall, John. *George Eliot: European Novelist*. Surrey: Ashgate, 2011.

Rorty, Richard. *Contingency, Irony, and Solidarity*. Cambridge: Cambridge University Press, 1989.

Rose, Jonathan. "How Historians Study Reader Response: Or, What Did Jo Think of *Bleak House?*" In *Literature in the Marketplace*, edited by John O. Jordan and Robert L. Patten, 195–212. Cambridge: Cambridge University Press, 1995.

Said, Edward. *The Question of Palestine*. New York: Vintage Books, 1992.

Sammons, Jeffrey L. "The Mystery of the Missing *Bildungsroman*, or What Happened to Wilhelm Meister's Legacy." *Genre* 14, no. 2 (1981): 229–46.

Schaeffer, John D. *Sensus Communis: Vico, Rhetoric, and the Limits of Relativism*. Durham, NC: Duke University Press, 1990.

Schneewind, J. B. "Moral Problems and Moral Philosophy in the Victorian Period." *Victorian Studies* 9 (1965): 29–46.

———. *Sidgwick's Ethics and Victorian Moral Philosophy*. Oxford: Oxford University Press, 1977.

———. "Whewell's Ethics." In *Studies in Moral Philosophy*, edited by Nicholas Rescher, 108–41. American Philosophical Quarterly Monograph Series. Oxford: Basil Blackwell, 1968.

Sedgwick, Adam. *A Discourse on the Studies of the University*. 5th ed. London: John W. Parker, 1850.

Shaftesbury, Anthony Ashley Cooper, Earl of. *Characteristicks of Men, Manners, Opinions, Times*. Edited by Douglas den Uyl. Vol. 1. Indianapolis: Liberty Fund, 2001.

———. *Characteristicks of Men, Manners, Opinions, Times*. Edited by Douglas den Uyl. Vol. 2. Indianapolis: Liberty Fund, 2001.

Shelley, Percy Bysshe. "Defense of Poetry." In *Shelley's Poetry and Prose*, edited by Donald H. Reiman and Sharon B. Powers, 480–508. New York: W. W. Norton, 1977.

Shiff, Richard. "Handling Shocks: On the Representation of Experience in Walter Benjamin's Analogies." *Oxford Art Journal* 15, no. 2 (1992): 88–103.

Shklovsky, Viktor. *Theory of Prose*. Translated by Benjamin Sher. Normal, IL: Dalkey Archive Press, 1998.

Shuttleworth, Sally. *George Eliot and Nineteenth-Century Science: The Make-Believe of a Beginning*. Cambridge: Cambridge University Press, 1984.

Siskin, Clifford. *The Work of Writing: Literature and Social Change in Britain, 1700–1830*. Baltimore: Johns Hopkins University Press, 1999.

Slaughter, Joseph R. *Human Rights, Inc.* New York: Fordham University Press, 2007.

Small, Helen. "Chances Are: Henry Buckle, Thomas Hardy, and the Individual at Risk." In *Literature, Science, Psychoanalysis, 1830–1970: Essays in Honor of Gillian*

Beer, edited by Helen Small and Trudi Tate, 64–85. Oxford: Oxford University Press, 2003.

Smart, J. J. C., and Bernard Williams. *Utilitarianism, For and Against*. New York: Cambridge University Press, 1973.

Smeed, J. W. "Thomas Carlyle and Jean Paul Richter." *Comparative Literature* 16, no. 3 (1964): 226–53.

Smith, Adam. *Theory of Moral Sentiments*. Edited by D. D. Raphael and A. L. Macfie. Indianapolis: Liberty Fund, 1982.

Snyder, Laura J. *Reforming Philosophy: A Victorian Debate on Science and Society*. Chicago: University of Chicago Press, 2006.

Soffer, Oren. "Antisemitism, Statistics, and the Scientization of Hebrew Political Discourse: The Case Study of *Ha-Tsefirah*." *Jewish Social Studies* 10, no. 2 (2004): 55–79.

Spencer, Herbert. "The Physiology of Laughter." In *Essays: Scientific, Political, and Speculative*, 2:452–66. London: Williams & Norgate, n.d.

Spivak, Gayatri Chakravorty. "Ethics and Politics in Tagore, Coetzee, and Certain Scenes of Teaching." *Diacritics* 32, nos. 3–4 (2002): 17–31.

Stephen, Leslie. *History of English Thought in the Eighteenth Century*. Vol. 1. London: Smith, Elder, 1876.

———. *History of English Thought in the Eighteenth Century*. Vol. 2. London: Smith, Elder, 1876.

Stephens, J. R. "Jack Sheppard and the Licensers: The Case against Newgate Plays." *Nineteenth-Century Theatre Research* 1 (1973): 1–13.

Stewart, Robert Scott. "Utilitarianism Meets Romanticism: J. S. Mill's Theory of Imagination." *History of Philosophy Quarterly* 10, no. 4 (1993): 369–88.

Stigler, Stephen M. *The History of Statistics: The Measurement of Uncertainty before 1900*. Cambridge, MA: Belknap Press of Harvard University Press, 1986.

Stone, Donald D. "Arnold, Nietzsche, and the 'Revaluation of Values.'" *Nineteenth-Century Literature* 43, no. 3 (1988): 289–318.

Stone, Harry. *Dickens and the Invisible World: Fairy Tales, Fantasy, and Novel-Making*. Bloomington: Indiana University Press, 1979.

Stone, Wilfred. "The Play of Chance and Ego in *Daniel Deronda*." *Nineteenth-Century Literature* 53, no. 1 (July 1998): 25–55.

Stoppard, Tom. *Rosencrantz and Guildenstern Are Dead*. Edited by Henry Popkin. New York: Grove Press, 1967.

Sutherland, John. *Is Heathcliff a Murderer? Puzzles in Nineteenth-Century Literature*. Oxford: Oxford University Press, 1996.

Taine, Hippolyte. *History of English Literature*. Translated by H. Van Laun. Vol. 4. Philadelphia: Henry Altemus, 1908.

Tave, Stuart M. *The Amiable Humourist: A Study in the Comic Theory of the Eighteenth and Early Nineteenth Centuries*. Chicago: University of Chicago Press, 1960.

Thackeray, William Makepeace. *Catherine: A Story by Ikey Solomons, Esq. Junior*. Edited by Sheldon F. Goldfarb. Ann Arbor: University of Michigan Press, 1999.

———. "Going to See a Man Hanged." *Fraser's Magazine* 22 (July 1840): 150–58.

———. "The English Humourists of the Eighteenth Century." In *The Works of William Makepeace Thackeray*, Vol. 1. New York: Pollard & Moss, 1881.

———. *The History of Pendennis*. Edited by John Sutherland. Oxford: Oxford University Press, 1994.

———. "Horae Catnachianae: A Dissertation on Ballads, with a Few Unnecessary Remarks on Jonathan Wild, John Sheppard, Paul Clifford, and — Fagin, Esqrs." *Fraser's Magazine* 19 (April 1839): 407–24.

———. *The Letters and Private Papers of William Makepeace Thackeray*. Edited by Gordon N. Ray. 4 vols. Cambridge: Harvard University Press, 1945–46.

———. "Thieves' Literature of France." *Foreign Quarterly Review* 31 (April 1843): 231–49.

Thrall, Miriam. *Rebellious Fraser's: Nol Yorke's Magazine in the Days of Maginn, Thackeray, and Carlyle*. New York: AMS Press, 1966.

Todorov, Tzvetan. *The Fantastic: A Structural Approach to a Literary Genre*. Translated by Richard Howard. Ithaca, NY: Cornell University Press, 1975.

———. "Narrative Transformations." In *The Poetics of Prose*, translated by Richard Howard, 218–33. Ithaca: Cornell University Press, 1977.

Tomashevsky, Boris. "Thematics." In *Russian Formalist Criticism: Four Essays*, translated by Lee T. Lemon and Marion J. Reis, 61–95. Lincoln: University of Nebraska Press, 1965.

Trollope, Anthony. *Barchester Towers*. New York: Oxford University Press, 1996.

Tversky, Amos, and Daniel Kahneman. "Belief in the Law of Small Numbers." *Psychological Bulletin* 76, no. 2 (1971): 105–10.

Vargish, Thomas. *The Providential Aesthetic in Victorian Fiction*. Charlottesville: University of Virginia Press, 1985.

Veyne, Paul. *Did the Greeks Believe Their Myths?: An Essay on the Constitutive Imagination*. Translated by Paula Wissig. Chicago: University of Chicago Press, 1988.

Wallach, Luitpold. *Liberty and Letters: The Thoughts of Leopold Zunz*. London: East & West Library, 1959.

Warhol, Robyn. *Gendered Interventions: Narrative Discourse in the Victorian Novel*. New Brunswick, NJ: Rutgers University Press, 1989.

Warnke, Georgia. "Hermeneutics, Ethics, and Politics." In *Cambridge Companion to Gadamer*, edited by Robert J. Dostal, 79–101. Cambridge: Cambridge University Press, 2006.

Watt, Ian. *The Rise of the Novel: Studies in Defoe, Richardson, and Fielding*. 2nd ed. Berkeley: University of California Press, 2001.

Weinstein, Philip M. *The Semantics of Desire: Changing Models of Identity from Dickens to Joyce*. Princeton: Princeton University Press, 1984.

Welsh, Alexander. *From Copyright to Copperfield: The Identity of Dickens*. Cambridge, MA: Harvard University Press, 1987.

Wesley, John. *The Works of the Rev. John Wesley, A.M.* 4th ed. Vol. 11. London: John Mason, 1841.

Wheeler, Burton M. "The Text and Plan of *Oliver Twist*." *Dickens Studies Annual* 12 (1984): 41–58.

Whewell, William. *Lectures on the History of Moral Philosophy in England*. London: J. W. Parker, 1854.

———. *Lectures on Systematic Morality*. London: John W. Parker, 1846.

White, Edward M. "Thackeray's Contributions to *Fraser's Magazine*." *Studies in Bibliography* 19 (1966): 68–85.

Whitley, Alvin. "Hood and Dickens: Some New Letters." *Huntington Library Quarterly* 14, no. 4 (August 1951): 385–413.

Williams, Bernard. *Ethics and the Limits of Philosophy.* Cambridge, MA: Harvard University Press, 1985.

———. *Moral Luck: Philosophical Papers 1973–1980.* Cambridge: Cambridge Unversity Press, 1981.

———. *Shame and Necessity.* Berkeley: University of California Press, 1994.

Williams, Edwin E. "Dr. James Drake and Restoration Theory of Comedy." *Review of English Studies*, 1939, 180–91.

Williams, Raymond. *Culture and Society, 1780–1950.* New York: Columbia University Press, 1983.

———. *Keywords: A Vocabulary of Culture and Society.* New York: Oxford University Press, 1983.

Wittenberg, David. *Time Travel: The Popular Philosophy of Narrative.* New York: Fordham University Press, 2013.

Wolin, Richard. *Walter Benjamin: An Aesthetic of Redemption.* 2nd ed. Berkeley: University of California Press, 1994.

Woloch, Alex. *The One vs. the Many.* Princeton: Princeton University Press, 2003.

Woolf, Virginia. *The Common Reader, First Series.* Edited by Andrew MacNeillie. New York: Harcourt Brace, 1984.

———. *The Second Common Reader.* Edited by Andrew MacNeillie. New York: Harcourt Brace, 1986.

Wrexall, Lascelles. "Gambling-Houses in Germany." *Dublin University Magazine* 77 (April 1871): 466–76.

Yeazell, Ruth Bernard. "Why Political Novels Have Heroines: *Sybil*, *Mary Barton*, and *Felix Holt*." *Novel* 18, no. 2 (Winter 1985): 126–44.

Young, Norwood. "Gambling at Monte Carlo." *National Review* 16 (1890): 486–95.

Zupančič, Alenka. *Ethics of the Real: Kant, Lacan.* London: Verso, 2000.

Žižek, Slavoj. *The Sublime Object of Ideology.* London: Verso, 1989.

INDEX